SCHOOL GUIDANCE SERVICES:
A CAREER DEVELOPMENT APPROACH

SCHOOL
GUIDANCE
SERVICES
a career development approach

Editors:
Thomas H. Hohenshil
Johnnie H. Miles

KENDALL/HUNT PUBLISHING COMPANY
Dubuque, Iowa

All royalties from the sale of this book are being donated
to the National Vocational Guidance Association.

Contents

Foreword

It is a pleasure to write a foreword for such an exciting new book. Although there have been variations on the theme the essential approaches in the past to writing introductory textbooks in guidance have been to:

1. have a book written by a single author or occasionally by joint authors around a general theme, or
2. have a book of readings pulled together in which many authors' previous writings are consolidated around a topical point of view.

In the first instance there is essentially one viewpoint, or at best two. In the second there is a healthy variety of viewpoints, but seldom written with enough overall purpose in mind to give a book solid continuity. In *School Guidance Services: A Career Development Approach* there is the best of both worlds—a positive theme set forth by editors Tom Hohenshil and Johnnie Miles *and* the different views and approaches of more than a dozen authors. Each of the authors has developed an original piece of writing for this book, therefore there is a real freshness of ideas built around the unifying theme of career development.

In addition, there is a careful blending of some new and veteran people in the field of education in the writing of the various chapters. Each reader should be able to find some new and significant concepts emerging out of this melding of theory and practice by the contributors. In short, the book combines fresh approaches and ideas interpreted by professionals for the guidance field.

Finally, this book has a unique feature in the bringing together for the first time of several key documents which are having great influence on the guidance field. Most texts leave these sorts of references to be checked out by the user/reader in the best ways possible. Often they are not available in the periodical literature or in libraries which are not completely up to date. So, there are the three major influences of national thought in this field in the mid-1970s: the U.S. Office of Education's *Position Paper on Career Education,* the American Personnel and Guidance Association's Position Paper entitled, *Career Guidance: Role and Functions of Counseling and Personnel Practitioners in Career Education,* and the National Vocational Guidance Association—American Vocational Association's *Position Paper on Career Development.* No further searching is necessary. These fundamental materials are here for users/readers to compare ideas with authors' conclusions and comments. Hopefully, this utilization will create a further opportunity for dialogue and discussion by the various reader groups.

Counselors, prospective counselors, teachers, administrators, and community leaders should all find much of value in *School Guidance Services: A Career Development Approach*.

Carl McDaniels
Virginia Tech
Blacksburg, Virginia

Preface

Guidance, as well as other socially oriented professions, must be responsive to societal change if it is to remain a viable service to contemporary individuals and institutions. During the last sixty years the profession has demonstrated its flexibility through continuing modification and expansion of services to meet the ever-changing needs of public school students. Although the formal guidance profession was developed under the banner of vocational guidance in the early 1900s, it has evolved through a number of cycles and changes in emphases, for the most part in response to societal demands. Today, one of the profession's greatest challenges is occurring. That challenge, being heralded by persons within as well as outside the profession, is the challenge of career development. The guidance profession has responded to this challenge through major position papers emphasizing the importance of career development and the necessity for all school personnel to be actively involved in the delivery of career guidance services. In addition, numerous career development conferences and in-service workshops have been conducted, and professional publications produced for use by counselors and other educational and community personnel.

This book was developed to describe how public school guidance services can be utilized to facilitate the career, educational, social, and personal development of students. The major theme throughout is to depict how guidance services can contribute to the career development of public school students. This is not to say that personal, social, and educational development are relegated to low-priority status. Rather, as noted in chapter 1, career development is viewed as an integral part of general human development, and thus includes the personal, social, and educational aspects. To refer to the term *"career development"* without also implying inclusion of personal, social, and educational development would indeed be a misinterpretation of this very important concept. Career development is envisioned as a common theme around which the entire educational enterprise can meaningfully rally. Career education and career guidance are seen as vehicles through which career development services are delivered to students. The delivery of career guidance and career education experiences is seen as a responsibility of all educational personnel.

Throughout this book efforts will be made to describe the roles of counselors, teachers, and other educational and community personnel in the delivery of guidance services to all students. The book begins with a brief overview of the major pupil personnel services and is followed by the historical development of guidance and a presentation of the basic guidance services with particular emphasis upon their implications for career development. Additional chapters are devoted to the career education concept, vocational education and guidance, legal issues in guidance, careers in counseling, and issues and trends in career guidance. Although this book was designed for use in an introductory guidance course for counselors, teachers, and administrators, it would also be a valuable resource for in-service education, and various courses regarding the roles of teachers and other educational personnel in the guidance process.

Thomas H. Hohenshil
Johnnie H. Miles

Chapter 1
OVERVIEW OF PUPIL PERSONNEL SERVICES

Thomas H. Hohenshil

From a historical perspective, pupil personnel services are a relatively recent phenomena in American education. The development of each of these services was, for the most part, a response to the evolving nature of education in a democratic society. Pupil personnel programs are composed of a constellation of services designed to facilitate the personal, educational, and career development of elementary and secondary school students. There are three basic components which comprise most American school systems. Instruction includes the basic content and teaching strategies for effective learning. Administration and supervision are responsible for the facilities, materials, staff, organization, and leadership which provide the setting for effective instruction. Pupil personnel services are designed to assist optimum student utilization of instruction (Hummel and Bonham, 1968). They are designed to benefit all students and are in support of effective instructional programs in the schools. Essentially they are services which assist students, educators, and parents to carry out their responsibilities in the educational process.

This chapter is designed to briefly present the most significant factors in the historical development of pupil personnel services, and an overview of the four major pupil personnel services. These include school psychological services, school social work services, school health services, and school guidance services. Each of these basic services was developed in an effort to adapt the school program to the needs of the students and to assist students to adjust to the school program. In the past, other types of specialized services were often included under the umbrella of pupil personnel programs. Depending on the author or school system, these might also include special education, speech and hearing therapy, child accounting and attendance, and remedial instruction. However, these services have now evolved into the primary domains of instruction and/or administration and therefore will not be considered as major components of pupil personnel services for purposes of this chapter.

Development of Pupil Personnel Services

The aims of education in a democratic society were, and remain compelling reasons for the development of pupil personnel services. A system of universal education forms the very foun-

Dr. Thomas H. Hohenshil is Associate Professor of Counselor Education at Virginia Polytechnic Institute and State University, Blacksburg, Virginia.

dation for participation in a democratic society. Freedom for individuals and the nation requires a free-access system of education which allows and encourages persons to fully develop their human potential. The primary aim of American elementary and secondary schools is to prepare educated citizens for full participation in the social, economic, and governmental spheres of this nation and the wider world community. The goals of pupil personnel services coincide with those of American education.

It was Ferguson's (1963) contention that compulsory school attendance laws had a profound effect upon the development of pupil personnel services and actually marked their beginning. By 1929, all states had enacted compulsory school attendance laws. This attempt to educate all the children of all the people brought many students into the schools who had no clear idea why they were there or what to expect from the experience. In an effort to meet the needs of this widely divergent student population, educators expanded curricular offerings. Because of increasing numbers of students and curricular choices, it was soon apparent that teachers and administrators needed assistance to provide individualized help for students. In addition, special assistance seemed to be required for students who did not appear to benefit from traditional educational practices. To meet these pressing needs, a variety of specialized pupil personnel services were integrated into the public schools. There is little doubt that compulsory school attendance laws were a major motivating factor in the development of these services (Peters and Shertzer, 1969).

The study of individual differences was the second major facilitating force behind the development of pupil personnel services. The second decade of the twentieth century brought about several developments of historical significance in this area. The study of individual differences and the apparent development of the necessary technology to assess these differences particularily affected the development of school guidance and school psychological services. Educators became aware that students differed widely and thus not all could be expected to progress at the same rate, nor benefit from the same curricular pattern. The testing movement, originating with the first widely accepted revision of the Binet Intelligence Scales, led to the development of group testing. The group testing movement appeared to offer educators the opportunity to economically assess individual traits in the hope that students could be better assisted in the selection of various courses of study. School counselors and school psychologists, trained in the use of these instruments, played a major role in the selection of students for various traditional school and special education curricula. It was not until the present decade that the entire underpinnings of the group testing movement were successfully challenged.

A number of other factors, to be covered in greater detail in later chapters, also facilitated the development of pupil personnel services. Social reform movements, the child study movement, the mental health movement, advances in medicine, world war and depression, improvement in public health, and federal and state legislation all signaled the need to provide a comprehensive set of pupil personnel services if the opportunity for optimum social, career, and educational development was to be a reality for all children in America.

School Psychological Services

The historical development of school psychological services in the United States might well be traced to a clinic established at the University of Pennsylvania by Lightner Witmer in 1896.

Witmer's clinic is often referred to as the first child guidance clinic in America and one of the landmarks in the development of clinical psychology. The clinic was closely allied with education because Witmer's goal was to prepare psychologists to help teachers solve the learning problems of children. A second landmark occurred in Chicago in 1899 when William Healy established a clinic for a juvenile court in the public school system. This clinic initiated the practice of including nonteaching personnel and specialists as part of the school system. While these clinics were being developed, a number of school districts were forming special classes for children who did not learn or "behave" well in regular classes. In reality, the formation of special classes for children exhibiting learning and/or behavioral problems was a result of acceptance of the concept of individual differences and the demand for universal education for all young people (Bardon and Bennett, 1974).

The testing movement of the early 1900s also had a significant effect on the development of school psychological services. Terman's 1916 revision of the Binet Intelligence Scale constituted a pioneering effort toward the measurement of intellectual abilities. This revision appeared to give schools answers to questions about pupils that educators wanted to know; that is, which children may require special class placement in order to progress satisfactorily in the educational system. Special class placement required that someone be responsible for deciding which children could benefit from this type of experience. The Binet and the later Wechsler Intelligence Scales seemed to be valuable tools to make these judgments.

During the intervening years growth in school psychology has been closely identified with the growth of special education. This has helped establish the image of the school psychologist as a "tester" and "classifier" of children for special education classes. The mental health and psychoanalytic movements did tend to add therapeutic and diagnostic elements to the practice of school psychology. One of the main by-products of the mental health movement of the 1950s and 1960s was the belief by many school personnel that mental health specialists could resolve children's learning and behavioral problems when teachers could not, and that referral to such specialists was the ultimate solution. School psychologists were often the specialists closest at hand.

During the last ten years school psychology has expanded its services in an effort to impact the school system on a broader basis. Psychologists are recognizing that if they are to offer solutions to the broad problems of education, reevaluation of their services is necessary and bold attemps for major involvement in the entire educational environment are required. In essence, they are attempting to apply the basic principles of learning theory and mental health to alleviate school conditions which interfere with effective student learning and healthy social and personal development. This approach is preventive in nature; the contention being that attempts should be made to eliminate the conditions which produce learning and behavioral disabilities, rather than merely treat them after they have already occurred. Consequently, contemporary school psychologists are seen as educational and psychological consultants to teachers and parents, curriculum consultants, developmental specialists, behavior modification experts, consultants in career and vocational education, and facilitators of educational change as well as the traditional diagnostic and therapeutic agents.

Diagnostic Child Study Service

School psychologists typically spend the greatest amount of their time conducting diagnostic case studies of students exhibiting learning and behavioral disabilities. These students are usually referred by teachers, administrators, and other pupil personnel professionals. It is not uncommon, however, for parents to also request this service for their children. The routine procedure following referral is for the psychologist to collect relevant information in reference to the presenting problem by analysis of student records, conferences with school personnel and parents, and interviews with referred students. A variety of educational and psychological assessment techniques are also utilized by the psychologist. These may include individual tests of mental functioning, visual-motor coordination, achievement, and personality development. On the basis of these types of information, the psychologist attempts to diagnose the cause of the learning or behavioral problem and makes recommendations to resolve or cope with the situation. It is also accepted practice for psychologists to follow up each case study to determine if recommendations were followed and if they were effective. In some cases referral may be made to other pupil personnel professionals or outside agencies for treatment.

Special Education

As noted previously, one of the fundamental reasons for the growth in professional school psychology can be attributed to the development of special education programs in the public schools. These programs were initiated in order to provide relevant educational services for students who did not appear to substantially benefit from traditional instructional techniques. Special education services may include separate self-contained classes, provision of various services for students within regular classes, or a combination of the two approaches. Following diagnostic case studies, school psychologists often recommend some type of special education service. This ranges from placement in a special class for the retarded, learning disabled, or emotionally handicapped, to some type of assistance (tutoring, behavior modification, or curricular revision) within the students' regular school program. In most states it is required that school psychologists evaluate all children before they are placed in separate special education classes, and that they be reevaluated periodically. With current estimates that 10-20 percent of all public school students could benefit from some type of special education programming, one can readily see the plight of psychologists in sheer numbers alone, especially when considering that a ratio of one psychologist for 5,000 students is not uncommon.

Consultation Services

A third major component of school psychological services is the provision of professional consultation services of an educational and psychological nature. These services are frequently provided to teachers, parents, and other pupil personnel professionals. They may range from helping a teacher design a behavior management program for one or more students, to assisting in general curriculum development. The current trend in school psychology is to expand the amount of time spent in consultation services and reduce the amount of time devoted to diagnostic child study. They are attempting to modify the school environment in an effort to reduce factors which tend to contribute to the development of learning and behavioral disabilities. Boehm and Weinberg (1972) contend that it is a major responsibility of the school psychologist to apply knowledge of human development and learning principles directly to the development of effective instructional materials and appropriate teaching techniques. In this manner the psychologist assists teachers to provide learning experiences which coincide with individual learning styles and developmental levels. Catterall (1970) has labeled this important role as "environmental intervention," where efforts in the curricular realm are viewed as attempting to assist the student by making adequate provisions in the total curricular/environmental setting of the school.

Counseling Services

Contrary to popular belief, most school psychologists do not spend a major portion of their time providing individual and group counseling services to students. When this type of treatment is in order, referral is often made to school counselors, school social workers, or a nonschool community agency such as a mental health center, family services, or rehabilitation services. This is due to the fact that most school psychology training programs are oriented toward training disgnosticians rather than therapeutically oriented psychologists.

Contributions to Career Development

The most recent development in professional school psychology is its involvement in career education and vocational education programs. Hummel and Hohenshil (1974) described the psychological foundations of career education and proposed several roles for the school psychologist in the development and implementation of these programs. Hohenshil (1974, 1975) proposed several functions for school psychologists in vocational education, and in fact, called for the "vocational school psychologist" as a new specialty in the profession. Basically the proposed roles revolve around the consultation function in program development, curriculum revision, and teacher consultation. Due to the funding provisions of the Vocational Education Act of 1968 for handicapped and disadvantaged students, special education, vocational education, and vocational rehabilitation are combining their efforts to provide appropriate educational programs for disadvantaged and handicapped youth. At the present time, nearly all students qualifying for special education services are also eligible for funding under the provisions of the Vocational Education Act of 1968 as well as funding under vocational rehabilitation statutes.

Another major function of school psychologists in career education programs is to serve as resource persons to teachers and students. For example, many psychologists volunteer to be guest speakers in various classes and describe the types of career opportunities in the field of professional psychology. The psychologist may also stress the importance of good mental health and effective interpersonal skills in the successful performance of any occupation. In addition, students particularly interested in a career in psychology might spend time actually observing a school psychologist at work. In this manner, interested students gain realistic information regarding career goals they may be considering.

School Social Work Services

School social work first appeared on the public school scene nearly seventy years ago. Boston, New York City, and Hartford, Connecticut simultaneously developed school social work services during the first decade of this century. In Boston and New York, the social workers were employed by community social agencies to work closely with the schools. The first school social work service to be established as an integral part of a school system was initiated by the Rochester public schools in 1913. This program was developed by granting a teacher leave to study at a school of social work. Upon returning, the teacher introduced visiting teacher services to the school system (Anderson, 1969).

Currently the titles of individuals providing school social work services vary. They may be called school social workers, home-school counselors, visiting teachers, or even attendance officers. The divergence in terminology is a result of the historical development of the services themselves. Attendance officers, the first of the home visiting specialists, were primarily concerned with problems of nonschool-attendance and their methods of operation were largely legalistic and authoritarian. Visiting teachers appeared later and, although they worked with many of the same kinds of problems, used a nonauthoritarian approach. Rather than force strict compliance with legalistic codes, they attempted to prevent attendance problems from becoming acute by helping parents and students understand their legal obligations and appreciate the value of the school experience. School social workers, a further evolution of the home-school-community concept, expanded their sphere of operation to include not only attendance problems, but also other factors which inhibit positive educational, social, and personal growth (Lundberg, 1964; Ferguson, 1963). A number of services are currently provided in a well-developed program of school social work.

Social Casework

Social casework with individuals and groups is one of the major functions of the school social worker. As a member of the school staff, the social worker receives referrals of students who are exhibiting symptoms of social and emotional difficulty which are interfering with learning, attendance, or social adjustment. Through interviewing techniques and the collection of relevant information, the social worker utilizes the resources of the school, home, and community while attempting to assist students to improve their adjustment to school. A distinguishing characteristic of school social work is the extensive utilization of home and community resources.

Coordination of Community Resources

The social worker frequently serves as the school based coordinator of community resources. In the development and implementation of plans to assist students with personal, social, and attendance problems, the school social worker functions as the prime liaison between the school, a variety of community social agencies, and the courts. These social agencies might include child welfare, vocational rehabilitation, family counseling, mental health centers, public health, and child guidance centers. Through this coordination function, the school has access to a wide variety of referral sources. This arrangement also provides community social agencies with a readily identifiable person on the school staff if coordination between the services provided by the school and the referral agency is required (Costin, 1975).

Consultation Services

The school social worker provides a variety of consultation services to teachers, administrators, parents, other pupil personnel professionals, and community agency personnel.

For teachers this might include assistance with child behavior management and the provision of insight into the effects the students' home environment might have on school functioning. Consultation with parents involves a number of areas such as behavior management techniques, development of effective student study skills, and physical and mental health practices. Consultation with referral agencies is necessary to provide them with feedback regarding the effectiveness of treatment provided to students and families. With knowledge of student functioning in the school setting, the school social worker is also in an excellent position to suggest treatment techniques which have a high probability for success to agency personnel (Berlin, 1969).

Contributions to Career Development

As with the school psychologist, the school social worker can assist in the career development of public school students. They can serve as resource persons to students and teachers by volunteering to be guest speakers in various classes and describe career opportunities in the profession of social work. Students interested in this area might also spend time observing the social worker at work to get a realistic view of the job. As a prime school liaison with community agencies, they may arrange for on-site work observations in a number of social professions as well as recruit resource speakers for classes. Finally, the social worker can play a central role in the work adjustment of handicapped and disadvantaged students enrolled in work experience and cooperative school-work programs.

School Health Services

School health is considered one of the oldest pupil personnel services. The 1850 *Report of the Sanitary Commission of Massachusetts* is a landmark in the development of school health services, for it recognized the school as an agency for the promotion of health. Physical examinations were initiated in the Boston schools in 1894. Connecticut law required teachers to test the vision of students as early as 1899. A school dentist was employed in Reading, Pennsylvania in 1903, and in 1904, Vermont initiated compulsory eye, ear, nose, and throat examinations for their students. By 1910, schools in more than 300 cities throughout the United States required medical examinations of some type (Anderson, 1972). Currently, every state has enacted laws to protect and improve the health of public school students.

School health services include a wide variety of related activities. Initially the primary emphasis was on the detection of communicable diseases and physical disabilities. In the intervening years health services evolved toward prevention by emphasizing health education and healthful school living. Courses in health education typically concentrate on physical hygiene, physiology, and first aid. Other topics often included are safety education, family life education, accident prevention, mental health, and the effects of alcohol, tobacco, and narcotics. The healthy school environment component attempts to assure the provision of a healthy school setting. It includes such elements as adequate lighting, heating and ventilation, water supply, toilet and shower room facilities, and school nutrition.

Contemporary school health services are provided in a number of ways. Some school districts enter into cooperative agreements with community agencies such as a county or city board of public health, while others employ their own health specialists. In most cases a combination of these two approaches is used. Few systems, for example, are able to employ full-time physicians and dentists, while most do employ their own teachers for health education programs.

School Health Specialists

A variety of health specialists work in the school on either a part- or full-time basis. School physicians and school nurses are the mainstay of the school health team. Their responsibilities are many and may include general medical examinations, organization of health screening programs, provision of emergency health care, development of communicable disease control programs, supervision of medical paraprofessionals, identification of handicapped and disadvantaged students, consultation in health education programs, examination of school employees, and evaluation of requests for medication to be administered in the schools. They also provide consultation to school personnel regarding the effects of various types of health disabilities on student behavior and learning styles (Fox and Harlin, 1974; Haro, 1974). Dental services are also provided in a large number of public schools. These services are usually confined to oral examinations conducted by school dentists, dental hygienists, or school nurses. Where examination reveals the need for treatment, referral is normally made to private dentists or community dental services.

The use of medical paraprofessionals and volunteers has expanded significantly in recent years. This movement can be attributed to the severe financial crises facing many school systems, the shortage of professional health personnel, and the expanded scope of school health programs resulting from state and federal legislation. Paraprofessionals and volunteers work under the supervision of school nurses and physicians. They normally assist in the delivery of a number of health services, including vision and hearing screening, and serve as nurses' aides and clerical assistants (Lum, 1973).

Contributions to Career Development

School health specialists, like school psychologists and social workers, can provide several types of supplementary career development services for public school students. They can serve as resource speakers to classes regarding career opportunities in the medical profession. They may also arrange for on-site work observations in medical facilities, or themselves serve as medical role models for students expressing interest in such occupations. The members of the school health team stress the necessity of good physical and mental health in career development. Finally, they can serve as consultants to educators in the planning and implementation of vocational programs including handicapped and disadvantaged students.

School Guidance Services

In terms of professional staff employed in the public schools, school guidance is clearly the largest of the pupil personnel services. Although there have been a number of models proposed for school guidance programs over the years (Shertzer and Stone, 1971), the authors of this book conceptualize "guidance" as a program of specialized services including: (1) The Individual Counseling Service, (2) The Group Counseling Service, (3) The Appraisal Service, (4) The Information Service, (5) The Placement Service, and (6) The Consultation and Intervention Service. These services are provided primarily for students, but some are also utilized by teachers, parents, administrators, and members of the community. Although the major leadership for guidance programs should be assumed by professionally trained school counselors, they are by no means the only persons involved in the *delivery* of these services. If guidance services are to be effectively provided for ALL students, then ALL educational personnel must be involved in their delivery. It is paramount that teachers, administrators, and other pupil personnel specialists accept the provision of guidance services as a regular part of their own jobs. The counselor, then, has a major leadership role in the development and coordination of each of the guidance services, should directly deliver some of the services, and should assist other educational personnel to participate in the delivery of such services. In this manner, teachers, counselors, administrators, and other pupil personnel specialists function as a team, with all recognizing and accepting their own roles and responsibilities in the guidance process.

The Career Development Concept

Contemporary school guidance programs are designed to facilitate the career, educational, social, and personal development of elementary and secondary school students. The major theme throughout this book will be to describe how basic guidance services can contribute to student career development. This is not to imply that personal, social, and educational development are relegated to low-priority status. Rather, career development is viewed as an integral part of general human development, and thus includes the personal, social, and educational aspects. To refer to the term *"career development"* without also implying inclusion of personal, social, and educational development would indeed be a misinterpretation of this very important concept. Career development is what happens to the individual. Simply put, it is a process of learning about oneself, about occupational alternatives, decision making, general education, occupational training, occupational performance, and the use of leisure. Career development is a *process* which is "cradle-to-grave" in scope, beginning well before individuals enter formal education and continuing throughout life. It is a theme around which the entire educational enterprise can meaningfully rally.

Career Guidance, Career Development, and Student Needs

Career guidance and career education are methods of intervention into the lives of students in an effort to facilitate the career development process. Through career education and career guidance activities, all students should be provided with opportunities as they progress through the educational system to insure that they:

1. Understand that career development is a lifelong process based upon an interwoven and sequential series of educational, occupational, leisure, and family choices.
2. Examine their own interests, values, aptitudes, and aspirations in an effort to increase self-awareness and self-understanding.
3. Develop a personally satisfying set of work values which lead them to believe that work, in some form, can be desirable to them.
4. Recognize that the act of paid and unpaid work has dignity.
5. Understand the role of leisure in career development.
6. Understand the process of reasoned decision making and the ownership of those decisions in terms of their consequences.

7. Recognize that educational and occupational decisions are interrelated with family, work, and leisure.

8. Gather the kinds of data necessary to make well-informed career decisions.

9. Become aware of and explore a wide variety of occupational alternatives.

10. Explore possible rewards, satisfactions, lifestyles, and negative aspects associated with various occupational options.

11. Consider the probability of success and failure for various occupations.

12. Understand the important role of interpersonal and basic employability skills in occupational success.

13. Identify and use a wide variety of resources in the school and community to maximize career development potential.

14. Know and understand the entrance, transition, and decision points in education and the problems of adjustment that might occur in relation to these points.

15. Obtain chosen vocational skills and use available placement services to gain satisfactory entrance into employment in relation to occupational aspirations and beginning competencies.

16. Know and understand the value of continuing education to upgrade and/or acquire additional occupational skills or leisure pursuits (*Position Paper of the Association for Counselor Education and Supervision,* 1976, pp. 7-8).

The remaining chapters in this book describe, in detail, how school guidance services can be used to insure that elementary and secondary school students have opportunities to engage in the above activities.

Summary

This chapter was designed to present the four major pupil personnel services provided by most school systems in the United States. The services provided by school psychologists, school social workers, school health specialists, and school counselors were briefly described, along with implications for career development. Pupil personnel services function best when the "team" approach is used. No one specialist in the school has a corner on the skills and knowledge needed to assist a widely divergent student population. Each specialist brings to the school a rather unique set of skills and competencies. In most instances several pupil personnel specialists may be involved with the same case or educational problem. Normally, through case conferences or staffings, all the skills of the individual specialists are brought to bear upon the presenting problem. Using this type of cooperative approach is the most effective utilization of the talents and skills of the entire pupil personnel team.

Beginning with chapter 2, consideration will be focused on one of the major pupil personnel services—school guidance services. The basic guidance services will be discussed with particular emphasis upon their implications for career development and career education. Additional chapters will be devoted to the career education concept, vocational education and guidance, legal issues in guidance, careers in counseling, and issues and trends in career guidance.

References

Anderson, C. L. *School health practices* (5th ed.). St. Louis: The C. V. Mosby Company, 1972.

Anderson, J. J. *Social work in schools*. Northbrook, Illinois: Whitehall Company, 1969.

Association for Counselor Education and Supervision. *Position paper of the commission on counselor preparation for career development/career education* (Approved, April, 1976).

Bardon, J. I. and Bennett, V. C. *School psycology*. Englewood Cliffs, New Jersey: Prentice Hall, Inc.,1974.

Berlin, I. N. Mental health consultation for school social workers: A conceptual model. *Community Mental Health Journal* 5 (1969):280-88.

Boehm, A. E. and Weinberg, R. A. The psychologist learns curriculum. *Journal of School Psychology* 8 (1970):19-21.

Catterall, C. D. Taxonomy of prescriptive interventions. *Journal of School Psychology* 8 (1970): 5-12.

Costin, L. B. School social work practice: A new model. *Social Work* 20 (1975):135-39.

Ferguson, D. G. *Pupil personnel services*. Washington, D.C.: The Center for Applied Research in Education, 1963.

Fox, G. and Harlin, V. K. Role and responsibilities of the school physician. *The Journal of School Health* 44 (7) (1974):369-70.

Haro, M. S. School health revisited. *The Journal of School Health* 44(7) (1974):363-68.

Hohenshil, T. H. Call for redirection: A vocational educator views school psychological services. *Journal of School Psychology* 13 (1975):58-62.

———. The vocational school psychologist: A specialty in quest of a training program. *Psychology in the Schools* 11 (1974):16-18.

Hummel, D. L. and Bonham, S. J. *Pupil personnel services in schools*. Chicago: Rand McNally and Company, 1968.

Hummel, D. L. and Hohenshil, T. H. The psychological foundations of career education: Potential roles for the school psychologist. *The School Psychology Digest* 3(1974):4-11.

Lum, M C. Current concepts in the use of nonprofessional assistants in school health services—A selected review. *The Journal of School Health* 43 (6) (1973):357-61.

Lundberg, H. W. *School social work*. Washington, D.C.: U.S. Department of Health, Education and Welfare (OE-31007, Bulletin no. 15), 1964.

Peters, H. J. and Shertzer, B. *Guidance: Program development and management*. Columbus: Charles E. Merrill Publishing Company, 1969.

Shertzer, B. and Stone, S. C. *Fundamentals of guidance* (2nd ed.). Boston: Houghton Mifflin Company, 1971.

Chapter 2

HISTORICAL DEVELOPMENT OF GUIDANCE

Johnnie H. Miles

Guidance is an emerging, growing, continually changing American concept, even though the idea of guidance, according to Bedford (1948), originated with the Egyptians around 2500 B.C. Close scrutiny of early writings does reveal some notions about individual differences, ideal societies, and the nature of life which indicate some of the foci of guidance.

Counseling and guidance services began in the United States as vocational guidance. Although it is difficult to designate a particular incident and time for the beginning of guidance, it is generally considered to have begun around the turn of the present century, evolving out of a history with a variety of influences. Brewer (1942) lists four conditions which were thought to have led to the rise of guidance: the division of labor, the growth of technology, the extension of vocational education, and the spread of modern forms of democracy. The guidance movement emerged as a natural consequence of the type of conditions existing during that time.

The early 1900s were characterized by urbanization, immigration, industrialization, and social evolution. The high influx of immigrants from other countries, hampered by the language barrier and lack of skills, were pushed into the slums of large cities already overcrowded by individuals migrating from the rural to urban areas in search of a better life. The development of industrialization led to the division of labor, the need for specialization contributed to a rise in unemployment, and led to massive changes in the pattern of American life. Add to these already burgeoning conditions the concern over child labor, compulsory school attendance, and the changing role of women, then the climate of social and economic reform becomes evident. Guidance evolved as a movement designed to help the individual resolve his difficulties and find personal happiness in his life, a humanitarian position which exists today in the guidance and counseling services.

Influences on the Guidance Movement

The beginning of guidance was influenced by a number of factors as previously mentioned, all contributing in a unique way to some aspect of guidance. Traxler (1966) traced the guidance movement to five divergent and highly dissimilar major sources: philanthropy or humani-

Dr. Johnnie H. Miles is Assistant Professor of Counselor Education at Virginia Polytechnic Institute and State University, Blacksburg, Virginia.

tarianism, religion, mental hygiene, social change, and the movement to know the pupils as individuals. Four of these sources will be discussed briefly in this section.

Philanthropy

The spirit of humanitarianism abounded at the turn of the century and highlighted the plight of slum dwellers who were unemployed and underemployed. The philanthropists stressed preparing young people for a productive life as a way of preventing continued slum dwelling. Schools were viewed as institutions capable of helping needy youth.

It was the spirit of philanthropy which was influential in the development of the settlement house movement. This movement was designed to promote more humane conditions for those in need. The humanitarian spirit abounded from Y.M.C.A.s, churches, teachers' associations, chambers of commerce, and philanthropic foundations. It was at Civic Service House, a settlement house in Boston, that Frank Parsons, often credited with the development of organized guidance, began his work.

Frank Parsons, a social activist of his time, was volunteering in the Civic Service House with out-of-school youth when he made a startling discovery. He found that young wage earners lacked the skills necessary for building a career. In cooperation with Ralph Albertson, he organized in 1905 the Breadwinners' College as an additional service of Civic Service House to offer young wage earners the experiences and training necessary for career building. Parsons continued his work with young adults through the organization of the Vocation Bureau of Boston in 1908. A philanthropist, Mrs. Quincy A. Shaw, provided financial backing for the Bureau (Brewer, 1942). Parsons, sometimes referred to as the "father of vocational guidance," provided the impetus for the movement from which most forms of guidance and personnel work seem to have evolved.

Mental Hygiene

Mental hygiene, like guidance, was a social reform movement well-grounded in the humanitarian spirit. Until the late nineteenth century, mentally ill patients were treated as criminals or devils and placed in prisonlike institutions and provided minimal care. Clifford Beers, a former mental patient, brought the treatment of mental patients to the attention of the public through a book about his own experiences as a mental patient. The book was entitled *A Mind That Found Itself* and was published in 1908. Beers became a social activist and instigated sweeping reform in the treatment of mental illness. He was influential in the founding of the Society of Mental Hygiene in 1908 which evolved into the International Committee on Mental Hygiene by 1919. According to Shertzer and Stone (1966), the committee originally concentrated on severe mental illness but gradually began to focus its attention on the study, treatment and rehabilitation of persons with less severe disorders. The committee also promoted the early identification and treatment of the illness. The work of Beers helped to change the relationship of the mentally ill to the larger society principally by helping to educate people about mental illness and the potentials for prevention.

Beers' contribution paved the way for the advent of another mental health reform in this country. Once the public was aware of the need for mental health services, the work of Sigmund Freud and his contemporaries was quickly adapted for treatment purposes. Freud's psychoanalytic approach was widely applauded in therapy circles. However, the approach did not immediately influence the development of guidance. It began to have some impact in the 1930s along with the proponents of laboratory psychology. Although psychotherapeutic and experimental efforts were potentially valuable, they were found to be unacceptable to many adherents to the humanitarian spirit who held fast to the notion that counselors should be concerned about the adjustment of all pupils in an educational setting, not just those with major problems. It was only after "normal" adjustment was linked with psychological well-being that the mental health movement began to influence school guidance work.

Social Change

Guidance responded in all its developing stages to the conditions and social change of the era. Traxler (1966) listed several such changes which stimulated the growth and direction of guidance. He stated that

> during the period between the two world wars technological unemployment, a worldwide depression, rising ethical standards with respect to child labor, compulsory school attendance laws, and similar forces drove into the secondary school thousands of young people who had no marked desire to be there, had no clear idea why they were there or what they expected to get from their secondary school training, and did not know where they were going when they were to leave school. Pressure of numbers and the essentially nonacademic character of these pupils created a whole set of new problems for administrators. (p. 4)

Schools, in an attempt to deal with increased enrollments, broadened curricular offerings and attempted to utilize guidance services to meet other needs. Guidance workers during that period lacked the skills necessary to respond effectively to the changing needs of students. If social conditions were static, guidance and curriculum could be designed to meet the resulting needs. However, the need for guidance continues to increase as social changes shift. Several more recent changes such as the launching of Sputnik in 1957, the knowledge explosion, development and use of computers, the Vietnam conflict, civil rights movement, women's rights movement, expansion of vocational education, political corruption, and the advent of humanistic or psychological education have demanded responses from schools in general, and guidance services in particular, to attend to needs of pupils created by these conditions.

These forces have altered and are continuing to change the social, moral, and economical structure of our society. There are numerous problems associated with attempting to meet the goal of education—that of training and guiding youth for life. The major factor contributing to the difficulty is that the society in which they will live is constantly undergoing change. Guidance programs and schools must focus more on preparing pupils to use their assets in coping with and contributing to a changing milieu. Consequently, guidance must be flexible and evolutionary if it is to continue responding to needs of individuals brought on by social change. The guidance movement has grown considerably since its beginning and the growth spurts seem to have reflected the growing needs of pupils brought on by the social conditions of the society.

Movement to Know Pupils as Individuals

The belief that the individual is of greatest importance undergirds the philosophical view out of which guidance evolved. Traxler (1966) purported that "the first duty of the school is to know its pupils as individuals and to enable each individual to understand himself" (p. 4). This approach recognizes the role information plays in better understanding an individual and the need to use all available resources to accomplish this task. This task requires that a vast amount of information be collected on each individual from a variety of sources and that the data be systematized in an easily comprehensible manner. Two assumptions in this approach are: (1) that once individuals know and understand their abilities, interests, and personal traits, they will use the information to make intelligent and productive choices, and (2) that schools, through pupil understanding, would be better able to realistically design programs to meet student needs.

Other changes and trends not mentioned by Traxler also contributed to the growth of guidance. Barry and Wolf (1963) stated that "industrialization, specialization, urbanization, the changing role of women, the growing need for education, rising enrollments, expanding curricula, rising secularism, the desire for useful education, and new educational theories as some of the changes and developments that created or intensified the need for guidance—personnel work" (p. 16). There are many descriptions on the development of guidance and one may note some overlapping influences among them. These trends point out the responsiveness of guidance to the individual and to the complex myriad of conditions in the environment. Some other influences had a profound effect on the guidance movement and will be added on to those previously discussed. They are: the measurement movement, government support, rise of vocational education, and the development of a national guidance organization.

Measurement Movement

Since Binet developed a test to identify retardation in school children in 1904, the testing movement has grown from the measurement of intelligence to measurement of every conceivable aspect of human learning and behavior. No attempt will be made to delve into the historical development of psychological testing. Testing is considered in this chapter only in reference to its relationship to and impact on the guidance movement.

During the first six months of Frank Parsons' work with the Vocation Bureau of Boston, he developed his procedure for vocational guidance. His conception of vocational guidance in counseling with clients included three broad factors: "(1) a clear understanding of yourself, your attitudes, abilities, interests, ambitions, resources, limitations, and their causes; (2) a knowledge of the requirements and conditions of success, advantages and the disadvantages, compensation, opportunities, and prospects in different lines of work; (3) true reasoning on the relations of these two groups of facts" (Parsons, 1909, p. 5). Borow (1973) summarized Parson's ideas as loosely resembling the modern services of appraisal of the individual, furnishing of occupational information, and provision of counseling. Williamson (1965) indicated that Parsons recognized the need for objective psychological techniques but the availability of instruments to assist in self-analysis was limited in his time. In this sense the development of psychological and educational measurement was helpful in meeting some of the goals of guidance.

The first thirty years of testing in this country was a period characterized by construction and refinement of tests. Tests were developed for measuring intelligence, achievement, interest, and personality. The expansion of available instruments, particularly in the first three categories, made testing more popular in schools. These instruments made a significant contribution to the movement to know students as individuals, supplementing data gathered from other sources. Miller (1961) characterized the postwar years of World War I to be the years of raw adolescence for intelligence testing in the schools. He saw testing as a band wagon affair with schools using IQ tests, ignoring the cautious attitudes encouraged in previous years. Many abuses resulted from naive practices, such as the promotion of students on the basis of test scores alone.

From the beginning, vocational guidance advocates were questioning the value of such tools to guidance and were particularly concerned about the dangers that could result from testing. Other professionals, while questioning the value of tests, felt some information could be gained from them and that their use should be continued (Crawford, 1934). Regardless of the criticisms, testing remained popular in educational institutions.

The testing movement received an additional stimulus with the passage of the National Defense Education Act in 1958. In order to receive funds each state had to submit a plan for the testing of secondary school students as part of the requirements for participation. This act ushered in another "boom" in testing. The use of tests through this act reemphasized the role that tests could play in identification and selection of students.

The impact of testing on guidance was not restricted to the schools. World War I stimulated increased activity in testing after psychologists devised the Army Alpha and Beta tests. The tests were used for the purpose of classification and assignment of men, selection of men for specialized training, and for identifying and placing men with special skills (Miller, 1961). Tests were also extensively used in the advising of veterans in the Veterans Administration Advising Centers following World War II. The United States Employment Service made use of tests in its counseling, selection, and placement efforts. An observation made by Williamson (1965) indicated that industrial psychologists understood Parsons' reasoning and need for tests more than others. Industrial psychology was involved in identifying abilities of workers prior to the 1909 publication of *Choosing a Vocation* by Parsons.

As can be seen, tests became a means by which information about an individual could be collected for use in guidance related activities. The measurement of traits and interests and their concurrent focus on the existence of individual differences is recognized as a significant element in the development of guidance.

Federal Government Support

Major federal legislation has contributed greatly to the development of guidance services through programs designed to meet occupational and educational needs. Through implementation of the legislation, guidance services received support, national recognition and prestige. The federal government has provided funding for guidance services within the educational enterprise and in noneducational settings. Brown and Srebalus (1972) implied that the guidance movement would have had little national influence in schools without federal support. Hoyt (1974) stated that. . .

> The availability of funds has been perhaps the major determinant of change and evolution in the counseling and guidance movement in general and vocational guidance in particular. Although it is true that such funds have represented outgrowths of various kinds of societal concerns, the fact is, nevertheless, that the responses of the guidance movement can be more correctly pictured as related to availability of funds than to any long-range, systematic attempt to develop this field as an effective part of the larger society. (p. 502)

Guidance has benefitted from federal support whether by way of indirect or direct means.

Direct Funding for Guidance. A direct source of funding for guidance not tied to other programs came in 1958 when the United States Congress, in a response to the launching of Sputnik, appropriated millions of dollars through the National Defense Education Act (NDEA) to identify, recruit, and encourage "gifted" pupils to pursue careers in science. Two sections, Title V-A and Title V-B, of the 1958 NDEA had far-reaching relevancy for guidance. Title V-A provided funds for support and development of local school guidance, counseling, and testing programs. Title V-B appropriated funds for Counseling and Guidance Institutes for the purpose of upgrading the qualifications of secondary school counselors.

Title V-A was narrowly interpreted to mean guidance for the "gifted." That interpretation was broadened in 1964 when the 1958 NDEA was amended. The 1964 amendments emphasized guidance and counseling programs for all students. The major intent was to help all students directly or indirectly, through parents and teachers, to achieve career development consistent with their abilities and interests. In addition, the 1964 act appropriated funds to train elementary school and postsecondary school counselors.

The major contribution of Title V-A was that it brought attention to the need to strengthen local guidance programs. Title V-B, on the other hand, influenced to a large extent counselor preparation programs as an outgrowth of the guidance institutes. According to Hoyt (1974), "in 1959 a small group of USOE Title V-B consultants initiated action through the National Association of Guidance Supervisors and Counselor Trainers (which became the Association for Counselor Education and Supervision in 1961) to undertake a five-year project aimed at building a set of standards for education in the preparation of secondary school counselors" (p. 505). He further suggested that the impetus for setting counselor education standards came from USOE's need to justify awarding NDEA Title V-B institutes to some institutions and not to others.

Title V-B was also instrumental in increasing the number of professionally trained personnel at the secondary and elementary levels. Furthermore, the 1964 amendments, by extending training to elementary counselors, reemphasized two important points:

1. the progressive or developmental nature of pupil needs, and
2. the need for a longitudinal guidance approach that can attend to needs at successive levels.

Shortly thereafter, the Elementary and Secondary Education Act (ESEA) of 1965 and its 1969 amendments designated funds for guidance and counseling purposes. The 1969 amendments combined the funds allocated for guidance through Title III of ESEA and Title V-B of NDEA into one appropriation. Guidance services through these legislations extended aid to the disadvantaged, emphasized outreach programs to parents, and began to reflect more of a career development focus.

Vocational Education. Conflicting reports have emerged relative to the relationship between vocational education and guidance. Brewer (1942) indicated that the origins of vocational education and vocational guidance seem to have had little direct connection. Contrary to this view, Stephens (1970) suggested that vocational guidance and vocational education were looked upon as unitary reforms with complementary functions. Both positions have merit and are not in direct conflict depending on the point of view taken. The position supported by the author in this chapter contends that neither approach contributed significantly to the other's origin. Nonetheless, there have been several periods in their history when there was close association and cooperation. The nature of federal support for vocational education and hence vocational guidance created and maintained, to some extent, that relationship. Vocational education is included within this section due to the role federal support has played in its development and in the development of guidance.

Early federal support to guidance was provided indirectly through vocational education in legislation such as the Smith-Hughes Act (1917), George-Reed (1929), George-Ellzy (1934), George-Dean (1936), and the George-Barden Acts (1946). Funds through these legislations, although not specifically identifying guidance as a grantee, implied reimbursable support for vocational guidance activities. The Occupational Information and Guidance Service was established under the Division of Vocational Education in 1938 in the Office of Education supported by funds from the George-Dean Act (Miller, 1961). The George-Barden Act did not authorize funds for teacher training or vocational guidance but each state board for vocational education was permitted to use monies for that purpose. The act did authorize salaries and expenses for state directors of vocational education, for salaries and travel expenses of vocational counselors, and other funds which were used for guidance related activities (Roberts, 1971). Vocational education and vocational guidance were very closely aligned from a funding base. Two significant elements that contributed to a breach in this relationship were the changing view of guidance and the transfer of guidance from vocational education to the aegis of state and local schools on the national level.

Guidance during the George-Dean and George-Barden periods was vocationally oriented and focused on the use of occupational information in job and curriculum selection and placement. The approach demanded knowledge of occupational fields, trends in the world of work, and a familiarity with training opportunities. This approach was a narrow view of guidance for guidance in schools was developing a broader base of services which included vocational counseling, educational counseling and some limited personal counseling. The influence of Carl Rogers's nondirective psychotherapy, and increased interest in psychometrics contributed to the change taking place. The change reflected somewhat of a merger between guidance and counseling.

Guidance services increased rapidly under Harry Jager's leadership as Director of the Guidance and Personnel Branch under the Division of Vocational Education from 1938 to 1952 when the branch was discontinued. A year later, the USOE created a Pupil Personnel Services Organization under the Division of State and Local School Systems. This act removed guidance from formal national attachments with vocational education. Harry Jager was appointed Chief of the Pupil Personnel Services Organization and continued to promote a broadened outlook of guidance.

This changing orientation of guidance and the transfer of national leadership of guidance from vocational education, along with other factors made for some shifts in guidance. Herr (1974) stated that the relationship between vocational guidance and vocational education "deteriorated, in part, because the National Education Association in 1918 accepted a craft rather than a technical training emphasis in vocational education and a guidance-for-education rather than for jobs conception of vocational guidance. Because of the ensuing identity split between vocational education and vocational guidance, each took increasingly independent pathways and pursued professional emphases unrelated to their earlier symbiotic relationships'' (p. 45). Even though vocational education and vocational guidance began a separate existence, vocational guidance continued its complementary functions relative to individual pupil needs and vocational education.

Federal support emphasized again the relationship between guidance and vocational education through the Vocational Education Act of 1963. The act provided funds for work-study programs, residential schools, and area vocational education programs while continuing support of traditional vocational programs. The act specifically stated that vocational guidance and counseling were to be provided to students enrolled in vocational courses and those planning to enroll. The 1963 act further expanded the groups eligible for vocational education by adding those persons who have academic, socioeconomic, or other handicaps that prevent them from succeeding in the regular vocational education program. The 1968 amendments to the 1963 act highlighted the need for career programs and rehabilitation for special needs groups, particularly the disadvantaged and physically handicapped. The 1968 amendments supported a broadened concept of guidance and counseling and its extension into elementary schools which was congruent with career development theory.

The 1963 act and the 1968 amendments have been instrumental in expanding the view of guidance and in the realigning of vocational education with guidance. The acts promoted career development notions and ushered in career education through the funding of exemplary projects out of 1968 monies. Hoyt (1974) noted the impact of the two pieces of legislation as consisting of:

a.   a number of national conferences on vocational guidance;
b.   a very large number of state and local conferences designed to improve relationships between guidance and vocational education;
c.   a significant number of innovative projects in career guidance, counseling, and placement implemented through Part D funds from the 1968 amendments; and
d.   the formation of the Guidance Division of the American Vocational Association. (p. 508)

As previously mentioned, federal support and influence was not limited to school settings. A brief notation of support for guidance and counseling in noneducational settings will be reviewed.

Funding for Noneducational Guidance. The guidance movement received some impetus through the numerous veterans assistance programs such as the Vocational Rehabilitation Act (1918), the Disabled Veterans Rehabilitation Act (1943), and the popularly known G.I. Bill (1944). Subsequent legislation enacted coverage for Korean Conflict veterans (1952) and for war orphans (1956). Later acts extended coverage to Vietnam veterans and others. These acts provided vocational advisement or counseling, and training for veterans. Vocational counseling was generally required prior to entrance into a vocational or educational training program.

An important contribution to guidance came through the Bureau of Labor Statistics of the United States Department of Labor when it published in 1939 the *Dictionary of Occupational*

Titles (DOT). The DOT briefly describes and codes thousands of occupations and is presently a major reference for counselors and personnel workers in a variety of settings.

The following year the Occupational Outlook Service was established within the Bureau of Labor Statistics. The major role of the service was to compile and disseminate occupational trends, characteristics, and opportunities through a document, the *Occupational Outlook Handbook*. The handbook was first published in 1948 and was revised on a regular basis and continues to be issued. The DOT and the *Occupational Outlook Handbook* contributed current and relevant information which was needed in choosing an occupation.

The United States Employment Services (USES), created on a national scale by the Wagner-Peyser Act in 1933, was instrumental in the growth of guidance. The USES broadened its placement function to include counseling around the early 1940s and also began conducting job classification, job analysis, worker analysis, testing, and the compiling and publishing of occupational information. The management of USES was later returned to state governments following the major wars.

These are only a few of the ways in which guidance activities have manifested themselves through federal support. In recent years, counseling has become a part of much federal legislation, particularly those social action programs which are geared toward upgrading employment skills, creating a positive sense of worth, and delimiting the influences of poverty.

The degree to which federal support has contributed to the development of guidance is difficult to determine for indirect results are as important as the direct. The real extent of governmental influences will take years to become evident.

Professional Organization Is Born

In the early 1900s guidance was spreading throughout the states and manifesting itself in a variety of ways—placement, occupational information, testing, moral guidance, and counseling. The Massachusetts Commissioner of Education, David Snedden, in 1910 suggested an annual conference to pull together all the varied interests in the guidance movement. Working cooperatively with Frank Thompson of the Boston Schools and Meyer Bloomfield of the Vocation Bureau, along with the Boston Chamber of Commerce, arrangements for a national conference were made (Brewer, 1942). In March 1910, delegates from thirty-five cities representing numerous organizations and institutions attended the first national conference on vocational guidance held at Boston.

The second conference was held in New York City in 1912. It was at the New York conference that organizational developments began toward the formation of a national vocational guidance society.

The National Vocational Guidance Association (NVGA) became a reality at the third national vocational guidance conference held at Grand Rapids, Michigan, October 21-24, 1913. A permanent constitution for NVGA was adopted at Richmond, Virginia in 1914 at the second meeting of NVGA and the fourth national guidance conference. The first publication of NVGA was released in 1915, the *Vocational Guidance Bulletin* (Borow, 1964).

The National Vocational Guidance Association continued to grow and was strengthened by its effective relationships with other organizations with similar or related interests. By 1951, the increased membership, spreading affiliations with other organizations plus a more explicit delimitation of what guidance was all about led to the merger among NVGA and other person-nel organizations to form the American Personnel and Guidance Association (APGA). The four merging organizations were: the National Vocational Guidance Association, the American College Personnel Association, The National Association of Guidance Supervisors and Counselor Trainers (now the Association for Counselor Education and Supervision), and the Student Personnel Association for Teacher Education (now the Association for Humanistic Education and Development).

In 1952, *The Vocational Guidance Journal,* previously NVGA's journal, became the major medium through which news of APGA was distributed. NVGA began the same year publishing a new journal, *The Vocational Guidance Quarterly.* The American Personnel and Guidance Association has quadrupled in membership since 1951 and the association includes twelve divi-sions which publish eleven journals and numerous newsletters. They are:

Division	Journal
American College Personnel Association (ACPA)	*The Journal of College Student Personnel*
Association for Counselor Education and Supervision (ACES)	*Counselor Education and Super-vision*
National Vocational Guidance Association (NVGA)	*The Vocational Guidance Quarterly*
Association for Humanistic Education and Develop-ment (AHEAD)	*The Humanistic Educator*
American School Counselor Association (ASCA)	*The School Counselor*
	Elementary School Guidance and Counseling
American Rehabilitation Counseling Association (ARCA)	*Rehabilitation Counseling Bul-letin*
Association for Measurement and Evaluation in Guidance (AMEG)	*Measurement and Evaluation in Guidance*
National Employment Counselors Association (NECA)	*Journal of Employment Counsel-ing*
Association for Non-White Concerns in Personnel and Guidance (ANWC)	*Journal of Non-White Concerns in Personnel and Guidance*
National Catholic Guidance Conference (NCGC)	*Counseling and Values*
Association for Specialists in Group Work (ASGW)	Journal in planning stage
Public Offender Counselors Association (POCA)	No journal

The national organization has had far-reaching influence on the growth and development of guidance. APGA has provided major impetus in the professional development of counselors through efforts related to training, certification, licensure, and to development of role and function of counselors. No attempt will be made to catalogue all of APGA's contributions. A greater understanding of the development of the organization may be obtained in *The History and Development of the American Personnel and Guidance Association* by Carl McDaniels (1964).

Historical Influences in Perspective

The many influences mentioned in this chapter have helped to shape the evolution of guidance. There were numerous other individual contributors, social conditions, and reform movements not mentioned here which also had some impact. Guidance has passed through several stages of development which, while highlighting unique aspects, have served to misrepresent and add to the misunderstanding of the nature of guidance.

Guidance and counseling, as we know it today, evolved from a vocational guidance framework. It grew out of concern over the debilitating conditions of urban life and its effect on individuals trapped in those conditions. Vocational guidance from the beginning was committed to the belief in the worth and dignity of individuals and their ability to be productive.

The guidance movement changed dramatically since the turn of the century. Guidance has somewhat diverted its social reform emphasis but remains attuned to the needs of the era. Guidance is closely identified with schools and education although the movement did not begin in schools. It began in social agencies and entered the schools to respond to needs of students. It continues that close association today.

Initially, guidance was narrowly oriented, focusing on vocational needs and interests. Vocational guidance emphasized selection of a vocation, occupational information, and placement. Between the 1920s and the 1930s there was a struggle to maintain the identity of guidance and to keep it separate from the curriculum and vocational education (Jones and Hand, 1938). The 1940s brought on an additional influence, life adjustment. It was perhaps natural that guidance would be considered as a process to enable youth to extract satisfaction from life and to also contribute to society as workers and citizens. The mental health movement was influential in the development of life adjustment focus. This period was also influenced by the work of E. G. Williamson and Carl Rogers, who contributed information about vocational appraisal and the nondirective counseling process respectively. This period was characterized by what seemed to be a merger between guidance and counseling. The description of guidance in the 1940s included educational and vocational guidance, testing, and personal counseling.

Developmental psychology and vocational development theory began to have increasing impact on school guidance programs in the 1950s. As theorists began to emphasize a developmental view of occupational choice, vocational development became popular as a way of describing occupational choice (Super, 1967; Barry and Wolf, 1957). The 1960s and early 1970s saw the term vocational guidance giving way more and more to vocational development and then to career guidance.

Guidance appears to have received additional impetus from the career education movement in the late 1960s and early 1970s. Career education has revealed itself in many ways from the traditional career information approach, ignoring guidance, to an approach which integrated career education and some aspects of guidance. If career education is to be successful, guidance and counseling must be involved in the process, for the dynamics of choosing a career are much more than considering occupational information.

Career education and guidance are considered to be a part of career development which has been proposed to be a part of human development. AVA/NVGA (1963) described career development as the interaction of psychological, sociological, economic, physical, and chance factors that shape the career or sequence of occupations, jobs, and positions that individuals hold during their lives. Hansen and Tennyson (1975) proposed that career development offers the most viable integrating base and unifying concept for career guidance and career education and for the work of counseling personnel. Whatever term is used—career guidance, vocational guidance, or guidance—the present view of guidance seems to reflect a career development focus.

The history of guidance has been traced from the time of Parsons around the turn of the century to the present. Many influences have been noted and several have contributed significantly to its change in emphases. Guidance seems to be responding to the conditions inherent in the changing social milieu and as a result—the ability to predict the future of guidance is extremely difficult. The author is in agreement with Borow (1964) in his projection of the future of guidance when he said. . .

> Whatever the responsibilities which ultimately devolve upon vocational guidance, it seems clear that they will be too broad to be supported by the older and limited concept of matching youth and jobs. (p. 20)

References

American Vocational Association/National Vocational Guidance Association. *Position paper on career development.* Washington, D.C.: National Vocational Guidance Association, 1973.

Barry, R. and Wolf, B. *Modern issues in guidance-personnel work.* New York: Bureau of Publications, Teachers College, Columbia University, 1963.

Bedford, J. H. History of vocational guidance in the United States. In O. J. Kaplan ed. *Encyclopedia of Vocational Guidance* (Vol. 1). New York: Philosophical Library, 1948.

Beers, C. W. *A mind that found itself* (5th ed.). Garden City: Doubleday, 1956.

Borow, H. ed. *Man in a world at work.* Boston: Houghton Mifflin, 1964.

———. *Career guidance for a new age.* Boston: Houghton Mifflin, 1973.

Brewer, J. M. *History of vocational guidance.* New York: Harper and Brothers Publishers, 1942.

Brown, D. and Srebalus, D. J. *Contemporary guidance concepts and practices: An introduction.* Dubuque, Iowa: Wm. C. Brown Company, Publishers, 1972.

Crawford, A. What about all these tests? *Occupations,* 12 (1934):13-18.

Ginzberg, E. *Career guidance.* New York: McGraw-Hill, 1971.

Hansen, L. S. and Tennyson, W. W. A career management model for counselor involvement. *Personnel and Guidance Journal,* 53(9) (1975):638-45.

Herr, E. ed. *Vocational guidance and human development.* Boston: Houghton Mifflin, 1974.

Hoyt, K. B. Professional preparation for vocational guidance. In E. L. Herr ed., *Vocational guidance and human development.* Boston: Houghton Mifflin, 1974.

Jones, J. J. and Hand, H. C. Guidance and purposive living. In G. M. Whipple ed., *Guidance in educational institutions.* Thirty-Seventh Yearbook of the National Society for the Study of Education, Part I. Chicago: University of Chicago Press, 1938.

McDaniels, C. O. *The history and development of the American Personnel and Guidance Association.* Unpublished doctoral dissertation, University of Virginia, 1964.

Miller, C. H. *Foundations of guidance.* New York: Harper and Row, 1961.

Parsons, F. *Choosing a vocation.* Boston: Houghton Mifflin, 1909.

Roberts. R. W. *Vocational and practical arts education* (3rd ed.). New York: Harper and Row, 1971.

Rogers, C. R. *Counseling and psychotherapy.* Boston: Houghton Mifflin, 1942.

Shertzer, B. and Stone, S. C. *Fundamentals of guidance.* Boston: Houghton Mifflin, 1966.

Smith, C. M. History of high school guidance. In O. J. Kaplan ed. *Encyclopedia of vocational guidance* (vol. l). New York: Philosphical Library, 1948.

Stephens, W. R. *Social reform and the origins of vocational guidance.* Washington, D.C.: American Personnel and Guidance Association, 1970.

Super, D. E. *A reconceptualization of vocational guidance.* Position paper prepared for Project Reconceptualization. Washington, D.C.: National Vocational Guidance Association, 1967. Mimeographed

Traxler, A. E. and North, R. D. *Techniques of guidance.* New York: Harper and Row, 1966.

Williamson, E. G. *Vocational counseling: Some historical, philosophical, and theoretical perspectives.* New York: McGraw-Hill, 1965.

———. A historical perspective of the vocational guidance movement. *Personnel and Guidance Journal,* 42(9) (1974):854-59.

Wrenn, C. G. *The counselor in a changing world.* Washington, D.C.: American Personnel and Guidance Association, 1962.

Yoakum, C. S. and Yerkes, R. M. *Army Mental Tests.* New York: Holt, 1920.

Chapter 3

THE INDIVIDUAL COUNSELING SERVICE

David E. Hutchins

Introduction and Historical Development

This chapter is concerned with the individual counseling service in the modern school. Counseling services in the schools are a relatively recent innovation in the educational process, having their origin in the early 1900s in the United States. The first section of this chapter begins with a brief outline of four major approaches to the counseling process along with an assessment of the usefulness of each approach in the school setting.

Psychoanalytic Approach

Psychoanalytic theory and practice stem from the original extensive work done by Sigmund Freud. Psychoanalytic concepts have been the basis for many of the most widely held notions of what happens in individual counseling or psychotherapy. As a result of books, movies, and television, the public has gained much information and misinformation about the counseling process. The psychoanalytic approach views personality as a function of exchanges of energy within the id, ego, and superego—constructs used to explain aspects of the mind's functioning. All kinds of protective (defense) mechanisms are unconsciously employed by the individual in the process of "adjustment" to life. To gain assistance and overcome blocks to productive living, one must undergo psychoanalysis with a highly trained therapist, a process which takes from several months to several years. In general, since psychoanalytic techniques were developed for use in the treatment of mentally disturbed individuals, the approach is not seen as particularly applicable in individual counseling in the schools where the focus is upon developmental and learning activities.

One important development out of a psychoanalytic frame of reference comes from the work of Alfred Adler. Adler emphasized the importance of the struggle for power, the fight against feelings of inferiority, the individual's life-style, and one's relationship to society. Adler was the first psychoanalyst to show a practical interest in child guidance. In the 1920s, Adler opened child guidance clinics where he worked with both difficult and normal children and involved teachers and parents in the process. Today, in the elementary schools, updated Adlerian techniques appear to be particularly useful in the process of individual counseling.

Dr. David E. Hutchins is Assistant Professor of Counselor Education at Virginia Polytechnic Institute and State University, Blacksburg, Virginia.

Trait-Factor Approach

The trait-factor approach to counseling grew out of the work of Frank Parsons and his colleagues in the Boston schools in the 1920s. The central idea was that various job skills could be factored into elements related to human traits. Through the development of appropriate kinds of tests, the traits and factors would yield an effective predictive index of human performance on the job. The goal was that each person could be matched to the kind of job in which individual potential and job satisfaction could be maximized. Though the early attempts to match people with jobs were plagued by inadequate kinds of tests and gross errors in interpretation, the search continued to develop more effective predictors.

The trait-factor approach received the greatest boost from the work of E. G. Williamson and his associates at the University of Minnesota where sophisticated research was conducted into various aspects of assessing human potential, particularly through the use of tests. Known by many as a kind of "test-them and tell-them" approach to individual counseling, the Minnesota point of view became one of the most widely accepted and used techniques in the schools in America. In the writer's opinion, combinations of the trait-factor and client-centered approaches constitute a major counseling style used by schools today, largely because of the numbers of practicing counselors who have been trained in the use of these two individual counseling approaches.

Client-Centered Approach

The client-centered approach to individual counseling is one of the most frequently used methods of practicing counselors in the schools today. Client-centered theory and practice gained its first major impetus with the publication of Carl Rogers's *Counseling and Psychotherapy* in 1942. The approach utilizes a positive and developmental point of view toward the individual. The person's perception of self and the environment is all-important. The individual is seen as being able to effectively deal with problems of living if freed from perceptual barriers. The basic means of counseling is through establishing a therapeutic relationship in which the counselor sets the conditions in which the client is free to explore aspects of self and environment. The counselor is genuine, warm, empathic, and demonstrates unconditional positive regard for the client, mirroring the essence of the client's concerns so as to facilitate a clearer understanding of the situation. Much research into client-centered counseling has been conducted by investigators looking for key elements of the counseling process. Working with relatively normal and intelligent students in the school setting, counselors find the client-centered approach to individual counseling to be both practical and effective.

Behavioral Approach

"The basic assumption of most current behavioral conceptualizations is that behavior is a function of its antecedents and, consequently, that behavior is lawful" (Goodstein, 1972, p. 245). The behavioral movement had its start when John B. Watson wrote an article titled, "Psychology as the Behaviorist Views It," which was published in the *Psychological Review* in 1913. A decade before Watson's work, E. L. Thorndike was conducting experiments with animals which led to the principle called the law of effect. The behaviorist school of psychology continued to expand through experimentation done by others including Hull, Tolman, and

Skinner. Today, B. F. Skinner's work exerts the most significant impact on the area of behaviorism. His popular novel, *Walden Two,* illustrates the application of principles of learning and conditioning to an ideal social system.

In behavioral counseling, principles of learning and conditioning are applied to the understanding, prediction, and control of human behavior. John Krumboltz and Carl Thoresen have been two of the leaders in the application of behavioral principles to the school counseling setting. The job of the counselor is to work on any problems for which the client requests help and to do so in whatever ways will accomplish the objectives (Krumboltz, 1965). Contrary to how some saw the earlier behavioral counselor, the modern behavioral counselor establishes an effective interpersonal relationship with the client in order to facilitate the client's movement toward achieving counseling goals. Behavioral approaches to counseling are becoming increasingly popular among the schools today for a variety of reasons, one of which is the ability to demonstrate changes in behavior which occur as a function of the counseling process.

Individual Counseling Defined

Individual counseling is (a) a process in which (b) a trained professional (c) utilizes appropriate resources to (d) assist in the client's development according to (e) mutually agreeable guidelines. Each of the five elements in this definition will be briefly addressed in this section. First, *individual counseling is a process*. It is not something which suddenly happens or which is "done to" the client. The process aspect of counseling takes into consideration the constantly changing nature of the individual within the context of society. Counseling may include a single encounter or a series of interventions in the client's life designed to assist in the student's personal, social, educational, and career development. Changes that occur for an individual are a function of the continuing interaction between the client and specific elements in the environment, of which counseling is one part.

A second element in the counseling definition lies in the fact that *the counselor is a trained professional* proficient in the use of counseling theory and techniques to assist a client in changing behavior. The counselor operates according to standards of professional organizations such as the American Personnel and Guidance Association. Because of the counselor's training, what is done and how it is done clearly differentiate the professional from others who may be important in the client's life.

The criterion for successful counseling is that the client's behavior changes as a function of the counseling process. Although the training of counselors varies somewhat, a modern training program is likely to include (1) counseling theory and practice, group counseling activities, measurement and appraisal techniques, and experiences designed to enhance the understanding of individual differences including learning and environmental factors of different cultural groups; (2) interpersonal relationship skills: listening and attending to verbal and nonverbal behavior, empathy training, reflection, clarification, summarization, probes, systematic inquiry, and initiating and terminating interviews; (3) problem-solving and decision-making skills: conceptualizing client concerns, establishing realistic and achievable goals, designing effective procedures, evaluation and follow-up; and (4) outreach experiences: consultation and intervention strategies, onsite field studies in business, labor, industrial, educational and governmental organizations. As a result of training, the modern counselor is a professional individual capable of assisting the client in changing behavior.

A third element in the counseling definition is that *the counselor utilizes appropriate resources*. One resource is the counselor's ability to interact effectively with the client. However, the modern counselor does not limit effectiveness by relying only upon interpersonal skills with the client. The counselor asks the question: what kinds of resources including data, people, and things could be brought to bear on the client's situation? The answer to this question suggests all kinds of possibilities which could have a significant impact upon the client, including appropriate elements of the home and family, school, and larger community.

In writing about comprehensive education, Lawrence Cremin (1975) states, "We must consider policies with respect to a wide variety of institutions that educate, not only schools and colleges, but libraries, museums, day-care centers, radio and television stations, offices, factories, and farms" (p. 7). Counselors can increase their potential effectiveness by utilizing all possible resources including the counseling relationship, school, and community to assist in the client's development.

A fourth element is that *counseling assists in the client's development*. Especially in the schools, counseling tends to be a clarification and learning process which assists in a student's total growth. Counseling is differentiated from psychotherapy in that counseling (1) is conducted with relatively normal individuals; (2) tends to rely on only the essential relatively recent background of the individual rather than delving much into an extensive past history; (3) dwells more on how to effectively cope with or eliminate concerns rather than on the cause of the concern; (4) is utilized to bring about specific kinds of behavior changes within a relatively brief time period (e.g., a few weeks or a school term); and (5) is conducted in an explicit and open manner with the counselor and client agreeing on both goals and procedures. In every situation the counselor makes a personal and professional judgment on the probability of being of assistance to the client. Viewed in this light, individual counseling is a process of invited intervention in the client's life which is designed to result in more effective personal and career development.

Finally, in the definition of counseling, it is important to recognize that the *counselor and client mutually agree on the guidelines for change*. Such guidelines include both the goals of counseling and the procedures which will be used to achieve goals. Goals should be realistic and achievable for the client. In addition, the client and counselor agree that the goals are appropriate both individually and in terms of the society of which they are a part. The client should understand the nature of all procedures which will be undertaken to assist in the change process including direct action and intervention with others in the home, school, and community. Thus, goals and procedures to be used are explicit and the counselor and client mutually agree about what will be done and how it will be done.

How Does Individual Counseling Differ From Other Interaction?

The counseling process differs from other kinds of interpersonal relationships because of several unique conditions, seven of which are outlined below. *First*, the client receives the total attention of the counselor. Although there may be appropriate occasions for involving other persons in parts of the counseling process, usually the only other individual present is the counselor. The individual counseling process may be one of the few times when a student is able to receive the total attention of an adult. The concern of this adult counselor is that the client's concern is understood as much as possible so that all appropriate resources can be utilized to assist in the client's development.

Second, the counselor is specially trained to assist in clarifying the client's concerns. The counselor listens carefully to what the client says (cognitive aspects) and how it is said (affective aspects). Both cognitive and affective elements of the client's communication furnish important cues to understanding the situation. Often in typical noncounseling interaction, each person may actually be competing to get their own "two-cents-worth" into the conversation. Very little attempt is made to really understand the other person.

As an example of the kind of situation which may occur, a parent or friend may say, "Let's have a heart-to-heart talk. I'm really interested in what you're doing," and then proceed with a virtual monolog starting with something like, "Back in my day, I remember what it was like. . . ." At this point, the other person realizes that the real message should have been, "Let *me* tell you a thing or two about *my* experience or ideas." Teachers may unwittingly give different messages than they wish. For example, the teacher asks if there are questions from the class and immediately turns toward the blackboard to write something down. The message students get is, "I'm not really interested in what you have to say." More often than not, perhaps, is the situation where the teacher, parent, administrator, etc., are just too busy with other important matters to take the time to really listen (and **hear**) what students are saying. In counseling, the counselor really tries to understand and clarify what the client's situation is as the client experiences it.

A *third* unique aspect of the counseling situation is that the client is primarily responsible for the content of what is talked about. The counselor facilitates the process in whatever ways are possible, serving as a guide in systematically helping to explore the most relevant aspects of the client's situation. The process is aimed toward understanding the client's concerns so that later, specific steps toward resolving the concerns can be undertaken.

A *fourth* aspect of individual counseling is that all concerns are confidential, limited only by the counselor's concern for assisting the client within the guidelines of the school and social system in which they live. Thus, the client is free to relate concerns of a highly personal nature, secure in the knowledge that the counselor's discretion regarding the content of the counseling session can be trusted. If there are specific limitations upon the counselor in a particular school system, these are shared with the client in an open manner during the initiation of the counseling interview. The counselor accepts the client's behavior as a given, which does not necessarily mean approval of the behavior, and assists the client in working toward future productive kinds of behavior while respecting the confidentiality of the counseling relationship.

Fifth, counseling is action-oriented. There is a constant, though subtle, push for the client to do something about the concerns expressed; telling them to another person is not enough. In the counseling process, the client has a unique opportunity to get to know aspects of self through a thorough examination of interests, abilities, attitudes, feelings, values, etc. As a result, both test and nontest data are combined in many ways to assist in this self-knowledge; but knowledge is not enough. The question still remains as to what will be done with the information the client has gained. For one thing, the client has had an opportunity to examine current styles of behavior and their consequences. Synthesizing information gained through counseling, the client is able to project probable consequences of alternative kinds of behavior, plan, and make decisions for the future in ways calculated to enable the client to live more effectively in terms of thinking, feeling, and acting.

The *sixth* characteristic of individual counseling which makes it different from other kinds of interaction is the opportunity for the client to try out (rehearse) new behavior and get immediate corrective feedback from the counselor prior to trying out the behavior in a typical social situation where there is a risk of public failure. One of the reasons many ineffective personal behaviors continue to persist, even though one might like to change, is because the person is so pressured by the immediacy of the situation that time is not taken to carefully assess the situation, weigh alternatives, and act in the most appropriate manner. Thus, one tends to do what has always been done: follow the path of least resistance. Individual counseling offers the opportunity to try out new behavior in a logical, rational manner. As an example, a client who has never interviewed for a job may wish to rehearse certain aspects of job interview behavior with the counselor before engaging in the actual situation. By rehearsing new behavior in a private counseling situation, the client reduces the chance of failure while learning appropriate skills and increasing confidence in the ability to succeed in the actual situation.

Seventh, counseling differs from other interactions because the client is able to learn a generalized method of decision making and problem solving. In individual counseling, the client and counselor mutually work to resolve immediate and specific concerns of the client, but perhaps a more important long range result is that these specific concerns are used to teach a method of effectively handling one's own problems for the future. In many cases, as a result of working through one or two problems, a parent or teacher assumes the student has "learned a lesson," but this is a hazardous assumption to make since the important *general principles* may not be understood, thus allowing for similar kinds of problems to occur in the future. In many cases the old adage of the politician is quite relevant: "Tell people what you're going to say, say it, then tell 'em what you said." The long range objective of individual counseling is similar to this, since the counselor clearly outlines the kinds of things which *will be done,* insures the fact that the client understands what *is being done,* and then reviews steps which *were* taken in the process in order to help the client learn the method. To learn a generalized approach to decision making and handling one's own concerns is thus a major goal of the individual counseling process.

In summary, individual counseling differs from other kinds of interpersonal relationships for a number of reasons. The client receives total attention from the counselor who is a professional trained to assist in understanding concerns from the client's point of view. The client is primarily responsible for the content of the interview, concerns are confidential, and counseling is action oriented. The client can rehearse new behavior in a nonthreatening situation and learn a generalized method of problem solving and decision making.

The Counseling Process

The counseling process can be thought of as involving five phases: (1) conceptualizing the client's concerns, (2) establishing mutually acceptable, achievable goals, (3) designing effective procedures, (4) evaluating counseling in terms of behavior change, and (5) following up the progress which has occurred. In the *first phase,* the counselor's attention is primarily focused on trying to *conceptualize the client's concerns* to the greatest possible extent. The counselor utilizes all appropriate skills to get to know the client in terms of the client's perceptions of the situation. The counselor learns as much as possible about the client's present functioning so as to assist in changing pertinent aspects of behavior including how the client thinks, feels, and acts.

Throughout the entire individual counseling process, the counselor utilizes all appropriate techniques while continuously attempting to understand the client's way of looking at things. The counselor assists the client in relating and organizing relevant data in ways which enable the client to see things more clearly than before. This clarification in conceptualizing concerns enables the client to really begin to think systematically about the situation. Because of a clearer picture of the situation, the client may be well on the way to resolving concerns in a number of cases. Clarification often leads to insight (recognition of relationships) and then to specific action on the part of the client.

The *second phase* in the counseling process is that of *establishing mutually acceptable, achievable goals.* There are several important aspects of this process. First, goals are acceptable to both client and counselor. If both cannot agree on goals, then further exploration of the situation must take place or counseling, with this counselor, must terminate. Perhaps in a specific termination, a referral to another source would be appropriate. In individual counseling in the school, the client and counselor are members of a prevailing social system and both need to operate within the acceptable parameters of behavior if they are to continue to function. Of course, if the system needs to be changed, that may be a desirable goal to work toward, but within the guidelines for socially and legally appropriate behavior.

Second, goals must be achievable in terms of the client's situation. Goals set will therefore be realistic, given the interest, values, abilities, and other aspects of the client and environment. It would be unrealistic, for example, to work with a client four feet ten inches tall who wished to become a professional basketball player, unless the person happened to be that height and growing in the fourth grade. If a person were very shy and wanted to go into public relations work, the client would need to realize that public relations typically involves more outgoing persons. The client could learn to become more outgoing or become involved in other related elements of public relations work such as advertising design, finance, accounting, etc. In setting goals with the client, there must be some kind of probability that the individual will be able to successfully engage in whatever kinds of activities will assist in achieving the goals.

Third, goals need to be specified in terms of observable outcomes. In many cases the client has only a very fuzzy notion of what it is that is desired. The counselor assists in clarifying the client's desires in terms of observable and verifiable results. If the goal cannot be verifiable in some way, how would one know whether it had been achieved? This is not to suggest that everything has to be directly observable to someone else in order to be useful in the counseling process. For example, in changing one's thinking or attitudes, the client may be the most appropriate person to judge the extent of change which has taken place by accurately reporting fewer headaches or stomach problems in testing situations where the counseling goal was for the client to be more relaxed on such occasions. However, it is still essential that some kinds of specific data can be observed, even if only by the client. In most cases, the behavior changes illustrated above could be verified indirectly by noting reductions in the amount of time spent worrying about tests, increases in test grades, increased amounts of effective study time, etc. Goals need to be established in terms of verifiable outcomes, even if the outcomes are by-products or indirect measures of the behavior.

Related to the notion of specifying goals is the process of breaking larger goals into appropriate components or subgoals so that the important prerequisite elements can be dealt with appropriately. If an individual wants to change behavior, very little progress tends to be made in terms of global personality change, except by approaching the process in relevant and sequential steps. Once the components have been learned, these components can then be integrated into the whole, thus enabling the individual to achieve the larger goals. For example, in playing basketball for the first time, the individual does not suddenly go out onto the playing court and become a member of the team. First, component skills such as shooting baskets, dribbling the ball, and teamwork need to be acquired. Once these skills have been learned, the person then attempts to integrate them into playing the game of basketball. The same principles are used in setting goals related to interpersonal behavior. If a client wishes to become proficient in interpersonal social skills, the goal behavior is stated and specific subgoals are identified, such as learning how to express one's self, inquire about others, and keep a conversation going for a certain length of time. Once these subgoals have been learned, the client puts them together and practices integrating the component skills. As a result of acquiring these skills and becoming increasingly proficient in interacting with others, the individual might be viewed by some people as having a "change in personality." In reality, it would be a change in specific methods of interacting with people. Goals must be realistic, observable, and able to be broken down into relevant components in order to be achieved.

Another important consideration in establishing goals is a mutual discussion of the consequences of changes for the client. For example, if a student who is shy (rarely if ever interacts with others) and wishes to become more outgoing and socially active, the possible implications which might result from the changes in behavior are fully discussed before initiating activities designed to reach the goal. Is the client prepared to accept and deal effectively with the consequences of specific kinds of behavior changes? If so, work toward designing procedures to reach the goal can begin.

In the *third major phase* of the individual counseling process attention is focused on *designing effective procedures*. The objective of the counselor is to work closely with the client in carefully constructing a sequential series of steps which can be taken to assist the client to achieve the desired goals. The principle in designing procedures is deceptively simple. Procedures are designed to insure a high probability of client success in reaching each step in the process. Too often, people assume too much about the client's abilities. In designing procedures, it is important to know what kinds of things the client does and does not do at the present time. Too often, a well-meaning teacher, when presented with a student problem, tends to send the student away with a smile or pat on the back saying, "Go ahead, I know you can do it." The only thing wrong with this kind of encouragement is the fact that if the client could "do it," the problem would not exist. In many cases, some of the most seemingly elementary kinds of skills are not in the present behavioral repertoire of the client. Unless such skills can be learned, not being able to engage in the relevant behavior poses major problems for the student. An application of this kind of situation is illustrated in example 1.

Example 1: Analyzing goals in terms of specific component behavior.

Concern: Client does not associate with other students outside the classroom.

General Goal: Learn how to make friends with others.

Specific Goal: To be able to talk with at least two other students between classes each day for at least three minute periods.

Question A: What kinds of things does the client do or not do which relate to the goal?

Question B: What kinds of things does the client need to do or not do which relate to the goal?

A: Behavior now	B: Needed behavior
a. Does not.	give appropriate eye contact to others.
b. Does not.	say "hi" or "hello" to others between classes.
c. Does not.	share information about self with others.
d. Does not.	learn information about other people.
e. Does not.	initiate conversations with other people.
f. Does not.	engage in conversations with others for more than one minute at a time.

Procedure to Reach Specific Goal: Teach the student how to engage in needed behavior *a* through *f* in a sequential series of steps designed to result in a high probability of successful experiences.

In example 1, once the concern and goal had been established, two questions were asked: (A) What kinds of things does the student *do* or *not do* which relate to the goal?, and (B) What kinds of things does the student *need to do or not do* which relate to the goal? By specifying the behavior the student presently engages in as well as what behavior is needed, a hierarchy of events can be set up which will assist in designing appropriate strategies for behavior change. There is a third question (C) which needs to be asked: What kinds of action need to be taken for the client to acquire the behavior suggested in question B? As an illustration, let us use behavior *a* in example 1. The situation is that the student does not give appropriate eye contact to others, but needs to do this as a part of the process toward the eventual goal. For some clients who have never learned to look another person in the eye, learning appropriate eye contact is the first place to start in learning to be effective in interpersonal relationships. A sequential learning process (STEP) for behavior *a* is then established which has a high probability of the client being able to achieve the needed behavior. An illustration of the process is provided in example 2.

Depending on the likelihood of the client being able to successfully engage in a specific behavior, the counselor might suggest adding additional activities to what the client will be doing. The guideline for adding elements to what the client will be doing is this: Is there a high probability that the individual will be able to successfully engage in the specified behavior? If so, then any number of additional behaviors can be added to the process outlined in example 2. The STEP process can be summarized as follows:

S: *SEQUENCE* and discuss the behavior.

T: *TRY OUT* and practice behavior during the interview.

E: *EVALUATE* the trials and outline steps to be taken outside the interview situation.

P: *PRACTICE* the behavior in appropriate situations, making notes which can assist in the following counseling session.

Example 2: The STEP process applied to behavior *a*.

Needed Behavior a: Client needs to give appropriate eye contact to others.

Question C: What kinds of action need to be taken for the client to acquire the needed behavior?

> *S—Sequence Events:* The counselor outlines what will be done to help the client achieve the specified behavior. As an example, the client might be instructed to give constant eye contact to the counselor for two or three minutes while the counselor is talking. The client then gives feedback about what it felt like, problems encountered, etc. Then, the counselor might relate to the client that in trying out any new behavior it will seem "different" or even "silly" but that with more practice, the behavior will "come naturally," meaning the client will no longer have to think about specific steps before engaging in the behavior.

> *T—Try Out:* With the counselor, the client tries giving eye contact in different kinds of typical situations: sitting, walking past each other as if passing in the hall between classes, etc. This technique is called behavior rehearsal.

> *E—Evaluate:* Counselor and client assess the trial behavior, giving feedback on how it went, how it felt, suggestions for improving the behavior to make it look more natural, etc.

> *P—Practice:* Following several trials and evaluations, the counselor and client mutually work out a verbal and/or written contract in which the client agrees to practice specific behavior outside the counseling interview in situations where the client will be likely to encounter a high probability of success with minimal negative results. Aspects of the contract include (a) what the client will be doing, (b) circumstances in which it will be done, such as when and where, and (c) the frequency of the behavior.

> The following illustrates a verbal contract between the counselor and client following the counseling session focusing on giving appropriate eye contact to others.

Counselor: I'd like you to summarize in your own words just what you will be doing between now and next time we meet.

Client: Well . . . let's see. (Pause) I'm going to practice giving good eye contact to at least two others when I meet them in the halls between classes. And, ah . . . just after getting into class I'll write down what happened and how I felt.

Counselor: Good! Do you have any other questions at this time?

In the STEP process of *S*equencing, *T*rying out, *E*valuating, and *P*racticing the new behavior, the overall pattern will look like a set of stairs with as many different steps in it as are necessary to achieve the specified counseling goals, as example 3 indicates.

In designing effective procedures, there is virtually no limit to the kinds of activities which might be used in assisting in the change process. Krumboltz and Thoresen (1969) and Krumboltz and Krumboltz (1972) outline many specific kinds of strategies which have been used successfully in working with individuals ranging from elementary through high school levels. Included in some of the strategies the counselor uses to assist clients are the following: direct suggestion, demonstration and social modeling, roleplaying, behavior rehearsal, relaxation,

Example 3: The sequential STEP process of designing effective procedures to reach a goal is illustrated by five individual steps which need to be taken to move from the client's concern to goal achievement.

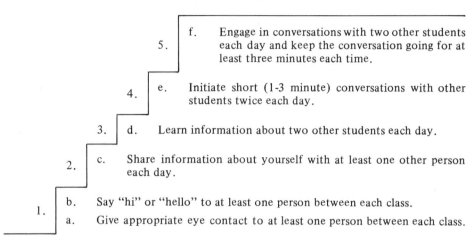

GOAL: To be able to talk with two other students between classes each day for at least three minute periods.

5.

f. Engage in conversations with two other students each day and keep the conversation going for at least three minutes each time.

4.

e. Initiate short (1-3 minute) conversations with other students twice each day.

3.

d. Learn information about two other students each day.

2.

c. Share information about yourself with at least one other person each day.

1.

b. Say "hi" or "hello" to at least one person between each class.

a. Give appropriate eye contact to at least one person between each class.

CLIENT'S CONCERN: Not being able to talk with other students in school.

assertive training, outside assignments, brainstorming, interpretation, exploration, contracts, behavior modification, and coordination, consultation, and intervention on behalf of the client. These strategies used by the modern counselor are briefly described in example 4, but are by no means exhaustive in describing the means available for assisting the client in the process of individual counseling in the schools today.

Thus far, three major phases in the individual counseling process have been outlined: conceptualizing client concerns, establishing realistic, achievable goals, and designing effective procedures to reach the goals. The next two phases, evaluation and follow-up, are very much tied into the first three. First, *how is the individual counseling process to be evaluated* ?

Earlier it was noted that the criterion for successful counseling was a change in the client's behavior. In order for one to know whether a change has occurred, the initial behavior had to first be recorded and assessed. The concise description of initial behavior provides a yardstick against which progress in counseling can be measured. When the ultimate goal is reached, the objectives of counseling would have been 100 percent achieved. However, even falling short of the ultimate goal, progress can be accounted for because of the contrast between the initial and current behavior.

The fact that progress toward counseling goals can be observed is important for at least two reasons. First, the client is able to note progress. The client can see, feel, and otherwise experience changes in behavior as they occur. As the goal comes closer, the client is increasingly

Example 4: Selected counselor strategies.

This is a list of counselor strategies which can be used in the individual counseling process to assist in various phases of the client's development. The list is by no means exhaustive, but is intended to suggest some of the kinds of options which may be used by the counselor.

Assertive Training: Specific training and practice on how to become more outgoing or aggressive in positive ways: e.g., how to apply for a job, conduct an interview, approach people, stand up for what one rightly deserves, etc.

Behavior Modification: Specific kinds of procedures used to accomplish certain tasks. Frequently behavior modification takes place in the elementary schools to overcome certain kinds of behavior problems which are clearly counterproductive for the individual.

Behavior Rehearsal: Trying out particular kinds of behavior in a simulated situation prior to engaging in the behavior in the real situation.

Brainstorming: Rapidly listing as many things as possible which may relate to a given situation, but without judgment as to the quality or appropriateness of the items. This technique is often used to get clients out of a rut or very narrow way of thinking about things.

Consultation: Contact with others to acquire additional specific data concerning aspects of the client's situation.

Contracts: Counselor and client make verbal and/or written agreements that certain kinds of behaviors will be done under specified conditions. Appropriate others may be involved in the contract, including parents, teachers, students, and administrators.

Coordination: The counselor becomes instrumental in pulling together data, people, and things for the benefit of the client.

Demonstration or Social Modeling: Counselor or others actually show the client the desired kinds of behaviors. This technique capitalizes on the demonstrated power of imitation as an influencer of behavior.

Direct Suggestion: Counselor or client may have a good idea about what should be done in a situation: all that's needed is encouragement to pursue the idea.

Intervention: The counselor, with the client's consent, initiates contact with others who can assist in resolving the client's concern, including people from the home, school, and larger community. Sometimes intervention means cutting bureaucratic red tape or direct manipulation of events to assist in the client's development.

Outside Assignments: Behaviors the client engages in, often in preparation for the next counseling interview. Such assignments might include:
   Information gathering from books, pamphlets, and other printed materials.
   Interviews to obtain information or points of view.
   Practice of new behavior: talking with people, engaging in a specified activity, etc.
   Test taking to assess additional kinds of information essential to the client's situation, such as aptitude, interest, and personality testing.

Relaxation Training: Systematic training in how to relax. Usually associated with reducing specific kinds of tension or anxiety as in test taking, giving speeches, confronting specific people, etc.

likely to continue working on the necessary behavior. Successful performance becomes a motivator of continued effort in the desired direction.

A second reason why progress toward the goal is important is the fact that the counselor is able to note individual client behavior change in the ongoing records which are maintained (in a confidential manner) as a part of the accountability process. In addition, others in the school, home, and elsewhere are likely to notice changes in the client's performance in ways which can assist in making an increasing difference in how they react to the client. These observations of changes can be added to the counselor's log of events in the change process for particular clients. By keeping track of the kinds of changes which occur in individual counseling, the counselor is able to account for work with students in ways which are likely to be directly linked to the school budget.

The *fifth major phase* in the counseling process is that of *following up the progress which has been made*. While some concerns of clients are temporary and specific, others tend to be more general and longer lasting. It is highly desirable to arrange for periodic follow-up meetings in order to (1) assess continuing progress, (2) suggest changes which may further assist in the developmental process, (3) correct certain other maladaptive behavior before it gets to be a problem for the client, and (4) reinforce the positive kinds of behaviors the client is engaging in which assist in living a productive personal life style. The follow-up process also enables the counselor to evaluate and make changes in the ways of working with particular kinds of situations, with an eye toward improving the process for clients in the future.

This section reviewed a generalized individual counseling process in which five major phases were described. The first phase was to conceptualize concerns in order to understand the client's point of view; second, to establish realistic, achievable goals; third, to design effective procedures which will lead to goal achievement; fourth, to evaluate counseling in terms of the client's success in reaching established goals; and finally, to follow-up and assess continuing progress, suggest changes, make corrections, and reinforce positive kinds of behavior. The continuing evaluation and follow-up allows the counselor to become increasingly effective in the individual counseling process.

Contributions of Individual Counseling to Career Education and Career Development

In general, counselors see individuals who are either self-referred or referred by others, including teachers, parents, and students. Within these two categories may be found individuals who can be grouped according to the degree of self and career direction, ranging from those who know who they are and where they are going to those who are totally confused. In reporting patterns of self and career awareness of college students, Irwin and Roberts (1974) indicated that 20 percent had reached a point of vocational security where little assistance was needed from outside sources; 21 percent had acquired both self-knowledge and occupational knowledge necessary, but desired further validation prior to making a commitment; 37 percent lacked ability to translate knowledge of self into career planning activity; and 22 percent expressed total confusion, lacking knowledge of self, career options, and decision-making skills. Extrapolating from these results and combining information about secondary school students, the writer proposes four general groups of students and indicates how individual counseling can make a contribution to the career education and career development of such individuals. Each description includes aspects of career education, the vehicle through which one's overall career (life) development can be facilitated.

Group I—Self-Initiators

Students in this group have realistically assessed themselves in light of the social system and career options available. The counselor serves as a sounding board, reinforcing anticipated activities of individuals designed to lead to personally satisfying kinds of behavior. The counselor may provide additional information and insure the fact that the individual's goals are realistic; however, the main focus of counseling activity with this group is to provide support and reinforcement for the individual to continue positive personal and career development. The relative time spent in individual counseling for persons in this group tends to be minimal, as illustrated by example 5.

Example 5. Relationships among groups of students seen in individual counseling, relative counseling time, and the major focus of counseling techniques.

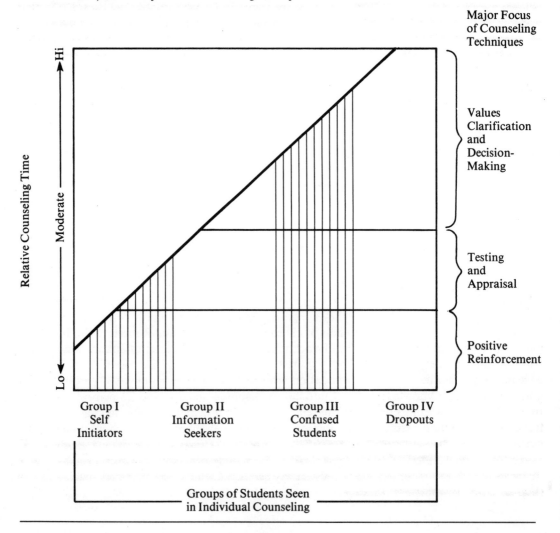

Group II—Information Seekers

These students include those who have some knowledge of self and careers but need further corroboration of ideas, often through additional individual appraisal and assessment devices. Therefore, the counselor assists the individual in clarifying elements of self-concept, interpersonal awareness, interests, skills, and values which allow the client to make informed choices based on more accurate data. The client reviews a problem-solving process which can be used in making immediate and long-range decisions in order to maximize future options. The individual not only learns elements of coping more effectively with the environment, but also how to change elements within the environment to enhance personal and career opportunities. The emphasis is on providing the client with an information base from which to take personal action to change ways of thinking, feeling, and acting in order to live productively within society.

As a part of career education activities, the individual counseling service works to help students clarify concerns, set goals, and design procedures which will lead to increased personal productivity. Personal and career exploration are encouraged so as to provide a realistic basis upon which to plan for the future. Activities are structured to increase individual awareness of paid and unpaid work, ranging from full or part-time jobs to leisure options. In this regard, a careful analysis of hobbies, interests, aptitudes, employment, etc., provides important clues to consider as a part of planning for the future. Typically, the major counseling focus with this group of individuals tends to include testing and appraisal and time demands are low to moderate as illustrated in example 5.

Group III—Confused Students

In this group are individuals who seem to be confused about many aspects of life. They flounder around from one thing to another in a state of continual change. Change, in itself, is not necessarily undesirable. However, to be in a constant state of random activity, without assessing how it relates to one's self, is very likely to lead to a minimally satisfying, highly frustrating existence. For such individuals, counseling builds upon components outlined for Groups I and II, and focuses upon values clarification and decision making as illustrated in example 5. Random activities are able to be systematically examined in light of their consequences. The time demands for individual counseling with Group III individuals tends to be moderately high.

Group IV—Dropouts

In this group, students are characterized as having lost interest in the mainstream of activities relating to themselves and society. If they haven't already, they are close to becoming dropouts by withdrawing from typical kinds of social participation and increasingly engaging in personally and/or socially destructive activities. Such persons tend to be perceived by others (and sometimes by themselves) as having so many things going against them that any kind of positive change appears to be remote. To make a difference, a great deal of time in counseling is demanded. The major focus of counseling activities includes extensive values clarification and decision-making activities as well as other aspects outlined in example 5. The career education of individuals in this group cannot proceed without first establishing a reality orientation to life. Without such a base, the broad options for individual career development are likely to be severely restricted. It is frequently desirable and necessary to supplement individual counseling with appropriate group counseling activities in addition to consultation and intervention strategies as outlined elsewhere in this book.

Within Groups III and IV exist a subgroup of individuals who are affected by peer pressure, but who do not know how to effectively deal with it. Sometimes the individual counseling process helps these clients by providing a reflective setting away from the counter-productive influence of peers long enough to explore aspects of personal and career development which are not possible to do in the immediacy of peer pressure. Frequently such individuals seek counseling because they do not know how to say "no" to activities others "force them" to engage in. Through clarifying attitudes and values and learning effective decision making, the individual client can learn to become instrumental in making positive personal and career choices. Furthermore, the client can develop effective methods of resisting negative influences while taking assertive action to facilitate personal and career development for the future.

Summary

Four categories of individuals have been briefly described as self-initiators, information seekers, confused students, and dropouts. In addition, specific elements of the individual counseling process were outlined as they related to each group. Individual counseling was seen as contributing to the overall career (life) development of students by teaching aspects of career education focusing on information, appraisal, values, and decision making as related to the individual and society. The major individual counseling goal was seen as assisting the student in developing the kinds of goals and activities which will lead to personal changes likely to enhance personal options in the future.

Roles of Various Personnel in the Delivery of Individual Counseling

Although the counselor takes the primary role in assisting with the client's development in the individual counseling service, other persons play important supportive roles in facilitating the objectives of counseling. This section briefly outlines contributing roles of key personnel in the individual counseling process.

Teachers

Within the school system, teachers are likely to have more direct personal contact with students than any other group of professional people. Because of the proportion of time students spend under the direct supervision of the instructional staff, it is imperative that teachers and counselors work together for maximum impact upon student development. The teacher is in an ideal position to notice various kinds of student behavior which may differ from the norm in terms of social, legal, or statistical ways. Some kinds of individual differences may be highly desirable and should be cultivated. However, other differences may tend to result in personal and interpersonal difficulties for the individual. If such deviant behavior is not recognized by the individual student, it may be the teacher's responsibility to refer the person to the counselor. In the counseling process, appropriate elements of the individual's behavior can be examined in confidence and appropriate action taken, depending upon the outcome of the counseling contact. Another situation closely allied to this is the case in which the *teacher* initiates contact with the student about behavior which the student may talk about first with the teacher. Later, if it seems desirable, referral may be in order. Teachers are also in an advantageous position to contribute observations about the student's behavior in the classroom setting, thus providing another dimension, and point of view to an overall assessment of the client's behavior.

If an individual is being seen in counseling, the teacher can also assist in the process of change through actions which support the goals of the student. Through negotiating specific kinds of activities with the classroom teacher, the counselor and/or student increases the probability that classroom behavior will reinforce other kinds of action taken to assist the client in achieving personal, social, academic, and career goals. Similarly, the teacher can also provide feedback to the client and/or counselor about specific kinds of action which take place and suggest corrective behavior if certain kinds of activities do not appear to be working as well as planned. It may be desirable to reemphasize the fact that goals and procedures involved in the counseling process are mutually agreed upon by both the client and counselor. Therefore, the efforts of the teacher are likely to be supportive of the counseling process. By providing feedback to the counselor and/or client, the teacher can enhance the overall effectiveness of the individual counseling process.

Students

Other students in school can provide a tremendous impact in supporting the efforts of the individual counseling service. The impact of peer pressure on student behavior is well known. Working with the counselor and/or client, other students can be a source of information, facilitate client change, act as direct interventionists to help the client, or serve as peer helpers for various kinds of learning, remedial, or supporting assistance. In addition, other students can often be effective as models of desirable behavior. The modeling effect on student behavior has been extensively reviewed by Krumboltz and Thoresen (1969) and Bandura (1969). Furthermore, various kinds of client behavior can be directly effected through the use of role playing and behavior rehearsal in which other students have active roles. The effective use of group counseling activities as an adjunct to individual counseling is discussed elsewhere in this book.

Parents

Parents can contribute to the effectiveness of individual counseling in various ways which are likely to have a marked effect upon the client. First, because of the amount of time and quality of interaction with the youth, parents are likely to have an effect on the client which directly relates to school behavior. Actions initiated at school can be increased, maintained, or extinguished through the influence of parents. Additional observations crucial to the counselor being able to assist the client can be gained through contact with parents. Specific kinds of consultation, intervention, and other activities with parents are discussed extensively in chapter 8. In some cases, parents can be instrumental in referring the student to the counselor in the first place.

Citizens Within the Community

A source of potential assistance in the individual counseling process is that of citizens otherwise not directly involved with the schools. Volunteer individuals and groups can be instrumental in acquiring needed assistance in various situations. In many schools, service organizations assist in providing equipment (glasses, crutches, wheelchairs) or funds (grants, scholarships, loans) which can be used to provide specific kinds of assistance to the counseling and instructional process. Volunteers of various kinds may be able to assist with tutorial, remedial, and developmental activities which supplement the individual counseling process. Interested adults can assist the counselor through volunteer work or through paraprofessional training programs which allow them to engage in certain record keeping activities as well as evaluation, follow-up, and placement operations.

Administration

Within the school system, administrators hold an important key to action which can be taken in individual counseling. Among other activities in support of the individual counseling service, the administration can make referrals, contribute observations of student behavior, facilitate changes in policy, cut red tape, and engage in other behaviors which greatly enhance the work of the counselor. Frequently, working with the administration, the counselor is able to negotiate cooperative efforts to assist the individual client through contacts with outside organizations and individuals including probation and parole officers, parents, social welfare organizations, employment agencies, and other groups. As persons who facilitate the action of many different people and organizations, the administrators play an important supportive role in the individual counseling service.

Differential Aspects of Individual Counseling

At all levels, kindergarten through high school, the individual counseling service is concerned with student development. However, there are some important differences between the elementary, junior high or middle school, and high school levels which will be briefly mentioned in this section.

Elementary School

In the elemenatry school, more than at any other level, the work of the counselor is primarily preventive and developmental (Nelson, 1972). Activities of the counseling service are directed toward assisting with individual student growth and development which tries to insure that students acquire basic educational, personal, social, and career development skills consistent with the goals of the elementary school. The counseling service acts primarily in a supporting role to the central thrust of the school by working with individual problems in a manner designed to encourage the positive development of each child. The service is often utilized by teachers as a referral source. The counselor then assists in resolving problems or suggesting appropriate consultants or resource persons who may be better able to assist the child. The individual counseling service works with children in appropriate age-level tasks related to *becom-*

ing aware of values and attitudes, methods of changing individual behavior and/or the environment, and learning elements of decision making.

Junior High/Middle School

To a certain extent, the activities of the junior high/middle school are an extension of those at the elementary school level. Counselors are still very much concerned with developmental aspects of students. Individual concerns related to adolescent problems of a physical and psychological nature frequently result in youngsters seeking assistance through counseling. At this level students are increasingly responsible for making decisions about their personal behavior. The counseling service assists in the transition from childhood to young adult status by providing opportunities for *exploring* various kinds of options related to educational, personal, and career goals. Attitudes, values, and decision making are specific topics dealt with in individual counseling at this stage of development. The client is encouraged to make responsible choices, try out different kinds of activities of potential interest, and examine the consequences of the options available. The student is *not* programmed into specific educational or potential career options, but is given a basis upon which to systematically examine and explore potential avenues of personal, educational, social, and career development.

High School

Building upon the skills acquired up to this point in time, the high school counseling service continues to assist students in their overall development while recognizing the importance of individual differences. Aspects of career awareness and exploration in earlier stages of the educational process now become the basis upon which students begin to make *tentative choices* about the kinds of things they may wish to do while completing high school studies. Students are helped to make choices which will insure appropriate academic and career preparation for opportunities beyond high school, including options for those who stop out of school, those who take entry level jobs upon graduation, and those who continue various forms of continuing education. Increasingly more accurate and helpful kinds of testing and appraisal methods are available to assist students in making personal, educational, and career decisions at the high school level. Important activities of the individual counseling service at the high school level involve assisting students in coping with or changing relevant aspects of personal behavior or the environment, making positive and effective interpersonal and social adjustment, and developing sound strategies for educational and career preparation while increasingly perfecting decision-making skills which will assist in enhancing the potential for personal and career development in the future.

Evaluating the Individual Counseling Service

In any evaluation, the question arises as to who evaluates what kinds of things. In assessing the effectiveness of the individual counseling service, the counselor, client, teaching staff, administration, and students may all have a role to play. Certainly teachers and administrators continuously evaluate the service by observing the differences counseling makes on the behavior of individuals with whom they come into contact. Such differences may be reflected in terms of the client's academic performance, attendance, classroom behavior, and in other ways directly observable by teachers and administrators.

The activities, interests, motivation, aptitudes, and attitudes of the client tend to relate directly or indirectly to most other behavior. Since all of these qualities are dealt with in individual counseling, they can be used as a part of the evaluation of the service. Frequently there are specific measures of such variables which can be used in assessing before and after differences in clients.

Clients who utilize the services involved in individual counseling are in a primary position to evaluate the differences to themselves in terms of how they think, feel, and act. Certainly, resolution of concerns brought to counseling should be one of the critical elements in any evaluation of the service.

The number of students who take advantage of various aspects of the counseling service is an important measure of effectiveness. By recording the number of students who seek assistance with specific kinds of concerns, counselors are in a better position to assist students in the future. Measures assessing the degree of client satisfaction or dissatisfaction with specific aspects of the service are important in planning to meet student needs in the future. The extent to which individuals experience success in working through specific kinds of concerns should be reflected in increased demand for such assistance by others. The student "grapevine" is also an important source of information about the service and may have the greatest impact on students who take advantage of the service for specific kinds of assistance. As individuals receive help in resolving problems, they will be likely to use the service in the future to obtain assistance with minor concerns rather than waiting until they become major problems. As a result of getting data on aspects of the counseling service such as those mentioned above, the counselor can become more effective in daily operation and future activities.

Frequently, one of the responsibilities of the counseling service is that of placement of students in various curricular opportunities in the school. As a result of comparing initial placement data with subsequent information on curriculum changes, student satisfaction, and entry into related areas in the future, guidelines for more accurate placement activities can be designed. When students leave the school, interviews relating to their impressions of the individual counseling service can be useful in planning. Finally, follow-up data relating to post-high-school experiences can be useful in an evaluation of the relative effectiveness of the counseling service. As a result of gathering and analyzing data such as outlined above, members of the individual counseling service obtain information which can be useful in evaluating the relative effectiveness of various options available to students. Further, they can use the data in planning a more effective operation in the future. Finally, the information and evaluation of the service can be a powerful tool in demonstrating the worth of individual counseling to individuals and groups who make decisions about personnel, budget, and resources. In these times of the increasingly tight dollar, it is imperative that the individual counseling service engage in activities to demonstrate its important role as an integral and essential part of the total educational program in the schools.

References

Bandura, A. *Prinicples of behavior modification*. New York: Holt, Rinehart & Winston, 1969.

Cremin, L. Public education and the education of the public. *Teachers College Record* 77 (1) (1975):1-12.

Goodstein, L. Behavioral views of counseling. In B. Stefflre and W. H. Grant eds., *Theories of counseling*. New York: McGraw-Hill, 1972.

Irwin, T. J. and Roberts, R. K. *The concept of student career self-evaluation*. Unpublished report, Counseling Center, Virginia Polytechnic Institute & State University, 1974.

Krumboltz, J. D. Behavioral counseling: Rationale and research. *Personnel and Guidance Journal* 44 (1965):383-87.

Krumboltz, J. D. and Krumboltz, H. B. *Changing children's behavior*. Englewood Cliffs, New Jersey: Prentice-Hall, 1972.

Krumboltz, J. D. and Thoresen, C. E. eds., *Behavioral counseling: Cases and techniques*. New York: Holt, Rinehart, & Winston, 1969.

Nelson, R. C. *Guidance and counseling in the elementary school*. New York: Holt, Rinehart, & Winston, 1972.

Chapter 4

THE GROUP COUNSELING SERVICE

Sally Ann Tschumi

Introduction and Historical Development

School counselors function in many group situations. However not everything they do in those situations is "group counseling." Group counseling is not a guidance hour in a classroom or homeroom, an orientation assembly, a Future Farmers of America Club meeting, a human relations seminar, a parents information meeting, or a field trip to an industrial plant. However all of these and more are group activities which may be part of guidance services in public schools. The more global term to describe the functioning should be "group work." The social work definition of group work used by Klein (1972) can easily be applied to educational systems.

> Group work is a method of helping people through a group experience—a form of social helping directed toward giving people a constructive experience of membership in a group so that they are able to develop as persons and be better able to contribute to the life of the community. A group is a social system consisting of two or more people who are in face-to-face interaction at both the cognitive and psychic levels within which the people perceive that they belong to the group. By virtue of it being a social system, it is understood that there are common goals, common norms, reciprocal relationships, social structure, and cohesion. It is agreed that the interrelationship of all the components of the system are so interdependent that change or action of any one component influences every other. (p. 26)

"Group guidance" has been used historically to describe the guidance activities usually taking place within the classroom that were informative or instructional in nature. The term "group counseling" should be reserved for the small, person centered groups of approximately four to twelve members which meet over a period of time to work on developmental or remedial problems. The thrust of this chapter will focus on group counseling but the activities and potential of other aspects of group work in guidance will be briefly discussed.

The meaning of many terms in group work have become less precise as they have become more popular. In one of the earlier books on group guidance Glanz (1962) defines a group as "a collection of persons operating together to achieve a mutually related purpose or functioning" (p. 326), and group dynamics as "the interactive forces operating within a group" (p. 327).

Dr. Sally Ann Tschumi is Assistant Professor of Counselor Education at Virginia Polytechnic Institute and State University, Blacksburg, Virginia.

These are simply stated but basically good definitions. The latter term is also used to mean a field of inquiry about the nature of groups (Cartwright and Zander, 1968). The term "group processes" will be defined as:

> a set of techniques, such as role playing, buzz-sessions, observation and feedback of group process, and group decision, which have been employed widely during the past decade or two in training programs designed to improve skill in human relations and in the management of conferences and committees. (Cartwright and Zander, p. 4)

"Group processing" is interchangeable with "read-out" and "clinicing" and refers to the group discussion of the intra- and interpersonal reactions to an experience or activity. It includes the processes of observation, feedback, analysis, projected application, and the resulting interactions.

Historical Development

The history of the development of group work in the schools may be traced in two ways: (a) the growth of various group methods and sciences and (b) the application of this knowledge and skill in the public school systems. As in all developments, many people get into the act, but few get recorded for posterity. Only those who have contributed to the literature directly or indirectly can be traced.

Group counseling has roots in psychiatry, psychology, philosophy, sociology and religion as well as in education. Dreikurs and Corsini (1954) suggest that "collective counceling" *sic* was developed in Europe between 1900 and 1930 and that Alfred Adler was probably the first psychiatrist to formally use "collective counceling" in his child guidance clinic in Vienna. According to Schutz (1973) group psychotherapy started with Pratt in 1907 and was given great impetus during World War II. Regardless of who was first, the unique properties of the group were revealed in clinical experience which showed group psychotherapy to be more than a poor substitute for individual therapy. The terms "group counseling" and "group psychotherapy" appear in the literature in the early 1930s and are attributed to R. D. Allan and J. L. Moreno, respectively (Gazda, 1971).

Social group work was one of the earliest professions to recognize that groups could be managed to promote desired changes in members. The study of group dynamics (i.e., what takes place in groups, laws of their development and operation) continues to draw from this field.

> Group dynamics began, as an identifiable field of inquiry, in the United States toward the end of the 1930s. Its origination as a distinct speciality is associated primarily with Kurt Lewin (1890-1947) who popularized the term group dynamics, made significant contributions to both research and theory in group dynamics, and in 1945 established the first organization devoted explicitly to research on group dynamics. (Cartwright and Zander, 1968, p. 7)

J. L. Moreno's major contributions to this field include psychodrama and sociometrics.

It is a little remembered fact that the National Training Laboratories (NTL) had their origin in education at a National Education Association (NEA) Conference. Students of Lewin founded the organization in 1947 as part of NEA's Division of Adult Education Service to emphasize group process and group dynamics in training (T) groups. The change to personal growth labs and inclusion of nonverbal techniques began quietly in the 1950s and led to the use of the term "sensitivity training." This became a popular movement in the 1960s. The late sixties and seventies have seen a mushrooming of growth centers, group movements, group techniques and training programs which need to be carefully evaluated. Those such as Values Clarification which grew out of Dewey's philosophy of "learning by doing" have a legitimate place in the schools. Adlerian, Behavioral, Client-centered, Gestalt and Transactional Analysis therapies have all developed group approaches which are also appropriate.

One of the earliest recorded guidance classes was started by Jesse B. Davis, principal of the Grand Rapids, Michigan, High School. In 1907 he took a weekly period from English composition and devoted it to "Vocational and Moral Guidance" (Glanz and Hayes, 1967). Courses in vocations and occupational information, and homeroom guidance periods quickly followed.

> The 1930s became the era of the group guidance class, where units on character, vocation, and citizenship were prominent. Hardly a city junior high or senior high school was without such a program, and the guidance literature of the era was saturated with texts on "group guidance." (Glanz and Hayes, 1967, p. 3)

The sincerity of the counselors or guidance workers in these early efforts did not always make up for the lack of training. Regular classroom teachers were told to do "group guidance" in classes of 35-100 pupils. The lack of real knowledge of the dynamics of groups, and the attempts to apply regular teaching devices poorly suited to the problems of guidance, so twisted the concept of "group guidance" that some administrators, teachers and counselors became disenchanted and dropped the programs. The National Defense Education Act of 1958, stressing guidance needs and the increased enrollment of students in school classes, caused school personnel to reconsider ways of working with larger numbers of students. Federally funded programs for innovation and training have given impetus to the group guidance and group counseling movement. The current emphasis on career education has continued that momentum. The question today is will these programs deteriorate as earlier ones did or have we learned to develop staff to use techniques appropriately? Currently there are no requirements for course work in group dynamics in teacher education and minimal offerings in many basic counselor education programs.

Content of the Service

This will necessarily be a brief overview of group counseling and a limited look at other activities in the group work aspects of guidance services. The reader is encouraged to investigate the references and other texts for expanded knowledge and to develop specific skills in this area.

Gazda (1971) uses a preventive-remedial continuum to distinguish between group guidance, group counseling and group psychotherapy. Figure 4.1 is his model. He indicates the typical setting for group guidance is a classroom of twenty to thirty-five, that providing information is the main concern, and that it should be available for all students on a regularly scheduled basis.

Group guidance is organized to prevent the development of problems. The content includes educational-vocational-personal-social information which is not otherwise systematically taught in academic courses. . . Providing accurate information for use in improved understanding of self and others is the direct emphasis in group guidance, whereas attitude-change frequently is an indirect outcome or goal. (Gazda, 1971, p. 7)

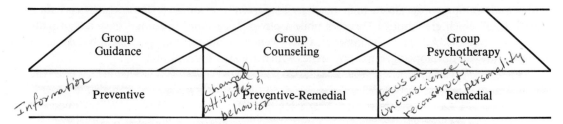

Information   *changed attitudes & behavior*   *focus on unconscience & reconstruct personality*

Figure 4.1. The relationships among group guidance, group counseling, and group psychotherapy. Source: Gazda, 1971, p. 9.

Group counseling differs from group guidance in that the groups are small enough for cohesiveness and intimate sharing to develop. Changed attitudes and behaviors are the direct focus rather than information which might lead to this change and it is recommended only for those students experiencing a problem that is best aided with the process. From a survey of literature and current practice the following definition of group counseling was formed.

Group counseling is a dynamic interpersonal process focusing on conscious thought and behavior and involving the therapy functions of permissiveness, orientation to reality, catharsis, and mutual trust, caring, understanding, acceptance, and support. The therapy functions are created and nurtured in a small group through the sharing of personal concerns with one's peers and the counselor(s). The group counselees are basically normal individuals with various concerns which are not debilitating to the extent requiring extensive personality change. The group counselees may utilize the group interaction to increase understanding and acceptance of values and goals and to learn and/or unlearn certain attitudes and behaviors. (Gazda, Duncan, and Meadows, 1967, p. 305)

Group psychotherapy is generally left to the psychiatrist or psychologist outside the school system. It serves the neurotic or severely disturbed, is long-termed, may focus on the unconscious and attempts to reconstruct the personality. Counselors and most school psychologists have not been educated to function at this level.

Group Counseling

Group counseling should not be part of the guidance service unless at least one counselor has some special preparation in the process. While some individual counseling and even teaching techniques are used, the major skill is knowing when and how to facilitate the group dynamics that lead to growth. The definition of Dinkmeyer and Muro (1971) seems to reflect this philosophy and explain the value of group counseling.

Group counseling is an interpersonal process led by a professionally trained counselor and conducted with individuals who are coping with typical developmental problems. It focuses on thoughts, feelings, attitudes, values, purposes, behavior, and goals of the individual and the total group. The group process permits the individual to examine and share self with others. Group transactions and group mechanisms facilitate increased understanding of self and others. Group counseling creates the conditions and climate for re-evaluating one's thoughts, feelings, and behavior. Through changing one's perceptual field, attitudes and feelings, or actions, one is better equipped to experience and cope with the tasks of life. (p. 1, 2)

Ohlsen (1970) recommends that the average number of participants in a counseling group be between four and eight. Dinkmeyer and Muro (1971) suggest five to six, Gazda (1971) five to seven, and Dye (1968) an optimum of five to seven in elementary school and twelve in high school. Four seems to be the smallest number that allows for support versus having two members pair up against a third. Beyond eight, the group tends to function like a class being more dependent on the leader than on themselves. The age and maturity of the members, the purpose of the group, the counselor's skill, and time available are some of the factors which determine size. Consideration should be given for attrition following selection. The group should be large enough to sustain interaction yet small enough to be cohesive and provide each person with an opportunity to be heard.

The suggested time allowed per session runs from twenty minutes (Ohlsen, 1970) to two hours (Dye, 1968). Sufficient time must be allowed in each session to establish the climate for work. All too frequently the academic class period controls the time available. Groups should meet at least once a week to maintain continuity. Primary school children may have as many as three brief sessions weekly. Gazda (1971) suggests forty minutes to one hour in a weekly session over three to twelve months for play group counseling of a preventive nature, and two sessions a week for six to nine months for one which is primarily remedial in nature (pp. 83, 84). Smaller groups, more frequent sessions, and less time per session characterize groups for younger children. Larger groups, less frequent sessions with more time in each are characteristic of groups for older children and adults.

Scheduling time for group counseling is one of the major problems in this service. Children who would form a natural group or who have similar problems do not always have the same schedule. Academic schedules often need to be adjusted to find group time slots. If the counselors plan for and legitimize group counseling as part of their own schedules, not as an occasional extra assignment, then they can probably influence administrators and teachers to also plan for this.

Volunteers and referrals for group counseling should be carefully screened before assignment to a particular group. An intake interview is suggested during which the counselor explains the process, expected behaviors and possible outcomes to the student, and assesses the individual's readiness, commitment, and appropriateness of the group to meet the presenting problems. In the behavioral group counseling intake interview the student and counselor agree on specific goals to be reached and ways of measuring progress toward the individual's goals.

At the first session of a new group, the freedoms, responsibilities, and limitations should be clearly communicated. These may be verbalized or provided in handouts. Minimal ground rules may be as brief as "We are allowed to do or say anything we want as long as no one is in-

jured physically or otherwise. Gossip injures people so we do not talk about what happens or is discussed here outside the group.'' The limits in play therapy have been expressed by Ginott (1961) as:
1. No toys are taken from the room.
2. No physical attacks on the counselor or on other children.
3. No leaving the room.
4. Limits on time. (pp. 109-13)

Details of group dynamics and the group processes which facilitate them in counseling groups may be found in many texts (Dinkmeyer and Muro, 1971; Dye, 1968; Gazda, 1971; Hansen and Cramer, 1971; Lifton, 1972; Mahler, 1969; Ohlsen, 1970; etc.). Some of the elements in the traditional group (Humanistic/Existential) which are therapeutic are:
a. The leader:
- initiates, models, teaches, and continues to move the process.
- safeguards members from undue attack or damage.
b. The group members:
- provide a variety of mirrors to reflect self.
- provide feedback.
- provide opportunities to experience vicariously.
- provide an opportunity to try out a variety of roles. (one is not always in the position of patient)
- provide support.
- provide a microcosm of interpersonal relationships experienced outside the group.
c. The atmosphere of trust and openness:
- defenses can be dropped.
- anything can be revealed and accepted.
- opportunity to try out new behavior.
d. Feedback:
- one is confronted with one's own behavior.
- one is able to check out self with perceived self and learn to work to bring the two closer together.
e. Here and now emphasis:
- really encounter self as you are.
- in touch with reality.
- provides the greatest potential for immediate change.
f. Responsibility for own actions:
- with insight gained in the here and now a person can go back and defuse the impact of past experience but he cannot go back and remove them. He learns to live with the consequences.
- learns he is in command and responsible, therefore he has power to be what he wants to be.

Ohlsen (1970) feels the therapeutic potential of a group is realized best when:

(1) clients begin with a commitment to discuss their problems openly, to change their behavior, and to help others change their behavior; (2) they know before they begin counseling, what is expected of them, insofar as this is possible in advance; (3) they accept responsibility for helping to develop and maintain a therapeutic climate, for their own behavior within their counseling group and outside of it, and for changing their behavior; (4) they sense genuine acceptance within their counseling group; (5) they perceive their group as attractive; (6) they feel that they truly belong; (7) they feel safe enough within their group to discuss whatever bothers them; (8) they experience enough tension to want to change, believe that they can cope with their tension, and are convinced that the results will be worth the pain and effort; and (9) they accept their group's norms. (p. 96)

Counselors may be educated in one of a variety of counseling theories and the style of group will usually reflect techniques consistent with this (i.e., Behavioral, Rational-Emotive, Gestalt, Transactional Analysis, Client-centered). Some unique aspects of behavioral group counseling might be mentioned here:

1. The goals for group counseling are distinctly specified and agreed upon in advance by each member individually and the group collectively.
2. The goals are specified according to behavioral terminology so that the outcome of the goal may be observed and evaluated at the conclusion of the group sessions.
3. Only one unit of behavior is dealt with at one time. Successive behaviors may be considered in turn which may lead to the performing of more complex units of behavior.
4. A systematic plan for achieving the goal is developed by the counselor, before the group counseling begins, involving a choice of techniques that will be used for counseling.
5. Both verbal and nonverbal techniques may be used.
6. The counselor takes an active and important role in the process, frequently taking the lead in directing the discussions. (Varenhorst, 1969, pp. 137-38)

Groups may also be developed around art, music, drama, and dance as well as play media. The T-group (Bradford, Benne, and Gibb, 1964), C-group (Dinkmeyer and Muro, 1971), and encounter group (Schutz, 1973) are other popular styles. The "T" stands for training and emphasizes learning about group dynamics and one's self from the way a group evolves from an unstructured situation. "C" represents the initial letters of the factors collaborating, consulting, clarifying, confronting, concern, confidentiality, caring, and commitment involved in examining the transactions between child and teacher. "Encounter" may be used to describe either Carl Rogers' nondirective approach or William Schutz's very active "open encounter" which stresses nonverbal techniques, body methods, and guided daydream fantasies.

Time limits concerning the life of the group should be established before the group begins and clearly stated. Care must be taken to see that a counseling group operates long enough to be effective, but does not go on endlessly. In some instances effective work can be done in a few sessions. Other counseling groups may run for a semester or a year. Nonproductive groups should be confronted with their level of functioning. If it does not improve then the group should be terminated earlier. Occasionally productive groups may want to continue beyond the original limit. A reminder several sessions before termination often stirs up participation as the members are encouraged to get their work done before the group finishes. Time should be allowed at the close of a counseling group for members to verbalize how they have grown and consider applications of this growth beyond the group.

A group counseling program should be initiated only after proper approval and support have been obtained from the administration. To do this a counselor must be able to clearly communicate the process, goals, and requirements of group counseling, the cost to the system (work load, space, disrupted schedules, etc.) and the anticipated benefits. Mahler (1973) suggests some goals that a school district might specify for its group counseling program:

1. To assist academic underachievers.
2. To assist students who have ineffective social skills.
3. To train all students in more efficient decision-making skills.
4. To assist students with excessive fears and anxieties.
5. To help students to explore life-style and career possibilities.
6. To reduce interpersonal hostilities in our school. (p. 22)

Maximum growth in group counseling can be assisted if parents and teachers are consulted regularly, and if they understand and accept what is expected in the group. Informational meetings held for the parents and teachers of the target group will gain support for the program. It is suggested that the first group be established to work on a developmental problem common to all children (such as to learn how to work better with other people). It should be advertised as a special opportunity for normal children to develop skills and that enrollment will be limited. The counselor's visits to classrooms will explain the same to the students. Volunteers should be screened by an interview to determine the appropriateness of the group, the readiness and commitment of the student. With older children a group centered on this problem will almost develop and work by itself if the counselor stays out of the way. It gives the beginning group counselor a chance to develop and refine skills before handling more difficult groups. Both the ongoing process and final outcomes should be evaluated to provide local data on what really happens in a group. A successful group experience will get good peer publicity (student to student, parent to parent, teacher to teacher) for a continued program.

Group Guidance

Definitions of group guidance usually indicate the classroom as the setting, and presentation of information the major concern and process. In the past the differentiation between teaching and group guidance was that the latter covered topics not taught in academic courses (i.e., educational-vocational-personal-social) and was done by counselors. Counselors are still active in the classroom making some presentations. However teachers are once again involved in the process. Training teachers for this is part of the counselor's role. The current approach is that not all information is presented *to* children. Values clarification strategies (Simon and Kirschenbaum, 1972) and other experiential learning techniques are helping children supply their own information. Some of the information is even being presented in academic courses in an attempt to make career education more relevant.

Group guidance takes many forms. Activities outside the classroom may take the form of informational meetings, seminars, special interest groups, clubs, special training sessions, group testing (e.g., CEEB, ACT), field trips, etc. In the classroom the counselor may conduct an informative session, work on a special unit, assist the teacher in using a particular group technique, or teach a course around a guidance theme. Guidance hours or units may be established as a regularly scheduled activity in each class/grade. Another approach is for the counselor to use a period from a required subject when it is necessary to present something to all students. These should be planned well in advance so that course instruction is not disrupted. With consultation and collaboration on a systems approach these interruptions may not be necessary. Logical places could be found in the normal curriculum for these developmental guidance activities.

The variety of group activities and techniques that can be used in group guidance (and sometimes in group counseling) is expanding rapidly. The group counselor should be familiar with, skilled in, and able to instruct teachers in the use of these activities. Miller and Leonard (1974) list over ten such practices which might be used for the disadvantaged giving the technique, an example, the career development goals, age level, and references. These include achievement motivation training, group assessment techniques, career days, decision-making training, field trips, role playing, simulation, social modeling, value clarification, and work experience programs. All of the activities are appropriate for the general school population as well as the disadvantaged. A few that are appropriate to both group counseling and group guidance will be discussed here.

Role play is a natural process for children. Normal play frequently begins "You be the daddy and I'll be the mommy. . ." and the stage is set to try out the thoughts, feelings, and actions of these persons. The same procedure takes place in role play. Someone decides on the problem or scene, roles are assigned or selected, and the participants act it out. Learning may come through actual participation or vicariously. Participants may switch roles to experience both sides of an argument, or try the same role several times to practice behavioral alternatives. The variety of techniques used are only limited by one's creativeness (Hawley, 1974; Dyer and Vriend, 1973). Role play can be developmental or therapeutic as well as diagnostic. It is developmental as it provides a safe place to practice future behaviors—a job interview, asking for a date, etc., Dyer and Vriend (1973) prefer to call its therapeutic side "role-working."

> Role-working in a group counseling session is a deliberately, though spontaneously, contrived helping structure in which group members receive assistance by working through old behavioral patterns and trying out previously unselected alternatives in a snug social enclave minimizing risk and maximizing involvement, feedback and openness. The group members seeking help are provided with an opportunity to check their own defenses, reactions, strengths and weaknesses in a simulated environment, and to develop insights into their own behaviors in given settings. Role-working is a total group process in which a variety of methods can be utilized for the purpose of helping individuals to observe and feel, on the spot, how they characteristically comport themselves in troublesome circumstances, and to learn fresh approaches to handling themselves in the presence of significant others in their lives which were not previously incorporated into their repertoires of behavioral alternatives. (p. 33)

It is diagnostic in that players frequently reveal their own life-styles in the role-playing activity. The leader can also assess areas of interest or concern, evaluate material learned and plan appropriate learning experiences.

Simulation games are a more structured, formalized way of playing a role. There are usually definite rules which limit roles, participants, time, space, equipment, and the acceptable behaviors. Abt (1970) defines a game as "an *activity* among two or more independent *decisionmakers* seeking to achieve their objectives in some limiting *context*" (p. 7). Because there are usually winners and losers in games or at least specific pay-offs, they are highly motivational. Simulation games are often divided into two types dealing with the way people operate in: (a) their social environment or (b) their physical environment. The possible objectives to which games relate are categorized into three groups by Adams (1973):

1. An understanding of the structure of knowledge.
2. Connecting subject matter (cognitive) and emotional (affective) learning.
3. An appreciation of group dynamics. (p. 11)

Simulation games may be purchased in kit forms, adapted from texts, or designed by the teacher and/or students.

Values clarification is a variety of instructional activities and strategies to help a person prize and choose one's beliefs and behaviors and then act on those beliefs (Simon, Howe and Kirschenbaum, 1972, p. 19). A number of steps are included in this process:

1. defining values so students understand what values are,
2. introducing students to a range of possible values,
3. indicating the importance of values and the impact they have on decisions and behavior,
4. giving students the opportunity to consciously select a set of personal values,
5. helping students learn to act on their values, and
6. helping students modify values over time as change is indicated. (Miller and Leonard, 1974, p. 51)

The leader of these activities should remain nonjudgmental to allow students the freedom to explore and select from a wide range of values.

Experiential learning through structured activities is the basis for the last two preceeding types of group processes. It is also called the laboratory or scientific method of learning. A hypothesis is generated and an experimental design or activity selected. In this the individual or group does something. The process is observed and reported from the various participants' viewpoints. They then analyze how it happened and what the dynamics were behind the experience. Conclusions drawn may be used to change behavior or apply the learnings to new situations. This process is inductive rather than deductive as the learner is actively involved in a personalized experience.

There is a wide variety of resources from which to select these activities. A limited number are listed in the references (Bessell and Palomares, 1967; Adams, 1973; Jones and Pfeiffer, 1972-1975; Otto, 1970; Pfeiffer and Jones, 1969-1975; Simon, Howe and Kirschenbaum, 1972). The users are cautioned to (a) have a specific goal or purpose, (b) select an activity that is an appropriate vehicle for reaching that goal, (c) be sure the activity is appropriate for the age group, the time, and space available, (d) use appropriate group skills to facilitate the experience, and (e) allow time for group processing.

A cartoon published several years ago depicted an interesting experience with a little girl and boy of elementary school age. In the first panel they were facing each other. The second panel showed the girl pouring a pail of water over the boy while saying "Here, have an experience!" The third and last scene had the dripping boy, standing passively, wondering what had happened. This cartoon illustrates some of the problems in experiential learning. Experiences, methods, and techniques are frequently used without any understanding of their appropriateness or power, and the learner is given little or no assistance in "processing" the event or analyzing the experience and making appropriate applications. Used appropriately these activities can facilitate learning.

Contributions of the Service to Career Development and Career Education

Group Counseling

The major contributions of group counseling to career development and career education are in the area of self-development. Counseling groups work on identifying one's strengths and changing self-defeating attitudes and behaviors. Students with behavioral problems such an nonachievement or acting-out can be assisted in overcoming these factors which block them from acquiring basic skills ultimately needed for their careers. The verbal communication and interpersonal skills learned in counseling groups have a direct carryover to acquiring and keeping a job. The dynamics of close association and learning to know a variety of people intimately in a group help a person open up to more positive relationships on a job. Groups for older students may deal more directly with the world of work. Seniors who appear unusually anxious or fearful of leaving high school or who are exhibiting no or inappropriate job-seeking skills may be referred for group counseling. Frequently programs in cooperative-education or work/study include a weekly group counseling session to discuss work habits, employer-employee relationship, expectations, etc. This type of assistance is usually not available to the average worker upon leaving school. Career-planning skills such as setting realistic goals, decision making and accepting responsibility for one's actions can also be developed in the counseling group. Parent groups can help families learn and support these behaviors in their developing children.

Group Guidance

Group guidance in the classroom is now a shared responsibility of teachers and counselors. It is here that most of the planned sequential, developmental approach to self, the world of work, and career planning is done. Individual schools, school districts, localities, and states have been actively working on these sequential plans. This has resulted in guidelines, suggested career emphasis in individual courses (e.g., math, English), units, and full courses. There has been a tremendous growth of commercial products to support this emphasis.

Through discussions, structured activities, and other experiential learning designs, students learn to know themselves and how to relate to others. Understanding and accepting their interests and personal skills enables them to later use this knowledge in making appropriate career choices. Simulation activities and games can be used at all age levels to explore the world of work. Role plays allow students to rehearse needed skills, try out alternate behaviors, and develop an affective understanding of work relationships. Visits to businesses and industries, educational institutions, and job placement centers help establish a realistic view of work situations. Discussion groups following these activities can help maximize the learnings. The *School To Employment Program* (STEP) considers the group guidance activity so important that they have mandated: "Students shall meet at least one period each school day with a qualified instructor to consider topics designed to facilitate adjustment to school and work" (1963, p. 7). College night and career day programs provide brief exposure to a variety of careers in a short period of time. Factual information needed for career planning can be presented in mass meetings, large groups, or repeated at various times for small groups. Values clarification and decision-making strategies help students get in touch with personal and environmental data needed for effective career planning.

Roles of Various Personnel in the Delivery of the Service

The public schools are basically set up to deal with people in groups. It is difficult to separate the roles of various personnel as each one, at some time, may be a participant, leader, teacher, facilitator, organizer or administrator of, or in different groups. Role responsibilities commmon to all school staff in the delivery of this service are: (a) to be aware of group dynamics operating in the role situations, (b) to be knowledgeable of the developmental stages and tasks characteristic of the target groups, (c) to be able to select and use appropriate group processes to facilitate that development, and (d) to cooperate with other staff to plan and carry out a comprehensive and integrated approach to group counseling and group guidance.

Teachers

The role of classroom teachers places them in prolonged daily contact with one or several groups of students on a usually consistant schedule lasting up to ten months each year. The younger the age group, the more time one teacher has with a group. Specialty teachers (e.g., art, music, physical education) may have students over several years, in a variety of groupings, on a more flexible schedule and in less formal settings. This prolonged contact means the classroom teacher has the best opportunity to identify and refer students who could benefit from group counseling. It also means that these classes are ongoing groups and the teacher should understand the group dynamics which influence them and become skilled in group processes that facilitate learning. The teacher can use this skill to help shape the class to provide support for a child in group counseling.

Teachers usually assume their first role responsibility is for the *content* to be taught in their classes. Unless the *climate* is given first priority, assimilation of the content may be blocked. The problem is illustrated in Dr. Gale E. Jensen's study of small group counseling for underachieving primary school children.

One explanation of under-achievement asserts that interpersonal or social relationships of the pupils are so unsatisfactory that most of the pupils' energy are diverted to work on these problems. Thus there is little or no time and energy left for working on the learning tasks in school. (Cited in Driver, 1958, p. 286)

Carl Rogers speaks to conditions which facilitate this learning climate in chapter 7 of *Freedom to Learn* (1970). Dinkmeyer and Arciniega (1972) suggest the use of "C" groups for teachers to affect the learning climate. The *Teacher Effectiveness Training* programs (Gordon, 1975) are also helpful in understanding this role.

Classroom teachers can become familiar with group processes and activities such as role play, values clarification (Simon, Howe, and Kirscnenbaum, 1972), simulation games (Adams, 1973), Achievement Motivation (Alschuler, Tabor, and McIntyre, 1970), Magic Circle (Helfat, 1973) etc., through reading, in-service training, workshops and consultation with counselors. They might also invite a counselor into the classroom to direct such activities when appropriate.

Counselors

The counselors' roles are to: (a) be properly prepared in group counseling and guidance techniques as well as in career education, (b) develop a program that relates to the needs of people in a particular school or system, (c) secure administrative approval and support, (d) publicize and promote the program, (e) assist with in-service training of staff (also peer counselors when available), (f) facilitate counseling groups, (g) lead group guidance activities, (h) assist teachers to integrate group counseling and guidance in the classroom, (i) consult with and supervise others who are using group processes, (j) establish and maintain evaluation procedures, (k) publicize results and use them to revise the group program, and (l) refer those needing group therapy or assistance beyond the program to outside resources.

Counselor-educators at North Texas State University prepared a 1973 monograph (NTSU) for the American Personnel and Guidance Association that lists the competencies expected in preparation programs for guidance associates (prepared at bachelor's degree level) and professional counselors (graduate degree). Perhaps the most extensive and detailed compilation of goals, abilities and activities for service identified with school counseling and guidance currently available, the monograph lists ten specific competencies for guidance associates and eighteen for professional counselors that integrate group processes and career education.

A sampling of these activities shows the focus of the guidance associate's role on informational and classroom guidance groups.

Demonstrating the ability to prepare audiovisual aids to be used in individual and group career development presentations. (p. 39)

Demonstrating the ability to plan and conduct classroom guidance activities.

Demonstrating the ability to provide assistance to classroom teachers in carrying out guidance activities. (p. 15)

Demonstrating the responsibility for the organization of programs such as:
1. Orientation to junior and senior high school;
2. Orientation to guidance services;
3. Orientation to the world of work;
4. Orientation to opportunities in higher education. (p. 23)

Demonstrating the ability to rate the facilitative and action oriented dimensions of group interaction on the Carkhuff Communication Scale. (p. 13)

The professional counselor is expected to have these skills at an advanced level plus the ability to do staff training, small group counseling with parents and students, and integrate these processes in the school system.

> Demonstrating the ability to assist teachers in correlating the teaching of career awareness within their respective subject matter. (p. 43)

> Be able to use the dynamics of group counseling and the various group activities that can facilitate attitude and behavior change according to the age level of the client. (p. 17)

> Demonstrating a working knowledge of group dynamics such as:
> 1. Content and process variables;
> 2. Typical stages of group development;
> 3. The various leadership styles;
> 4. The conditions under which groups promote healthy growth. (p. 17)

> Demonstrating an adequate knowledge of developmental tasks and coping behaviors of children and youth of different age levels and the skill to use various techniques appropriate for various age levels including:
> 1. Play group counseling;
> 2. Modeling—social learning techniques;
> 3. Role playing (sociodrama and psychodrama). (p. 18)

> Demonstrating the ability to provide individual and group counseling for the student as he studies himself and his future. (p. 43)

> Demonstrate the ability to conduct group counseling with parents on education and vocational plans for their children. (p. 43)

> Demonstrating the ability successfully to conduct and participate in T-group sessions with professional staff members. (p. 28)

The entire monograph is well worth reading by counselors as they consider their education and skills, and by administrators as they look at staff roles and competencies. The minimal school counselor certification requirements in most states do not require preparation that leads to competencies in these areas. The majority of school counselors were certified before some group work was required. Many counselor education programs have only recently added a beginning course in group guidance. Thirty to forty-five class hours does not begin to prepare one to facilitate a counseling group. The role of the counselor, then, must be to seek out appropriate education and experience. It must be remembered that just having an experience in a group does not qualify one to lead such a group. Counselors should know the theory behind what they do in groups, how to facilitate maximal learning from the activity, and how to handle potential psychological outcomes of that process.

Group counseling or group guidance activities should not be introduced into a school system because they are the current fad. The system or school should be studied and particular group procedures introduced to meet specific needs. The role of the counselor is to work with teachers and administrators to identify these needs and plan a comprehensive group program that responds to them.

Counselors may find it more helpful to a larger number of students if they make in-service training and group counseling with significant adults a high-priority role. Demonstrating techniques in the classroom may encourage teachers to attend in-service training programs. Gerler (1973) presents a five step approach for getting teachers started in the Magic Circle program. Gordon's (1975) *Teacher Effectiveness Training* is a commercial program that is helpful.

To fulfill their evaluation role, counselors should be able to use some method for recording or identifying what is happening in the process. Bales (1950) *Interaction Process Analysis* classifies what group members say to each other in twelve categories, three each for positive reactions, attempted answers, questions, and negative reactions. The *Hill Interaction Matrix* (Hill, 1965 a and b) categorizes content of the group work on a four by four matrix showing content moving from topics to relationships and style moving from prework to work.

Administrators

The primary role of the administrator is to select qualified staff and provide the climate to maximize their functioning. The counselor "promoted" from the teaching staff with minimal credentials is not adequate to function as a small group facilitator or group counselor. This means the administrator should: (a) encourage counselors to continue their education in group techniques and (b) promote an in-service training program to update faculty on maximizing their group process skills. The Province of Manitoba, Canada (1973) employs a full-time group work consultant to conduct workshops, training programs and provide consultation services in their schools to integrate and upgrade group skills. Large school systems might consider this type of a position.

Administrators fortunate enough to have qualified group counselors should provide time for their maximum service in this area. This means first of all an adequate support staff to do clerical, routine work so the counselors are free to counsel. Unless they are well prepared, many counselors will stick with the security these neccessary routines require rather than experiment with more developmental group functions, and the school system loses the potential value of a well-paid specialist. The school deserves and can get more for its money if specialists spend their time at their specialty. Counselors are usually assigned to certain grades or a proportionate number of students in several grades. Assignment by function on the basis of interest and preparation allows the most qualified to work with groups, and not be penalized by a disproportionate share of other departmental duties. Some adjustment should be made because the group counselor frequently works with students assigned to someone else.

Another way of providing the climate concerns the student or school schedule. More flexible time slots might be made available so that pupils could meet some of their guidance needs as they develop, and not when the calendar says it is appropriate.

Counselors, teachers and administrators should be encouraged to work together and plan a systems approach. A good administrator will know what the counselors are doing in the group area, the goals of their programs, how this benefits students, and be able to interpret this to parents, teachers, school boards, and the public in general. Administrators should also know the limitations of their programs and the community resources available for referrals.

Students

The student is the major consumer and target of the school's group counseling effort. This does not mean the role of the student is limited to participant or passive receiver. At any age level students are capable of expressing their wants, problems, and needs. These should be considered in setting up any group counseling program. As a participant in any group the individual student should be expected to make a commitment to the group, to set personal goals, and to assist other group members. During and following their participation, student evaluation of the group experience is vitally important. Students may also function in public relations and referral roles. The recommendation or approval of a peer often bears much more weight than that of the professional in adolescent and preadolescent circles. Students who have had a good group experience will influence others to participate. Beginning a group counseling program with groups that help normal students with normal stages of development aids in establishing the positive attitude and good peer publicity. Using group counseling only for problem students or crisis management tends to stigmatize the participants and eventually the group process. Students who have had a successful group experience and have been trained to be peer helpers can be used as cofacilitators in counseling groups, and in group guidance activities.

Community Persons

The roles that may be filled by community persons are only limited by the size of the community and the counselor's imagination. Individuals may appear as role models or presenters in group guidance classes. Local firms may arrange for group tours of business and industry. Other business firms or community groups may want to finance equipment used in the group programs. This might range from play materials, kits, stimulus slides, films and tapes, to video taping and playback equipment. There may be professionals outside the public school system (e.g., psychologists, social and mental health workers, ministers, educators, management personnel) who have specialized training in group work. They could fill roles as consultants and advisors, instructors for in-service training of school staff, leaders for *Parent Effectiveness Training* groups (Gordon, 1970), facilitators for counseling groups, and resources for referrals and therapy where necessary. The training, experience, and skills of these professionals should be carefully assessed before assignment to group responsibilities. Those who participate in any of these roles should also assist in the evaluation process. Beginning group counselors may want to use a local professional to critique their work.

Parents

Parents are part of the community so all of the above may be roles they would play. Parents are also the target population for certain groups. These may be informational groups on child development, career development, or orientation to a new school; less formal group activities as in Parent's and Career Nights; instructional groups such as *Parent Effectiveness Training* (Gordon, 1970); or even counseling groups ranging from educational and vocational plans to problem areas. Shaw (1969) reports a successful program involving fifty-three counseling groups for parents of first and seventh grade children in five school districts. The focus of the groups was "on the kinds of concerns that parents normally have about their growing children and about the educational development of their children" (p. 45). Parents who have participated in successful discussion groups on children may be encouraged to establish and lead such groups in their own neighborhoods. This would be particularly helpful in meeting needs in areas where perceived bias of the counselor's race, social class, or ethnic background might hinder communication with the target population. Some counseling groups may include parents and children of several families or concentrate on the members of one family. If parents are adequately informed of the purpose and potential of the group counseling program they can be helpful in referring their children, supporting them in the process, providing feedback to the counselor on their progress, and evaluating the program.

Differential Aspects of the Service for Various Levels of the Educational System

In very general terms the career education focus in elementary school is on career awareness, self-awareness, and acquiring the basic educational tools, social, and career development skills. The junior high school is a transitional stage where the focus is on career exploration and decision-making skills. In high school the focus is on preparation for work or post secondary education. The goals and techniques of group counseling and group guidance may be similar, but the processes should be adapted to the maturity and skills of the children and the stage of their career development. Gazda (1971) has three chapters which discuss group procedures at various age levels from preschool to adults based on developmental tasks, vocational developmental tasks and coping behaviors.

Elementary School

Children who are shy, have difficulty participating in class discussions, want to make friends and are performing below ability profit most from group counseling (Ohlsen, 1971). Dinkmeyer and Muro (1971) suggest that children who are compulsive, restricted, constant do-gooders, conduct problems, have specific fears (such as of tests), and effeminate boys could be grouped for counseling. Assignments to a group should not be made randomly. A mix is needed so that there is strength in one child that may assist another child weak in that characteristic.

Groups centered around play materials and other action oriented techniques (art, role play, puppets, etc.) are best for the early grades. Some of the appropriate uses of play techniques are described by Ohlsen (1970).

> Play techniques can be used effectively by counselors to help the children convey what bothers them, to communicate feelings and reactions that are difficult for them to express verbally, and to discover new ways of relating to significant others. They also can be used to help them reveal material that is difficult for them to express directly in face-to-face relationships. For example, some children can talk freely about a problem with the counselor or another client on a play telephone (or do so when pretending to be talking to a trusted friend on a telephone). They also can use puppets and dolls to show how their families live together and relate to each other. (p. 227)

In verbal oriented groups, young children need more structure and assistance from the counselor. They are sensitive to other's feelings but need to learn how to be both helpers and helpees. There are two current models of guidance discussion groups which come close to group counseling but involve intact classrooms and are usually led by the teacher. The *Magic Circle* (Bessell and Palomares, 1970; Gerler, 1973; and Helfat, 1973) seats groups of eight to ten children in a circle with an adult leader. The leader initiates the topic and give permission to talk. Three rules are observed: sit quietly, talk only after receiving permission from the leader, and listen when someone else is talking (Bessell and Palomares, 1970). A group meets daily for twenty to thirty minutes. The goals of the group are to facilitate growth in awareness of feelings, self-confidence, and social interaction. The rest of the class may sit in an outside circle

observing the inner group or at their desks. Glasser (1969) takes the whole class seated in a tight circle with the teacher. The focus is on solving the educational problems of the individual, the class, and the school. Discussions are directed toward solutions which do not find fault.

There are several commercially prepared kits of guidance activities for elementary school children. *Developing Understanding of Self and Others* (DUSO) (Dinkmeyer, 1970, 1973), *Focus on Self Development* and *Toward Affective Development* are representative of these models. *DUSO I,* using hand puppets to introduce stories and lead discussions, is appropriate for grades kindergarten through two. *DUSO II,* for ages seven through ten, has career activity cards not found in the first kit. Both have large poster pictures, stories on tape, puppet activities, role plays, and other supplemental activities to stimulate participation. Counselors frequently bring these activities in during a classroom guidance or health period. The materials are presented in such a form that teachers can quickly learn to use them at other times. *Focus* has six, five-minute filmstrips to introduce some units in each of its three stages: Stage I Awareness (grades kindergarten through two), Stage II Responding (grades three and four), and Stage III Involvement (grades five through six). Topics which cut across the series are feelings, family relationships, problem solving, and peer or social relationships. Stage I spends more time on self and environment while Stages II and III bring in the world of work. There are recorded stories, photo boards, and a variety of learning activities that stimulate and involve students. Another program, *Toward Affective Development* (TAD) (Dupont, Gardner, Brody, 1974), is aimed at grades three to six or ages eight to twelve. It contains many good starter activities dealing with self-understanding, feelings, working together, and decision making. Ditto masters and discussion posters are provided for a series of 191, twenty to thirty-minute lessons. Strong emphasis on careers is expressed in the section on Me: today and tomorrow. Thirty-five illustrations of gestures and body expressions are a unique contribution of this kit to the study of feelings and communication.

Career awareness can be stimulated by field trips exploring the occupational possibilities in the local community. Parents who are representative of various occupations can be invited in as role models (Campbell, Walz, Miller and Kriger, 1973). Play materials should allow for acting out simple roles and trying out skills related to careers. Class projects may be long term simulation activities such as running a store, bank, postoffice, etc. Role plays can focus on children's contacts and involvement with the wide variety of workers who serve them.

Junior High School

The younger children in junior high are in the latter years of the latency period. Natural groupings are of the same sex. Manual activity, creative expression, free play, and interaction are still better mediums for group counseling and guidance activities than those requiring verbal expression and insight. Gazda (1971) describes two types of group counseling that use group games, both physical and sedentary, as the best media for free and spontaneous communication. In activity-interview group counseling an activity (e.g., darts, volleyball, chess) is used to involve the members, stimulate interaction, lower inhibitions and defenses, etc. A discussion follows the activity focusing on the interaction. Activity group counseling relies more on the effect peer group members have on each other and less on formal discussion with the counselor. The makeup of the group is "engineered" so that each member has a peer who can be a reinforcing model. Camping, swimming, crafts, and field trips are some of the suggested activities. Discussions take place in the midst of the activity.

The puberty and early adolescence periods bring about a concern with bodily changes, sexual development, and independence from the family. The sexes should not be separated in counseling groups which deal with these problems. Role plays or role rehearsals are appropriate techniques here. Behavioral group counseling (Varenhorst, 1969) tends to provide structure that facilitates growth at this level. Achievement motivation (Alschuler, Tabor and McIntyre, 1970) also lends itself to this age group.

Group guidance activities that focus on career exploration are field trips, interest inventories, hands-on simulation experiences, etc. Career days usually reserved for high school can be adapted to be rewarding at this level. Prevocational exploratory programs relate basic academic skills to various occupational areas and provide experiences in work activities related to a number of occupational areas (Miller and Leonard, 1974). *A World of Choice—Careers and You* is an example of a one-year course that helps middle or junior high school students identify styles of work suitable to their personalities, select in and out of school experiences that will assist in making tentative career choices, and involve them in realistic simulation activities based on styles of work and USOE Occupational Clusters. Simulation games such as the *Life Career Game* give students an opportunity to experience situations similar to real life, to experiment with behaviors, and get feedback on the results.

Values clarification techniques are helpful self-development strategies in the struggle for independence and identity. Minicourses on personality development, social skills, study skills, etc., can be elective and alternate with other short-term courses such as art, home economics, shop, etc.

The junior high school age group is in a transition stage. For the first time they are confronted with some educational choices leading to effecting career decisions. They need decision-making skills to assist them in planning and choosing wisely. The CEEB *Deciding: A Decision-making Program for Students* is one commercial curriculum available. This may be used in a classroom, or as a guidance course. Some schools use it as part of their orientation program. Student workbooks provide stories to be analyzed. The roles of values, information, and strategies are emphasized in the decision-making process, and students are helped to apply this process to their own life decisions.

Senior High School

The verbal and interaction skills of high school students open up a wider variety of counseling groups and counseling group strategies. The typical developmental-remedial groups on academic, personal-social development, career development, and educational problems should be offered. *Human Potential Seminars* (Otto, 1970) and T-groups (Bradford et al., 1964) can be developmental in approach. Encounter groups (Schutz, 1973) may be used to work out conflicts between advantaged and disadvantaged groups whether it be on the basis of social class, religion, race, or ethnic origins. *Encounter-tapes for Vocational Education Groups* (Berzon and Solomon) provide ten one and one-half hour experiential learning sessions based on interpersonal exercises for people planning to begin work.

The group guidance activities in high school often focus on preparation for work. For those going on to higher education, it means search, selection, application, possible interview, consideration of alternatives, and decisions. Similar skills are needed for those going directly to employment. Lifton (1972) encourages schools to get out of the lock-step method of providing the same information to many students at one time.

> But if we recognize that information is incorporated best at the point where need is perceived, individuals will differ markedly not only in the timing of their desire for the data but also in their need for it to be presented in a different form. (p. 251)

Instead of using classroom groupings as the delivery system, differential scheduling of informational and skill groups could be considered. Tests could be interpreted in small groups when students are ready to hear and make use of the information provided. A student should not have to wait for Unit 3 in English 12 to learn how to write a resume, complete a job application form, and respond to an interview if the need occurs in the sophomore or junior year. Role play and simulation activities are appropriate techniques to be used whenever these topics are considered.

Decisions and Outcomes is the CEEB program for training high school students in decision-making skills. Again this could be offered in a short-term course, or integrated into various classes. The *Life Career Development System* (Walz) is limited to schools that will participate in their training program. This is a comprehensive program that provides career education for the normal career development process of this age group.

Methods for Evaluation of the Service

Evaluation methods should be built into the program as each activity is in the design stage. Activities should be selected as the best possible means for meeting specified objectives and aiding a particular group of people to move toward specified, attainable, and measurable goals. Before a group begins, the decision should be made as to how the activity will be evaluated. One of the effects of this disciplined approach is to keep the leader and participants honest. "Teaching for the test" then becomes legitimate.

Within limits, participants should be involved in deciding on goals. If they have not been, a clear statement of purpose at the beginning of and occassional reminders during an activity will assist in keeping the group on target. In group counseling, goal statements made by each person before the group help the other participants focus in and use their resources to provide assistance, and makes it easier to measure individual progress. It is not always possible to measure the growth resulting from, or the effectiveness of a group with instruments that combine individual responses. If combined on a scale of "frequency of verbal input" the scores of a student who has learned to control excessive talking would negate the scores of a student who has learned to speak up, and statistically the group would show no gain.

Dye (1968) has listed a wide variety of evaluation measures commonly used in group counseling on a two by two matrix comparing the source of data with the person reporting (see figure 4.2). The use of several methods which measure the same factor will add to the effectiveness of the evaluation.

SOURCE OF DATA

As Reported By:	Within Group	External to Group
Self	Checklists, ratings of personal behavior, reactions Continuing log of group sessions Q-sort of actual, ideal behavior, attitudes, etc. Spontaneous statement of growth, progress, etc.	Problem checklists, inventories (pre- and post-counseling) Autobiography Curricular and career decisions made Personal communications to counselor, teachers Post-group rating, surveys, questionnaires

Others	Peers:
	    Ratings of group behavior, attitudes, etc.
	    Performance checklist
	    Sociometric procedures
	Counselor ratings, log
	Formal analysis of sessions by counselor, observers (tapes, typescripts)
	Group's summary of each session
		Teachers:
		    Rating and checklist procedures
		    Informal, open-ended written reports
		    Counselor-teacher feedback sessions
		    Citizenship, behavior
		Others:
		    Attendance, grades, disciplinary histories, etc.

Figure 4.2. Illustrative evaluation procedures. Source: Dye, 1968, p. 52.

The oldest and best known resources for information concerning standardized tests which may be used to evaluate individuals as they grow through the group processes are the Buros *Mental Measurements Yearbooks.* If they seem to be overwhelming in scope there are two books which discuss a limited number of instruments popular in current group research. In 1973, Lake, Miles, and Earle presented systematic reviews of eighty-four different instruments for measuring social functioning in *Measuring Human Behavior.* University Associates are the current leaders in the field for collecting and publishing useful materials in human relations training and group facilitation. Their handbook, *Instrumentation in Human Relations Training* by Pfeiffer and Heslin (1973) reviews seventy-five instruments. This is a very practical guide in that it discusses uses, theory, development, and application that is easily understood by the beginning practitioner. The *1972, 1973, 1974, 1975 Annual Handbooks for Group Facilitation* (Jones and Pfeiffer) and Volumes 1-5, *Handbook of Structured Experiences for Human Relations Training* (Pfeiffer and Jones, 1969-1975), will also give some excellent ideas concerning various observation forms, checklists, rating scales, etc. Consulting the above resources will assist counselors in choosing appropriate instruments or designing their own.

In a comparison of research versus evaluation, Benedict (1974) suggests that research is attempting to explain causes while evaluation attempts to look at specifics that indicate what is happening. The beginning group counselor should emphasize the latter first. While not speaking to group counseling per se, Benedict points out the need for continual evaluation data so that "ongoing decisions regarding an educational program may be made while the program is in progress and not after it has been terminated" (p. 3). In addition, evaluation data may be fed back to the group and assist the members in taking responsibility for their growth.

Many groups are evaluated only at the end of the program. Dye (1968) warns that counselors deal with values, attitudes and understanding that develop over a lifetime and are not easily subject to change during a brief period of group contact. In a 1973 study, students who had just completed a forty hour group process workshop were significantly lower in stability of self scores than the reference group. However, ten weeks later they were higher than the reference group and the change was significant. Had only the posttest been considered, the wrong assumption regarding the values of the group workshop would have been made (Tschumi, 1973). The same is also true of the Mallison (1964) study of gifted underachievers which showed that academic improvement followed rather than coincided with adjustment. Gurman (1969) identified five studies which showed the existance of an "incubation period" before there were any noticeable effects from group counseling. Longitudinal studies are needed to allow for this delayed effect of treatment.

Professional journals and periodicals which might be consulted in addition to those of various affiliates of the American Personnel and Guidance Association are: *Comparative Group Studies, Group Leader Reports, Group Psychotherapy, Interpersonnel Development,* the *Journal of Applied Behavioral Science,* and the *Journal of Humanistic Psychology.*

The readers of this chapter have been exposed to some ideas on group counseling and group guidance as it relates to career education. These tools can be very effective in responsible hands and also very rewarding. In group work one should hold back the natural tendency to tell people answers or what to do and facilitate the process instead. The reward for doing this is the opportunity to see people grow to accept themselves and share their potentials with others. "The greatest good we can do for others is not just to share our riches with them but to reveal theirs to themselves." *Full Circle* (1969)

References

Abt, C. C. *Serious games.* New York: Viking, 1970.

Adams, D. M. *Simulation games: an approach to learning.* Worthington, Ohio: Charles A. Jones, 1973.

Alschuler, A. S; Tabor, D.; and McIntyre, J. *Teaching achievement motivation.* Middletown, Connecticut: Education Ventures, 1970.

Bales, R. F. *Interaction process analysis: A method for the study of small groups.* Cambridge, Massachusetts: Addison-Wesley, 1950.

Benedict, L. G. *Traditional research versus evaluation.* Amherst, University of Massachusetts, 1974. (ERIC Document Reproduction Service No. ED. 100 959).

Berzon, B. and Solomon, L. *Encountertapes for vocational educational groups.* Atlanta, Georgia: Human Development Institute, Inc.

Bessell H., and Palomares, U. *Methods in human development.* San Diego: Human Development Training Institute, 1967.

Bradford, L.; Benne, K.; and Gibb, J. *T-group theory and laboratory method.* New York: Wiley, 1964.

Buros, O. K. (ed.). *The mental measurements yearbook.* Highland Park, New Jersey: Gryphon, 1970.

Campbell, R.; Walz, G. R.; Miller, J. V.; and Kriger, S. F. *Career guidance: A handbook of methods.* Columbus, Ohio: Merrill, 1973.

Cartwright, D. and Zander, A. *Group dynamics* (3rd ed.) New York: Harper and Row, 1968.

College Entrance Examination Board. *Deciding: a decision-making program for students.* Princeton, New Jersey: Publications Order Office, CEEB, Box 592, 08540.

———. *Decisions and outcomes.* Princeton, New Jersey: Publications Order Office, CEEB, Box 592, 08540.

Dinkmeyer, D. C. *Developing understanding of self and others* (DUSO) D1, D2. Circle Pines, Minnesota: American Guidance Service, 1970, 1973.

Dinkmeyer, D. C. and Arciniega, M. Affecting the learning climate through "C" groups with teachers. *The School Counselor.* 19 (1972):249-53.

Dinkmeyer, D. C. and Muro, J. J. *Group counseling theory and practice.* Itasca, Illinois: Peacock, 1971.

Dreikurs, R. and Corsini, R. J. Twenty years of group psychotherapy. *American Journal of Psychiatry,* 110 (1954):567-75.

Dupont, H.; Gardner, O. S.; and Brody, D. S. *Toward affective development.* Circle Pines, Minnesota: American Guidance Service, 1974.

Dyer, W. W. and Vriend, J. Role-working in group counseling. *Educational Technology* 13(2) (1973):32-36.

Dye, H. A. *Fundamental group procedures for school counselors.* Boston: Houghton Mifflin, 1968.

Focus on self-development. Chicago: Science Research Associates, 1970, 1971, 1972.

Full circle. New York: Full Circle, 1969. (32 E. 51st Street, New York, N.Y. 10022)

Gazda, G. M. *Group counseling a developmental approach.* Boston: Allyn and Bacon, 1971.

Gazda, G. M.; Ducan, J. A.; and Meadows, M. E. Group counseling and group procedures—Report of a survey. *Counselor Education and Supervision* 6 (1967):305-10.

Gerler, E. R., Jr. The magic circle program: How to involve teachers. *Elementary School Guidance and Counseling* 8 (1973):86-91.

Ginott, H. G. *Group psychotherapy with children.* New York: McGraw-Hill, 1961.

Glanz, E. C. *Groups in guidance.* Boston: Allyn and Bacon, 1962.

Glanz, E. C. and Hayes, R. W. *Groups in guidance* 2nd ed. Boston: Allyn and Bacon, 1967.

Glasser, W. *Schools without failure.* New York: Harper and Row, 1969.

Gordon, T. *Parent effectiveness training.* New York: Wyden, 1970.

———. *Teacher effectiveness training.* New York: Wyden, 1975.

Gurman, A. S. Group counseling with underachievers: A review and evaluation of methodology. *International Journal of Group Psychotherapy* 19(4) (1969):463-74.

Hansen, J. C. and Cramer, S. H. eds. *Group guidance and counseling in the schools.* New York: Appleton-Century-Crofts, 1971.

Hawley, R. C. Exploring student concerns through open-chair roleplaying. *The School Counselor* 21(5) (1974):358-64.

Helfat, L. The gut level needs of kids. *Learning,* 2(2) (1973):31-34.

Hill, W. F. *HIM, Hill interaction matrix.* Los Angeles: University of Southern California, Youth Studies Center, 1965 a.

———. *HIM, Hill interaction matrix scoring manual.* Los Angeles: University of Southern California, Youth Studies Center, 1965 b.

Jones, J. E. and Pfeiffer, J. W. eds. *The annual handbook for group facilitators* (4 vols.). La Jolla, California: University Associates, 1972-1975.

Klein, A. F. *Effective groupwork.* New York: Association Press, 1972.

Lake, D. G.; Miles, M. B.; and Earle, R. B., Jr. eds. *Measuring human behavior.* New York: Teachers College Press, 1973.

Life career game. Western Publishing Company, School and Library Department, 150 Parish Drive, Wayne, New Jersey.

Lifton, W. M. *Groups: facilitating individual growth and societal change.* New York: Wiley, 1972.

Mahler, C. A. *Group counseling in the schools.* Boston: Houghton-Mifflin, 1969.

———. Minimal necessary conditions in schools for effective group counseling. *Educational Technology.* 13(2) (1973):21-23.

Mallison, T. J. Gifted underachievers: A follow-up study of four types of treatment. *Subscription Service,* National Training Laboratories, National Education Association, 3 (1964).

Miller, J. and Leonard, G. E. *Career guidance practices for disadvantaged youth.* Washington: National Vocational Guidance Assoc., 1974.

North Texas State University, Denton, College of Education, Division of Counseling Education, the Guidance and Counseling Staff. *Preparation of guidance associates and professional counselors within the framework of a competency based program.* Washington, D.C.: APGA Press, 1973.

Ohlsen, M. M. Counseling children in groups. In Hansen, J. C. and Cramer S. H. eds., *Group guidance and counseling in the schools.* New York: Appleton Century Crofts, 1971, 297-304.

———. *Group counseling.* New York: Holt, Rinehart and Winston, 1970.

Otto, H. A. *Group methods to actualize human potential.* Beverly Hills, California: Holistic Press, 1970.

Pfeiffer, J. W. and Heslin, R. *Instrumentation in human relations training.* Iowa City, Iowa: University Associates, 1973.

Pfeiffer, J. W. and Jones, J. E. eds. *A handbook of structured experiences for human relations training* (5 vols.). Iowa City, Iowa: University Associates, 1969-1975.

Province of Manitoba, Canada, Department of Education. *Group work consultant,* Job description, March 1973.

Rogers, C. A. *Freedom to learn.* Columbus, Ohio: Merrill, 1969.

Schutz, W. C. *Elements of encounter.* Big Sur, California: Joy Press, 1973.

Shaw, M. C. The feasibility of parent group counseling in elementary schools. *Elementary School Guidance and Counseling,* 4(1) (1969):43-53.

Simon, S. B.; Howe, L. W.; and Kirschenbaum, H. *Values clarification.* New York: Hart, 1972.

STEP School to employment program. Second Annual Report. Albany: The New York State Education Department Bureau of Guidance, 1963.

Tschumi, S. A. Changes in self-concept resulting from a crisis intervention marathon group process treatment for nonachieving two-year college freshman. (Doctoral dissertation, State University of New York at Albany, 1973). *Dissertation Abstracts International* 34(9) (1974):5647-A. (University Microfilms No. 74-6943, 164).

Varenhorst, B. Behavioral group counseling. In Gazda, G. M. ed., *Theories and methods of group counseling in the schools.* Springfield, Illinois: Charles C. Thomas, 1969.

Walz G. R. *Life Career Development System.* Ann Arbor, Michigan: Human Development Services, Inc.

A World of Choice—Careers and You. CACO Project, VPI and SU, Blacksburg, Virginia. 24061, 1975.

Chapter 5

THE APPRAISAL SERVICE

Benjamin D. Silliman

Introduction and Historical Development

The appraisal service, like many of the areas which come under the leadership domain of the counselor, is many faceted. In older textbooks on guidance services, this particular aspect was often termed the individual inventory. Typical aspects discussed under this title included group and individual testing, the case study, the cumulative folder or record, the autobiography, health information and attendance data. Often, considerable space was devoted to examples of forms which could be utilized for the collection and organization of this information. However, since counselors should now be working with group models as well as the older individual model, the "individual inventory" title is no longer appropriate. But that is fairly recent history. Perhaps a quick review of the earlier history of appraisal will add the perspective necessary to facilitate greater understanding of this particular service.

Since there are really two main paths which converged to create what we now call those activities contained in appraisal, it seems appropriate that they be discussed from their separate perspectives and then merged at the appropriate time. The first of these paths is that of testing or what is sometimes referred to as the psychological term, psychometrics. The second path, to be discussed only briefly, is that of the vocational guidance movement.

Origins of Testing

Most texts which discuss testing to any extent (e.g., Anastasi, 1968; Helmstater, 1964; Goodenough, 1949; and Peterson, 1926) describe the early Chinese "civil service exams" and the ancient Greeks' assessment of educational attainment as some of the earliest forms of what we today think of as tests. Yet, little is specifically known of the form of these examinations. The modern history of testing is usually traced to the mid to late 1800s. It was at this time, both in Europe and in America, that the names of those people considered to be the "fathers" of testing as we now know it came to light.

In France there were a number of scientists whose interest was in the study of those who deviated from normal. Typically, the group under study was composed of people who exhibited

Dr. Benjamin D. Silliman is Assistant Professor of Counselor Education and Research at Virginia Polytechnic Institute and State University, Extension Center, Reston, Virginia.

behavioral extremes and were termed "insane." At about the same time, but in Germany, experimental psychologists led by Wundt began to systematically study uniformities of normal adult human behavior. Wundt's early work was primarily concerned with physiological aspects such as reaction time. In the field of mathematics Gauss was developing his formulation for what we now know as the normal curve. Many of the later defined psychometric characteristics of this distribution have been incorporated into the majority of standardized tests.

Of those who have been given the title of "father of mental testing" there are three who appear in nearly all references. The first of these is Sir Francis Galton. Not only did his early efforts to explore individual differences have a profound effect on the work of Charles Darwin, but he is also credited with the development of the concept of statistical correlation. The mathematical development of correlation was later established by Karl Pearson (Pearson Product Moment Correlation). Thus the correlation approach, initiated by Galton, was later carried on by such notable measurement specialists as Charles Spearman and Cyril Burt in England and by L. L. Thurstone and J. P. Guilford in America. The use of statistical inference was adopted and developed as an aspect of the testing movement.

Another "father" title is attributed to J. M. Cattell. Having been a student in Wundt's experimental laboratory in Germany, Cattel naturally brought the methodology of experimentalism with him to America. He did, however, have a difference of opinion with his mentor as to the proper focus of the experiment. While Wundt was concerned with normal adult functioning and found the errors or deviations to be a nuisance, Cattell found the differences to be appropriate for further study. He spent much of his time and energy developing and refining what he termed in 1890 as "mental tests." In congruence with the concern in the Wundt laboratory, much of Cattell's early "testing" was carried out in the sensory difference area.

In the area of testing more closely parallel to the form of testing as we know it today, Alfred Binet is clearly seen as one of the major forebearers. Binet and a colleague, Victor Henri, had been conducting studies into the area of individual differences also, though of a different nature. They had turned from the sensory approach which was so prevalent at the time and in 1895 began actively challenging the scientific community for its rigidity in measuring such things as reaction time. It was in 1904 that the French government appointed a group to study the educational approach to subnormal students. To meet one of the requirements of the group, Binet and Theodore Simon published the first thirty problem test to aid in the differentiation of normal from subnormal school children. Since its original publication in 1905, the instrument has gone through numerous revisions and translations. The resulting instrument, most familiar to Americans, was originally revised at Stanford University by L. M. Terman and is known as the Stanford-Binet. It is with this revision, first available to the public in 1916, that the term intelligence quotient (IQ) was first used. As used in many instruments today, IQ is the ratio or relationship between mental or tested age as the numerator and the chronological age as the denominator. Although many acknowledge Binet as the father of mental testing for his recognized efforts, there are those (e.g., Anastasi, 1968, Greene, et al., 1954) who point out that in 1887, eighteen years prior to the first form of the Binet-Simon instrument, an American physician named S. E. Chaille had published an article in a rather obscure medical journal with limited circulation which specified a series of tests and standards for establishing the mental levels of children through age three. Apparently this early development of the concept of mental age went unrecognized.

While the major focus of experimental psychologists and other scientists was either with "mental testing" or with the mathematical-statistical analysis of the information resulting from mental testing, there were those with other interests. According to Green, et al. (1954), who quote Caldwell and Courtis (1923), ". . .the first examinations of note in this country were those of Boston in 1845 (p. 23)." These were written replacements for the oral examinations conducted by the visiting examiners. Horace Mann, who was at the time (1845) the secretary of the Massachusetts School Board, published his reasons for supporting the written examinations:

1. It is impartial
2. It is just to the pupils
3. It is more thorough than older forms of examination
4. It prevents officious interference of the teacher
5. It determines, beyond appeal or gainsaying, whether the pupils have been faithfully and completely taught
6. It takes away all possibility of favoritism
7. It makes the information obtained available to all
8. It enables all to appraise the ease or difficulty of the questions (In Greene, et al., 1954, p. 23)

One of the earliest American forms of the objective test was developed by J. M. Rice in 1894. He compiled a list of spelling words and administered this "test" to school children in many school systems. The results of his study of spelling achievement played a large role in the further evolution of achievement testing. There was also the development of the College Entrance Examination, which was initiated in 1900. These appear to have been an evolution from the earlier (1865) Regent's Examination in New York.

As can be seen, numerous people and factors have had an impact on the development of the testing aspect of appraisal. Brief attention to the vocational guidance movement should provide insight as to how testing became more specifically incorporated into the schools as an aspect of guidance.

Vocational Guidance Impact

Many authors have traced the development of vocational guidance in detail. Some volumes which may be available to the reader include Borow (1964), Ginzberg (1971) and Stephens (1970). However, perhaps the most thorough and complete efforts are to be found in Williamson (1965). If any credibility is to be found in the brief historic perspective which follows, it is due in large measure to the labor of love presented by Williamson.

This historic perspective is not intended to establish again all of the historic antecedents of vocational guidance and counseling. The intent is to single out those incidents which have had strong influence on the development of appraisal services as offered today.

The name most frequently associated with the explicit foundation of vocational guidance is Frank Parsons. He was so involved with social and economic issues of his time that he was discharged in 1899 from a college faculty post. It is not surprising to find him involved in the Breadwinners College in Boston teaching "career-choosing" classes or in 1908 establishing the Vocations Bureau in Boston. As stated in his posthumously published book of 1909, Parsons conceived of a three step process of vocational guidance:

First, a clear understanding of yourself, aptitudes, abilities, interests, resources, limitations, and other qualities. Second, a knowledge of the requirements and conditions of success, advantages and disadvantages, compensation, opportunities, and prospects in different lines of work. Third, true reasoning on the relations of these two groups of facts. (p. 5)

As can be seen quite readily, the first step represents what is conceived of here as the appraisal process in counseling. What this amounted to for Parsons, however, was not the use of objective tests, but the directive and subjective evaluation of the client by Parsons. It should be remembered that at the time there was little sophistication available in objective testing.

Though Parsons is generally given credit for the foundation of vocational guidance, Williamson adds the names of several others to the origins of vocational counseling. Most notable among these are W. P. Harper, whose efforts as founder and first president of the University of Chicago (1899) to provide scientific study of individual students prior to instruction as well as efforts to provide faculty advisement for students seem quite comparable in their possible impact on vocational guidance to the work of Parsons.

The Merger

While many events transpired both before and after the work of Parsons and Harper, none are considered to have had quite the impact on appraisal as two major world wars (World War I and World War II).

The First World War brought about a need to provide a massive integration of psychometrics and guidance due to the numbers of men taken into the armed services. The main question seems to have been, what do we do with all these men? What resulted surely derived its impetus from the work of earlier psychometrists, psychologists such as Binet, industrial psychologists who had begun to classify various work tasks within industry, and the various people engaged in vocational bureaus. In point of fact, mass testing with two levels of a specifically designed instrument (the Army Alpha and the Army Beta) occurred. The purpose of the mass testing was to respond to the question—What do we do with all these people? The Army Alpha was used with the literate group and the Beta was used with the illiterates. In effect, screening, selection and assignment to role and function in the army were all facilitated by the results of this testing.

At the time of the Second World War, many refinements had taken place in the earlier selection instruments. To facilitate placement during this war, the Army General Classification Test (AGCT) was evolved. It should be recognized that both of the war-time tests were constructed to meet a need and that their structure was oriented toward an assessment of mental ability.

By the end of World War II, with large numbers of service personnel returning to civilian life, there was again the need to place people in vocations—only this time they were civilian jobs. Those seeking to get back into the system were met with a much broader range of help including test instruments. Strong and Kuder had developed interest inventories during and prior to the war. Personality inventories followed the First World War model, called the Personal Data Sheet, which was developed by Robert Woodworth. Aptitude, ability and achievement testing had proliferated by the end of the war, and greater concern was being voiced regarding the value of testing.

There were other nontest types of developments which had also occurred by the end of the

Second World War. Initiated by the United States Employment Service (USES) at the time of the depression, the basic form of the Dictionary of Occupational Titles (DOT) became available in 1939. This was a major effort to classify occupations and the characteristics of workers. Industrial psychologists had begun performing time and motion studies and assessing the relationships of job characteristics and worker traits. These and other aspects of nontest data gathering and evaluation procedures have been incorporated into the appraisal service as it is found in our schools today.

Content of Appraisal

Perhaps the most appropriate way to discuss the aspects of appraisal is to acknowledge that any information, gathered by any means, about one or more students can be an important part of appraisal. Typically, the types of information are grouped into two broad classifications: information resulting from "tests"; and information resulting from nontest sources. It could be said that these two classifications represent attempts to maintain both objective and subjective sources of data.

Testing Sources

The most frequently discussed aspect of appraisal is testing. The two polarized ends of the discussion are reflected in the following two statements: tests are great and can provide us with much valuable information; tests are inherently evil and should never be used as nothing can be gained from them. Yet testing is generally carried on in the schools and is frequently mandated by the various states under statewide testing programs. Assuming this to be the case in most school situations, the following is an attempt to speak to the general question of what should be known about testing.

Types of Tests

The types of tests available can be grouped by the following titles: aptitude, ability, achievement, interest, and personality. In the following material each of the five types of testing will be briefly discussed, beginning with a specific definition of each type to aid in differentiation. It should be pointed out early in the discussion of instruments that it is not always the type of tasks or items which differentiate types of tests, particularly aptitude, ability and achievement tests. That which most readily distinguishes these three first types of tests is the intended use or purpose.

Aptitude tests. Aptitude tests as defined by English and English (1958) are "a set of tasks so chosen and standardized that they yield an estimate of a person's future performance on other tasks not necessarily having evident similarity to the test tasks" (p. 40). In the case of ability measures it can be seen that the specific purpose is prediction of future performance on the same or related tasks. Ultimately, this is very important to understand as a given test may be valid (to be discussed later) for one purpose and totally inappropriate for another. Some would argue that since the content of most measures of aptitude, ability and achievement instruments comes from information available in the environment, all three of these types of instruments are really measures of achievement or experience with the environment. At one level of thinking, philosophic, this is essentially true. However, at a scientific or psychometric level of thought, the function or purpose must be considered; considering this aspect *does* differentiate the instruments.

The *Differential Aptitude Tests* or DAT (The Psychological Corporation) is a widely used example of an aptitude test. The DAT is a case in point for a well-researched instrument. Its technical manual presents a wealth of information on the predictive nature of the various subtests which make up the instrument. Separate subtests cover: verbal reasoning; numerical ability, abstract reasoning, clerical speed and accuracy, mechanical reasoning, space relations, spelling, and language usage. A score is reported for each subtest and the verbal reasoning and numerical ability scores are combined to form a score (VR + NA) which has been shown to have a high degree of correspondence to general mental ability scores. Even in one of the most widely used aptitude measures there is the merging of purposes.

It should be recognized that the above is but one example of an aptitude measure. There are single aptitude instruments available on most subject matter areas taught in the schools, and many have been developed for specific occupations and occupational settings.

Ability tests. Frequently, test publisher's catalogs do not provide a separate heading or grouping for ability measures. Instead, they are often included in the category with aptitude measures. A possible reason for this can be hypothesized on consideration of the English and English (1958) definition of this type of measure: "A test of maximum performance designed to reveal the level of present ability to function" (p. 2). In the same definition they go on to clarify the same position taken here. That is, that the purpose for constructing the instrument is of great importance: Is the focus to be on past (achievement), present (ability), or on future (aptitude) levels of functioning? As with the DAT, is it surprising that test users and publishers would wish to have tests suitable for more than one purpose?

It should be remembered that tests of mental ability were of the first type to be developed. In this category are both individual and group measures of "intelligence" as well as specific areas of ability such as creativity. Since many of the ability measures require specific training as well as supervised practice in their use and interpretation, particularly in diagnostic situations, routine knowledge of this type of instrument is not acquired by many certified staff members in the schools. Whereas mass testing with a group ability measure such as the *Henmon-Nelson Tests of Mental Ability* (Houghton Mifflin) was a very routine matter until the mid-sixties, serious questions have been raised about this approach in recent years. The basic issue is centered around the educational purpose and adequacy of IQ tests. In particular, this has evolved from the use of ability measures with the disadvantaged. This aspect will be discussed later.

Achievement tests. The most broadly administered type of test used in the schools is achievement. As defined by English and English (1958) this is "a measure of proficiency level gained by testing the performance actually displayed in a given field. . . . It is so constructed as to bring to light the relative excellence of the individuals' past learning" (p. 6). Again, there is the issue of purpose. In this particular type of test, the item content should reflect the subject matter content of what has been taught in each specific area of achievement assessment.

Specific examples of widely used achievement measures are: the *Metropolitan Achievement Tests* (Harcourt Brace Jovanovich), the *SRA Achievement Series* (Science Research Associates), and the *Iowa Tests of Basic Skills* (Houghton Mifflin). These instruments offer assessments in the "solid" subject matter areas (language arts, social studies, science, and math) and in many cases there are both whole and part scores, i.e., math usage and math concepts combine to form total math.

Interest measures. The field of interest measurement has undergone serious examination in the last four years. The center of the controversy has been the challenge of sex bias in interest measurement. This aspect will be discussed at greater length in a following section.

Many people have attached a totally inappropriate word, test, to the assessment of interest. From the standpoint that there are no right or wrong answers, measures of this type can hardly be called tests. However, Super and Crites (1962) do list tested interests as one of the four ways information is gained. The examples they offer for tested interest deal with using objective testing to assess the amount and type of information retained in specific fields. The underlying assumption seems to be that the more information one has retained about an occupational area, such as science, the greater is the individual's interest. They also state that testing for vocational interest has not received much attention since just after World War I. The other three they list are: expressed interest, manifest interest, and inventoried interest. The obvious difference between these four approaches is the method used to gather the data. The confusion on the topic of interests is also noted by English and English (1958) who devote considerable space to the subject. Since the focus here is on the more widely used form of interest assessment, the inventory, only their definition of that aspect follows: "A series of questions concerning the objects or activities which the individual likes, prefers, or in which he has interest" (p. 271).

As is apparent from the above, most forms of interest measurement are highly subjective; it is basically a statement of what one likes and dislikes. The format of item presentation is usually either of the forced choice style as in the *Kuder* inventories (SRA) or of open format as in the *Strong-Campbell Interest Inventory* or SCII (Stanford University Press), *Self-Directed Search* or SDS (Consulting Psychologists Press) and the *Ohio Vocational Interest Survey* or OVIS (Harcourt Brace Jovanovich). In the Kuder forced choice format, items are presented in triads or trios of activities; and the person responding to the instrument is asked to specify which of the three activities is liked most and which is liked least. There are many forms of the Kuder available for use with differing age levels of people. Forms C and E are frequently used with middle school age youth to stimulate their thinking about the process of career development.

In the open format of the SCII, the person responding to the inventory is presented with a series of activities, job titles and school subjects and asked to specify whether each is liked, disliked, or whether the person is indifferent to each separate item. Though the item format of the SCII remains quite similar to the older *Strong Vocational Interest Blank* or SVIB, the wording used, particularly in job titles, has been unisexed and both males and females respond to the same test booklet. The item format for the SDS and OVIS is similar to that of the SCII though the option of being indifferent is not offered in quite the same way. Both the SDS and the OVIS make use of the *Dictionary of Occupational Titles* or DOT in the exploration of the meaning of scores, whereas the SCII uses known groups of occupational workers and their assessed interest responses as norm or reference groups.

Personality measures. Unlike the other forms of appraisal of traits held by students, personality measures are not frequently used in the schools. Basic to the infrequency of use in the schools is the personal incroachment possibility of most instruments. Not only can the instruments be viewed as threatening by school youth, but considerable research has supported the ease with which most can be faked.

As with the field of interest, English and English (1958) devote a considerable amount of space to the many and varied definitions of personality. The definition offered for personality inventory is: "A check list, usually to be filled out by a person about himself, consisting (a) of many statements about personal characteristics which the subject checks as applying or not to the ratee, or (b) of questions to be answered *Yes, No* or *Doubtful*" (p. 383).

One of the more thoroughly researched personality inventories is the *Minnesota Multiphasic Personality Inventory* or MMPI (Psychological Corporation). However, as with the individually administered ability measures, its use is usually restricted to those with special training in the use and interpretation of the MMPI. As such, the instrument has seen wide usage in mental hospitals, for which it was originally developed, and in postsecondary counseling centers as well as in the private practice work of psychologists and psychiatrists.

Personality inventories which are sometimes used in the schools would include the *Edwards Personal Preference Schedule* or EPPS (Psychological Corporation) and the many measures of self-concept now on the market. Considerable thought should be given prior to the administration of a personality measure in the schools. Questions such as: Do I possess the skills needed to wisely use the results?; Will this assessment provide information which is unavailable through any other means?; and Is this the time to make a referral?; should be asked prior to most administrations.

While only the personality inventory has been discussed to this point, there are other methods of personality assessment. The theraputic technique of free association, a form of verbal evaluation, is sometimes used by a trained psychologist or psychiatrist. Another form would be to place the person in a situation and have a trained observer evaluate the actions or interactions. Some aspects of this form are used regularly by school personnel. Yet another form, the projective approach, is another which requires a background of training prior to utilization. An example of this approach is the *Rorschach Technique* (Psychological Corporation).

Other groupings. While the preceding five types of tests are viewed as the most useable form for ready information, there are other ways of classifying tests. There are several dichotomies that can be used to describe tests: speed vs. power, individual vs. group, performance or verbal vs. pencil and paper, objective vs. subjective, and normative or criterion referenced vs. ipsative. All but the last of these five should be self-explanatory in their differences. In the case of the last comparative pair some definitions are in order. In the first case, normative, the explicit implication is that there is a large comparison group of appropriate background which becomes the standard against which all other or later scores are compared. It should be quite apparent that having clear information regarding the makeup of the norm group is very important, particularly when it comes to deriving meaning from the score. The second term used was criterion referenced. The implication here is that some external authoritative group has established a yardstick and with the yardstick some type of minimum measure of acceptability. Through ongoing collection of data from repeated testings it is possible to develop norms for this type of test as well. In the case of an ipsative measure, though there are other (usually psychometric) forms of ipsativity, the implication here is the contrast with normative. Instead of being compared with an external group, personal trait aspects within a given individual are compared for their relative strength or regnancy. The EPPS is an example of such an instrument. The results from the EPPS eventuate in a profile on which the relative strength of the current status of fifteen psychological needs is depicted for an individual. Both types of tests, normative and ipsative, are or can be of value. However, the person administering either type of test needs to know the purpose for the testing and the intended use of the resulting information. It should be recognized by all of those who administer tests or in any way use the results of testing that those results represent simply a *sample* of all possible behavior; in many cases a very small sample.

Psychometric Issues

One of the major psychometric considerations, norm group, was discussed in the previous section. However, since the nature and characteristics of the norm group are so important to test interpretation, there are a few additional aspects which need to be discussed. From the scores of the norm group, organized into a distribution, the score format for all those to be tested later is devised. If the characteristics of the norm group, such as age, grade level, sex, and cultural background, are not representative of the group to be tested, then the value of the resulting or projected scores could be highly suspect. Most test publishers are currently doing a laudable job of selecting a norm group which is truly representative, but this aspect does need to be assessed by anyone with responsibility for using or interpreting test scores. It is assumed that those selecting the instruments will have done this also.

Other items of psychometric consideration would include such things as a knowledge of the score form. What is a percentile and how should it be interpreted? How does a percentile score differ from a standard score, or a decile or a stanine? It seems that the most often misinterpreted score is the grade equivalent score; how should it be interpreted? At least some acquaintance with the difference between score forms and what can be said about each should be attained by all of those working with tests and/or test results.

There are also some very basic kinds of psychometric information which should be common knowledge. These would include the concepts of reliability and validity. Basically, reliability speaks to the issue of the faith which can be attached to the repeatability of a given score. Validity on the other hand, relates to the purpose of the test.

All forms of reliability are the result of the applications of the statistical technique of correlation. The results, whether of test-retest, split-half, alternate form or any other approach, are stated as a decimal value from $+1.00$ to 0.00. The test-retest form of reliability relates the stability of score levels over time. The split-half form of reliability relates the internal consistency of the group of items within a given instrument. The parallel or alternate form type of reliability relates the equivalence of scores between two forms (e.g., A and B) of the same instrument. Generally, the closer the number is to 1.00 the greater is the test's reliability. The question, How high is enough?, is responded to by Helmstadter (1964), who lists minimum reliabilities for four different purposes:

1. To evaluate level of group accomplishment, .50
2. To evaluate differences in level of group accomplishment in two or more performances, .90
3. To evaluate level of individual accomplishment, .94
4. To evaluate differences in level of individual accomplishment on two or more performances, .98 (p. 84)

A very close cousin to reliability is the standard error of measure or SEM. The SEM is derived by using a measure of reliability and can do for an individual's score what the standard deviation does for the scores of a group of people. It can aid in the interpretation of a given score by placing it not as a point on a line, but within a band of possible points. Test scores do represent a *sample* of behavior and do have sources of error connected with them.

The validity of an instrument can help establish the purpose for which the scores may be used—valid for what purpose(s)? As there are many possible purposes for testing, there are also many forms of validity. The two primary distinctions are described by the labels "statistical" and "nonstatistical." The statistical or empirical label indicates that the validity statement or outcome is one arrived at mathematically. All types of statistical validity employ some form of correlation approach. As with reliability values, the resulting number will vary from + 1.00 to 0.00. In effect, the validity of a measure is statistically calculated by relating or correlating the scores from one group of people on two different measures. Whether these measures are taken at roughly the same time (concurrent validity) or the two measuring points are spread out in time (predictive validity), both are expressing the correspondence between the measure under question and some other criterion. Thus, the purpose of the measure can be in part determined by the type of validity data presented.

The nonstatistical or subjective forms of validity include face validity, and content and curricular validity. Basically, face validity is inferred by all test users by scanning the item or task content of the instrument. We arrive at a conclusion that the instrument appears to assess X, whatever X is. Though highly desirable in most types of tests, it is often necessary to obscure the intent of a measure of personality and eliminate its face validity so that it is not easily faked. Content and curricular validity are qualities which are highly desirable particularly in achievement measures. Every attempt is usually made to have an instrument reflect the curriculum and specific course content of the areas assessed. This is usually accomplished by test companies employing recognized experts to assist them with the item development.

A third classification, construct validity, is frequently utilized. As this type of validity is somewhat complicated by comparison with the previous two types, it is suggested that those interested in this and possibly other forms of validity seek a general measurement text (e.g., Helmstadter, 1964 or Nunnally, 1967).

It is readily recognized that the above material on what may be perceived as the statistical aspects of testing have been presented in a rather sketchy manner. Yet, in order for any member of the school team to be able to use tests and test data accurately, the very least which needs to be common knowledge are the "nuts and bolts" presented here. Without this minimum knowledge base, assuming an ability to interpret test results appropriately, the students as recipients of testing are going to be better off if the given staff member is not involved in testing in any manner.

Uses and Abuses of Testing

There are many issues which could be discussed under this heading. In fact, there are now available entire texts as well as many commissioned papers on specific issues which involve testing. One such text, *Crucial Issues in Testing* (Tyler and Wolf, eds, 1974) does a rather complete job of stating and discussing many of the larger issues. Some of the section headings include: testing and minority groups, using tests in selecting students for educational opportunities, tests and the grouping of students, and tests and privacy. The American Personnel and Guidance Association (APGA) has continually attempted to speak to the many issues which frequently cloud the issue of testing. In 1972 one of the branches of APGA, the Association for Measurement and Evaluation in Guidance (AMEG), presented a position paper entitled "The Responsible Use of Tests." Subsequently the APGA appointed a Commission on Standardized Testing and Evaluation of Potential Among Minority Group Members. Among the issues discussed in the commission report are those of: dangers of misclassification, difficulties of psychometric consideration, and test fairness in test construction.

As stated earlier, the use of ability measures, and particularly those reporting an IQ score, with disadvantaged groups has been the focus of much of the debate. In some cases, states, e.g., California, have passed legislation which seriously restricts the use of IQ measures.

There appear to be four major topics of the ongoing debate. In the first instance, the questions or tasks presented to the person being tested have been spoken to by test publishers as well as professional counselors. What has resulted so far has been increased development of criterion referenced tests, culture free and culture relevant tests. Yet the specific tasks required of those who are tested are one of the smaller aspects. Another topic comes under consideration when norm referenced tests are administered. Until very recently the majority of available ability measures were normed on white middle-income students. This approach has been modified of late by test publishers and there are now many instruments available which do include a much broader comparative base in their norm group. There remains a great deal to be accomplished in this area however. Turning to the third point, there is less clear evidence that the manner in which a given instrument is administered, in terms of whether a like minority or disadvantaged person is in charge, has an effect on the outcome or test score. On the other hand, it has been shown that disadvantaged students and others can profit (increase their test scores) through learning test-taking skills. This does not mean teaching the test. It does mean such things as preparing the student for the type of task which will be presented. Simply working with an IBM type answer sheet can throw a student who is unfamiliar with what is expected. Many students can learn to work more rapidly under the IBM type answer sheet condition by being taught the most efficient method of filling in the space. Many students could also profit from gaining skills in working with multiple choice type tasks. The last major topic or task, and perhaps the most difficult to deal with, is that of the interpretation and use of scores. It is in this area that the most persistent and insidious forms of bias often exist.

Another major issue which has come to the surface with the emergence of the women's movement and general concern for sexual equality is that of sex bias. While many aspects of appraisal and testing in particular have come under scrutiny for possible sex bias, none have received as much attention as has the field of interest assessment. Many groups came together under the leadership of the National Institutes of Education (NIE) and their efforts have resulted in a number of papers and sets of guidelines. One of the older interest inventories which seemed to be the center of the criticism was the Strong Vocational Interest Blank (SVIB)—one for men (the test booklet was blue), and one for women (the test booklet was pink). Unfortunately, the issue of the pink and blue test booklets seemed to have received more attention than the fact that men and women were responding to different items and that each sex group had different kinds and numbers of vocational interest group comparisons on the resulting score profile. The SVIB has been modified both in form (a new single booklet), profile (both sexes now receive scores on the same occupational groups), and in the name of the instrument itself (it is now the *Strong-Campbell Interest Inventory* or SCII). Where possible all of the remaining items of the SCII have been desexed in an attempt to reduce the implication that only one sex could gain entry into a particular vocation.

Perhaps the most pervasive abuse of tests comes through the misuse and misinterpretation of test scores. The old story of one parent comparing the amount of intelligence of his or her child with another parent of another child seems appropriate here. The story usually ends: My child is smarter than yours because his/her IQ is 109 and your son/daughter only has 107. It is obvious that the parent suggesting this has an inappropriate understanding of testing in general or of intelligence testing in particular. Most tests have a SEM of three to six points, which, if that had been applied in the story case, would have depicted the probable lack of any real difference in the two scores.

It seems reasonable, however, that if the public, including the news media, does have difficulty placing appropriate interpretations on test data, then the responsibility for the deficiency must be shared in large measure by the schools and school staffs. There are still schools and school systems making judgments which have long-term effects on students based on a single test score. This is just a single example of the manner in which the schools have and in some cases continue to misuse or misinterpret test data. Another example could be of the teacher who prepares the class of students to respond to a standardized testing situation by explaining how worthless and time consuming tests are; yet wonders why the scores which result from the subsequent testing are so much lower than expected. In light of these and many other possible examples, it seems that the time has come for school districts to devote greater in-service efforts aimed at modifying attitudinal states and general testing knowledge of the school staff.

As can be readily seen, there have been and probably will continue to be many issues in need of resolution in connection with the field of testing. Yet until some better alternative to testing surfaces, it seems much more profitable to deal openly with the issues than to hide from them in hopes that they and testing will go away.

Other Resources on Testing

There are many different titles of workers in the field of education who have various parts to play in respect to testing. Yet the purpose of this section has not been to totally spell out all that each of those groups of people need to know about specific tests or tests in general. Each school system and for that matter each school will have its own unique methods of dealing with tests and test data. It is assumed, though, that there is a need to have at hand some ideas as to where to turn should you need to have information which goes beyond what has been presented here. To that end, the following sources are offered.

For specific information about any given test or assessment device, the first source which should be considered is the manual for that instrument. While manuals and tests differ considerably, the American Psychological Association (APA) (1966) has published a set of standards for tests and test manuals. Each test or assessment manual should contain all of the essential information on the development, standardization, norming, scoring, and interpretation of the given instrument. It should also provide information on the reliability and validity of the instrument as well as its cross-validation. It should spell out how the members of the norm or reference group were selected if it is a norm referenced instrument or should spell out the development of the items and the criterion if it is a criterion referenced instrument. Frequently, these types of information are not found in one single manual, or in a manual at all, and anyone wishing to evaluate an instrument will need to look elsewhere.

One of the major accumlated sources of information on tests may be found in a series of reference books which were first published in 1938. The Mental Measurements Yearbooks, (1938-72) or Boros as they are frequently spoken of (after the name of the editor) contain an invaluable source of information about the majority of tests published in English speaking countries of the world. At present there are seven volumes available with the current volume containing so much information that it was necessary for the first time to present it in two parts. Current yearbooks (the third through the seventh) include critical reviews of instruments as well as reference citations where other information may be found regarding a specific instrument. Each listing also provides the name of the publisher, the date of publication, the cost, the forms and levels available and the names of the subtests if more than one single score is reported. One of the weakest aspects of the information provided is on the cost. In our current inflationary period the costs of all materials associated with testing are changing so rapidly that even test publishers sometimes have difficulty making current pricing information available to potential users. Publishers' catalogs should be consulted for current pricing information.

Boros has edited a number of other very useful resource books on testing which may also be consulted. *Tests in Print II* (1974) contains a comprehensive listing of tests in print as of early 1974, as well as a cumulative index to the more than 70,000 documents in the *Mental Measurements Yearbooks* and selected references on each specific test listed. *Personality Tests and Reviews II* (1975) is a monograph which deals specifically with the field of personality testing. Like its counterparts, it contains both reviews and references on specific instruments. There are also monographs available on testing in many of the curricular areas.

Another source of information of both general and specific nature may be found in the periodic publications of two of the major test publishers. Both Harcourt Brace Jovanovich, Inc. (HBJ) and The Psychological Corporation (Ψ) have responded to the need for information on the general and specific aspects of testing in the forms of Test Service Notebooks (HBJ) and Test Service Bulletins (Ψ) which are made available to those using tests at no cost. For a listing of currently available titles, each publisher should be contacted.

Educational Testing Service (ETS) also has produced a number of booklets which have recently been combined into a "Tests and Measurement Kit." To obtain the titles of the materials in the kit and the current price, the Office of ETS, Princeton, New Jersey 08540, should be written.

Another organization which has published materials of a research nature as they relate to testing is The American College Testing Program (ACT). Their *Research Report* series offers a wide variety of titles. A list of currently available titles and their cost may be obtained from ACT, P.O. Box 168, Iowa City, Iowa 52240.

Nontest Appraisal Sources

In contrast with testing sources of appraisal data, nontest sources of or for appraisal are more diverse in their nature. The breadth of personnel who assume responsibility for the collection and use of the resulting data is also extensive. Whether assigned or assumed, conducted explicitly or implicitly or carried out at a conscious or preconscious level, all school personnel are or can be involved in the collection and utilization of nontest forms of appraisal data. The assumption made herein is that the student(s), faculty, and in fact community at large can gain more from explicit conscious efforts to gather and utilize nontest appraisal information.

As mentioned earlier, many texts discussing appraisal, at the formative stage of the guidance movement, have dedicated a large portion of space to the presentation of various forms which may be used for the collection of nontest information. That approach will not be presented in this chapter, but should information regarding forms for recording appraisal data be desired, a possible starting point which may prove helpful is Froehlich (1958).

Whereas all of the data resulting from testing sources of appraisal can be said to be objective, only a small portion of the nontest sources of appraisal are considered to be objective. The majority of nontest sources are, at least on the surface, highly subjective. This is not to say that the subjective nature of this information is bad or somehow less valuable than the other objective elements, but to acknowledge that it may also have some sources of error.

Administrative and management sources. One of the major sources of objective nontest data results from typical school management functions. Knowing which students are where is an important aspect of the functioning of a school. Each student's daily schedule is maintained in some form of record in one or more places in the school building. By federal, state and often local regulations, all schools must maintain some system of attendance monitoring. It can frequently be very telling to compare the absences and tardies of various students or groups of students with the teachers' perceptions of that student or group of students. Frequently school staff members infer many attitudinal qualities from different levels of class attendance. Yet how frequently do these attitudinal states become the topic of explicit communication between students and staff?

Another aspect of some objective quality that is often maintained in a number of places is the student's grades or marks. It will usually depend on the philosophy of the school, though, as to the connotation of any specific grade. Are grades received for attendance, for trying, for subject mastery or competence in general?

Other categories of information may be found which could be grouped under the management function, whether carried out by teachers, counselors, administrators, secretaries or even paraprofessionals. Whether the student is bussed to school, for any number of reasons, may be important to know. Somewhere in each building there are probably copies of each bus route. The number of referrals to the office is usually maintained by someone in the office. Also, the number and types of awards and other forms of positive recognition are also on record somewhere in the building.

The foregoing should have led to a feeling or statement regarding management-types of information. Hopefully a question will be raised about what each staff member is doing with this type of data. All too often the result is a set of labels and expectations which greatly facilitates one type of student (just as "good" test scores do), while at the same time acting as additional stumbling blocks for other students (as in the case of "bad" test scores). Suggestions on how to deal with all of the information on students will be dealt with later.

Health information. In most, if not all, schools there is some form of nursing service provided. The person responsible for this service usually keeps records on the physical characteristics as well as the special health needs of given students. This would usually include information on height, weight, vision, hearing and in some cases special information related to dietary control and disease innoculations. It is not unusual for parents to communicate with the nurse who in turn communicates with the faculty regarding special medication or situational aspects of a student's health. This may include knowledge of heart conditions, respiratory problems or postoperative recovery.

Observational data. All staff members in a school are in a position to either formally or informally observe the daily activities of students. Typically, at least until there is some crisis, the students who are the focus of most observation are those who carry the label of "problem." Yet all students deserve our attention. Yes, we do pay attention to students, but how frequently do we make a conscious effort to observe the behavior and attitudes of all or even a majority of students? The need for this approach and the possible positive outcomes has been well-spelled out by the Model School Project (Trump and Georgiades, 1970).

A great deal of ambiguity remains on how best to deal with the observational data. A major aspect of this will be discussed under the section on the cumulative record. However, it can be said here that placing untested assumptions about a given student, gained through observation, in a written form can be very hazardous to the well-being of both the student and the staff member. It is one thing to say in writing that Jerry or Jane fell asleep in class on a given day for a period of roughly twenty minutes; it is quite another to make an extension of the data and suggest in writing that the falling asleep is symptomatic of some deep-seated emotional problems for which Jerry or Jane ought to be seeking professional help.

Situations which can provide valuable observational data would obviously include the classroom. Yet how many faculty members really observe the hallways during passing periods and before and after school? Often one of the most distressing duties which can be assigned to a staff member is cafeteria supervision. Yet what golden opportunities there are in that situation for observation. How are students responded to by their peers? How or to what extent do they interact with peers? These and other types of situations offer many opportunities to observe the attitudes, values and behavior patterns of students.

One way to formalize to some extent the levels of peer interaction is through use of the sociogram. Any staff member who works with a group of students can develop a series of questions which ask the members of that group to pick other members with whom they would desire to work, or talk with or be talked to by, or be led by or any other form of activity. The type of question could be stated in the negative also, but students seem to feel freer if the directions are in the positive. Once the question or questions have been responded to by all members of the group, the next step is to plot the results. To do this, each student's name can be assigned a number and that number placed in a circle on a piece of paper. Those students picked most frequently can be grouped near the center of the page and for each choice by one student of another an arrow can be drawn from the chooser to the chosen. If two students pick each other, an arrow can be drawn on both ends of the line. What results are the peer perceptions of leaders, followers and isolates. Other names may be used depending on the questions asked, but the resulting pictorial display may add considerable understanding of the dynamics of a given group and may also make it easier for the staff member to formulate objectives which utilize group talents and purposively begin to incorporate the student who is frequently left out but not ever noticed. Peer interaction with most school youth can be a very potent determiner of behavior.

The cumulative folder. This particular aspect of appraisal, while not specifically either test or nontest oriented, is included here because of its overall impact on appraisal. As such, the cumulative folder or record has recently come under scrutiny from sources as general as Sunday newspaper supplements, through support of foundations such as Russell Sage, and from the floor of Congress itself through the Buckley-Pell Privacy Rights of Parents and Students Amendment (93-380).

For those who, as either student or parent, have attempted to view or gain access to the contents of the cumulative record, the reasons for the scrutiny are quite clear. The ability to gain access to all or even a portion of the contents was not evenly applied at all. Some schools and school systems have had an open door policy to the school's cumulative records for some time, though in most cases this has meant that the records were open to anyone but the parents and certainly not to the student. This attitude has been fostered by the anticipated confidential nature of the set of records, which by the time a student reached the senior year often contained recommendations for postsecondary entry into jobs or further education and training. Yet, seldom has there been the opportunity for assessing the accuracy of the contents by the parent or the student.

Earlier statements regarding the cumulative folder would seem to shed some light on a part of the problem. As stated in an HEW publication (1963), "A pupil's record grows as the pupil grows and provides a permanent scoreboard that should follow him from year to year throughout his school career" (p. 14). Grow most of them did, at least until the middle to late sixties. One of the primary questions raised regarding the record has been the relevancy of the material contained in it. There has been little concern for keeping the results of standardized testing, only with the use and interpretation of them. Yet, special testing whose value diminishes rapidly over time was often routinely kept in the folder and followed a student, often to his or her detriment, throughout the school career. Disciplinary notes and letters of suspension or parent conferences seemed to never be thrown away, even though they also had a useful life span of at best one year. In short, the "fat" cumulative record aided in building expectations for the behavior of students. All too often this became a self-fulfilling prophecy.

With the advent of the Family Educational Rights and Privacy Act, which became effective on November 20, 1974, the fat files suddenly became very thin. In *Education U.S.A.* of October 7, 1974, a discussion of the impact of the new act was offered. That document stated that, "A massive throw-away campaign is underway to cull personal and irrelevant material from students' cumulative files. School administrator groups are urging their members to remove from their files all materials that do not appropriately serve the student and the school." The implication was quite clear that schools had kept materials that they were not too sure they wanted parents or students to see.

Though the federal regulations for this act were due early in 1975, they are not yet available and 1975 is nearly past history. A recent phone call to the office of Thomas McFee at HEW, who is coordinating the development of the regulations, determined that the regulations should be coming out soon, but no date was given. In the absence of any federal guidelines, schools and school systems have been left on their own to develop policy. Just how all of the concerns surrounding the privacy act will be resolved is in doubt at this time, but what has been assured is that parents and students of legal age do have the right to inspect the contents and to challenge their accuracy if such is necessary. When they become available, the federal regulations should be studied carefully.

The preceding material has presented the content of appraisal through its two major aspects: testing sources, and nontest sources. Yet to know what the aspects of a given guidance service are is only half of the story. In order to respond to the question, Why bother to appraise?, the following section, dealing with the contribution of appraisal to career development is offered.

Contributions of Appraisal to Career Development

Career development, in the context of this section, is taken to mean and be synonomous with the total life development of an individual. Quite naturally this includes the aspects of school, home and community as each of these sectors of society has a profound effect on the development of an individual.

What are some of the relevant assumptions that can be made about career development as that process is affected by appraisal? The first of these would quite obviously be an extension of Parsons's (1909) first step of vocational guidance. *All individuals need to have a clear understanding of themselves, their strengths as well as their limitations.* This is not to say that all people need the same information or that any specific information is needed at any given time in their lives. To say this would be to contradict the whole foundation of the developmental nature of people. Another assumption stemming from the first is that *all people make decisions regarding their lives, and that to make these decisions sound information is clearly a necessity.* Having a clear picture of yourself is but part of the means by which decisions are made. The other part is information about how the self might fit into the world out there—learning the range of possibilities. Another assumption related to the schools, is that *all schools need to know as much as possible about all students in order to be able to develop a curriculum that is relevant to the needs of those students as well as to societal needs.* We can no longer afford the luxury of only educating the chosen few for the "good life." All students are entitled to relevant education that prepares them to be responsible choosers.

The major tenets of career development are quite clearly spelled out in the joint position paper of the National Vocational Guidance Association and the American Vocational Association. This paper may be found in the appendix of this text. The three previously stated assumptions reflect the major areas in which appraisal should be expected to have an impact on the field of career development.

In the case of the first assumption, relating a need for self-understanding, there are a number of ways by which this activity may be facilitated by the appraisal service. At the earliest point, the entry into school, many systems are now moving away from some arbitrarily established age for that entry. In its place many schools are using school readiness tests which are available or are developing their own. The information resulting from this testing should be shared with the parents of the potential student so that they might participate in the decision for school enrollment. A factor in the modification of the school entry age has been the increased numbers of working mothers and the greater availability of preschool experiences. If children can be shown to be socially and emotionally ready for entry into school, through the testing and observation processes, they should be accepted by the school system. However, the need for information on which to make this decision is quite clear.

Having once established the students' status there are ongoing needs for information about the "self" of all students. The periodic testing at the elementary grades helps parents, the student, and the school staff to assess the special needs of all students. This information comes not only from the standardized achievement, aptitude, and ability testing, but from teacher made tests and nontest sources, as well. Since there are not that many options available to students at the elementary level, the primary use of the appraisal information is to insure that each student acquires the maximum possible prerequisite skills. Appraisal information at this level should help the parents, students and school staff members to capitalize on the individual strengths which all students have, as well as providing possible direction for upgrading perceived areas of weakness.

At the junior high or middle school years, the student continues to have a need for self-understanding. It is during these school years that students may find a desire to obtain information about their vocational interests, as this may be of use in educational planning. Interest measures offered at this time should report broad areas of interest, such as mechanical, rather than the narrow or specific fields such as engineering. There are a number of well-constructed interest measures which do provide appropriate data for the purpose of aiding the individual in narrowing his or her vocational planning. Testing, observation and the appropriate use of the data by students, parents and school staffs should provide potential direction for all students.

By the time students reach the senior high years (ten to twelve) they usually have some rough idea as to who they are and the possible directions they would like to consider traveling. In prior years, the majority of efforts by both administrators and counselors (and often by teachers as well) were directed to helping those students who were collegebound. As more counselors and administrators become more aware of the career development needs of all students, this trend should be greatly reduced. This is not to suggest that counselors, teachers and administrators reduce or no longer respond to the needs of collegebound youth, but rather that they also begin devoting more time to that growing number of youths who are seeking short-term special instruction or electing to enter the world of work at the completion of their senior year of high school.

There are many special tests for postsecondary decision making which should be available to all students at the eleventh and twelfth grades. This would include the numerous interest measures which report more specific types of information. It would also include the many postsecondary school placement tests (ACT, PSAT, SAT AND CEEB), as well as a number of special aptitude batteries such as the General Aptitude Test Battery (GATB) offered through the Employment Service, and The Armed Services Vocational Aptitude Battery (ASVAB) which is available through the military.

The schools should also become more involved in the placement process, in which students who choose not to go on to further postsecondary education may receive assistance in securing employment in a field which is commensurate with skills, interests and work values of the student. Since placement will be considered in another chapter, it will not be elaborated on here. Yet all students need information about themselves and the environment to assist them to become responsible choosers.

Though already incorporated in the previous material for assumption one, it should be obvious that there are a number of decisions made by the student; particularly educational and vocational decisions. To the extent that these decisions have been made by the student through assessing all of the relevant information available through the appraisal and information service functions, the student will in most cases assume responsibility for those decisions.

In the case of the third assumption, curriculum relevance, the ongoing evaluation of students' progress through the use of achievement testing can be of considerable value in curriculum planning. A primary example would be the last five to ten years of mathematics instruction. With the introduction of "new math" and its emphasis on the conceptual approach, there was a rather large shift in resulting test scores in the areas of problem solving and math concepts. The overall score on math concepts rose considerably and the overall average score on problem solving fell considerably. This caused a number of newspaper editorials on the failure of the schools and/or the tests. Many schools however, took the approach that test results frequently reflect the emphasis of the curriculum and set about to rethink the decision to emphasize concepts at the exclusion of problem solving. At this point, many of the achievement instruments have been renormed and schools have modified the curriculum to again include the learning of math facts for problem solving. Curriculum modification has been influenced by test results.

There are other ways of course in which the curriculum for individual students has been modified. Through testing and observation the special learning needs of individual students can be assessed. What should result from the appraisal of students is an individual curriculum geared to the needs of the student. There are some practical considerations involved however. Not all schools are large enough to have the variety of offerings and special classrooms needed to approximate the needs of all students. In those cases schools rely on the professional competence of school staffs to do the best job that is possible with the available resources. To accomplish the most desirable end, schools need the most well-developed appraisal process they can muster, supported by a competent well-functioning staff.

Roles of School Personnel

Every member of the school staff and many members of the community can be important aspects in the appraisal service. Considered in this manner, it is apparent the appraisal service should be a team effort. While all members of the team will have a number of common roles, i.e., general concern for the welfare, growth and development of all students, each member will also have some very specific roles and training.

Roles of Teachers

The teacher's role in the appraisal process usually encompasses both the testing and nontest aspects. It is usual for the teacher to act as the test administrator in the classroom, or to at least have a proctoring or monitoring function. In the capacity of administrator the teacher needs to adhere to the time limits specified in the manual, and to make it easy for the students to function at their optimum level. This type of testing, particularly at the elementary level, makes a different type of demand on the teacher. The usual classroom behavior of the teacher includes providing assistance to students who are having difficulty with the assigned task—this cannot be the case during standardized testing.

In the case of those school situations where the classroom teacher is in charge of the testing, an appropriate activity which should take place prior to the testing is the development of test-taking skills. This would include such things as reminders of the need for a good night's rest and a good breakfast prior to the test, how to work with multiple choice-type questions, how to work with an IBM-type answer sheet, and the most appropriate way to fill in the selected spot on the answer sheet.

During the test itself, the teacher should keep a log of any unusual events which transpire during the testing period. This would necessarily include the observations of individual students. This log should make the process of deriving meaningful information from the resulting scores considerably easier.

It was recommended earlier that teachers should begin to purposively observe the behavior of all students. Though it may be somewhat difficult, it would be highly desirable for each teacher to keep a log of day to day student activities which could be added to when there appeared to be a need to do so. This could be done by class in a manner similar to the grade book. Obviously all teachers do observe their students, the point taken here however, is that this process could be completed in a more explicit manner.

Where teachers are placed in the position of interpreting test results to parents it is strongly recommended that they recognize their level of competence and resist the urge to go beyond that point. However, in order for this approach to be successful with students or parents, the teacher needs a next-level source to whom parents or students may be referred when the need for information surpasses the teacher's level of competence. This source should be located before the fact, not after, as it clearly facilitates making a referral.

Roles of Counselors

Ideally the counselor should be the most knowledgeable person in any given building regarding the subject of appraisal. Given the knowledge as a base of operation, the counselor should also provide the leadership function for the activity, through planning and coordinating in-service training for the rest of the staff, as it relates to the gathering and utilizing of test and nontest data.

The counselor is usually expected to coordinate the standardized testing program, including in many cases the selection of testing materials, ordering of materials, maintenance of their security, sharpening of pencils, and the shipping of answer sheets for scoring. While this is a type of management function, it needs to be completed by someone who cares about the outcome of testing as any of the above factors may have an influence on the test results. From this position, the counselor is usually responsible for selecting the specific time and place for the testing program and securing the cooperation of the faculty.

As with teachers, counselors should recognize their limits of competency in interpreting test results and resist going beyond that point. They should also have a known referral source should a parent, student, or staff member need more information than they are equipped to offer. In many situations, there are possibilities for group test interpretation to students which can be followed up by individual or small group sessions as the needs arise.

In keeping with the need of the parents and community at large for information regarding testing and test results, the counselor can work with the local PTA or other school parent group to make presentations on the topic of appraisal. This should be limited to class profile and test characteristics in general. This approach can be a positive stimulator of parent and community interest which acknowledges the lack of specifics and yet opens the counselor's door to those parents who wish to learn more or to discuss more specifically the test results of their child.

Counselors, particularly at the secondary level, often use the results of appraisal in individual and small group counseling and guidance sessions with students. This may be originated from any or all aspects of appraisal as they relate to school behavior, selection of future classes or to vocational planning and other postsecondary possibilities.

The counselor is often called upon by other staff members to assist them in interpreting appraisal data for a class or an individual student. As such, the counselor, in the role of consultant to the staff, facilitates the development of individualized curricula and learning experiences. In the instance of an individual student, the counselor may gather a group of staff members together for the purpose of conducting a case study on that individual. This process would attempt to bring all of the relevant information together so that it may be seen as a whole. This should lead to decisions for future activities of a planned nature as they relate to resolution of the specific concerns regarding the student.

One of the primary administrative roles comes at very the earliest possible point, the actual hiring of the counselor. At this point administrators need to clearly spell out a professional role financial or leave time support of the administration, but if a professional staff is desired, it also deserves support. Counselors need to continue their formal and informal education through classes, seminars, workshops and convention involvement. They need to keep up to date on techniques of appraisal. As a part of the skill-upgrading of most secondary counselors, it is highly desirable for them to maintain an open dialogue with the business, industry and labor employment aspects within the community and to transmit the needs of this group for specific skills, knowledge and behaviors back to the faculty and students of their respective schools.

Roles of Administrators

One of the primary administrative roles comes at the very earliest possible point, the actual hiring of the counselor. At this point administrators need to clearly spell out a professional role and incumbent responsibilities which will build appropriate expectations for the functioning of the counselor. All too often counselors have been and continue to be utilized as assistant administrators and paper shufflers much to the detriment of the students, staff and eventually the counselor.

Another administrative role is implemented through the continued support of the counselor's efforts in the area of appraisal, including the administrator's keeping in touch with what is being carried out and how actions and attitudes of the school can be positively influenced by the counselor. As the administrator works in the aspects of planning he or she should assist the counselor in planning and scheduling the standardized testing program.

From the leadership position, the administrator should work with the counselor to develop curriculum development strategies, public relations activities and release time arrangements. The administrator should also request from or develop with the counselor a set of objectives for the appraisal service, against which the strengths and weaknesses may later be evaluated. Ideally, the administrator would be enough of an advocate of a strong guidance department in general and appraisal service in particular that he or she would work to secure sufficient support personnel for the program. This may mean additional clerks or secretaries or even developing a plan for some form of student help.

Roles of Students

There are two primary student roles which should be activated in the area of appraisal. The first is to become an active participant in the process, as this approach will yield them the most appropriate and valuable information for current and future decisions. The second role is to become as active a consumer of appraisal data as they are able to become.

In the case of the first role, students may sometimes need to push on faculty or counselors to gain active participant status. It may be that little is being done in the way of preparing students to acquire test taking skills as an example. The students themselves, because of their own needs, may have to request that special types of testing, such as interest inventories or postsecondary admissions exams be available to them.

In the case of the second role, they may need to request or seek out the meaning of any number of aspects of appraisal. In particular, this might originate by way of a need to know more deeply the relationships between a given test score and their future educational or vocational planning. Students need to be active and resourceful consumers of appraisal data.

Roles of Community Members

The basic role of community members is one of utilization and input to the appraisal service. As stated earlier, there is a great need for continuing dialogue between the employing aspect of the community and the school. There are many opportunities in the schools today for students to gain work experience as an aspect of their secondary education. The supervision of that work can be a valuable opportunity for observational data which can be shared with the school supervisor and the counselor.

To speak to the utilization aspect, community members need to have a clear understanding of what can be gained through appraisal. This is particularly true when one looks at the manner in which test scores are usually reported by the media. Employers in the community could work with the schools to develop profiles of different types of workers which could then be used by the schools to provide additional information by means of which students could make reasonable decisions and future plans.

There is another rather large issue which will not be discussed at any length, that is having a considerable impact on employers. That is the whole process of personnel selection through the use of tests. There have been two major court cases, *Griggs* v. *Duke Power Company* and *Moody* v. *Albernarle Paper Company,* the results of which have ". . . tightened the screws on employers by stating that when a test, even if valid, has adverse impact, every effort should be made to find an alternative, less adverse, selection device" (Holden, 1975, p. 37).

Roles of Parents

Parents have two major roles in the domain of appraisal. The first of these is to help their children gain the most from the appraisal data collected by the school. In the second case, parents need to participate with the school in the appraisal process, both to learn more about the strengths and weaknesses of their children and to protect their children from those few situations in which inappropriate data is placed in the cumulative record or when appropriate data are used in an inappropriate manner. The important thing for parents to remember is that students, despite their protestations to the contrary, need the support of their parents in order to become responsible citizens.

Differential Aspects of Appraisal

In as much as there are or may be differences in the extent and type of appraisal activities which are carried out at various levels of the educational system, the following material will present the contrasts of the three major subdivisions.

Elementary School

Despite the fact Carlson and VanHoose (1971) specify that there has been ". . . substantial and consistent growth in the number of elementary school counselors. . .(p. 43)," there are many elementary schools which are faced with the problem of operating without a counselor. The contention here is that considerably more is usually accomplished in the area of appraisal in those schools where a competent elementary counselor is employed. This is not to say that the elementary counselor will be at all akin to the older secondary model, for as Muro (1975) states regarding appraisal aspects:

> To deliver this he will become a tester, but not one who fits the traditional Stanford-Binet model. He will be knowledgeable in detecting self-images, developmental ages, and interaction patterns. He will learn of the child's world and help make the school fit the child rather than have the child fit the school. He will be one of a number of child advocates who will help the elementary school to at least begin to initiate what it has so long espoused (p. 9).

The appraisal service in the elementary school has several unique aspects. Irrespective of who is responsible for delivery of certain phases, the focus of the service at this level is usually related to screening and readiness, diagnosis, and curriculum revision. In the first instance, screening and readiness, appraisal is usually an aspect of admission to the public schools. This is particularly true in those school systems where the historic age requirement for entry has been modified. In the case of diagnosis, most school systems use several types of appraisal data to determine the educational needs of students. The data gathered in the diagnostic process is usually an aspect of the selection and placement activity. This should definitely amount to more than putting a new label (e.g., learning disabled) on a student. It should result in a program of planned experiences which are geared to the needs of the student. In terms of the remaining focus of appraisal at the elementary level, curriculum revision, data gathered through the achievement testing process can readily be of use in evaluating the present curriculum at large against national and local standards. Data from achievement testing can also be an aspect in assessing the curricular needs of specific students through looking for the strengths as well as the weaknesses as related in both test scores and daily classroom performance.

Middle or Junior High School

As experienced by most if not all staff members of junior highs, these particular years of student development (with their struggles for identity development and independence) can be very difficult for both students and staff members. Though the appraisal services found at the elementary grades are in some cases also found at the junior high, there is a unique aspect available here which seeks to respond to students' needs for assistance with tentative identity formation. Specifically available at this level are instruments, which may be routinely administered or may be available on request of individual students, of use in the process of career development and exploration. While most of these instruments would fall under the heading of interest inventories, other types of instruments are adding sections or additional aspects which respond to the needs of students at this level. In the case of interest inventories, the appropriate ones for the level would provide students feedback on general as opposed to specific areas of interest. An example of another type of instrument, in this case an aptitude test, which has added a component to assist with the career development process would be the Differential Aptitude Test (DAT). As of 1973 a Career Planning Program has been available as an optional aspect of this instrument. Through use of this specific aspect a report is provided which interprets the current educational and vocational thinking of students in light of their DAT scores.

The preceeding is not intended to minimize the importance of appraisal information in general as it might be utilized by students in their educational planning. Whereas it was previously noted that elementary school staffs made use of appraisal information in curriculum planning, it is usual for the focus of use to shift to the student at the junior high.

Senior High School

In addition to many of the appraisal aspects noted for the lower grades, students at this level have often extended their needs for data to assist them with career selection and narrowing their career development. This requires that the senior high schools not only have available those career development instruments which may also be available at the junior high level, but that they also have the expertise to administer additional instruments which provide students with more specific information and were thus inappropriate for use in lower grades.

While some of the appraisal data available at this level is utilized in the curriculum development and revision process, it is more frequently conducive to the process of educational and vocational decision making on the part of students. As another aspect of this process, the senior high schools frequently assume responsibility for the administration of specialized testing for entry into postsecondary education. While the resulting data is usually forwarded to institutions selected by the student, it is usual for the student to also receive a copy of the scores. This aspect of appraisal frequently serves as yet another point of contact between the counselor and the student as it relates to interpretation of the test results in light of the student's educational and/or vocational planning.

Evaluation of Appraisal

One of the most important aspects of all of the guidance services and the appraisal service in particular is the obvious need for evaluation. Yet this is one aspect that all too frequently is overlooked or put together in an inadequate manner. As a result of this overlooked or inadequate response to the evaluation of services provided, others have stepped in and performed this aspect, usually to the displeasure of the counselor. In light of the public demand for accountability and the increased competition for school dollars it is highly desirable that well-thought-through and team-type evaluations of the appraisal service be conducted.

As with most activities, evaluation of appraisal services begins with the first step. In this sense, as with most evaluation procedures, the first step must be the establishment of objectives before taking any action. The objectives for the appraisal service may come from any sources, the primary concern is to have them expressed more formally, i.e., explicit rather than implicit. In harmony with the rest of this chapter, the position taken here is that a team approach for the development of objectives is highly desirable.

One likely place to start the process of developing objectives is with the school guidance committee. Typically this committee functions at the discretion of the building principal and is composed of one or more counselors, an administrator and two or more teachers. It could include student members, possibly from the student council or a parallel type of student organization. It is also possible to include community representation in the form of parents or from the potential employer ranks. Regardless of the makeup, the committee can function as a task group with the task in this case being the development of general and specific objectives for the appraisal service. This should lead to school wide expectations for the service, as well as the elaboration of the counselor's role.

Another team that can develop objectives for appraisal is the counselor and his or her individual clients or groups. This might be termed heresy by some, but if students are to benefit from the service, why should they not be involved in determining what it is that they will receive.

Parents, either through their guidance committee involvement or in conference with the counselor could also become involved in the process of developing objectives for appraisal. Their input may be of any nature, but it is most likely that their needs would center around becoming better consumers of appraisal data and supporting the concerns and needs of their children. This can also be a positive public relations tool.

Once any of the above activities has taken place and objectives have been arrived at and agreed to, the activity phase may begin. As an outgrowth of the objectives, action steps and strategies can be developed which would be expected to lead to the attainment of the objectives.

Either at the time of the development of the objectives or along with the development of action steps and strategies for attainment of objectives, a plan needs to be developed for the data collection to determine if the objectives have been met. At present, there seems to be a proliferation of the need to count things and through the total count claim accountability. This is not to play down the value of keeping track of how many people have used a given service, but to acknowledge that there are other means.

While the counselors can subjectively respond to how the appraisal service has been effective and can frequently quote numbers, they have really missed the point if that's where the evaluation stops. The point, as viewed here, is the word service itself. This clearly indicates that something is being provided to or for someone. This someone is really the most appropriate focus for gaining evaluation data. This means that the responses and/or reactions to the appraisal service by staff members, students, parents, and community members should be included in the formal evaluation.

Just how the data are specifically accumulated from the users of the appraisal service is another matter. As stated earlier, whatever the means, there ought to be an obvious correspondence between the original objectives that were formulated, and resulting data gathering technique. If this indicates that a questionnaire could be developed to fulfill that correspondence, so be it. If it requires that recall of past history type data be acquired and used as some form of base line, that should be an acceptable starting point. It may be possible to conduct a form of poll of selected users through the school newspaper. There are also more elaborate and possibly sophisticated forms of data collection such as developing a semantic differential approach. The basic issue is that the method of obtaining the data should fit the objective(s) and should be within the evaluator's level of competence to comprehend.

Many types of elaborate statistical procedures are also available. Their application depends in part on the type of data gathered and the level of statistical competencies available to the evaluator. The ready availability of computers has made most techniques of data diddling nearly a fingertip response. The difficult part yet remains, however, since the results still need to be interpreted in light of the objectives, and then a restructuring or modification of the service provided should take place.

References

Anastasi, A. *Psychological testing.* (3rd ed.) New York: Macmillan Publishing Co., 1968.
Boros, O. K. ed., *The mental measurements yearbooks.* Highland Park, New Jersey: Gryphon Press, 1938-72 7 Vols.
———. ed., *Personality tests and reviews II.* Highland Park, New Jersey: Gryphon Press, 1972.
———. ed., *Tests in print II.* Highland Park, New Jersey: Gryphon Press, 1974.
Borow, H. ed., *Career guidance for a new age.* Boston: Houghton Mifflin Company, 1973.
Caldwell, O. W. and Courtis, S. A. *Then and now in education, 1845-1923.* New York: World Book Co., 1923.
Carlson, J. and Van Hoose, W. H. Status of elementary guidance in large cities. *Elementary School Guidance and Counseling* 6 (1971):43-45.
English, H. B. and English C. *A Comprehensive dictionary of psychological and psychoanalytical terms.* New York: David McKay Co., 1958.
Education U.S.A. Washington, D.C.: National School Public Relations Association, 1974, 17 (6).
Froehlich, C. P. *Guidance services in schools.* 2nd ed. New York: McGraw Hill, 1958.
Ginzberg, E. *Career guidance.* New York: McGraw-Hill, 1971.
Goodenough, F. L. *Mental testing: Its history, principles, and applications.* New York: Rinehart, 1949.
Greene, H. A.; Jorgensen, A. N.; and Gerberich, J. R. *Measurement and evaluation in the secondary school.* New York: Longmans, Green and Co., 1954.
Helmstadter, G. C. *Principles of psychological measurement.* New York: Appleton-Century-Croft, 1964.
Holden, C. Employment Testing: Debate simmers in and out of court. *Science,* 190 October 3, 1975.
McLaughlin, K. F. ed. *Understanding testing: Purposes and interpretations for pupil development.* U.S. Department of Health, Education, and Welfare, 1963.
Muro, J. J. Elementary school guidance: The state of the art. *Virginia Personal and Guidance Journal* 3 (10) (1975): 5-9.
Nunnally, J. C. *Psychometric theory.* New York: McGraw-Hill, 1967.
Parsons, F. *Choosing a vocation.* Boston: Houghton Mifflin, 1909.
Peterson, J. *Early conceptions and tests of intelligence.* New York: World Book, 1926.
Position Paper: The responsible use of tests. *Measurement and Evaluation in Guidance* 5 (2) (1972):385-88.
Report: APGA committee on standardized testing and evaluation of potential among minority group members. Washington, D.C. American Personnel and Guidance Association, 1975.
Standards for educational and psychological tests and manuals. Washington, D.C. American Psychological Association, 1966.

Stephens, W. R. *Social reform and the origins of vocational guidance.* Washington, D.C.: American Personnel and Guidance Association, 1970.

Super, D. E. and Crites, J. O. *Appraising vocational fitness.* (Revised edition) New York: Harper and Row, 1962.

Trump, J. L. and Georgiades, W. Doing better with what you have—NASSP model schools project. *The Bulletin of NASSP* 54 (1970):106-33.

Tyler, R. W. and Wolf, R. M. eds. *Crucial issues in testing.* Berkley, California: McCutchan, 1974.

Williamson, E. G. *Vocational counseling: Some historical, philosophical, and theoretical perspectives.* New York: McGraw-Hill, 1965.

Chapter 6

THE INFORMATION SERVICE

Carl O. McDaniels and Ruth Swann

Introduction and Historical Development

In this chapter an overview of the accumulated understandings of the information service, its functions, and the features which implement, develop, manage, and evaluate it are discussed. The intensity with which the topics are treated was determined by the chapter's purposes, spacial considerations, and the needs of users of an introductory guidance textbook.

Traditionally, the information service has played a primary role in guidance programs. What is known about its role in guidance can be traced from 1908, when Frank Parsons articulated the concept of vocational guidance, to the modern era. In the years since, an enormous body of opinions, descriptions of practices, and reports of research findings have become evident in published literature and conference papers.

Many readers, scholars, and critics place great value on recency in judging the worth of ideas, practices, and materials. The authors of this chapter believe that value should come first, and that guidance services still are indebted to the creative mind of Parsons and others whose thoughts of yesterday about the function of information in guidance services are embedded in more sophisticated phrases than those in which the original author first articulated them.

In *Choosing a Vocation,* written nearly seventy years ago, great emphasis was placed on providing the individual with information about self and jobs. The primary functions of information in vocational guidance were outlined by Parsons (1908) in these words:

> In the wise choice of a vocation there are three broad factors: (1) a clear understanding of yourself, your aptitudes, abilities, interests, ambitions, limitations and their causes; (2) a knowledge of the requirements and conditions of success, advantages and disadvantages, compensations, opportunities and prospects in different lines of work; and (3) true reasoning on the relations of these two groups of facts (p. 5).

Thus, according to several histories (McCracken and Lamb, 1923; Patterson, 1938; Brewer, 1942; Hutson, 1958; Williamson, 1965; Shaw, 1973) a framework for collecting, disseminating, and publishing vocational information, conducting group and individual study of occupations and self, and introducing vocational guidance into American schools was provided by Parsons.

Dr. Carl O. McDaniels is Professor of Counselor Education and Director of Graduate Studies in Education, and Ms. Ruth Swann is a Doctoral Candidate at Virginia Polytechnic Institute and State University, Blacksburg, Virginia.

Shaw (1973) describes Parsons' formulations of the role of information in guidance as brilliant, when:

> . . . the following factors are taken into account. At that time knowledge of human behavior was limited, no psychometric devices of any kind were in existence in this country, formalized occupational information did not exist and the idea of self-understanding had not been articulated (p. 13).

Nevertheless, leaders in American education caught the significance of Parsons' contribution almost immediately (Hutson, 1958) and acclaimed the value of occupational information and guidance for the individual and society. Helpful and illuminating literature in the field of vocational guidance began to appear and has continued to the present.

Brewer (1942) directed attention to the definitive contributions of four tributaries of historical significance. These agencies labored for wider understanding and acceptance of the values of occupational information in guidance and for improvement in methods of securing, managing, and using information pertaining to work and self. They are: (1) the National Occupational Conference organized by the Carnegie Corporation which from 1933 to 1939 published *Occupations* (now, the *Personnel and Guidance Journal).* These publications served the purpose of making more people acquainted with the information function, in addition to providing a useful tool; (2) the Minnesota Employment Stabilization Research Institute organized in the early 1930s to make detailed analyses of unemployed persons. It generated techniques of ascertaining occupational potentialities and tested the validity of the processes used; (3) the Adjustment Services of New York City functioned from 1933 to 1934 carrying out an experiment similar to the Minnesota Project; and (4) the United States Employment Service, Research Division, created in 1934 carried out a systematic analysis of occupations according to human abilities required. Its greatest work, *The Dictionary of Occupational Titles* (DOT), currently contains more than 21,000 separate titles and has enjoyed two revisions and continuous publication since 1939.

A number of other persons labored to extend and supplement the achievement of the DOT. They focused upon the publication of psychometric devices and other aids to facilitate analysis, study, and interpretation of individual potential (Patterson, 1930; Bingham, 1937; Rothney, Danielson, Heimann, 1959; Goldman, 1961; Holland, 1966; Traxler, 1966, Meyering, 1968). Thus, beginning in the early thirties and continuing to the present era some need has been seen for using scientifically developed instruments and procedures to solve the problems of ascertaining more precise diagnostic data regarding individuals' school and work capabilities. The pattern of thinking regarding the contribution of these tools to the information services has undergone considerable debate and refinement, but still remains among the controversial topics in contemporary American education. Fortunately, innovative experimentations with the proper uses of test data in the information services are expected to continue well into the future. Additional information pertaining to the use of tests as sources of information in guidance can be reviewed in the chapter dealing with Appraisal Services.

The works of E. G. Williamson (1926-1975) and Joseph Samler (1961) placed Parsons' trait-factor approach to using guidance information in a psycho-social context; while those of a number of others (Kitson, 1925; Hollingsworth, 1926; Patterson, 1938; Super, 1955; Hoppock, 1949; Holland, 1959; Isaacson, 1973) have served to survey, categorize, clarify, and present resources, techniques and knowledge that each educational practitioner and all who participate in the guidance program should have available for effective operation.

The contributions of professionals over the years have made it possible for present day counselors, employment service and student personnel workers to have insights, understandings, and techniques to help individuals make the most of their abilities and opportunities. These efforts have helped meet the manpower needs while helping productive workers seek self-fulfillment through satisfactory employment.

Although historical and cultural in nature, the contributions cited here provide support for the extensive development of content for the information services and the establishment of an effective methodological system through which the content could be articulated in meeting individual and societal work needs. It is, therefore, germane that attention be directed to the functions, relevance, and nature of information service content, and in addition to strategies for securing and evaluating these resources. The discussion which follows embraces these concerns.

Content of Service

Information as a special service area in guidance is of uttermost importance, in that decisions made by students and concerned adults should be based upon accurate, relevant, readily available information. Therefore, one of the most important functions of the information service is to provide for the collection, maintenance, and dissemination of current educational, occupational, and personal-social information for use by students, teachers, administrators, and parents on a developmental basis.

Developmental Concerns

According to Norris and others, specific objectives for determining the content and activity needs of the information service should be developed by counselors in each school in cooperation with other staff members. These objectives will be valuable as guideposts in developing and evaluating the comprehensiveness and effectiveness of materials and activities used in meeting the informational and developmental needs of students at all levels of educational and vocational development. In order to provide guidance for educators in the development of appropriate objectives, Norris (1966) proposed six general objectives:

1. To develop a broad and realistic view of life's opportunities and problems of training at all levels.
2. To create an awareness of the need and an active desire for accurate and valid occupational, educational, and personal-social information.
3. To provide an understanding of the wide scope of educational, occupational, and social activities in terms of broad categories of related activities.
4. To assist in the mastery of the techniques of obtaining and interpreting information for progressive self-direction.
5. To promote attitudes and habits which will assist in the making of choices and adjustment productive of personal satisfaction and effectiveness.
6. To provide assistance in narrowing choices progressively of specific activities which are

appropriate to aptitudes, abilities and interests manifested and to the proximity of definite decisions (p. 136).

Differential Aspect of Content for Various Levels and Development Needs

Peters and Shertzer (1974) state that the information needed by teachers and students for educational guidance purposes must be differentiated according to students' educational levels and provided on a continuous basis from the day individuals enter school until the day they terminate. They point out that at certain key points pupils' need for information and guidance will be more critical than at other times. Such times occur as pupils progress to an organizational phase of the curriculum new to them—when they enter elementary school, junior high, or senior high school. The new phase demands of pupils "new" ways of acting, planning, and responding (Peters and Shertzer, 1974).

It should be emphasized here that the content, level, and amount of information are not equally the same for pupils at the three levels, nor are the information and guidance needs for all pupils within these levels the same. Therefore, when counselors seek to organize and routinely provide a program of information services for all students, it must be remembered that provisions must be made to consider each student's needs on an individual basis over developmental periods from kindergarten through grade twelve.

Most writers (Hill, 1974; Glanz, 1974; Kowitz and Kowitz, 1968) agree that the objective of educational guidance is to facilitate better adjustment of students on the basis of actual individual need and capacity and that the information needs of most students, regardless of educational level, can be met in part by providing the following types of information:

1. The school's physical plant and environment
2. The school's schedule, including plans for school days, holidays, and vacations
3. The content of what is to be taught in any one year or subject
4. Regulations regarding attendance, decorum, safety, and traffic patterns
5. Grade report schedule, policies, and practices
6. Curricular and extra curricular activities

In addition, differentiated types of information may be needed by students at the various levels. Teachers and counselors will also need to develop specific strategies, resources, media and materials for interfacing career information and curriculum concerns. Such specific concepts as self-awareness, educational awareness, career awareness, decision making and employability—skill awareness should serve as the primary concepts by which students at the various levels are provided such categories of career information as follows:

Elementary School Pupils

1. The awareness and appreciation of work roles in the home, school, community and society.
2. The awareness of the role of self-knowledge in perceiving, appreciating and performing career related activities.
3. The awareness and understanding of the similarities and differences between life roles and skills learned in schools.

4. The understanding of relationships between the roles of workers, work environment and occupational clusters.
5. The relationship between factors involving self-concepts, aspiration and expanding career-planning-options.
6. The processes of identifying and planning for junior high educational and career development experiences.

Junior High School Pupils

1. The art of acquiring and employing career and educational data in futuristic planning.
2. The knowledge and understanding of how the school environment relates to society in general, and to the structure of work and employability skills.
3. The identification, understanding and exploration of interest, attitude values, and abilities as they relate to career clusters and work environments.
4. The techniques for making, analyzing and implementing career decisions based on counseling classroom activities, leisure, work and organizational experiences.
5. The impact of work on such personal factors as: life styles, friends, place of residence and employment.

Senior High School Students

   The extensive curricular offerings, special programs and courses, and variety of extra-curricular activities necessitate that students examine their in-school opportunities, their interests, strengths and weaknesses, plans for the future, and select courses and activities in the light of these data. Information of the following types should prove to be helpful:

1. The analysis of curriculum offerings as they relate to educational options, life goals and career planning.
2. The application of self-awareness experiences to realistic post-high-school, career and life-style planning.
3. The ways of exploring career clusters, based on work modes and environments, as well as interests, values, abilities and all available self-data.
4. The mastery of the tools necessary for applying decision-making processes to the study of careers and educational and job preparation options.
5. The assessment and implementation of a plan for securing admission to post-high-school educational or work preparation institutions.
6. The identification and understanding of the economic implications and financial requirements of postsecondary occupational and professional education programs.

   The problem of delivering this information to students has been addressed by Ohlsen (1974); Isaacson (1973); and Norris, Zeran, and Hatch (1966). They observed that some of this information can be disseminated through teacher, counselor, and parental contacts, while that of a more personal nature can best be communicated through individual counseling. Group techniques which include orientation programs, discussion groups, audio-visual presentations, college days, career conferences, industry and campus visits, assembly programs, study units within courses, and homeroom programs or activity interest periods have been proven useful approaches.

Leisure and Recreation Information

The area of leisure pursuits and related job opportunities present strong implications for guidance information and activities programming. The information service should make students increasingly aware of the multiplicity of contemporary forces which are producing more leisure for individuals in massive quantities and creating a greatly increased need for workers to produce and manage leisure related companies and to organize and service leisure facilities and equipment. McDaniels (1974) has pointed out the assistance needed by individuals in utilizing school and community facilities to meet leisure needs in the career development process.

Consequently the whole area of leisure and work in career development merits inclusion in the information service thrust. Counselors have a responsibility to help students acquire first hand as well as symbolic, vicarious leisure-time experiences. In an approaching era of increasing discretionary use of time, money, and life styles, counselors should seek opportunities to sensitize students to the choices open to them for pursuing leisure-skill development opportunities.

McDaniels and Simutis (1975) have provided a comprehensive overview of leisure activities and careers. The data is presented in the form of a wall chart. The chart addresses such concerns as: education for leisure; leisure activities open to high school and college students; examples of careers related to part-time pursuit; interest and experience in the visual and performing arts; individual and team sports; out-of-school community groups; in-school and extra curricular activities; and in addition, leadership and career clubs.

Teachers and counselors should find this chart, in addition to treatments of the topic in textbooks, film/film strips and publications like Green's (1968) *Leisure and the American Schools* helpful in designing developmental materials and activities suggesting how a person might build careers or part-time work opportunities around leisure activities which are compatible with a main job.

Decision Making and Career Planning

Another important function of the information service is providing vocational information and assistance in its use to enable students to make decisions and vocational plans that are appropriate for them. It is through their use of information and advice on the part of counselors that students will be able to deal effectively with the complexities of the work world and the affective aspects of their future involvement in it. Herman and Molen (1959) claim that appropriate decisions are made when individuals are cognizant of their strengths and weaknesses. They present the following formula for guiding the counselor in gathering the necessary information and assisting the student in formulating positive conclusions: (1) The equation of awareness. Students must have knowledge of their abilities, their real interests, and their performances; (2) The equation of self-knowledge. The knowledge of one's potential is combined with self-knowledge and work experience which results in a measure of possible job opportunities open to the student; and (3) The equation of vocational understanding. The knowledge of those previously discussed equations makes known the possibility of numerous vocational opportunities that are applicable to a person's abilities and interest.

Herman and Molen (1959), in addition, present a vehicle for integrating developmental strategies into the vocational counseling processes. Samler (1966) expressed four reservations pertaining to the nature and use of information in counseling. They are: (1) vocational counseling and its use of occupational information is based upon a theory (trait and factor) that is unsatisfactory and incomplete; (2) informational resources used in counseling are incomplete; (3) occupational investigation is not psychologically based; and (4) even with proliferation of occupational materials, there is reason for concern that the realities of work, the work force, and the labor structure are not really considered. These reservations led Samler to identify and present seven proposals for occupational exploration in counseling:

1. Occupational exploration is not a separate part of the counseling process.
2. The client's needs should be identified and their strengths assessed.
3. The client's potential for commitment to task is assessed.
4. The client is helped to become aware of the nature of career development and progression. His potential for orderly career development is assessed.
5. The working world should be seen as a totality. Within it the individual should be seen as psychosocial as well as an economic entity.
6. The process of occupational exploration is psychological in the sense that the client's perceptions are taken into account.
7. Occupational exploration should provide a model for decision making, not necessarily the decision itself (1966:413).

Hoppock (1967) observed that students will differ in their knowledge of occupations. Some will have a definite choice of an occupation that seems appropriate for them. Others will be seeking aid from the counselor and will want to know: (1) the range of vocational opportunities open to them, (2) the sources of vocational information available and how to appraise their accuracy, (3) how to choose an occupation, (4) how to find a job, and (5) the significant specific things about an occupation. On the basis of this observation and the availability of more than 22,000 occupations, Hoppock suggested that the counselor would need to separate a core of essential information from that not quite so essential. The essential information would include: (1) the first jobs of the school's dropouts and graduates, (2) the principal employment opportunities for graduates and dropouts, (3) those occupations that are being seriously considered by students, (4) sources of information about occupations and how to appraise their accuracy, and (6) labor legislation. Once counselors have learned this core of information about their students, according to Hoppock, they can extend further their knowledge of occupations.

Baer and Roeber (1964) listed seven uses of occupational information in counseling interviews:

1. *Exploratory use.* Occupational information is used to help the counselee to make an extensive study of the world of work.
2. *Information use.* Counselees are assisted to make a detailed study of a few occupations.
3. *Assurance use.* The counselor uses occupational information to assure the counselee that they have made an appropriate or inappropriate choice.
4. *Motivational use.* Occupational information will be used to arouse the counselees' interest in school work or in vocational planning.

5. *Holding use.* Occupational information will be used to retain counselees in counseling situations until they gain some insight into their real needs and into their behavior.

6. *Evaluative use.* The counselor will check the accuracy and adequacy of the counselees' knowledge and understandings of an occupation.

7. *Startle use.* The counselor will ascertain if counselees are uncertain or anxious after they choose a particular vocation (p. 468).

At this point in our discussion, if not earlier, it must have become apparent that providing occupational information, and developmental counseling for those who have reached the point of specific needs, such as those implied by Baer and Roeber (1964), the counselor would need, in addition to specialized training in the developmental aspects of vocational counseling, to have a basic supply of educational and occupational materials on hand. A realistic question might be: What guidelines might be provided to assist counselors in securing and appraising guidance information materials and activities?

The Counselor's Professional Library

According to Peters and Shertzer (1974) guidance counselors need to maintain a professional library if they are to keep up with the constantly changing educational and occupational scene in America. They state that counselors must be alert to collecting material providing such things as the ever-changing requirements for admissions to colleges, technical schools and training programs, advance placement and early admissions practices, and scholarships and other forms of financial aid. Their library will of necessity consist of materials that are ever changing and will have to be continuously replaced or supplemented. Peters and Shertzer proposed the following list of materials as representative of those judged by experienced counselors to be minimally essential for conducting educational and vocational guidance activities.

Educational Counseling Materials

1. One copy of a catalogue from each post-high-school educational and employability skill training institution in the state in which the school is located (other states providing that the catalogues are free).
2. A general directory of colleges which gives brief descriptions of the institution and specific information of cost, entrance requirements, degree conferring, facilities and where to write for information.
3. A general directory of scholarship and financial aid.
4. Guides to planning and preparing for college.
5. A general directory of home study and correspondence courses.
6. Materials dealing with how to study.

Career Counseling Information

1. *The Dictionary of Occupational Titles.*
2. *Occupational Outlook Handbook and Quarterly.*
3. *The Vocational Guidance Quarterly.*
4. Literature introducing the psycho-social concepts and relationships in occupational materials.

5. Literature based on job, career family, clusters and ladder approaches.
6. Literature about the military services, personal and public services, skilled and semi-skilled occupations.

There are many good materials available from which counselors may select to build up a professional library. Examples of some of these materials and sources from which they may be obtained are cited at the end of this chapter. It is obvious that only a brief list of suggested sources of information can be provided and that these are intended only as examples. For extensive lists of information materials and sources, the reader is encouraged to consult standard references in the field.

Closely related to the identification of commercial sources of information materials and appropriate types of library resources is the recognition of the need to develop local information resources.

Developing Local Information Resources

Information from national sources such as commercial publishers, professional and technical societies, and national industries and agencies has always been valuable, but it has to be supplemented with information pertaining to regional and local conditions. Local information regarding education and employment can be obtained from two primary sources; namely, (1) local surveys planned and conducted by the counselor(s) on a school or system-wide basis and (2) information supplied by state departments of education, state employment agencies, local boards of education, local unions and industries, Chambers of Commerce, and local or regional industrial development agencies.

In their endeavor to develop and maintain an up-to-date local information file, counselors will find reciprocating relationships with the local office of their state employment commission invaluable. Since 1933 this agency has assumed responsibility for ascertaining data denoting the availability of jobs in the state and nation on the basis of manpower shortages and long-ranged, as well as seasonal needs. Through the use of the General Aptitude Test Battery (GATB) state employment agencies, supply in- and out-of-school youth and adults with information relative to their interests and aptitudes; and, in addition, these agencies assist them in using this "self-data" in making wise choices among available placement data and projected employment opportunities.

Since the school's prime responsibility in this respect is guidance based on future, as well as immediate needs, recognition should be given to the here and now aspects of the information and placement functions of the state public employment agency. This function includes providing assistance with needs related to part-time work, apprenticeship, and entry level industrial skill development opportunities.

In addition, through the Manpower Research Division of the Virginia State Employment Commission, bulletins entitled, *Occupational Profiles, Labor Market Trends,* and *Labor Turnover in Manufacturing* may be published monthly. These materials are supplied on request as a courtesy to counselors and vocational educators, librarians, placement offices, schools, colleges, and other appropriate institutions and organizations in each state.

Additional sources of local information include surveys of occupational, educational, community services, health and social services conducted by civic groups and public agencies, as a part of their services on or in conjunction with guidance personnel and vocational, technical, and industrial program coordinators.

In recent years, many communities have witnessed the development of computerized information banks. Some of these are school-based while others are available to the general public, through the state employment services as well as special groups and institutions. These resources have been established with care, and concentrate on keeping educational, employment, health and social information up-to-date and accurate. Assistance in many instances is just a telephone call away.

In discussing general goals to be considered in securing information materials, Baer and Roeber (1964) provided five suggestions which should prove helpful in selecting local as well as national materials. The suggestions are that the materials provide: (1) realistic and accurate information, (2) up-to-date information, (3) many types of information, (4) appeal to various levels of ability and experience, and (5) coverage of characteristics of any given kind of work or training opportunity.

Evaluation of Information Materials

The successful implementation and management of the functions of the information service—obtaining, disseminating and interpreting occupational, educational and social information require the acceptance of a standard of excellence which has been provided for such purposes.

In the past, a number of authors of guidance textbooks have listed standards for use in preparing and evaluating occupational materials (Baer and Roeber, 1964; Norris, Zeran and Hatch, 1966; Hoppock, 1967; Peters and Shertzer, 1974). The importance of improving the quality of information has claimed the attention of the National Vocational Guidance Association (NVGA) for over fifty years. Since 1924, NVGA's Career Information Review Committees have spent considerable time developing guides for evaluating occupational materials and reviewing materials according to criteria established by NVGA (NVGA, 1973, 1964). Every school should have multiple copies of *Guidelines for the Preparation and Evaluation of Career Information Media* published by NVGA in 1971.

Selecting Materials

Most schools possess occupational, educational and social information. No matter how adequate the collection of books, pamphlets, catalogs, and audio-visual aids appears to be, the school staff (counselors, teachers, and librarian) must constantly assess whether the materials needed by their students are available. Periodically, procedures should be executed to inventory resource materials, to identify gaps and to eliminate out-dated materials. Ohlsen (1974) provided the following questions to be used in screening new materials.

1. Who published the materials? Are they reputable publishers?
2. Who wrote the materials? Is the author qualified in the field?
3. What was the author's motive in preparing the materials? Was the author obligated in any way to present a point of view or to recruit for a sponsoring organization?
4. When was the material published? Is it up-to-date?

5. Is the material well written? Is it on the reading level of those who will use it?
6. Is the material well illustrated? Will it appeal to students? (p. 274)

In addition to providing detailed criteria for evaluating and preparing vocational materials, NVGA publishes in each issue of the *Vocational Guidance Quarterly* "Reviews of Current Career Literature and Career Films and Filmstrips" which classify each new product listed by type, reading level, and quality.

Contributions to Career Education and Career Development

Thus far in this chapter, the information service has been shown as occupying a place of paramount importance in educational and occupational guidance. In addition, the service's potential for becoming the core around which the conscious elements of career development unfold were highlighted. Therefore, it appears that the information service's contribution to the current career education movement deserves special attention.

The major contributions of the information service to career education and to career development are providing: (1) a background of information about occupational opportunities, (2) research data on job satisfaction, job task analysis, employment trends and vocational development and choice theories, and (3) a repertoire of activities and strategies found to be effective for helping individuals prepare for, enter into, and progress in job and career development situations.

It has been traditionally assumed that the probabilities of wise choices, job satisfaction, employment stability, and progress in an occupation or a career would increase with individuals' knowledge of jobs they may be able to ascertain if the vocational developmental tasks of relating occupational, self and opportunity data were properly executed at the appropriate developmental stages. Because educators acted on this assumption, the contributions of the information services are not only valuable indications of what has been done in the past but provide insight, justification, and tools for facilitating career development and incorporating career education activities into the totality of life-centered experiences.

In addition, the research findings and publications of Williamson (1926-1975), Hoppock (1955-1975), and Super (1955-1975) provide evidence supporting the assumption on which the information service has traditionally operated; thus providing a theoretically sound foundation on which counselors can design, implement, and test career development and career education programs and research studies.

Other noteworthy contributions of more recent origin are: (1) the sensitizing activities of The National Vocational Guidance Association; (2) the emergence of career information centers; (3) the leadership role adopted by the National Institute of Education; and (4) the special emphasis given to the career information and career developmental needs of special groups (i.e., disadvantaged, handicapped, elderly, and women). At this point it is considered necessary to spell out some of the contributions alluded to in the categories enumerated.

National Vocational Guidance Association Programs

Sponsorship of National Career Guidance Week and the National Career Guidance Week

Poster Contest are facets of the leadership program in which the National Vocational Guidance Association takes great pride.

> NATIONAL CAREER GUIDANCE WEEK is set aside each year to inform the public of career guidance services, how these services help youth, as well as adults, to make sound choices, where counseling and career guidance may be obtained, and why the further development of these services needs public understanding and support (excerpt from the 1975 Career Guidance Week Information Brochure).

Through the office of the National Career Guidance Week Chairperson, an appropriate theme and guidelines and materials for planning, implementing, and conducting a week of career guidance activities are provided to schools, employment agencies, libraries, churches, and other interested organizations. In addition, NVGA state divisions are encouraged to sponsor statewide observations. Traditionally, since the National Career Guidance Week program was operationalized under the leadership of Earl Klein in 1965 (known then as National Vocational Guidance Week) the program activities have included such activities as proclamations from mayors and governors, radio and television presentations and spot announcements, public programs, a series of activities sponsored by schools and colleges, in addition to in recent years, congressional recognition.

The National Career Guidance Week Poster Contest originated during the presidency of Carl McDaniels in 1973-1974. At that time NVGA saw a need to extend the participation of school and college students in the observation of Career Guidance Week; through the leadership of Ruth Swann, the association launched a pilot poster contest in the Norfolk Virginia City Schools. The poster project proved to be a valuable medium for increasing the awareness of students, teachers, administrators, parents, and the need for public support. In addition, it encouraged students to engage in research, link and portray aspects of self and career developmental opportunities. The Career Guidance Week Poster Project, now an on-going national component of NVGA's career education endeavors, illustrates one way of getting students involved in self and environmental and occupational research, data analysis, and career decision-making activities.

The Career Information Center

In recent years, the concept of delivering occupational and educational information in the school, college, and community setting has expanded to embrace the idea of providing comprehensive resources centers. This concept advocates providing physical space other than the library for the housing and use of career resource materials with students and other interested persons on group or individual basis. In addition, the concept mandates the employment of a differentiated staffing pattern which includes volunteers, paraprofessionals, students, learning resource and career counseling specialists, and outreach service personnel in the development and maintenance of such centers.

Although the availability of space, equipment, facilities, and an adequate staff are the prerequisites for developing a career resource career, a number of centers are beginning to emerge in all parts of the country in varying degrees of sophistication. Advocators and pioneer developers of comprehensive career resource centers suggest inclusion of information systems for storage and retrieval of information, curriculum linkage and carefully developed guidance strategies, and assistance in the use of these centers. Some of the persons who have provided directions and examples of developmental strategies are: Circle (1968), Hansen (1971), Indiana Career Resource center (1971), Ohio State University, Division of Vocational Technical Education (1972), Waltz (1972), Jacobson (1972), and Burtnett (1974).

Perhaps one of the most far reaching justifications for the career resource center idea is the capacity and potential of the center for serving large numbers of people. A significant and supporting contribution to the career resource center thrust was the establishment and development of the National Career Information Center by the American Personnel and Guidance Association.

In addition to its onsite activities, the National Career Information Center through its director, Frank Burtnett, has prepared and distributed "Guidelines for Establishing a Career Information Center." This publication presents and discusses nine sequential steps to be utilized in the development of a local career resource center in a school or a community setting. Also, a description of how two ongoing centers were implemented, operationalized, and developed are presented, with pictures of some of the effective activities.

According to Burtnett (1974), it has been demonstrated that:

> When good career information materials are collected and made available as a part of an organized career information Center, students will voluntarily seek them out. Counselors, teachers, and parents can refer students to such a center for exploratory purposes and to determine answers to specific educational and occupational questions (p. 1).

It appears that bringing all of the career resource materials in the school to a central place is an activity believed by center advocates to focus greater attention and provide increased visibility, availability, and usability of the multitude of printed materials, films, and filmstrips, etc.

The National Institute of Education's Contributions

The National Institute of Education (NIE) through contractual arrangements with prime sponsors is making a valuable contribution to career education and career development. Two of the major contractual programs under development are the career decision-making study and developmental career education research undertaken by the developers of four exemplary career education model projects. The American Institute for Research is currently, under NIE contract, conducting empirical studies that promise to provide a synthesis of theoretical statements and add to our understanding of the many influences in the career decision-making processes.

The exemplary projects are currently attempting to research and develop school-based, employer-based, home/community-based, and rural/residential-based models projects. The underlying objectives of the projects are focused on developing programs and materials to facilitate the development of some of the many skills individuals need in order to move rationally and effectively through the various career developmental stages. These skills should include: (1) an awareness and acceptance of self; (2) an awareness and understanding of the world of work; (3) an understanding of the relationship between school experiences and the world of work; (4) a knowledge of the skill necessary to cope with change in futuristic planning; (5) an awareness of goal-setting, decision making, and self-development skills; (6) an understanding of the components and influences of life style; and (7) the ability to see self as constructive. Since the focus here is on awareness, it is obvious that the contributions of the information service are central. Without information properly presented there can be no awareness nor selective perception of self, environment, opportunities, and options.

It is apparent that accurate and appropriate information is the core of career education programs. Therefore, it can be reasonably concluded that the role of the information service is to ensure that the vast reservoir of occupational information and vocational guidance and counseling techniques that the guidance services possess is used in providing effective career counseling and career education experiences in the best of possible ways. The best way possible suggests that counselors and teachers who perform career development, career education, and career counseling functions in the schools should have responsibility for the successful implementation and evaluation of materials and strategies used in their work.

Occupational Information for Special Needs Groups

Another major challenge to the information service is the development of occupational materials and delivery strategies which focus on the specific career developmental needs of women and girls, and minority, handicapped, and disadvantaged groups.

It appears that until recently, many educators felt that students needed information and advice to assist them in moving in the educational and occupational directions in which they were destined to go. Consequently, students, possessing characteristics indicative of positive self-concepts and the capacity to develop vocationally relevant educational and career goals were provided ample information and counseling experiences which tended to encourage the development of rationally determined educational and occupational behavior patterns, appropriate to their needs. On the other hand, too many of the students who possessed less sophisticated educational, occupational and career developmental understandings and inadequate self-concepts "were programmed" to satisfy their vocational needs, interest and choices by aspiring to work roles traditionally ascribed for their social, economic, cultural, ethnic and sex status. Others (the so-called run-of-the-mill, or poor background students) were left to carve out vocationally-relevant behavior patterns based on insights developed through incidental information and chance factors.

Today educators are being challenged to provide members of these previously neglected groups information, and career counseling geared toward the development of what people are calling "positive-occupationally-relevant self-concepts," "occupational values" and the meaning of "variance in values between and within occupational clusters." Therefore, as providers and coordinators of the information service, counselors must make a decisive effort to (1) assist girls faced with the perplexing problem of developing occupationally relevant self-concepts, positive attitudes toward devoting a large share of their adult lives to work outside of the home, transcending the barriers imposed by limited job opportunities and assess to upward mobility career developmental experiences, in setting meaningful career goals, (2) assist minorities, handicapped and disadvantaged individuals in developing confidence in their abilities to advance beyond current social, economic and educationally handicapping situations and restrictive ranges within employment and job categories, and in addition, (3) provide these individuals with assistance in developing appropriate coping strategies, ascertaining successful learning and work experiences and in setting and moving toward the achievement of realistic educational and career goals.

In order to attain the levels of educational and occupational achievements commensurate
with their capacities, females and disadvantaged groups must be provided materials and experiences that are especially meaningful to them. These materials must speak to their specific
needs in a coherent, forthright and pragmatic manner. Counselors have several responsibilities
in this regard. They include:

1. assisting publishers and significant others in addressing the special information needs
   of all students.
2. developing or selecting materials for special needs groups which address (a) understanding and appreciation of values regarding work, (b) relating work values to life-
   styles, (c) identifying need-meeting qualities of specific occupations, (d) prioritizing
   occupational values, (e) tailoring occupational, educational and career goals to
   specific personal and societal work needs.
3. utilizing occupational counseling and guidance approaches to provide sensitizing,
   stimulating and supporting career developmental behavior experiences.
4. contributing to the current thrust to make occupational materials more readible, and in
   addition checking materials provided these students for readibility, until such times as
   occupational literature materials reflecting job analysis, working conditions, trends,
   wages and projected manpower demands, etc., are written at the appropriate reading
   level of potential users.

It is the opinion of the authors of this chapter, that a notable lag exists between materials
and occupational delivery strategies and the needs of females, disadvantaged, handicapped and
minorities. Hence, in order to more fully provide an information service that is commensurate
with the demands of career education, counselors' action must be directed toward providing information services which capitalize on "human-vocational-behavioral" needs.

The Roles of Various Personnel in the Information Service

The wide-spread emphasis on implementing career education into school programs from
kindergarten through high school suggests a renewal of interest in the guidance roles and functions of all school personnel. It is expected that the traditional information service roles
ascribed to educators will be expanded as career education takes on additional vigor in educational programming. Therefore, it is fitting that special attention be given to the dimensions of
roles and guidance information services performed by counselors and others in the school setting.

Role of Counselors

Although the primary role of counselors in school settings is counseling, they assume such
information provisional roles as consultant, resource person, and researcher, each of which
contributes to planning, developing, conducting, and maintaining an effective information service. Effective school counselors will not only follow the basic guidelines set down for all of the
services, but will show initiative in finding new ways to carry out their responsibilities in
meeting the objectives of the information service. However, they will not view these guidelines

as restrictive and will endeavor to enhance the service by articulating the roles to be played by significant others.

In planning approaches to enlist the support of teachers, students, parents, business, industrial, and civic leaders, counselors must arrive at clear-cut ways in which they can be helpful. This can be achieved by the organization of an advisory committee composed by representatives of each of the group identified as potential contributors. Together the members of the advisory committee can explore, identify, and commit themselves and/or the groups they represent areas of service and support.

Consulting. In consulting, the counselor: (1) helps teachers to secure educational, occupational, and social materials and develop procedures for a variety of classroom group guidance uses, and (2) provides materials and information concerning such matters as characteristic and needs of the student population, student post-high school behavior, and employment trends for use in curriculum study and revision.

Resource person. As a resource person the counselor assumes major responsibility in: (1) identifying community referral agencies and services; (2) assisting parents and students who need such services to become aware of, accept, and secure the needed service; (3) providing student, teachers, and parents with an understanding in relation to educational and occupational opportunities for the students optimal growth and development, and to promote self-direction; and (4) collecting and disseminating to students and parents information concerning careers, opportunities for further education and training, and school curricular offerings.

These activities should be provided through a carefully planned information dissemination program of activities. The program may include such activities as: group and individual sessions with students; parents and teachers; guidance newsletters; bulletin boards; special programs; up-to-date guidance information files; career resources centers or nooks; mobile libraries, exhibits and displays; continuing visual presentation in appropriate areas for free-time use; and information seeking tours of educational institutions, business and industrial establishments.

Another vital activity is the use of individual and group strategies to provide students and parents with information and assistance in understanding application procurement and processing procedures for admissions to colleges, trade schools apprenticeships, college entrance, and civil service examinations, in addition to those for securing financial aid, employment, and volunteer experiences.

Public relations. At this point, it should be pointed out that most aspects of the information service and the counselors accompanying responsibilities have a potential public relations value. Therefore, it is expected that counselors would: (1) participate in public programs sponsored by the school and civic groups; (2) prepare articles on information for school, community, and national publications; (3) assist in the preparation of programs for radio and T.V.; and (4) willingly interpret the service components comprising the guidance and counseling program to interested persons.

Of great importance from a public relations and research point of view is the considerations given to ethical standards by the counselor in the delivery of information services. Therefore, the applications of professional ethics to the utilization of information in guidance, research, and counseling activities deserve special consideration in this discussion of the counselor's role in the information service.

Ethical Considerations

The program concerns of the information service necessitate the counselor assuming the ethical responsibility of keeping current. Beck (1966) provides this probe for the practicing counselor:

> Have I tried to stay current on legislation, information retrieval, new theories of counseling, socioeconomic development, industrial developments, race problems, important research, now disproven assumptions and new research techniques?

Keeping up with these developments is a professional responsibility in addition to an ethical responsibility and embraces the ethical consideration set forth by Hoppock (1963) for professional guidance in executing the information service function. Hoppock's five ethical admonitions follow:

1. A counselor should never encourage a person to enter or prepare for a specific occupation or field of work if the counselor has not recently inquired about the opportunity for employment.
2. A counselor should never rely upon his/her own personal impressions source of occupational information without first verifying the accuracy of his impression.
3. A counselor should never recommend a piece of occupational literature which the counselor has not examined for evidence of accuracy.
4. A counselor should never refer a person to a library for occupational information without first warning the person to examine copyright data of all publications before reading them.
5. A counselor should never refer a person to recruiting literature from employers, unions, educational institutions, military service, etc., without pointing out that recruiting literature frequently exaggerate advantages and minimizes disadvantages (p. 463).

The ethical codes cited here are viewed as necessary, but only define the broadest limits of professional and personal responsibility of the guidance information function, relative to the acquisition and dispersion of information.

Research

An area in which the counselor has a unique opportunity to utilize scientific methods, exercise high ethical sensitivity, and preconsideration is local research. In conducting local studies and in working with school evaluation and planning committees, the counselor will do well to consider ethical elements in seeking data to answer relevant questions regarding the information service. It must be borne in mind, however, that guidance information services are usually observed as a component of the total program. Rarely ever, except in specialized research studies, are guidance service areas syphoned off for research or assessment purposes because of the inter-relatedness of the components.

In a sense, the most important research done in local guidance programs dealing with information is that done by students with the help of counselors as they seek self-understanding, awareness of the environment, and realistic decisions. It stands to reason that the best portrayal of the impact of the information service can be obtained from a synthesis of case studies dealing with youngsters' efforts to utilize data to better understand "the self" and "the world" in which they live. In this relationship, the counselor should make a judicious effort to provide developmental experiences for client and counselor. Here the goals may be dual: (1) a search for data to further the development of the individual and the counselor, and (2) to determine the information needs of the program, students, and/or counselors.

It is apparent that for whatever reason counselors collect data, the source of information for case studies and other research approaches is people. In research endeavors care must be exercised to let students, parents, teachers, and others know why information is desired, and the context in which it will be used. In the solicitation of information from business, civic, school, and community groups, honesty must prevail regarding the way in which the educational and work world will be interpreted in the research report. If a climate of honesty and objectivity characterizes the information gathering process, the counselor, students, school, and community will profit from these contacts, both as contributors and as users of data about the individual, the school, and the community.

It is apparent from delineations of the counselor's functions in the information service that in the past counselors have exercised a dominant role in the securing and dissemination of guidance information. In addition, according to Hill (1974), counselors have been expected to define the role and functions of other school personnel. This entailed securing the support and cooperation of teachers, administrators, other pupil personnel workers, parents, pupils and the community. Determining the roles and functions of other members of the educational team involves considerable problems. On the other hand, providing leadership and/or participation in the decisions contributes to an integrated approach to information program development. Consideration will be given to the types of roles given workers play in helping students to achieve those goals for which guidance information is needed.

Teacher's Information Roles

Apart from the parent, teachers constitute the school staff member most closely in contact with students and are, therefore, in a good position to make valuable contributions to this guidance service area.

Perhaps the most important contribution the teacher makes to the information service in guidance is that of communicating to the individual student, through the instructional processes, a sense of personal worth, the value of the subject being taught, and the contribution that learning makes to the achievement of life goals. Through individual conferences and group guidance discussions, teachers support the work of counselors and contribute to increased self and environmental understandings. Also, through the rendering of assistance in orienting new students to the school, and the acquainting of students with prospective new programs and course offerings, and the purposes and requirements of their courses, teachers help to disseminate information.

Teachers in many schools contribute directly to the information service by teaching units or courses that contribute to students' understanding of the world of work, the world of education, the processes of decision making, and planning for one's future. The processes used in these endeavors are somewhat different from those employed in academic course teaching, therefore, assistance from counselors as resource persons or in an in-service context are important.

There are, however, many things that teachers can do systematically in the teaching of their subject matter that contribute greatly to the school's information and career guidance efforts. In their regular classes, they can assign occupationally oriented readings, writings, interviews, research and evaluation reports, bulletin boards, demonstrations, observations and, in addition, conduct group discussions on such topics as: "What Will I Be?"; "Education and Work"; "The Processes of Life Planning"; and "Opportunities for Training and Employment in Their Subject Field."

 *Vocational teachers* are in a unique position to address the vocational developmental needs cited in their classes and as consultants to counselors and academic teachers in the development of relevant career guidance activities based on current and authentic data. In addition their close identification with the world of work and contacts with local places of employment put them in an ideal position to carry out the following roles and functions:

1. Serve as a liason between guidance personnel and the local employers.
2. Share information with guidance counselors relative to potential placement and cooperative work opportunities.
3. Help counselors and other classroom teachers to establish contact with business and industrial representatives to serve as guest speakers and resource persons for career guidance activities.
4. Assist counselors in determining focus for information sensitizing activities based on input from employers and onsite co-op training personnel.
5. Assist in bridging the gap between the contribution of academic and vocational information and experience to facilitate career development and futuristic planning.
6. Provide group guidance to college bound and work bound students in home rooms, interest group, rap sessions, subject matter clubs and interested vocational and leisure oriented groups of students.
7. Serve as a member of the school's guidance information coordinating committee.

In the development of activities and career guidance units, teachers and students will need the help of the school librarian. The librarian's contribution to an effective classroom information program can be real and substantial. Therefore, at this point a look will be taken at some of the ways the library service functions of the librarian are related to the information service.

Role of the School Librarian

The information service functions of the school librarian are of uttermost importance and relate to guidance in the following ways:

1. The identification, ordering, classifying, housing, and distribution of guidance materials used by counselors, teachers, and students.
2. The providing of assistance in the prompt selection of materials desired and in making effective use of other relevant and appropriate materials.
3. The arrangement in cooperation with counselors and teachers of exhibits and special displays, designed to motivate fuller use of guidance materials and to supplement individual and group guidance and counseling experiences.
4. The providing of assistance to teachers and counselors in the development of guidance

courses, learning package modules, and activities through the identification of appropriate aides and materials.

5. The encouragement of voluntary reading on the part of students and occasionally providing career developmental programs, such as book reviews, film and filmstrip presentations pertaining to students' occupational, leisure, and social interest and needs.
6. The providing of consultative services to students seeking assistance in identifying data for assignments which have a strong potential for integrating self, environmental, and futuristic data in their development and preparation.

Another member of schools' guidance information team whose supportive and consultative functions in the information service are similar to those of the librarian is the chief building administrator. Perhaps the most difficult task is that of developing in cooperation with the librarian, counselors, and teachers a statement of policies and practices governing the securing, utilization, and care of information materials and equipment. A list of some of the roles in which the principal should exercise responsibility and be creatively involved follows.

Role of the School Principal

The building principal can support the information service by:

1. Providing adequate space for housing and utilizing guidance materials.
2. Stimulating the staff to become more sensitive to the value of using guidance information in their on-going instructional programs.
3. Lending administrative support in keeping guidance materials up to date and the information service functioning effectively.
4. Becoming deeply involved in the establishment of procedures for the collecting, processing, and disseminating of guidance materials, and scheduling of information program activities that will be profitable for students.
5. Appointing a school-wide guidance information committee.

In addition, the principals' leadership and public relation roles demand that they serve as information resources for students, teachers, counselors, and parents; and as liaison members of the team, help to develop community, parental, and student support and participation in the development, conducting, management, utilization and evaluation of the service.

Role of Students

Many persons may look upon students as strictly the recipients of the information service. However, students as recipients and contributors have been observed to have a profound effect upon the achievement of the services' purposes. Typical ways in which student involvement have been witnessed are:

1. Expending energy and time to help other pupils understand the services, and interpreting the services to parents while serving as information aides.

2. Promoting guidance goals and activities through participation in assembly programs, PTA programs, preparing bulletin boards and exhibits.
3. Assisting in the organization and conducting of community surveys, follow-up studies, and writing up research reports.
4. Serving as guidance library aides, receptionists, orientation aides, host for visitors, and audio-visual equipment operators.

The information service, counselors, and students can benefit in numerous ways from the supportive, leadership, and public relations task performed by students. Counselors should not hesitate to explore with students ways in which they can contribute to the administration, management, and evaluation of the information services. Students should also be encouraged to enlist the support and assistance of their parents.

Role of Parents

Parents can support the information service in the following ways:

1. Encourage their children from time to time to use the information and counseling services provided by the school to solve developmental problems.
2. Encourage other parents to seek the help of school counselors and other school personnel to facilitate the development of apparently normal youth and to assist troubled youth in making the essential adjustment.
3. Provide teachers, counselors, and other school personnel with pertinent information about their children to enrich the appraisal service.
4. Support the role of the counselor and the function of the information service through interpretative dialogues with their children, their friends, neighbors, and community groups.
5. Serving as a volunteer or as a paraprofessional aide in the securing, housing, and disseminating of guidance information in the school and at PTA functions.
6. Represent their field of work as: career day consultants, Job Fair and hobby exhibitors and speakers or discussion leaders for subject area career guidance activities.

Thus far, the roles of counselors, teachers, principals, parents, and students in the information service have been discussed. It should be noted that it would be impossible to provide in the space provided for this topic, a complete list of all the possible contributors to the information service or a comprehensive list of how various personnel can be employed to enhance the information service. The potential resources are almost without limit. It should be noted that local conditions regarding assessibility, needs, and other situational factors would suggest that counselors in each school should generate their own list.

Role of Community Organization

Community organizations have an important role to play, if counselors are to expand the information services to include concrete occupational information and experience. Such organizations as the Chamber of Commerce, Sales Executive and Marketing Association (SEM), and the National Alliance of Businessmen (NAB) are in a position to assist counselors in the implementation of a number of feasible programs to better serve the information needs of counselors, students, and teachers.

In recent years these organizations have developed or adopted excellent models of community-school support approaches. These include: (1) NAB sponsored career guidance institutes for counselors and teachers; (2) Rotary's speaker bureau; (3) SEM's career guidance liaison and scholarship committees; and (4) the Chamber of Commerce's expression of support of activities to stimulate the implementation of career education into all schools. In many localities these organizations and others facilitate and reinforce the schools' efforts to secure the support of local business, labor, professional and community leaders.

A few ways in which some school and nonschool personnel can become involved in the information services were delineated. It is important to note that although there is limited coverage in the literature relative to roles that may be performed by many persons, every school should promote the concept of active involvement of students, parents, representatives of business, industry, government, civic and social organizations, in addition to a corps of volunteers in seeking to provide meaningful information for the occupational, social, and educational needs of children and youth. The aspects of involvement of schools, student and community personnel in the development and management of the information service should begin with the initial planning stage and extend through the evaluation phases. Attention at this point will be given to a review of the literature dealing with the assessment of information service activities and strategies for its evaluation as a total component of the guidance service.

Evaluation and Research Studies of Information Program Activities

The importance of and the necessity for conducting evaluation research studies of guidance and counseling programs and services have been repeatedly stressed in the literature. But, according to the literature search reported by Farwell and Peters (1960); Patterson (1962); Sinick (1970); and Sinick and Hoppock (1971) evaluation studies of the information service are few in number, but appear to be increasing. The continuing paucity of research reports dealing with the information service specifically may be attributed to, in part, the shift in emphasis during the fifties from occupations to career psychology and in the sixties to the impact of social forces and career development theory. According to Tiedeman (1975) each of these trends had a decided impact on the use of information and appraisal data in carrying out the counseling function.

Patterson (1962) and Glanz (1974) report an increase in experimental investigations, in addition to follow-up and survey studies of the effectiveness of counseling and appraisal services. In addition to the counseling and guidance activities, occupational courses have been considered for many years by schools and guidance personnel at the elementary, secondary, and college levels to be a meaningful component of the information service. Consequently, Hoppock (1963) and Sinick (1970) and a number of other researchers have been able to provide through a survey of especially relevant literature and research data substantial evidence of the continuing merits of occupational information courses.

In order to illustrate the kinds of informational research activities that practicing counselors may adapt to their school settings, a few selected investigations will be presented. Most of these studies will be taken from the publications of Robert Hoppock (1963) whose observations, research, and writings on relevant aspects of the information service spans several decades. The reviews follow:

Career Guidance Information for Adults was found by Logie, Humiston, and Ballin, according to Hoppock (1963) to have been favorably received and positively acted on by a group of two hundred adults who participated in an information program two evenings a week for a six week period. Forty-one percent of those involved reported job changes yielding greater satisfaction six months after the program.

The Impact of Occupational Information on Occupational Choice was shown by Hoppock (1963) to have a positive effect. After learning about employment opportunities in their hometown, the percentage of students in Nick's study who chose some overcrowded occupation was cut in half, while the percentage who chose appropriate occupations doubled.

The Effects of Occupational Information Upon Job Satisfaction ascertained from two follow-up studies was described by Couny (Hoppock, 1963). High school alumni who had a senior year course in job finding and job orientation were better satisfied and earned more money than comparable students who had not had the course. The second report, a five year follow-up study, indicated that these same students were superior in job satisfaction and earnings, and had suffered less unemployment. The difference between the two groups in terms of employment and job satisfaction was greater at the end of the fifth year than at the end of the first year.

The Influence of High School Information Courses on College Adjustment was studied by Lowenstein (Hoppock, 1963). He reported that college freshmen who had had a high school course in occupations made a better adjustment to college than comparable students who had not had such a course.

The Appropriateness of Occupational Plans of high school students who had had both counseling and a course in occupations when compared with students who had received only counseling were judged by Lincoln (Hoppock, 1963) to have been the best, while students who had received counseling without the course were next best. Students who had received neither were judged poorest.

Observation of Workers in Students' Preferred Occupations according to Washville (Hoppock, 1963) resulted in 14 percent of sixty-seven high school students who spent one day observing such workers, stating that they would change their occupational goals as a result of the experience.

Try-out Work Experiences. King (Hoppock, 1963) reported that when boys in their last year of formal schooling spent two weeks in factories in jobs selected by themselves, 48 percent said they would change their occupational goals as a result of the experience.

Closed-Circuit Television Systems were found by Wease, Eberly, and Isconetti (1963) to be an effective medium for the dissemination of information to a very large group of students and served as a stimulus for research. The research findings indicated that the students preferred a series of television guidance information programs to their regular homeroom programs.

Now, in order to include the works of others, update the illustrations presented here and to summarize the research generalization, a few additional studies of guidance information activities will be cited. These studies utilized such activities as: a series of counseling sessions with more than one counselor (Moore, 1969), a manual and a guide, "You Today and Tomorrow" (Katz, 1959); a test of readiness for utilizing vocational information and counseling (Gribbons and Lohnes, 1968: Flores and Olsen, 1967; Drogers, 1968; and Hales and Fenner, 1972); growth in self-comprehension (Miller and Tiedeman, 1972). The findings indicate that the approaches resulted in the acquisition of information or knowledge related to guidance concepts.

Therefore, we can conclude that the research tells us that counselors should utilize a variety of information service program activities to achieve guidance and counseling goals for each individual. And in addition, the outcomes of their information program activities should be evaluated to extend knowledge of what works best and to further clarify and define the content and processes of the information service activities. Within this frame of reference, problems usually encountered in developing and carrying out information service evaluation activities and sources of assistance will be discussed next.

Evaluation of the Information Service

Evaluation of the guidance programs or of either of the service's components takes a great deal of ingenuity, time and effort. Thus too often, it remains undone. Among the complicating factors are:

1. The tendency to look at the service rather than the results of the services rendered.
2. The difficulty of finding answers to such questions as
   a. What does the information service accomplish?
   b. How does it contribute to the total guidance program?
   c. How does it contribute to the instructional process?
   d. How does the information service influence students, teachers, counselors, administrators, and parents?
3. The difficulty of finding ways to assess the impact of the information processes on the development of students.

An examination of the foregoing evaluation concerns suggest that without clarity of purpose and objectives that can be specifically defined as outcomes, that can be identified, answers to the questions raised will of necessity be more or less subjective.

Most schools have a good deal of utilization of information taking place. Therefore, they can profit from the use of evaluation instruments which help to observe or assess the information service processes and products independently. Process evaluation looks at what is done and product at what gets done. This distinction is a useful one and should be recognized and utilized by school counselors to determine what information practices are good and desirable.

Aids to process and product evaluation for program components and elements of the services can be obtained from rating devices prepared by the U.S. Office of Education such as:

Criteria for Evaluating Guidance Programs in Secondary Schools and How to Use the Criteria for Evaluating Guidance Programs in Secondary Schools (Washington, D.C., Federal Security Agency, Office of Education, 1949) Nos. 3317 and 3317A

Evaluation Criteria, National Study of School Evaluation, Washington, D.C., 1970.

In addition, standards for evaluation are traditionally published by state departments of public instruction. These guidelines can usually be obtained from the local board of education office, as well as from the state educational agency. Many guidance textbooks contain evaluation guides that may adapt well to local conditions. And finally, it should be noted that process and product evaluation conducted with the assistance of any of the guides, is a matter of staff judgment regarding what is done in the name of the information service. This is an important point, in view of the fact that the elements of many of the services appear to be similar or overlap.

There is little or no doubt that each counseling staff can devise noncomplex, uncontrolled means of examining the impact of the information service on students' educational and vocational developmental behavior, interpret the results and supply the findings to program improvement. Thus the latter is the main purpose of evaluation. The outcomes of the improved service, in terms of student development, reveal what the information service achieved.

Summary

In this chapter all effort has been made to chronicle in brief the events, theoretical concepts, evaluation, and research findings, procedures and practices which led to the expansion of the information services in guidance, counseling, and instructional programs in schools and colleges throughout these United States over the last seventy years.

It was noted that during the past five years, the information resources have had an extensive growth and promise to be of even greater importance during the ensuing decades, when the problems of providing sufficient and efficient materials and methods to meet career education program needs must be solved. Of special concern was the current emphasis on the development of career resource centers and the providing of programs designed to meet the information needs of the disadvantaged, handicapped, and females.

The continuing and expanding needs of students, educators, and the general public for accurate and appropriate career developmental information was emphasized. In addition, the attributes of the information service having direct bearing on the individual's career developmental needs were highlighted. This focus on individual needs, according to Glanz (1974) is the information services' unique characteristic:

> . . . in guidance concern for aiding the individual learner in the acquisition, ordering, and integrating of related and unrelated data regarding self, others, work, education, opportunities, leisure, and options into meaningful concepts . . . Concepts that are useful in formulating the problem-solving and decision-making patterns, that establish values and life objectives (p. 42).

References Cited

Baer, M. F., and Roeber, E. C. *Occupational information.* Chicago: Science Research Associates, 1964.

Beck, C. E. *Guideline for guidance.* Dubuque: William C. Brown Company Publishers, 1966.

Bingham, W. V. *Aptitudes and aptitude testing.* New York: Harper, 1937.

Brewer, J. M. *History of vocational guidance.* New York: Harper, 1942.

Burtnett, F. E. *Guidelines for establishing a career information center.* Washington: American Personnel and Guidance Association, 1974.

Circle, D. F. *The career information service: A guide to its development and use.* Newton: Newton Public Schools System, 1968.

Drogers, R. Occupational aptitude of high school dropouts. *Vocational Guidance Quarterly* 16 (3) (March 1968):185-87.

Farwell, G. F. and Peters, H. *Readings in guidance for counselors.* Chicago: Rand-McNally and Company, 1960.

Flores, T., and Olsen, L. Stability and realism of occupational aspiration in eighth and twelfth grade males. *Vocational Guidance Quarterly* 16 (1967).

Gribbons, W. D. Changes in readiness for vocational planning from eighth to tenth grade. *Personnel and Guidance Journal* 42 (1964).

Gribbons, W. D., and Lohnes, P. R. *Emerging careers.* New York: Teachers College Press, 1968.

Glanz, E. *Guidance foundations, principles and techniques* (2d ed.). Boston: Allyn and Bacon, Inc., 1974.

Goldman, L. Information counseling: A dilemma. *Personnel and Guidance Journal* 36 (1967):42-46.

———. *Using tests in counseling.* New York: Appleton-Century-Crofts, 1961.

Hale, L., and Fenner, B. Work values of 5th, 8th and 11th grade students. *Vocational Guidance Quarterly* 20 (1972).

Hansen, L. S. *Promoting student career development through utilizing volunteers in a career resource center.* Progress report, Minneapolis: University of Minnesota, 1971.

———. A model for career development through curricula. *Personnel and Guidance Journal* 51 (1972):4.

Herman, J. J., and Molen, R. V. An equation for use in vocational counseling. *Vocational Guidance Quarterly* 8 (1959):1.

Hill, G. *Management and improvement of guidance* (2d ed.) Englewood Cliffs: Prentice-Hall, Inc., 1974.

Holland, J. A theory of career choice. *Journal of Counseling Psychology* 6 (1959):35-45.

———. Exploration of a theory of vocational choice. *Vocational Guidance Quarterly* 12 (1962):17-21.

Hollingsworth, Leta S. Musical sensitivity of children who test above 135 IQ (Stanford-Binet) *Journal of Educational Psychology* (February 1926):95-109.

Hoppock, R. *Occupational information* (2d ed.) New York: McGraw Hill, 1963, 4th ed. in press.

———. *Group guidance principles, techniques and education.* New York: McGraw-Hill, 1949.

Huston, P. W. *The guidance function in education.* New York: Appleton-Century-Croft, Inc., 1958.

Isaacson, L. E. *Career information in counseling and teaching* (2d ed.) Boston: Allyn and Bacon, Inc., 1973.

Jacobson, T. J. Career guidance center. *Personnel and Guidance Journal* 50 (1972):599-604.

Katz, M. R. *You: Today and tomorrow.* Princeton, N.J.: Educational Testing Service, 1959.

Kitson, H. D. *Psychology of vocational adjustment.* Philadelphia: Lippincott, 1925.

Kowitz, G. T., and Kowitz, N. *Operating guidance services for the modern school.* New York: Holt, Rinehart and Winston, Inc., 1968.

McCracken, T. L. and Lamb, H. E. *Occupational information in the elementary school.* Boston: Houghton-Mifflin, 1923.

McDaniels, C. The role of leisure in career development. *Proceeding of the Fifth World Congress of the International Association for Educational and Vocational Guidance.* Quebec: IAGVT, 1974.

McDaniels, Carl, and Simutis, Cathy. *Leisure activities and careers.* Garrett Park, Maryland: Garrett Park Press, 1974.

Meyering, R. A. *Use of test data in counseling.* Boston: Houghton Mifflin Co., 1968.

Miller, A. L., and Tiedeman, D. Decision making for the 70s: The cubing of the Tiedeman paradigm and its application in career guidance. *Focus in Guidance* (September 1972):1.

Moore, Lorraine. A developmental approach to group counseling with seventh graders. *The School Counselor* 16(4) (1969):272-76.

National Vocational Guidance Association. *Guidelines for the preparation and evaluation of career information media.* Washington: APGA Publication Sales, 1971.

Norris, W. L., Zeran, F., and Hatch, R. *The information service in guidance* (2d ed.). Chicago: Rand McNally Co., 1966.

Ohlsen, M. M. *Guidance service in the modern school.* New York: Harcourt, Brace and World, 1974.

Parsons, F. *Choosing a vocation.* Boston: Houghton Mifflin, 1908.

Patterson, C. H. *Counseling and guidance in the schools: A first course.* New York: Harper and Row Publishers, Inc., 1962.

Patterson, D. G. The genesis of modern guidance. *Education Review* 19 (1938):36-46.

Perrone, P. A., and Thrush, R. S. Vocational information processing system, a survey. *Vocational Guidance Quarterly* 14 (June 1969):255-66.

Peters, H. J., and Shertzer, B. *Guidance programs development and management* (3rd ed.). Columbus: Charles E. Merrill Publishing Co., 1974.

Rober, E. C. The school curriculum and vocational development. *Vocational Guidance Quarterly* 14 (1956):87-91.

Rothney, J., Danielson, P. J., and Heimann, R. A. *Measurements for guidance.* New York: Harper & Row, 1959.

Rothney, J. *Guidance practices and results.* New York: Harper, 1958.

Samler, J. Psycho-social aspect of work, a critique of occupational information. *Personnel and Guidance Journal* 2 (1961):458-65.

———. A new psychological speciality: vocational counseling. *Vocational Guidance Quarterly* 12(2) (1966):82-88.

Shaw, M. C. *School guidance systems.* Boston: Houghton-Mifflin Co., 1973.

Sinick, D. *Occupational information and guidance.* Boston: Houghton-Mifflin Co., 1970.

Sinick, D., and Hoppock, R. Research on the teaching of occupations. *Vocational Guidance Quarterly* 20 (1971):129-37.

Super, D. E. *The psychology of career.* New York: Harper, 1957.

Tiedeman, D. V. Structured personal integration into career education. *Personnel and Guidance Journal* 53(9) (1975).

Traxler, A. E., and North, P. D. *Techniques of guidance* (3rd ed.). New York: Harper & Row, 1966.

Waltz, G. *Information analysis and targeted communication program for improving the quality and expanding the amount of occupational exploration and career planning.* Ann Arbor: University of Michigan Press, 1972.

Wease, Jean; Eberly, Glen; and Iaconetti, Louis. Counselors on Camera, *Bulletin of the National Association of Secondary School Principals* 47 (September 1963):27-31.

Williamson, E. G. To avoid waste. *Journal of Higher Education* 8 (1937):64-70.

———. An historical perspective of the guidance movement. *Personnel and Guidance Journal* 42 (1964):854-59.

Annotated Bibliograpy

Borrow, H. ed. *Man in a world of work.* Boston: Houghton Mifflin, 1964. This book summarizes what is known about work in one's life, the processes of vocational development and educational endeavors to actualize vocational guidance. (NVGA—50th Anniversary Edition).

Herr, E. L. and Cramer, S. H. *Vocational guidance and career development in the schools: toward a systems approach.* Boston: Houghton Mifflin Company, 1974. Detailed analysis and synthesis of specific guidance services goals, objectives and methods in a behavioral framework. Focuses on guidance as a subsystem within the formal social-system—the school. (NVGA 60th Anniversary Edition).

Hoppock, R. *Occupational information: where to get it and how to use it in teaching and counseling.* New York: McGraw-Hill, 1967 (4th ed. in press). This revision of one of the classics in guidance literature presents a more comprehensive treatment of the subject than found in any other guidance information resource textbook. Very practical and carefully written and well-documented.

Isaacson, L. *Information in counseling and teaching* (2d ed.). Boston: Allyn and Bacon, 1973. The major thrust of the book is on applied areas of providing adequate educational and occupational information. It provides an excellent summary of research on vocational development, the mechanized and computerized information system and working with clients in school and nonschool settings.

Norris, W.; Zeran, F. R.; and Hatch, R. M. *The information service in guidance* (3rd ed.). Chicago: Rand McNally and Company, 1972. A worthwhile reference for school counselors. Discusses uses and types of guidance information and identifies kinds and sources of the various types.

Peters, H. J., and Hansen, J. C. eds. *Vocational guidance and career development* (2d ed.). New York: The Macmillian Company, 1971. A collection of articles by national figures discussing the problems and achievements of vocational guidance; societal and cultural factors affecting work; career development theory; information processes and resources; and aspects of career development for women, the disadvantaged and adults.

Counselor's Personal Library

Bureau of Employment Security *Dictionary of occupational titles* 3 Vols. (4th ed. in press). Washington: Government Printing Office, 1965.

Bureau of Labor Statistics *Occupational outlook handbook* 1974-75 edition. Washington: Government Printing Office, 1974. (See latest edition).

———. *Manpower report of the president.* Washington: U.S. Government Printing Office, 1975.

———. *Jobs for which a high school education is preferred, but not essential, Jobs for which high school education is generally required, Jobs for which apprenticeships are available, Jobs for which junior college, technical institute or other specialized training is usually required,* and *Jobs for which a college education is usually required.* (5 Pamphlets) Washington: U.S. Dept. of Labor, 1974.

Hopke, William E. ed. *The encyclopedia of careers and vocational guidance.* Chicago: J. G. Ferguson, 1967.

House, Elaine ed. *Facilitating career development for girls and women.* Washington: NVGA-APGA Publication Sales, 1975.

Liston, Robert A. *On the job training and where to get it.* New York: Julian Messner Press, 1967.

Miller, Juilet and Leonard, George *Career guidance practices for disadvantaged youth.* Washington: NVGA-APGA Publication Sales, 1974.

How to visit college, Washington: NVGA, APGA Publication Sales, 1972.

Personnel and Guidance Journal. American Personnel and Guidance Association, Washington.

Pitts, G. D. *How to select a private vocational school,* Washington: APGA Publication Sales, 1975.

Strohmenger, C. T. *How to complete job application forms.* Washington: APGA Publication Sales, 1975.

Super, Donald E. ed. *Measuring vocational maturity.* Washington: APGA Publication Sales, 1974.

U.S. Department of Labor, *Guide to local occupational information.* Washington Government Printing Office, (4th ed.) 1973.

U.S. Employment Service, *Task analysis inventory.* Washington: Government Printing Office, 1973.

———. *Handbook for analyzing jobs.* Washington: Government Printing Office, 1972.

Vocational Guidance Quarterly. National Vocational Guidance Association, Washington.

Occupational Information Indexes

Career guidance index, Careers, Largo, Florida: (A monthly, October through May annotated bibliography of free and inexpensive materials).

Career index, Chronicles Guidance Publications, Inc., Moravia, New York: (A monthly September through April, annotated bibliograpy of free and inexpensive materials).

Counselors guide to manpower information, U.S. Department of Labor, Washington.

Counselors information service, B'nai Brith Vocational Guidance Service 1640 Rhode Island Ave. N.W., Washington: (Annotated bibliography, books, pamphlets, periodicals and press releases on occupations, guidance and counseling).

Educators guide to free films, educators guide to free filmstrips and *educators guide to free tapes, scripts and transcripts.* Educators Progress Service, Randolph, Wisconsin. (List of sources of educational, occupational and social A-V materials).

Guidance exchange, Occu-Press, 489 Fifth Ave. New York: (A bimonthly digest of current guidance literature.)

NVGA bibliography of current occupational literature, National Vocational Guidance Association, 1605 New Hampshire Ave. N.W., Washington: (Contains approximately 100 pages of career resource listings: literature, film reviews and publishers. Periodic revisions published, in addition to quarterly supplements in each issue of the *Vocational guidance quarterly).*

Occupational index, Personnel Services, Inc., Box 306, Jaffrey, New Hampshire (Quarterly issues cite current sources).

Science Research Associates Chicago, Illinois (Variety of occupational and educational materials).

Community Occupational Surveys

Hoppock, Robert *Occupational information* (2d ed.). New York: McGraw-Hill 1963, 16.

Eldsr, L. A. An in-service community occupational survey. *Vocational Guidance Quarterly* 17 3 (1969):185-88.

Educational Information

A handbook for counselors of collegebound students The Association of College Admissions Counselors, 801 Davis St., Evanston, Illinois. (Comprehensive data on over 700 members of sponsoring organization; published biennially).

American universities and colleges, American Council of Education, Washington, (emphasis on four year degree granting colleges, abstract submitted by the institutions contain basic information for the ensuing year).

College blue book. Christian E. Burckel Co. and Assoc., Yonkers-On-Judson, New York (3 vol. main section, contains data on universities, colleges, junior colleges, technical institutes, and seminaries. Profiles for institutions consist of 59 information items listed in tabular form).

College testing programs bulletins, The American College Testing Program (ACT); The College Entrance Examination Board Program (SEEB-SAT & CBAT) College Entrance Examination Board, Educational Testing Service, Princeton, New Jersey.

Directory of vocational training sources, Science Research Associates, Inc., Chicago, Illinois (contains basic data on more than 5,500 vocational training sources arranged in 45 occupational areas.

Educational directory, part 3: higher education, Office of Education, Dept. HEW, Government Printing Office, Washington: (a directory of colleges and universities, published annually).

Lovejoys college guide, Simon and Schuster, Inc., (published biennially; supplements published monthly by the author, C. E. Lovejoy, between revisions of the Guide; contains descriptive materials for over 23,000 institutions of higher education).

The college handbook, College Entrance Examination Board, 475 Riverside Drive, New York, New York (contains descriptive data on member colleges and universities, revised biennially).

Apprenticeship training programs, Bureau of Apprenticeship Training, U.S. Dept. of Labor, Washington: or state Employment Commission and Apprenticeship Agencies, (see latest edition).

Baron's Profile of American Colleges, Baron's Educational Series, Inc., Woodbury, New York.

Cooperative education programs, National Commission for Cooperative Education, 8 West 40th Street, New York, New York.

Accredited insititutions of higher education, Federation of Regional Accrediting Commissions of Higher Education, Washington: 1971-72.

Home study blue book, National Home Study Council, Washington, (see latest edition).

Job Training suggestions for women and girls, U.S. Department of Labor, Washington.

Scholarships and Financial Aid Information

A chance to go to college, College Entrance Examination Board, 475 Riverside Drive, New York, New York.

College opportunities for southern negroes, Scholarship Information Center, University of North Carolina, Raleigh, North Carolina.

Financing a college education: a guide for counselors College Entrance Examination Board, Princeton, New Jersey.

National defense education act student loan program Office of Education, Department of Health, Education and Welfare, Government Printing Office, Washington.

Parents confidential statement College Scholarship Service, Princeton, New Jersey.

Patterson, Ray ed. *Need a lift* (25th ed.) Indianapolis: The American Legion Education and Scholarship Program (Revised, annually).

ROTC-Financial Assistance Bulletins. Air Force ROTC, Navy ROTC, Army ROTC.

Student aid annual: scholarships available to entering college freshmen, Chronicle Guidance Press, Moravia, New York.

Summer employment in federal agencies, Government Printing Office, Washington.

The national register of scholarships and fellowships World Trade Academy Press, New York, New York.

Additional Sources of Information

Printed materials

Appalachia Educational Laboratory, Inc., P.O. Box 1348, Charleston, West Virginia.

Bellman Publishing Co., Box 172, Cambridge, Massachusetts.

David McKay Co., Inc., 750 Third Avenue, New York, New York.

Education Progress Service, Randolph, Wisconsin.

Julian Messner, 1 West 39th Street, New York.

McKnight and McKnight Publishing Co., Bloomington, Illinois.

Vocational Guidance Manuals, 235 East 45th St., New York, New York.

Films

Career Center Filmstrips, Thomas J. Jacobson, 5945 Highgate Court, La Mesa, California.

Churchill Films, 622 N. Robertson Blvd., Los Angeles, California.

Coronet Instructional Films, 65 East So. Water Street, Chicago, Illinois.
Counselor Film, Inc. CFI, Career Futures, Inc., 2100 Locust St., Philadelphia, Pennsylvania.
Educators Progress Service, Randolph, Wisconsin.
Encyclopedia Britannica, Educational Corp, 4424 Oakton St., Skokie, Illinois.
Guidance Associates, Pleasantville, New York.
McGraw-Hill Book Co., Inc. Text-Film Dept., 330 W. 42nd St., New York, New York.
Singer, Education Division, 1345 Deversay Parkway, Chicago, Illinois.
Vocational Films, 111 Euclid Avenue, Parkridge, Illinois.
Charts, Posters, and Pictures,

American Hospital, 840 North Lake Shore Dr., Chicago, Illinois.
Career Posters, Careers, Largo, Florida.
Chronicle College Charts, Chronicle Guidance Inc., Moravia, New York.
Garrett Park Press, *Career educational wall charts,* ed. Carl McDaniels and Cathy Simutis, Garrett Park, Maryland.
Glamour Magazine, 420 Lexington Ave., New York, New York.
Posters, National Career Guidance Week Posters, NCGW Kits Publicity Kit NVGA (order from Dr. Sally Spedding) National Career Guidance Week Cordnator P.O. Box 892 Southill, Michigan.
National Industrial Conference Board, 845 Third Street, New York, New York.
Science Research Associates, 259 E. Erie St., Chicago, Illinois.
The Guidance Center, Ontario College of Education, University of Toronto, Toronto, Canada.
U.S. Department of Labor, Bureau of Labor Statistics, Washington, D.C.

General Bibliograpy

Berg, I. *Education and jobs; the great training robbery.* New York: Preager, 1970.
Borow, H. ed. *Career guidance for a new age.* Boston: Houghton Mifflin Co., 1973.
Crites, J. O.*The maturity of vocational attitudes in adolescence.* Washington: APGA Publication Sales, 1971.
Green, T. *Work, leisure and the American schools.* New York: Random House, 1968.
Ginzberg, E. *Career guidance.* New York: McGraw-Hill, 1971.
Hansen, L. S. *Career guidance practices in school and community.* Washington: APGA Publication Sales, 1970.
Holland, J. L. *The psychology of vocational choice.* Waltham, Massachusetts: Ginn-Blaisdell, 1966.
Leach, L. A. *Manpower requirements for national objectives in the 1970s.* Washington: National Planning Association, 1968.
National Vocational Guidance Association. *Guidelines for the preparation and evaluation of career information media.* Washington: AFGA Publication Sales, 1971.
National Vocational Guidance Association. *NVGA bibliography of current career information,* 6th ed. Washington: APGA Publication Sales, 1973.
Neff, W. S. *Work and human behavior.* New York: Atherton Press, 1968.
Norris, W., et al. *The information service in guidance* (2d ed.). Chicago: Rand McNally, 1966.
Osipow, S. H. *Theories of career development.* New York: Appleton-Century-Crofts, 1968.
Pearls, A., and Riessman, F. *New careers for the poor.* New York: The Free Press, 1965.
Peters, H. J. and Hansen, J. *Vocational guidance and career development.* (Selected Readings). New York: The Macmillan Company, 1966.
Tennyson, W. W., et al. *The teacher role in career development.* Washington: APGA Publication Sales, 1965.
Silberman, C. E. *The myths of automation.* New York: Harper & Row, 1966.
Splaver, S. *Your career if you're not going to college.* New York: Julian Messner Press, 1963.

Venn, G. *Man, education and work.* Washington: American Council on Education, 1964.

Whitfield, E. A., and Hoover, R. *Guide to careers through vocational training.* San Diego: Knapp, 1968.

Whiteley, J. M., and Resnikoff, A. *Perspective on vocational development.* Washington: APGA Publication Sales, 1972.

Wolfbein, S. L. *Occupational information.* New York: Random House, 1968.

Zyotowski, D. G. *Vocational behavior.* New York: Holt, Rinehart, and Winston, 1968.

Chapter 7
THE PLACEMENT SERVICE

Carl O. McDaniels and Cathy L. Simutis

Introduction and Historical Development

Historically placement has ranked as one of the high priorities of vocational guidance. In the *Principles of Vocational Guidance* adopted over fifty years ago by the National Vocational Guidance Association (1924) there is a strong statement of support for placement as a part of the process of vocational guidance—not the whole. There are numerous references to placement in high school vocational guidance programs in the early 1920s. See for example Dorothy DeSchweinitz (1923) *Practical Problems of the Placement Office;* Mary Stewart (1924) *Placement and the Central Placement Office.* More recently Lillian Buckingham (1972) in the *American Vocational Journal* described in detail the centralized high school placement activities of the City of Baltimore, Maryland, since 1928. She reported that they now have a staff of over forty-six professionals to provide a free year round service to students.
Vocational Journal described in detail the centralized high school placement activities of the City of Baltimore, Maryland, since 1928. She reported that they now have a staff of over forty-six professionals to provide a free year round service to students.

More recently, most (but certainly not all!) of the major textbooks in guidance have devoted special sections or chapters to placement. Usually it is described as one of the several key services which a high school should provide for students. Arthur Jones (1945) whose book was probably the most popular professional text in the 1930s and 1940s always devoted a chapter or more to placement related activities with careful attention to the role of the counselor. In the 1950s Clifford Froehlich (1958) in his widely acclaimed book *Guidance Services in Schools,* devoted thirty pages to placement activities. In the 1960s Merle Ohlsen's *Guidance Services in the Modern School* (1964) and in the 1970s Shertzer and Stone's *Fundamentals of Guidance* (1971) both dwell at length on the important role of placement in the total guidance function in the schools. Specifically, guidance services are defined with placement as a significant part of the obligation of the schools to its students.

Besides the schools, other state and federal agencies have, for several decades, put placement in the forefront of their activities. Since its origin in the 1930s the U.S. Employment Service and its state affiliates have put placement first and have tried repeatedly to work with

Dr. Carl O. McDaniels is Professor of Counselor Education and Director of Graduate Studies in Education at Virginia Polytechnic Institute and State University, Blacksburg, Virginia. Ms. Cathy L. Simutis was formerly Director of Placement Services at Radford College, Radford, Virginia.

schools and colleges to fill their responsibility in this area. Vocational rehabilitation and various veteran programs have always ranked placement at the top of their priorities. When colleges and universities have established any student personnel service, placement has usually been the first to be funded. There seems to be no question about the significance of placement over the last fifty years and its defined role in the schools as a guidance function.

Flannagan (1974) in a recent issue of the *Vocational Guidance Quarterly* asked the question "Whatever Happened to Job Placement?" He speculates that interest in placement runs in cycles (something like the seven year locust!) and may be entering a new period of interest. Since concern has been off for several (seven?) years, maybe it is time for a renewal. Montgomery (1970) reports on the continuing activities of a state employment service agency in relation to providing placement services in some rural schools. There is evidence this interest is still high on the part of USES and its affiliates to provide a direct placement service in local schools.

There is an obvious need to take a fresh look at placement because of the wide interest in career education. Much of the concern for this area is coming from vocational educators. In Virginia, Vocational Education Act of 1968 funds are being used to support pilot placement programs—using former vocational education teachers as placement personnel—*exclusively*. In Tennessee (1972) a position of vocational guidance specialist with main duties as a placement counselor has been spelled out in a recently enacted state law.

Florida has created the position of "occupational specialist" and given this person placement related duties. In Ohio the area vocational schools have counselors who concentrate their efforts in vocational guidance with placement as a high priority. The recent American Vocational Association (December 1974) Convention in New Orleans devoted considerable time and attention to the subject of placement, giving a further indication of interest by the AVA and its members in this field. In contrast the American Personnel and Guidance Association's New Orleans Convention (April, 1974) devoted scant attention to the subject. There seems little question that there is increased interest in placement coming mainly from vocational educators—and a few counseling people. Public pressures also are beginning to mount, and they may yet represent the most significant influence.

It may be true that interest in placement goes in cycles. There are five good reasons behind a rise in interest regarding placement in the mid-1970s. One is because placement is, as Wasil (1974) has called it, the "Keystone in the Arch of Career Education." So, if career education is to be truly effective then students moving through such a program must be able to seek, find, and maintain meaningful employment. Backers of career education know placement must prove its true strength.

Second, the general public continues to clamor for better results from their tax dollars being spent on education. Many have generalized this pressure into the rubric of accountability. The demonstration of ultimate accountability is the success of the high school graduate being able to gain successful employment. Placement can be one of the main responses to outcries for accountability by showing how schools prepare students for meaningful careers. Feedback on school strengths and weaknesses through follow-up can and should be a part of the total placement efforts.

Third, the decreasing percentage of high school graduates going on to higher education is at a thirteen year low as reported by Michelotti (1973) in a recent issue of the *Monthly Labor*

Review. From a high of 55 percent of the nation's secondary school graduates going on to higher education in 1968, the statistics reveal only 47 percent went to various colleges and universities in 1973. The preliminary figures on 1974 show a continuation of the declining percentage. This clearly spells out a direct pressure from students themselves to get the same kind of help in finding jobs which the school has provided for those going on to higher education. The unemployment rate of 20 to 24 percent among young workers also must be viewed as a strong indictment of our current placement efforts.

Fourth, studies at the state and national level point out with clarity student desires for greater assistance in the area of career planning and placement. One of the most comprehensive investigations ever done in our field was reported by Prediger for the American College Testing Program (1973). In it he pointed out that students wanted and expected much more help from counselors and the schools in this area than they were getting. Only 15 percent of the national sample said they had any practice for job interview situations. Almost the same identical information came out in a 1973 Virginia study sponsored by the State Advisory Council for Vocational Education (1973). In this study approximately 65 percent of the counselors surveyed indicated they felt their work with individual and group counseling was not adequate with respect to job counseling. The results in state after state confirm that both counselors and students didn't feel very good about what placement services are available.

Fifth, there is a strange conflict emerging between vocational education people and counselors as to who should have the prime responsibility for school placement activities. Currently for example, vocational education funds in the state of Virginia are being used to support several pilot placement projects in high schools of various sizes. These projects are now in the second and third year of operation. The conflict part comes up when the people hired for the positions had to be vocational education teachers—not counselors. The pressure to resolve who is going to do what needs to be settled and soon. The National Vocational Guidance Association and the American Vocational Association (1973) agreed that it was the counselor who clearly had the responsibility for carrying out the school placement program.

Placement Services and Career Development

Placement is more than an employment service that matches available students to job openings. It is the educational institution's opportunity to assist the student with the transition from school to employment. For this reason, placement services should include the following five functions: needs assessment, job development, student development, job placement, and follow-up.

Needs assessment must be done both in terms of employers and students. The placement office has to be aware of national and local employment trends and be able to translate this information to school personnel and students. It is important that students have a realistic picture of the type of workers being sought and the industries where employment is available. At the same time, it is essential to know what the needs of the students are. The placement office should view the students as its primary clients.

Students will have different needs. Some students may need part-time employment while they are in high school for financial reasons. Other students may need job try-outs to clarify their thinking about occupations. For those students going on to college, volunteer work may be an appropriate method to learn about professions. Some students may have special problems that need to be considered and others will need assistance in learning how to go about looking for employment. The placement office has to be aware of these diverse needs before it can effectively serve the student population.

The process of job development has to be on-going. It involves continuous contact with potential employers in business, industry, and government. These people must be aware of the placement service if they are to list job vacancies there. And they must be pleased with the service if they are to continue placing vacancies there.

Other sources of job vacancy information must also be explored. Various civic groups, unions, the local Chamber of Commerce, and local professional organizations should be contacted by the placement office. Parents of students, alumni of the school, and school personnel should be aware of the functions of the placement office and encouraged to list job vacancies of which they are aware. Current information about apprenticeship and military openings must also be available to students.

The placement office has to be involved with student development in the area of job-seeking skills. It is a place students can go for assistance in planning an employment search. The skills offered should include interviewing, completing applications, making contacts, follow-up, and decision making.

Many students who are leaving or completing high school have never before sought full-time employment. They are unaware of even the most basic procedures that are usually followed. They need to be able to rely on one person who can take them through the job search and teach them the skills they will need throughout their lifetime. The placement office should teach the student to function independently of the placement office.

Interviewing skills can be taught to students in several different methods. One of the most commonly used is role playing with a staff member. The staff member simulates an employment interview, taking the role of the employer and the student is the applicant. The staff member can provide feedback with the student. Another effective way to use role playing is a triad where the students play the three roles of interviewer, applicant, and observer. In this way, they are provided with peer feedback. Interviewing skills have also been taught with closed-circuit T.V. and role playing. This can be highly effective with students who have the ability to analyze their own behavior. Students can also be taught to learn from actual interview experiences.

Job placement is done with all students but especially with the students who have particular problems. It is important that the staff member be familiar with students and work closely with students and potential employers. The staff member should intervene on the student's behalf only rarely. Ordinarily the staff member would encourage the student to place him/herself. Any support that is needed should be provided but ideally students should learn to function independently.

Follow-up is essential for evaluation of the placement office and can also act as evaluation of the academic, technical-vocational, and career education programs in the school system. The data collected should be immediate and longitudinal. The follow-up data is an integral aspect of the evaluation of the services. The special type of data collected would depend on the objectives established by the school system itself. The kinds of information collected usually include the number of students going on to college and choice of major, number of students employed, time of employment and suitability of employment, and number of students who choose not to work nor to continue their education. Information should also be collected on students going into the military, technical-vocational schools, junior colleges and apprenticeship programs. It is important to note which students avail themselves of the services offered by the placement office and to compare their placement with that of other students.

The placement office can also assist students by arranging and coordinating employment testing in the school for students. In many states, the entry level state civil service exams can be administered in the school. Much of the testing for college application, such as the College Entrance Examination Boards, the American College Testing Program and others can be coordinated through the placement office.

The placement office can also schedule recruiters to see students. These people provide the students with an opportunity to learn more about employment or educational opportunities in varied geographical locations. One of the traditional activities sponsored by placement offices is a career day, or a college day, which serves to bring large groups of students into contact with representatives from many career fields and colleges.

Because of the on-going contact with business and industry, the placement office is in a position to refer students and faculty to possible work experience sites. The faculty in technical-vocational programs should be encouraged to work closely with the placement office.

Students should also feel that the placement office can be of assistance with part-time and summer employment. For freshman and sophomores this may be a first positive contact with the guidance services program. Brief training sessions can also be arranged to prepare students for short-term employment after school and on weekends during the peak employment season around Thanksgiving and Christmas. Arrangements for "working papers" should also be a part of the placement office service.

All of the services of the placement office should be available to all students. It should not be limited to students who are seeking employment as opposed to those who are continuing their education, nor to those who are graduating as opposed to those who are leaving school before graduation. When it is possible, the services should be offered to alumni as well.

In-School Placement

Many school systems view arrangements for students to make course and curriculum selection as a placement function. This "in-school" placement activity is developmental in nature and fits neatly into the life span approach to career development. In this phase of the placement service *each* student is given assistance in knowing what the in-school choices are which are open to him/her and what the immediate and long-range implication of each subject is—both required and elective. Students are aided with career decision sessions which are aimed at clarifying career goals and values. Each year a review is made for each student of the four to six year plan of subjects and curriculum and tentative career objectives. This in-school placement function, which is developmental in nature, is what leads to ultimate success in placement once a student leaves the secondary school for further education, seeks full-time employment or both.

The differential aspects of the in-school placement have special meaning at each grade or age level. In the elementary school, placement may have a role to play in helping to assign students to special classes, special experience groups, or special leisure-learning groups. In the middle or junior high school the placement function of the overall guidance program may have a role to play in helping students to choose from among various curriculum choices, various exploratory experiences, various work-tryout experiences, or various part-time, summer or voluntary work experiences. In the senior high school the placement function may be most evident in assisting students to choose to prepare for full-time employment after high school or to continue immediately into some form of post-high-school education, or in some cases to try and combine both options into a meaningful continuing education *and* work situation. Placement may also be available to the student seeking part-time, summer, or full-time employment as well as placement in cocurricular activities or volunteer work.

Placement in Career Education

Given a half century of uneven interest in placement through vocational guidance it appears from an analysis of the past, the current situation and contemporary pressures, that it is time to set out some clear guidelines on how placement should fit into the total school setting and in particular into career education as it gradually becomes better established. A mistake to be avoided is to see placement as a single action or event in the life of the individual. It is part of the process of career development. In great measure the success of even the best placement efforts will depend on the events of earlier years. How well the student goes through the process of career exploration, awareness, inquiry, experience, preparation, etc., will determine how much advantage can be taken of any placement service available. The student also needs to know and understand how to go through the process of self-assessment, job search, and personal preparation—for lifetime use—not just to have someone find a job for him or her. As the old proverb goes, give a man a loaf of bread and you satisfy his hunger today, teach him to bake and he will eat forever.

The following steps should make placement a key part of career education. Here are the action elements:

1. Placement is a total school responsibility just like any other necessity in public education. It should be viewed as a vital aspect of the overall obligation American education has to each student. School authorities should move to establish programs where none exist and expand to adequate proportions where inequalities prevail. This is first of all the responsibility of a state department of education to spell out in general the standards of quality and expectations for the individual school districts to carry out.
2. Placement should be reestablished as a principal role of the counselor. This was agreed to by the National Vocational Guidance Association and the American Vocational Association in 1973. It has been a central mission for vocational guidance for over fifty years. All should quickly settle any dispute as to who has this responsibility and go about making sure counselors are well prepared to do the job and provided with the necessary time and facilities to perform the duties adequately. If further preparation is needed, then get on with it at once.
3. Placement in employment should be given immediate equity with placement in higher education. Each secondary school must provide the same resources for job assistance

through career development—both tangible and intangible—which goes into helping students get into colleges and universities. Placement for every student regardless of their post-high-school objectives should be a goal of each school.

4. Placement as a part of the process of career education should be built around a comprehensive five point plan carried out in every high school. The plan should include at least these elements:

a. Needs assessment:

finding out what the student needs with respect to placement
finding out what the employer needs with respect to placement

b. Job development:

working to get job orders from area business, industry and government
working to create community interest in the school as an immediate source of skilled employees

c. Student development:

teaching students decision-making skills
teaching comprehensive job skills in school
teaching job searching and job keeping skills

d. Placement:

helping bring together potential employees with employers
helping students with job search and job keeping skills

e. Follow-up:

providing the school with much needed evaluation data on the curriculum and guidance programs
provide an important continuing link between schools and employers

In addition, placement must be regarded as an integral part of a student's learning about the world of work. The actual process of seeking employment exposes a student to new aspects of the work environment. A great deal about occupations and the job market will be learned by the student. The placement staff also has an important responsibility to assist the student with the transition from an academic to a work environment.

Roles of Various Personnel

The wide scope of activities necessitates that all persons within the school system and the community be involved. Counselors, teachers, administrators, students, community persons, and parents are all involved in the delivery of this service.

Counselors

It is the writers' professional opinion that the counselors should be responsible for the school placement program. Others may assist in the school in placing their own students through vocational programs, but the duty of the counselor was and is to carry out the responsibility for the school's role in placement. Maximum cooperation should be expanded to the fullest with all available resources—outlined briefly in this section.

Teachers

In the classroom, teachers can work with students on direction following skills, and verbal and written communication skills. All of these are important to the student both in looking for employment and on the job. Specifically, teachers can make assignments in the area of completing applications, writing letters, and exploring the job market by reading (and writing) classified ads. Vocational teachers especially can be helpful with job contacts since they usually have excellent contacts with people in business and industry. Because of their general contacts in the community, all teachers may be a source of information about employment which they can share with the counselors in the placement office and students directly.

Administrators

The system-wide authority for a good placement program rests squarely with the superintendent. If this person is solidly behind the effort to maintain an adequate program, in all likelihood, it will be done. Administrative support is vital for budgetary assignments with time, physical resources and well-qualified professional staff. Building principals exercise the same specific leadership role in each school. They can establish priorities for the guidance program which put a premium on placement. Because central office staff and building principals have many contacts with potential employers they can assist the placement service by advocating the use of the service by employers and the importance of local employment needs and opportunities back into the schools.

Students

It is oftentimes a former student who helps a current student to find a job. It is also the former student who can help by coming back to school and sharing something of how the placement process went for them. Student-to-student help is sometimes the best kind. School placement services should make full use of this vital resource.

Parents and Community Persons

Parents, family and friends represent the best source of placement help for people of all ages—not just students. The school placement service should help students to understand what a valuable resource they have right at hand in these acquaintances. Often it is the people who know one best who can help one best—at least when it comes to placement.

In addition parents and community persons can serve a supplemental role to the school's main efforts by arranging volunteer help. The Memphis (Tennessee) Volunteer Placement Program is an outstanding example of how this is working in one large metropolitan area. In Memphis over 1,500 students in three high schools have been directly helped through school and volunteer planned college and career days as well as "job readiness" workshops and other activities. Willard Wirtz (1975), in his new book *The Boundless Resource,* calls for Community Education—Work Councils which will help schools, among other things, with placement activities.

Evaluation

Evaluation of placement services is at best difficult. One indication of the success is the return of employers for new workers in consecutive years. Another indicator is simply the number of students using the services and being placed. Feedback from employers can be solicited to find out how students are handling the employment interview and later how well they are doing on the job. A part of all programs offered should include evaluation by participants (students) as a matter of course. This may be done through exit interviews with all or a sample of all students leaving the secondary school.

The evaluation of the placement services is also, in a sense, an evaluation of the entire career education program in the school. It is therefore essential that follow-up evaluations be carried out after the student has left school and has been working for several years. A planned program of one, three, five and ten year follow-up is best. Only then is it possible to evaluate how well the student is adjusting to the world of work, how well he or she was prepared for employment, and how satisfied the student is with the decisions that were made. This type of evaluation of necessity involves longitudinal studies.

References

Buckingham, L. Job placement as a school program. *American Vocational Journal* 46 (1972):63-64.

Campbell, H. High-school placement and the central placement office. *Vocational Guidance Magazine* 3 (1925):132-34.

Cohen, I. *Principles and practices of vocational guidance.* New York: Century Co., 1929.

DeSchweinitz, D. Practical problems of the placement office. *National Vocational Guidance Association Bulletin* 1 (1923):124-28.

Flannagan, T. What ever happened to job placement. *Vocational Guidance Quarterly* 22 (1974): 209-13.

Froehlich, C. P. The service of placement. *Guidance Services in Schools.* New York: McGraw-Hill, 1958, 231-60.

Germane, C. E. and Germane, E. G. *Personnel work in high school.* New York: Silver Burdett Co., 1941.

Gray, K. Mt. Ararat finds the keystone. *American Vocational Journal* 49 (1974):33-36.

Jones, A. J. Placement. *Principles of Guidance* (3d ed.). New York: McGraw-Hill, 1945, 370-77.

McAlmon, V. The department of guidance and placement. *Vocational Guidance Magazine* 2 (1924): 176-78.

Michelotti, K. Employment of high school graduates and dropouts, 1973. *Monthly Labor Review* 97 (9) (1974):48-52.

Montgomery, T. Employment service in school counseling programs as seen by students. *School and Community* 57 Novmber (1970):294.

National Vocational Guidance Association. *Principles of vocational guidance.* Washington, D.C.: NVGA, 1924 (first adapted in 1921, then revised and adapted in 1924).

National Vocational Guidance Association—American Vocational Association. "Position paper on career development," Washington, D.C.: NVGA, 1973.

Ohlsen, M. M. Vocational placement and follow-up. *Guidance Services in the Modern School.* New York: Harcourt, Brace and World, 1964, 335-56.

Pate, R. Placement and follow-up—what role in the guidance program. *The High School Journal* 54 (1971):287-95.

Prediger, D. J., et al. *Nationwide study of student career development: summary of results* (ACT Research Report # 61). Iowa City, Iowa: The American College Testing Program, 1973.

Shertzer, B., and Stone, S. Career planning and placement service. *Fundamentals of guidance* (2d ed.). Boston: Houghton Mifflin, 1971, 373-83.

Stewart, M. Placement and follow-up as steps in the vocational guidance program. *Vocational Guidance Magazine* 2 (1924):158-62.

Tennessee, Chapter 27 of Title 49 of Tennessee Code as amended (1972) (Senate Bill 1091, House Bill No. 1203).

Virginia State Advisory Council on Vocational Education. *A study of counseling and guidance in the public secondary schools of Virginia.* Blacksburg: VSAC on Vocational Education, 1973.

Wasil, R. A. Job placement: keystone of career development. *American Vocational Journal* 49 (1974):32.

Wirtz, W. *The boundless resource.* Washington: The New Republic Book Co., 1975.

General References

Adler, K. A. *The job resume and letter of application.* Cambridge, Massachusetts: Bellman Publishing Co., 1971.

A guide to child labor provisions of the fair labor standards act. (Bulletin No. 101. U.S. Department of Labor, Employment Standards Administration, Wage and Hour Division Child Labor, Washington, D.C.: Government Printing Office, 1973.

A message to young workers about the fair labor standards act (W. H. Publication 1236). U.S. Department of Labor, Employment Standards Administration, Wage and Hour Division, Washington, D.C.: Government Printing Office, 1971.

After high school what? Nashville, Tennessee: R. L. Polk & Co., 1970.

Apprentices. Largo, Florida: Career, 1972.

Ashley and Roberts. *101 Summer Jobs.* New York: Tempo Books, Grosset and Dunlap, 1970.

Biegelson, J. I. *How to go about getting a job with a future.* New York: Grosset and Dunlap, 1967.

Blackledge, W. L.; Blackledge, E. H.; and Keily, H. J. *You and your job.* Cincinnati: South-Western Publishing Co., 1967.

Bush, D. O. *Occupational education program.* Greeley, Colorado Rocky Mountain Educational Laboratory, Inc., 1969.

Dreese, M. *How to get a job.* Chicago: Science Research Associates, 1971.

Eisen, I. *Seven steps to finding your place in the world of work.* Washington, D.C.: B'nai B'rith Vocational Service, 1971.

Employment of high school graduates and dropouts October 1973: the high school class of 1972 (Special Labor Force Report 155). U.S. Department of Labor, Bureau of Labor Statistics, Washington, D.C.: Government Printing Office, 1973.

Employment outlook: tomorrow's jobs. U.S. Department of Labor, Washington, D.C.: Government Printing Office, 1970.

Employment patterns for the 1970s. U.S. Department of Labor, Washington, D.C.: Government Printing Office, 1970.

Feingold, S., and Swerdloff, S. *Occupations and careers.* New York: McGraw-Hill, 1969.

Freitag, A. J. ed. *NVGA bibliograpy: current career information.* Washington, D.C: National Vocational Guidance Association, 1973.

Gelinas, P., and Gelinas, R. *How teenagers get good jobs.* New York: Richards Rosen Press, 1971.

Government internship programs (summer). New York: Alumnae Advisory Center, 1967.

Haight, P. *Careers after high school.* New York: Collier, 1971.

Handbook for young workers. U.S. Department of Labor, Bureau of Labor Standards, Washington, D.C.: Government Printing Office.

Handbook of job facts. Chicago: Science Research Associates, 1972.

Herr, E. *Decision making and vocational development.* Guidance Monograph Series IV. Boston: Houghton Mifflin, 1970.

———. ed. *Vocational guidance and human development.* Boston: Houghton Mifflin, 1974.

How to get the right job and keep it. Miami, Florida: Management Information Center, 1969.

Hummel, D. L. *The counselor and military service opportunities, Guidance Monograph Series VII.* Boston: Houghton Mifflin, 1973.

It's easy to hire teenagers. U.S. Department of Labor, Employment Standards Administration, Wage and Hour Division, Washington, D.C.: Government Printing Office, 1971.

Jacobson, T. J. *Knowledge needed to obtain work (Teacher/counselor guide).* Chicago: Science Research Associates, 1974.

Job training suggestions for women and girls (leaflet 40 revised). U.S. Department of Labor, Washington, D.C.: Government Printing Office, 1970.

Job seeking methods used by unemployed workers (Special Labor Force Report 150). U.S. Department of Labor, Bureau of Labor Statistics, Washington, D.C.: Government Printing Office, 1973.

Jobs for the 1970s slide series. U.S. Department of Labor, Bureau of Statistics, Washington, D.C.: Government Printing Office, 1972.

Jobs for which a high school education is generally required. U.S. Department of Labor, Washington, D.C.: Government Printing Office, 1973.

Jobs for which apprenticeship training is available. U.S. Department of Labor, Bureau of Labor Statistics, Washington, D.C.: Government Printing Office, 1968.

Jobs for which apprenticeship training is available. U.S. Department of Labor, Bureau of Labor Statistics, Washington, D.C.: Government Printing Offfice, 1968.

Jobs happen—careers don't. Arlington, Virginia: U.S. Public Health Service, 1967.

Job losers, leavers, and entrants: traits and trends (Special Labor Force Report 157). Department of Labor, Bureau of Labor Statistics, Washington, D.C.: Government Printing Office, 1973.

Kimbrell, G., and Vinegard, B. S. *Succeeding in the world of work.* Bloomington, Illinois: McKnight and McKnight Publishing Co., 1970.

King, A. F. *Help wanted: female: the young woman's guide to jobhunting.* New York: Charles Scribner's Sons, 1968.

Know your employment rights. U.S. Department of Labor, Washington, D.C.: Government Printing Office, 1970 (revised).

Lee, M. *Jobs in your future.* New York: Scholastic Book Services, 1973.

Liebers, A. *How to pass employment tests.* New York: Arco Publishing Co., 1966.

Loeb, R. H., Jr. *Manners at work: how they help you toward career success.* New York: Action Press, 1967.

Making the most of your job interview. Columbus: Ohio State Department of Education, 1968.

Manpower goals for Virginia in the 1970s. Richmond: Virginia Employment Commission.

Manpower report to the president: a report on manpower requirements, resources, utilization, and training. U.S. Department of Labor, Washington, D.C.: Government Printing Office, 1973.

McDaniels, C. *Finding your first job.* Boston: Houghton Mifflin, 1975.

———. *Leisure activities and careers.* Garret Park, Maryland: Garrett Park Press, 1974.

———. *Summer jobs: a checklist and guide for action.* Garrett Park, Maryland: Garret Park Press, 1974.

McDaniels, C., and Simutis, C. *Educational requirements for selected occupations.* Garrett Park, Maryland: Garrett Park Press, 1974.

———. *Job search pyramid: 15 steps to finding a career.* Garrett Park, Maryland: Garrett Park Press, 1974.

McKay, A. E. *The MacMillian job guide to American corporations.* New York: MacMillian, 1967.

Miller, J. V. *Intensive high school occupational guidance approaches for initial work and technical school placement.* Ann Arbor, Michigan: ERIC Clearinghouse on Counseling and Personnel Services, 1969.

The National apprenticeship program. U.S. Department of Labor, Manpower Administration, Washington, D.C.: Government Printing Office, 1972.

Navy training/civilian careers: to be someone special. United States Navy Recruiting Command, Washington, D.C., 1973.

Norton, J. L. *Sixty-five people tell what it's like on the job.* Chicago, Illinois: J. G. Ferguson, 1970.

Occupational outlook handbook (1974-75 ed., bulletin 1785). U.S. Department of Labor, Bureau of Labor Statistics, Washington, D.C.: Government Printing Office, 1974.

Parents' role in career development. Washington, D.C.: American Personnel and Guidance Association, 1970.

People and choices career folios. New York: Harcourt, Brace, Jovanovich, Inc., 1971.

Power is green. New York: I.P.D. Publishing Co., 1971.

Publications for women—self-guidance series. New York: Catalyst, 1973.

Publications for women—career opportunities series. New York: Catalyst, 1973.

Publications for women—education opportunities series. New York: Catalyst, 1973.

Reefe, J. *The teenager and the interview.* New York: Richards Rosen Press, 1971.

Service occupations. U.S. Department of Labor, Washington, D.C.: Government Printing Office, 1970.

Shertzer, B. E. *Career exploration and planning.* Boston: Houghton Mifflin, 1973.

Sinick, D. *Part-time, summer and volunteer jobs for Jewish and other minority youth.* Washington, D.C.: B'nai B'rith Vocational Services, 1970.

Skilled and other manual occupations. U.S. Department of Labor, Washington, D.C.: Government Printing Office, 1970.

Slocum, W. L. *Occupational careers.* Chicago: Aldine Publishing Co., 1974.

Splaver, S. *Careers through non-traditional education.* New York: Julian Messner, 1974.

———. *Non-traditional careers for women.* New York: Julian Messner, 1973.

———. *Your career if you're not going to college.* New York: Julian Messner, 1971.

The teachers' role in career development. Washington, D.C.: National Vocational Guidance Association.

The transition from school to work. *Princeton Manpower Symposium, May 9-10.* Princeton, New Jersey, 1968 (report).

The U.S. Labor force: projections to 1990 (Special Labor Force Report 156). U.S. Department of Labor, Bureau of Labor Statistics, Washington, D.C.: Government Printing Offfice, 1973.

Volunteers in ACTION (Action Pamphlet 4000-8). Washington, D.C.: Government Printing Office, 1973.

What students should know about interviewing. New York: General Electric Communications, 1973.

Wolfbein, S. L. and Goldstein, H. *Our world of work.* Chicago: Science Research Associates, 1970.

Working loose. San Francisco: American Friends Service Committee, 1971.

Young farm workers and the fair labor standards act. U.S. Department of Labor, Employment Standards, Admission, Wage and Hour Division, Washington, D.C.: Government Printing Office, 1971.

You're hired! Getting the right job for you. Austin, Texas: University of Texas, 1972.

Your social security (DHEW Publication no 55A-72-10035). Washington, D.C.: Government Printing Office, 1972.

Chapter 8

THE CONSULTATION AND INTERVENTION SERVICE

Johnnie H. Miles

Introduction and Historical Development

Recent emphasis on accountability and the evaluations resulting from educational research have stimulated school personnel workers to reanalyze the role of the school and their individual roles in the facilitation of human potential. All pupil personnel workers are reviewing their roles, particularly school counselors who have received considerable criticism in educational circles. It seems that the previously accepted role of the counselor as providing educational, vocational, and personal counseling is now being questioned. Criticism from the literature indicates that counselors need to expand their services, and become actively and visibly involved in the educational life-space of students and teachers (Mosher and Sprinthall, 1971; Blocher, 1966). Counselors can no longer be complacent nor remain insulated in the counseling office. They must become involved in the realities of the "total" school.

In the field of guidance and counseling there has been concern about and an impetus for a renewed emphasis in guidance. The call is for a new role definition as well as a new focus on prevention and development rather than remediation. Consultation is being viewed as the process with the greatest potential for realization of the developmental focus. Greater recognition is being given to the consultation process by researchers and practitioners in the field. However, the consulting activities being proposed are not necessarily new. Many activities of earlier counselors, although not identified as consulting, were aimed at the facilitation of student potential by encouraging school personnel to work in a cooperative and coordinated manner. The initial work of the Vocation Bureau of Boston was not primarily to undertake counseling, but was concerned with the training of teachers in the Boston schools through methods such as lectures, publications and conferences (Bedford, 1948). Eli Weaver was concerned with the youth leaving school early and giving "need to earn" money as a reason. He worked cooperatively with farms, community agencies, and industries to locate after-school, Saturday, and summer jobs for boys. His goal in the early 1900s was to keep students in school in order that they may secure broad cultural values and vocational training necessary for career building (Smith, 1948). Broadly evaluated, the two examples could be considered consultation.

A number of well-known guidance advocates have increasingly included consulting as a function of counselors. Patouillet (1968) suggested that guidance had changed from a remedial to a developmental approach and as such was concerned with the maximum develop-

Dr. Johnnie H. Miles is Assistant Professor of Counselor Education at Virginia Polytechnic Institute and State University, Blacksburg, Virginia.

ment of all pupils. He purported that all school personnel had responsibility for guidance and that the school guidance counselor should be a "consultant" in human relations who involves in a cooperative enterprise all those who affect the development of the child. Wrenn (1962) viewed consultation as being important and the medium through which the developmental needs of students could be met. In a later look at the role of counselors, Wrenn (1965) reemphasized the importance of consultation by suggesting that the "counselor may be able to help students more by providing assistance and understanding to the adults in the students' lives than by using the same amount of time with individuals or even groups of students" (p. 62). Although consulting-type activities have been occurring in schools for a long time, consultation still remains one of the least understood of the services.

Content of the Service

One of the basic issues stimulating the focus on prevention and development rather than remediation is the notion that guidance should be for all students. To provide counseling primarily whether individual or group, seriously limits the number of students who can benefit from the counselor's effort. In addition, counseling tends to focus on helping individuals cope with the school situation and the wider environment. This approach makes the assumption that those environments are conducive and that it is the individual who needs to adjust or change. Leacock (1968) indicated that school personnel should consider the sociological sources of pupil problems. As a practice, schools tend to conceptualize pupil problems as arising from the individual rather than from the societal context of the school or environment. People do not exist in a vacuum and to counsel clients while ignoring existing environmental contingencies, denies the reality of environmental influences. This approach does not suggest that people are totally influenced by their environment but it does acknowledge some environmental impact. Therefore, the recognition of environmental relationships and influences expand the intervention possibilities for assisting a client. The environment then becomes a target that can be modified or changed to allow for individual growth and development.

The notion of environmental influences on the individual is being considered more and more to have applicability to the field of education and counseling (Wrenn, 1965; Blocker, 1966; Stern, 1970; Banning, 1974). Dinkmeyer and Carlson (1973) suggested that "if school is to meet the challenge of developing creative, purposeful beings who actualize their human potential, then all aspects of the educational process must become humanized" (p. 20). Thus it is crucial that school counselors focus on clients as well as on the milieu in which they exist and that both be considered targets for intervention.

Consultation Defined

Consultation describes a number of relationships within and outside of educational settings. The consultation relationship is a voluntary relationship between a professional helper (consultant) and help-needing system (client) in which the consultant is attempting to give help to the client in the solving of some current or potential problem, and the relationship is perceived as temporary by both parties. Also, the consultant is an "outsider," i.e., is not a part of any hierarchial power system in which the client is located (Lippitt, 1959; p. 5). An implication from this definition is that the consultant is an outsider. The focus of the consultant as an outsider is not the view considered in this chapter. The financial situation of most educational institutions is such that funds are usually not available for hiring temporary personnel. As a result, needed services will have to be provided through presently existing staff.

In this chapter, consultation is viewed as a natural extension of the role of the counselor, an already identifiable member of the school system. The terms counselor and consultant will be used interchangeably in this chapter. Counselors functioning as internal consultants, are more likely to be accepted and have credibility guaranteed by their organizational status. In their discussion of an internal consultant, Dinkmeyer and Carlson (1973), state that "the type of professional identity we are suggesting, then, is one that is concerned and involved with the total school process. The consultant is not an ancillary or auxiliary service. He is in the mainstream of the educational endeavor, involved with the total environment and school milieu" (p. 20). Consultants provide service to all persons in the educational environment—administrators, teachers, specialists, parents, and children. As their major function, they participate in decision making regarding the most effective way to enhance the learning process for children.

Other implications from the definition by Lippitt are consistent with the 1966 report made to the American Personnel and Guidance Association on the role of elementary counselors, by a committee appointed jointly from the Association for Counselor Education and Supervision (ACES) and the American School Counselor Association (ASCA). The committee concluded that "counselors will have three major responsibilities: counseling, consultation, and coordination." Although this particular study was geared to the elementary level, it put into a conceptual framework the activities that were being performed by secondary school counselors as well. The role and functions of secondary school counselors were formulated by ASCA (1964) but the policy statement appeared not to be as concise, nor as flexible as the elementary model.

The ACES-ASCA Committee (1966) defined consultation as the process of sharing with another or group of persons information and ideas, of combining knowledge into new patterns, and of making mutually agreed upon decisions about the next step needed. Consultation denotes collaborative participation between significant others within a client system for the purpose of planned change on the behalf of a client. Broadly conceived, consultation is an approach to helping those persons (parents, teachers, administrators) who have some responsibility for students, facilitate students' development. This process may involve coordinating along with planning, designing and implementing new services to meet students' needs.

The three aspects of this definition, if taken separately, will help in the clarification of the consulting process. The first aspect of the definition, "the process of sharing with another person or group of persons information and ideas," identifies the nature of the consulting relationship. Consultation is a way of sharing information with another person for the purpose of decision making. Wrenn (1962) identified the other persons in the relationship to be significant adults within and outside of the school. These significant adults are considered to be teachers, parents, administrators and community persons and are labeled consultees when in the consulting relationship. The counselor and consultees work in a collaborative relationship, each contributing relevant information about a client who is generally external to the relationship. The client is considered to be an individual, a class, a family, or any other functioning unit.

The second factor, "of combining knowledge into patterns," refers to the process of synthesizing available information into a holistic picture. This process allows the counselor and the consultee to see the client in an ecological context. It may necessitate, in some cases, bringing together all those individuals who have access to pertinent information about the client including the consultee. It is within this type of context that the developmental needs of the client are best identified.

The third factor, "of making mutually agreed upon decisions about the next step needed," is the action-oriented aspect of the definition. Two major ideas emerge here: (1) there is mutual or reciprocal involvement of counselor and consultees and (2) a decision or action is determined. The consultation relationship is not the traditional "expert-helpee" relationship where the consultant tells the consultee what should be done. This is not intended to indicate that the counselor is not recognized as one having special skills and expertise. The counselor enters the system having had specialized training different from other professionals within the school. However, teachers, administrators, parents and other personnel are viewed as professionals in their own right with specialized skills in their areas of concentration which is recognized by the consultant. Consultation instead becomes a collaborative effort on the part of all those individuals involved. It becomes a way of capitalizing on the strengths of all available resources within the system. Decisions on the next step are also determined collaboratively, but the final action is left to the consultee to implement.

One may note that in the consulting relationship the client, the major beneficiary, is not directly involved. The counselor and significant others are working together to create the kind of milieu that will facilitate the client's optimal development. Consultation then denotes primarily an indirect approach to resolution of client problems.

In addition to the role of the counselor as a consultant, the counselor has responsibility for counseling and coordination. Oftentimes confusion exists when attempts are made to clearly differentiate among these role functions of the counselor. The following section seeks to bring attention to some of the areas of similarities and differences between the three functions.

Consulting and Counseling Differentiated

Counseling is defined by Hutchins (see chapter 3) as a process in which a trained professional utilizes appropriate resources to assist in the client's development according to mutually agreeable guidelines. Counseling is conceived as a process, initiated by the client, in which the counselor and client work together with the focus of their interaction being the client. Counseling may occur in a one-to-one or small group interaction. The client's self-understanding and decision making are the primary goals and the client is the major recipient of the collaborative effort. Counseling is a method of direct intervention in that the counselor is involved in the relationship with the client and works directly toward change in the client's behavior that is mutually desired.

Counseling is differentiated from consulting in two main ways: (1) counseling is a direct approach to problem solving in which the client is intimately involved while consulting is a more indirect approach involving significant others rather than the client (see fig. 8.1); and (2) the relationship, in counseling, between the counselor and the client focuses on internal variables of the client whereas consulting focuses on variables of the client and his environment that are external to the relationship between counselor and consultee. McGehearty (1969) indicated that perhaps the greatest difference between the two strategies is in the manner in which they are in-

COUNSELING

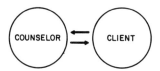

CONSULTATION

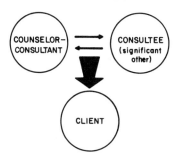

Figure 8.1. Counseling differentiated from consultation.

itiated. In counseling, the client usually initiates the contact and in consulation the contact is generally made by someone other than the client. These assumptions are but few of a variety of other differences regarding the nature of the consulting activity (Faust, 1968; Kaczkowski, 1967; and Dinkmeyer and Caldwell, 1970).

Consulting and Coordination Differentiated

Coordination is the method used to integrate all the guidance services and activities within a school program. The counselor, as coordinator, would organize all efforts to avoid duplication by school and related community personnel so that resources can be optimally utilized. Scheduling is one of the major coordination functions. Planning and developing programs in areas of need are also involved. Coordination is viewed as necessary if a guidance program is to operate smoothly.

The differentiation between coordination and consultation is not an easy task to accomplish. Both functions are related in that they emphasize making services available to all. A major difference between the two would be that coordination is primarily managing and organizing with some limited planning while consultation focuses more on planning and implementing with some management oriented aspects. It is to be noted that the two functions are more alike than different especially when the concern is bringing together available resources to meet student needs. On the other hand, coordination is an organizational strategy which is more administratively oriented as opposed to the service orientations of consulting and counseling.

Consultation in this chapter will include some programmatic aspects that might be considered coordination. The problem of differentiation is due both to the extreme difficulty of separating the two functions and to the broadened concept of consultation.

Although care has been taken to differentiate consulting from counseling and consulting from coordination, it is not meant to indicate a lack of relationship. In fact, the three functions complement each other and are highly interrelated. All three are needed to plan, develop and implement a meaningful pattern of guidance services within a client system.

Consulting: The Process

The rationale for consulting is based on the belief that counselors are accountable to the whole client system and that to facilitate the development of all individuals the environment must be conducive to healthy growth. From the view of consultation, then, the professional goal becomes that of helping to create and maintain learning environments in homes, schools, and communities that will nurture the optimal development of every student. As a result, consulting has become an active practice of school counselors that seeks to assist institutions to tune in to the developmental needs of students.

The actual consultation process is similar to the counseling process in that it follows a plan of action and is aimed at eventual change in clients' behavior. Counseling and consultation are both helping relationships or intervention strategies but they differ in focus, goal setting, and implementation. Consultation generally involves a series of stages which are interrelated and interdependent. These stages are basically the same as those found in counseling. However, a discussion of the stages reveals the differences in the processes beginning at stage two. Although there are differences, if consultation is to work, it must be based upon the same facilitative human interpersonal skills as counseling—empathy, respect, and open communication. The stages are:

1. developing a sense of need for change
2. initiation of the relationship
3. establishment of a helping relationship
4. conceptualization of the client's problem
5. examining alternative solutions
6. determining the "next step"
7. implementation
8. follow-up and evaluation

In the *first stage,* the consultee observes the milieu and perceives the need for change. The needs may vary significantly dependent upon the nature of the relationship between the consultee and the client and the nature of the problem. Generally speaking, individuals seek consulting because their life situation with the client is unsatisfactory in some way. They are seeking resolution of some circumstances whether it is internal or external to the self. They want the situation changed in some way and the expectation is that the change will be an improvement over what presently exists.

The *second stage,* initiation and establishment of a helping relationship, is approached by individuals in different ways because not all individuals have developed the same degree of skills and openness required to seek help. Consultation is initiated by consultees rather than by clients. Locating the person to provide the assistance is generally a simple task in most schools because there are only a few staff identified to provide such assistance.

Kaczkowski (1967) suggests that "several conditions must be present in order for one to seek help from a counselor: (1) the counselor must be seen as a person capable of giving help, (2) the school district must have both an explicit and implicit policy that it is both right and proper for school personnel to express themselves on a variety of topics without fear of being penalized, and (3) the principal must accept each staff member and respect his worth" (p. 131). Counselors, then, have to make themselves visible in the school by meeting teachers, parents, and students and opening channels of communication. In essence, the role of counselors must be to "sell" the idea of consultation to the potential consultees in the schools. Members of the school community must realize that the consultant is not an evaluator nor an authority, but one who is interested in and willing to become an advocate of all individuals within the school environment.

Although counselors, as consultants, plan to function out of a preventive or developmental model, they may have to initially respond to crisis requests from consultees in order to build a strong consulting service. In addition, some continual limited crisis intervention may always be necessary. The consultant would want to maintain a flexible schedule which will allow for open accessibility to the consultation service.

Consulting cannot be meaningful unless those who need help feel comfortable with the person giving help. To facilitate stage two and to provide a smooth transition for stage three, the counselor should respond to the consultee with empathy, respect, and openness the same as one would approach a client in the counseling process.

The consultant should use all the interpersonal dimensions and techniques necessary for establishing a helping relationship. However, if consultation is the goal, the focus should remain as much as possible on the client rather than on the personness of the consultee. In order to help the consultee feel less threatened and to encourage collaboration, the consultant focuses in on the consultee, by actively listening, attending, and responding in order to facilitate the consultee's information sharing about the client. For example, if a teacher were to approach the consultant for assistance with misbehaving students in her class, the consultant would actively work to make the teacher feel at ease in the relationship. The discussion will generally concentrate more on client behaviors than on the teacher's feelings. However, a part of understanding the consultee-client interaction may involve exploration of feelings about the situation.

Stage three is the information sharing phase in which consultees describe their perceptions of the client and the interactional field of forces. The consultant focuses on the relationship between the consultee and the client and on the client's problems. The consultant assists the consultee in structuring the data into relevant combinations and in clarifying the client's problem in as specific a manner as possible, taking into consideration individual client differences and needs. It may be necessary for the consultant to seek information from other sources and/or collect firsthand data through observation. Consultants avoid providing quick answers and advice giving as they assist consultees to recognize and strengthen their ability to formulate the client's problems. The consultee is to remain aware that the consultant will not make an independent decision on what to do about the client.

The *fourth stage* in the process is examining alternative solutions to the problem. The potential solutions result from mutual collaboration between the consultee and the consultant. The solutions take into consideration the client's problems, and the interactions between them. Creative thinking can be utilized in this phase to identify all possible ways which the problems of the client can be handled.

Stage five, determining the "next step," is the reality oriented stage. Determining the next step or the action to be implemented must take into consideration the realities of the situation, for what is possible is dependent on that situation and the environmental conditions in existence. Several important facets to consider are (1) the consultee's readiness to change, (2) the complexity of the goals set (goals should be specific, manageable, and short-term), (3) the consultee's expertise to perform the selected task, and (4) the conditions within the milieu which will have to be manipulated or controlled. If some approach is needed to resolve the client's problem that is outside the realm of expertise of the consultee, the consultant may provide the training needed by the consultee. Other alternatives such as the consultant performing the task within the milieu or seeking some other referral resource to provide the service are possible.

The *sixth step* involves putting into action the plan that was devised in step five. The consultee will implement the plan within the normal milieu of the client. This stage involves manipulation of people or things within the milieu to elicit a different response from the client. Teachers may change their behavior toward the client, may modify the classroom climate, or may alter instructional procedures in order to meet client needs and at the same time change client behavior. The overall goal is to create the type of milieu in which the client can make steps toward positive growth and development. The consultant does not terminate the consultee at this time but provides support and maintains contact throughout the implementation stage. The consultees, as a result, strengthen their problem-solving ability and feel more competent that there is a possiblity of bringing about change. In addition, the consultee is in a position to use the skills in the future to prevent client problems.

The *final stage,* "follow-up and evaluation," determines whether the consulting effort was appropriate. The needs of the client and the consultee, as well as the appropriateness of the plan for that milieu may be evaluated to make this determination. The feedback received on the process can be utilized to reformulate or refine the process for future use. Feedback also provides information on the effectiveness of the consultant. However, due to the unique nature of each consulting request, there is no general solution to all problems, but the techniques and strategies can be made more effective.

In summary, this section outlined the nature of the consultation process. Throughout the seven stages it was evident that consultation was putting counseling skills to use with consultees for developing understandings about client problems and to elicit commitment to new approaches and new relationships. The similarities and differences between counseling and coordination were highlighted. It was evident that consulting, like counseling, considered both the client's individual differences and needs. However, consulting utilized more the milieu or natural environment for creating growth possibilities for clients rather than utilizing the artificial environment of the counseling office.

Who Initiates the Consulting Process?

Consultation may be initiated in two basic ways: (1) consultee-initiated, and (2) consultant initiated. Consultee-initiated relationships usually result from some perceived need for change within the consultee's environment. The perceived need generally focuses on external concerns. Teachers, for example, may want to find out how to incorporate some specific technique in the instructional program such as career planning or decision making. Parents may seek help in determining how to encourage their child to study. Students may approach the counselor-consultant for assistance in changing some environmental influence which is blocking their development. Administrators may wish to determine student concerns about school regulations. Whatever the relationship, the consultant enters into it with the same basic goal—that of creating facilitative climates for student development. Consultants are system advocates and as a result must work with, through, and for all groups.

The second procedure—counselor initiation of the consulting process—involves the counselor taking the first step and intervening in an already functioning unit. This situation occurs when the counselor recognizes elements in need of change that have not been identified by other members within the unit and when some type of modification of the milieu is needed to enhance the counseling process. In the first situation, counselors may observe some students whose needs are not being met. Through the establishment of relationships with the significant others involved, change can be initiated. This change can take place successfully only when significant individuals recognize the effect the environment has on students, and this recognition may result from mutual information-sharing.

Occasionally the counselor needs the cooperation from significant others in order to further the counseling process. The cooperation needed may involve modifications in the environment to alleviate forces that impede the client's progress. This may be in the form of changing the client's class schedule, bedtime or curfew hours, or involvement in specific extracurricular activities. The counseling process is usually sufficient to bring about client change but sometimes needs environmental reinforcement in order to maintain the change. In the event significant others do not cooperate, then counseling is continued with the client and additional help is sought in other areas.

To initiate change requires that counselors know the organization in which they are a part and have high visibility along with a good reputation within the system. This approach does not give the counselor a free hand to initiate change independently. It does, however, indicate that counselors with established relationships with other system members can "act" collaboratively on the milieu to bring about changes. The major concern is not who initiates the relationship, but that it is initiated. Regardless of the initiating impetus the consulting process is the same and the final action is still dependent upon the consultee.

Consultation, as has been descibed, can operate effectively in a system where there is an atmosphere of trust. The consultation process can help build this trust through interaction with administrators, teachers, parents and students. Consultation can provide the avenue through which the guidance functions are integrated into the total life space of the client. To do so, consultation must focus on the unique needs and problems of the groups previously mentioned. The nature of the consulting relationship may be slightly altered due to the needs of the specific groups.

Consulting with Administrators

Administrative support is crucial to the work of the consultant. The establishment of the counselor as a legitimate professional within the organizational structure is due partly to support of administrators. As a result, the degree of collaboration between the administrators and counselors determine the kind of climate in which they must operate.

Research studies conducted with school principals indicated that consultation was considered by them to be a vital function of counselors (Smith and Eckerson, 1966). However, there seems to be a discrepancy between the research results and what occurs in practice. Often the work of the counselor with students is limited due to extraneous duties imposed on them in various schools. Consultation with administrators, must as a priority, involve developing an understanding of what the role and function of counselors should be. Counselors should also seek to obtain administrative support for appropriate facilities and funds. Consultants should impress upon administrators their desire to help them achieve the school's objectives for growth and development of pupils, at the same time impressing upon them the need for cooperation of every staff member.

The counselor as consultant would seek to develop administrative support from administrators for intervention and change in that administrators have responsibilities for schoolwide changes. Consultants would seek cooperation from administrators and others to design and implement in-service training for teachers by providing time for such training. In addition, there must be agreement on operational matters regarding the amount of time that would be provided for teacher in-service, and the counselor's relationship with others in the school, especially for the counselor in the role of consultant. If working with teachers is discouraged, then the role of consultant to the system is rendered ineffective. Administrators must demonstrate their full support of the consultant's work in actions and attitudes because teachers, parents, and students often take their cue from administrators on whether to support or ignore the guidance program.

Consultants discuss with administrators school policies and instructional practices and how they affect human development within the system. Concern is focused on system impact on both students and teachers. The consultant's role in this process may necessitate working closely with the Curriculum Committee, preferably as a full member of the committee. Consultants do not attempt to be specialists in content areas, although most have had teacher training. They do, however, share information regarding the developmental patterns and the dynamics of human behavior and their effect on curriculum development. Involvement on the curriculum committee can be the means to integrating guidance into the curriculum.

Consultation with Teachers

Consultation with teachers is high on the list of priorities within the school system. It has been noted that the teacher is central to the educational process and probably the most important member of the counseling team outside the counselor (Halpern, 1964). Faust (1968) implied that working with teachers is more economically feasible than working with students. He stated that. . .

> One teacher who is maximally effective in the learning process affects perhaps thirty children a year. That is, working with one teacher can effectively free thirty children to learn. Both the economics and the humaneness of this are obvious. One hour of work with an individual teacher can be worth thirty hours of child-counseling time. Even more, the same teacher can the following year take his gains to thirty more children. The teacher can be expected to remain in the profession for perhaps ten or thirty years. The individual teacher who can significantly alter his behavior as a result of work with the counselor may then assist the freeing of perhaps 300 to 1,000 children to learn. Work with one teacher can then be 300 to 1,000 times more economical than working with one child in a crisis situation (p. 118).

Faust suggests that work with groups of teachers further extends the possibilities for children to operate within effective learning climates. The goal of work with teachers would be to make the staff more assertive in responding to needs of students in a school setting.

Counselors work with teachers on an individual and group basis. However, due to time limitations and the advantages derived from social interaction, the group approach is deemed most feasible. The consultant seeks to provide assistance to teachers on two levels: (1) help with individual or group of students, and (2) providing in-service education.

Teachers may seek the help of consultants about an individual student or a group of students who may be disrupting the instructional process or who for some reason do not appear to be benefitting from the program. In this situation, teachers are assisted to develop a course of action that will help students operate successfully in the class. The consultant may be asked to observe the class in operation to help the teacher collect data needed to isolate contributing conditions. The consultant and teacher then determine a course of action to be taken by the teacher in the classroom. To complete this process it may require bringing together all the significant others in the life of the client in a case conference.

The in-service approach can play a major role in the development of teachers. Through in-service programs, teachers may improve previously developed skills and learn new skills which may be needed to accomplish their goal. The in-service should be continuous (above and beyond the professional education courses taken by individual staff members) and should be related to the goals and needs of a particular school system and its students and teachers. The overall plan for in-service, although unique to each school system, will probably show some similarities in programming. Topics usually concentrate on areas of concern such as individual difference, diagnosis in the classroom, career development, career education, discipline, parent involvement, use of appraisal data, classroom guidance, and many others.

In-service training is often the responsibility of the central office staff in most systems. Counselors may work collaboratively with that staff to develop programs to meet the needs peculiar to their schools. Teachers can also be instrumental in determining the nature of in-service by sharing their concerns with the counselor and by volunteering to participate in the planning.

The concept of "in-service" is preventive and developmental in nature. However, it can also serve a remedial function by incorporating specific information that is needed by persons experiencing some difficulty. Teachers sometimes seek consulting when they have access to the information needed to solve the problem but lack the skill in transferring the knowledge into practice. Therefore, the plan for in-service should be information and skill oriented.

In-service training needs to provide experiences that help teachers integrate their attitudes, perceptions, feelings and values with skill and knowledge into a workable instructional methodology. Research results are indicating more and more that it is not the knowledge and method of teaching that distinguish effective teachers from ineffective teachers (Ellena, Stevenson and Webb, 1961). There are results surfacing which indicate that effectiveness is influenced by the degree to which the teacher can be open, genuine, accepting, flexible and can communicate these interpersonal dimensions to others (Berenson and Carkhuff, 1967; and Combs, et al., 1969). Experiences through small groups open avenues for this type of self-development that usually does not occur in large groups.

A technique known as the "C"-Group, developed by Dinkmeyer (1971), is an approach that can provide for self-development of teachers. The model helps teachers to clarify their thinking about children and helps them to understand the relationship between teachers' beliefs, attitudes, and behavior and the beliefs, attitudes and behavior of students. The approach also seeks to develop better relationships among staff members while eliciting commitment to change. The "C" represents collaboration, consultation, clarification, confrontation, communication, concern and caring, confidentiality, commitment, change, and cohesion. The "C"-Group can provide the experience needed to personalize the information received through lectures and discussions in the in-service training program.

Another approach, Teacher Effectiveness Training (Gordon, 1974), provides an opportunity for teachers to develop other special competencies. Teacher Effectiveness Training (TET) is a twenty-four hour course designed to develop skills in active listening, sending I-Messages to communicate one's feelings about another's behavior, and problem solving so nobody loses. These skills, along with others from the course, make it possible for teachers to facilitate student development in a learning environment without the use of power. TET helps teachers develop empathic understanding, flexibility, and openness which according to Berenson and Carkhuff (1967) are the skills needed to facilitate growth.

Consultation with Students

Consulting with students may be either developmental or crisis-oriented. Students at different levels will require varying sorts of information and skills and developmental consulting concentrates on providing the kinds of information and skill needed through group guidance or related activities. Providing the information that students need and assisting them in applying it to facilitate their development is one of the basic functions of the counselor. Students at advanced levels become more interested in and able to interact and influence their environment. Consulting contributes to this process by assisting students to develop the leadership skills needed to participate democratically in the educational enterprise. Students are the individuals who can provide firsthand feedback about the impact of education on their lives and are willing to respond if the mechanism for open communication is established.

Consulting is available to groups of students on a crisis oriented basis when there are specific difficulties and needs which require more involved assistance. The relationship is initiated and the consulting progress is activated through the established stages.

The counselor should be accessible to students and make efforts to maintain close contact with them. Serving as a liaison between students, the administration, and instructional staff is one way to keep the flow of information moving, thereby increasing the possibility for prevention of milieu problems.

Consultation with Parents

Faust (1968) ranked the school and community personnel with whom the counselor-consultant works and the order described presented teachers as being the major recipients of the counselor's work and parents as being seventh on the list. The author agrees with Faust about work with teachers taking priority especially when attempting to build effective learning climates in schools but questions the lack of priority given to parent consulting. Faust apparently recognizes the benefit that could accrue from parent consulting but views it as an ineffective approach. He states that "when the counselor's major objective is to assist in building whole new worlds for children to live in through the school year, when he places major emphases on building new, effective learning climates for children, certain critical implications become obvious for his hierarchy of roles. Chief among these is the uneconomical and unrealistic character of attempting to invest much more than some 5 percent of his professional time and energy with parents. Parent counseling is uneconomical since there simply are not enough counseling hours available to undertake it. In order to conduct parent counseling on a dimension that would effectively reach a number of parents, we would have to present the taxpayer with an exorbitant bill" (p. 82). It is the author's premise that without some support from the environment (home and community) in which children spend most of their time, much of what is done in the "effective learning school climates" will be significantly wiped out.

The 1970 White House Conference on Children and Youth served to alert educators and citizens to the responsibility of the family unit as the first educational delivery system for the child. Funds have subsequently been expended in support of programs that are geared toward assisting the parents and family to recognize and provide for this responsibility. Educators, however, continue to demonstrate minimal awareness of their role in assisting families to meet the challenges of the future.

Recent research has focused on the involvement of the family in programs aimed at assisting in the development of children. These programs are increasing in number and the research results indicate that gains from interventions with families have more lasting effects than when the family is not involved. Gilmore (1971) agreed with involving parents in helping children. He asserted that parents, through parent counseling, could improve the home environment and make it more accepting, supporting, and nurturant. He further asserted that a secure and esteeming "total environment" was needed to enable a child to be productive and to make choices in a positive direction.

Love (1972) demonstrated clearly that intervention focused on parents was more effective in improving school performance of children than was individual psychotherapy. Taylor and Hoedt (1974) compared the effects of group counseling with significant adults (parents and teachers) to group counseling with elementary school children for reducing classroom behavior problems and found similar results. Their results revealed that indirect intervention or counseling with significant adults was more effective in reducing teacher-perceived classroom behavior problems than direct intervention with children. These and other results seem to indicate that working with parents and teachers is an approach worth consideration.

Counselors have recognized the importance of working with teachers but have seemingly neglected work with parents. It is important that work with parents be given more importance in a list of priorities, possibly third, having work with teachers and students within the school take first and second place respectively, particularly at the elementary and middle school levels. Not only does this approach broaden the potential "effective environments" for pupils but it decreases the potential for negation of the accomplishments of the schools.

Consultation with parents, often a responsibility of teachers, provides an opportunity for counselors and teachers and other pupil personnel specialists to work together and collaboratively with parents. If coordinated properly, school personnel can supplement each other's work with parents, increasing the efficiency of parent contacts.

Reactive Consulting

Parent consultation usually occurs when school personnel are seeking the support of parents in an intervention strategy prescribed for their child, and/or secondly to seek information about children to help in better understanding them. Often consultation is initiated in response to a crisis situation. Faust (1968) identified five basic kinds of parent consultation that usually are responses to crisis situations. They are:

1. Consultation with parents may be undertaken in order to collect data for increasing the consultant's own understanding of the child.
2. Consultation with parents may be designed for the purpose of interpreting the child to the parents.
3. Consultations with parents may be exercised in an effort to effect certain limited remedial measures in regard to their relationships with the child.
4. Parent consultation may be undertaken in a program that facilitates positive parent-school relationships where such relationships may have become impaired or where impairment could be expected to occur.
5. Parent consultation may consist of no more than an effort to obtain permission from parents to place their child in counseling with the school's counselor or some outside agency (p. 87).

In crisis situations, the counselor-consultants must be extremely cautious for they are likely to be viewed by parents as a threat, especially since school personnel traditionally do not meet with parents at any other time. Parents should be accepted and not criticized, and made to feel comfortable at the onset of consultation. The establishment of a good working relationship is necessary if effective consultation is to take place. The counselor-consultant should enlist the help of the parents in activities that will be of value to the child. Parents are generally interested in their children and are willing to cooperate in an effort to meet their needs. Once parents have agreed to participate in a continuance of the consultation, the rest of the procedure is the same as that described earlier in the chapter.

Counselor-consultants, in order to have some impact in a preventive or developmental manner, cannot respond in crisis situations only. They must take responsibility for acting on the environment and meeting needs of parents in ways which would have carry-over benefits for pupils.

Proactive Consulting

Parents of children who have social or academic difficulties often seek help from others, such as teachers or counselors, in dealing with the child's problems. Often these parents feel inadequate and view other professionals as having skills they lack in handling such problems. In order to assist parents in becoming more proficient, and to remain independent, counselors need to help parents develop the skills needed for working with their children. As a result, consulting might extend into parent education. Programs may be developed that help parents learn about their children's behavior and needs. The goal of consulting in this approach is to increase the ability of parents to function effectively with children. Several such approaches will be briefly discussed here:

Parent-Conference. The parent-conference allows the consultant to solicit information about the special interests, abilities, or problems of a child which parents have opportunities to observe. Consultants can also share information with parents about their children and their patterns of development in school. The acquisition of such information mutually helps parents and counselors better understand the child. This type of approach usually is handled by teachers in their consulting role but may be handled by counselors. It certainly is an area in which teachers and counselors can work together.

Parent Discussion Groups and Child Study Groups. These two approaches are similar in orientation. These groups provide opportunities for parents to explore specific issues or problems, to attain an understanding of the developmental stages their children are in, and how these stages may influence the family and the educational process in school. Parents, in a group atmosphere of trust, share their expectations, aspirations and knowledge of their children which can serve three basic purposes: (1) help parents better understand their children, (2) help other parents better conceptualize the problems of their children by realizing that certain behaviors and problems of children are universal, and (3) provide knowledge about children that the consultant can use in planning particular programs in school to meet student needs. The groups allow parents to develop an awareness of school and community resources available to help them and their children. In addition, parents try out new behaviors within the group in a supportive climate.

More in-depth but related parent education programs have emerged in recent years, many of which are possibilities for use in this area. Parent Effectiveness Training (Gordon, 1970), Fullmer's Family Group Consultation (Fullmer, 1972), Transactional Analysis (Harris, 1969), Adlerian Family Counseling (Dreikurs, 1964), Conjoint Family Therapy (Satir, 1967), Behavioral Consulting (Mayer, 1972), and the C-Group (Dinkmeyer, 1973) are some of the currently popular approaches for working with parents and families. The counselor will probably not be trained to conduct all the above programs but should have expertise in at least one approach. However, counselors can through program planning and coordination, locate available resources to conduct the training.

Study groups allow the counselor another opportunity to interpret the school's program to parents. Parents are generally eager to learn of new programs being developed in the schools as well as about the way in which regular programs are designed and carried out. It is through information sharing sessions such as these that parents begin to develop an understanding of and a commitment to school programs.

In summary, consulting with parents can be productive in that it provides an opportunity for parents and school personnel to work together toward improving the life situation for the child. Consulting through parent education helps parents achieve new parenting skills which in turn facilitates the child's development.

Consultation with Special Needs Groups

A number of groups exist within the school which may be considered to have special needs. Included in this category are groups of minority students, handicapped, disadvantaged, females, and a variety of other exceptional students. These groups of students will need assistance from guidance that is more dynamic and more intense than the guidance given to more advantaged students.

It has been apparent that for some special needs students the school environment has not been equipped to deal with their individual and group needs. It has also been evident that conditions within the environment in many cases have contributed to and caused the problems of these students. The counselor, through consultation, must work directly with teachers, parents, school administrators, and support personnel to create school climates that will maximize the possibilities for effective development of special needs students.

Special needs students have been discouraged by the reaction of the school and will need support and positive feedback in order to be productive individuals. They need an advocate to help them develop a positive concept of self and the influence skills needed to sensitize the environment to their concerns. To perform these tasks, consultants must assess the multiple and difficult socio-academic problems of special needs students. They must be aware of the successes and failures of special needs students in coping with their problems. Consultants must also be able to understand the students, their problems, the forces complicating those problems, and the need for intervention on their behalf.

Consultation on behalf of these students may involve a variety of individuals and activities. Consultation with administrators, for example, may involve identifying the special needs of the physically handicapped and requesting modification of school facilities to better meet their needs. Consulting with teachers may focus on creating the kind of teacher attitude and classroom climate that would be conducive to minority students (Atlas, 1975). There are times when consultants may have to serve as mediators between special needs students and administrators, teachers, and other students.

Consultants should work with special needs students to encourage their participation in planning and implementation of programs that have relevance for their needs and experiences. The consultant, in order to be effective for special students, is forced to function as a change agent in an active, dynamic fashion.

Consultation with Community Persons

All too often educators focus their work on the school and the home and avoid the wider community. Many of the contingent situations that exist for families and schools result from influences in the community and could be resolved by resources available in the community. As a result working with the community through a planned sequence of events would be highly recommended.

The counselor can be instrumental, in cooperation with the administration, in educating citizens about the goals of the school. Through a series of school-community discussion groups, community persons can learn about the curriculum at all levels, staffing patterns and problems, the developing students and their needs, as well as about the costs of the educational process to which they are contributing. At the same time, efforts should be made to increase community-wide involvement. Citizens should be invited to participate in the school and given an opportunity to plan and organize the ways in which they can be involved.

The counselor, in an attempt to expand guidance services beyond the school's walls, can serve as a liason between the community and the school. The consultant must identify first the needs of students and secondly the availability of relevant resources within the community. Once identified, consultants can proceed to enlist the cooperation of the school and community in providing the services and experiences for student development. Open lines of communication are fundamental to success of this type of endeavor.

Individuals within the community can be instrumental in the process of evaluation. However, the society's expectations of guidance workers and goals are not necessarily the same as the goals of guidance workers (Ginzberg, 1971). Consultants may seek to inform the public about the objectives of the guidance program through school-community discussion groups to alleviate any discrepancies that might exist.

Summary

Essentially, then, consulting is a process through which the counselor can provide service to individuals within the total system in a capacity above and beyond counseling. The relationship is collaborative and emphasizes mutual participation and problem solving by significant others for the benefit of the client. This process focuses on change in the milieu through the creative resources of teachers, administrators, parents and students.

Contribution of Consultation to Career Education and Career Development

Facilitating the career development of youth is a phenomenal task which cannot conceivably be accomplished by counselors alone. Career development activities should be infused throughout all the school experiences from orientation to instructional methodology. Promoting career development requires that attention be devoted to the process by the total staff—teachers, counselors, school psychologists, administrators, and school social workers along with parents and community persons. No attempt will be made to describe the unique contributions made by these other team members. However, it is important that each member of the team be recognized as playing a significant role in career development in their own way that is equal to and supportive of the contribution made by the counselor.

The counselor is in a unique position to contribute to the career development of students through the regular consultative activities. Unlike other pupil personnel workers, counselors are school-based which allows them to have firsthand knowledge of and experience with the total system. The counselor's role in human and career development has been described in detail in several chapters of this text. The authors have mentioned the role of the counselor in career development through the various guidance services such as individual counseling, group counseling, information service, appraisal, placement, and follow-up which will not be duplicated here, even though consulting is often viewed as extending the guidance services to the total system. The counselor's role in initiating and coordinating the career development program will be considered in this section.

In some communities, much of the planning, coordinating, and promoting of guidance and career development is left to counselors. They serve, like administrators, as representatives of the school to the community and can do much to assist students by promoting school-community-industry-business cooperation. Counselors can discuss the policies and programs of the school with community groups while focusing specifically on career education and career development.

In most schools, members of the staff are already performing tasks and activities that are career development oriented. Teachers are including units on career education or career development; school psychologists are providing information that students may use in career decision making; and principals are sharing information with parents about career education. Counselors can organize the existing efforts within and outside of school, into a pattern of activities with specified goals and delivery systems that make the programs available to all students. Once the activities are organized, consultants can identify additional areas of need that are not being met. Counselors then have the basis for planning and initiating, along with other interested individuals, the programs needed.

Planning the content of career development programs is a joint process among teachers, students, and counselors for in-school programs and among counselors and interested individuals in the community for out-of-school programs. In order for the content to be important and relevant to participants, they must be involved in the planning. Counselors may gain additional information for planning from system and community needs assessment.

A major factor in promoting career development involves the degree to which counselors can build cooperative relationships with significant adults. It is through open communication with teachers and others that gives meaning to guidance services and prevents it from becoming tangential and isolated. Teachers' importance in this process has been previously spelled out in earlier sections. Their cooperation in planning, promoting, and evaluating services is essential. Special effort should be exerted in establishing cooperative relationships with vocational teachers for they perform routine activities daily with potential value for career development. They also have information to share with teachers of other academic subjects about the selection, training, and placement needs of students. Counselors can maximize these relationships through in-service education and training in career development. Effective working relationships are essential if career development is to become an integral part of the educational process.

Consultants who work primarily with individual teachers to improve selected climates limit their impact to a few students. To achieve a high level of involvement, consultants must work beyond the crisis-intervention stage. The greatest impact for career development can be realized more fully through the curriculum. It is through curricular offerings that career development information and new instructional ideas become accessible to all students. Counselors should be full members of the curriculum committee and should encourage opening the committee to parents or other community persons and students so they, too, can participate in curriculum development.

Guidance consultants have access to data about students, (abilities, interests, goals, etc.), faculty, and community needs which they can bring to the curriculum committee. They also come equipped with information about human development, learning, career education and career development which can be shared with the committee. They can use their skill in feedback and other strategies to initiate change in curricula offerings and instructional methodologies.

The consultant is called upon to perform numerous tasks. Due to time limitations, consultants can only deliver directly a limited number of these services. However, the consultant is not limited to direct intervention. Through careful planning and the use of teachers, parents, pupil personnel workers, students, and volunteers, the consultant has expanded programming capabilities. Counselors have a high degree of interpersonal skill, knowledge of and skill in group process and career education and can use these tools in training others to perform career development activities, thereby providing indirect service.

Consultants, probably more through career development than other areas, can use the skills of volunteers or paraprofessionals as they are commonly called. Interested community persons, whether parents or not, may become involved in all levels of the career development process. Paraprofessionals may perform tasks such as (1) establishing and building school-community relations; (2) operating parent discussion groups; (3) planning and participating in career days, college days, and orientation; (4) coordinating community surveys; (5) generating needed information on local occupational and training opportunities for pupils; (6) providing continuous updating of occupational files; (7) identifying representatives from the community to participate in the career education program, and (8) scheduling visits to community and industrial sites which give students the opportunity to learn about and experience a greater range of career possibilities. These are just a few of the ways in which consultants can work with paraprofessionals.

Students can also fill the manpower needs in career development and should not be overlooked as resources. Students can responsibly participate in all the previously mentioned activities as well as provide direct service to other students as peer helpers and peer counselors, sharing with them information on how to conceptualize and use various experiences toward their own career development.

In summary, one method of promoting career education and career development is to utilize a team approach. Consultants work with other professional staff, paraprofessionals, and students to provide services needed by the client system. Consultants coordinate the team effort to increase effectiveness. A second method is to integrate career education and career development concepts into the curriculum. The latter approach is viewed as having the greatest potential for facilitating student development. When both aspects are operational, the potential for facilitating student and system growth is increased.

Roles of Various Personnel in the Delivery of Consultation

It is increasingly apparent that the members of the school staff must function as an integrated, coordinated team if the school is to obtain its goal—facilitating human potential. The counselor can serve as a resource for change with administrators, parents, teachers, and students but each member must make a unique and definite contribution.

Teachers

Outside the home, teachers are probably the most significant adults in the lives of students. The teacher is perceived as the key to the human development process in the school. The importance of teachers in human development has been highlighted in all the new reforms in education such as career education, psychological education, developmental guidance, and humanistic education. The ultimate success of these programs depends upon the teachers' willingness and ability to integrate these concepts within the classroom.

The teacher is essential to the extension and maintenance of any innovation in education. As a result, the teacher can and should be regarded as a resource and a catalyst for change within a school system. The teacher can contribute to consultation by opening channels of communication with counselors, utilizing the counselor as a resource in the classroom, and serving as a resource to the counselor. Teachers are in a unique position to observe, identify, and diagnose specific needs of pupils, particularly their academic performance. They are also aware of student strengths and weaknesses and have some suggestions for problem resolution. Teachers may integrate guidance techniques and career education materials in the curriculum as a way of creating opportunities for affective and cognitive growth of students.

Serving as consultants to parents in helping them to better understand their child is another role of the teacher. Teachers can share information about the student's interests, abilities, and performance in school with parents. Secondly, parents may be assisted in creating the kind of home environment that will be supportive of the school in general and facilitative of their child's development in particular. Teachers may also serve as consultants to other teachers and school personnel, sharing information that will help identify and better serve the needs of students. Consultation, viewed as a vehicle for facilitating change in the learner's environment, cannot be accomplished without the commitment and cooperation of teachers.

Administrators

Administrators are viewed by teachers and others as key variables in school climate, determining in a large part what the school climate would be (Halpin and Croft, 1962). In addition, administrators are essential to any change within the system because of the vested responsibility for change inherent in their positions. If the school is to respond to developmental needs of students, administrators must go beyond the traditional alliances with faculty and staff and provide support systems that include professional endorsement and a commitment to change. It is essential that the role of the administrator in public relations be emphasized. Administrators can sell the guidance program to the community at large through already established contacts.

Administrators must foster the kind of attitudes which inspire increased productivity from all the elements (teachers and students) within the school and that stimulate a climate of openness and flexibility.

Students

Students are the major recipients of the school's total efforts but seem to have little or no input in the program. Students, particularly at the junior high and senior high levels, are very much interested in their total environment and would like to have input in program development.

There is a growing movement for involvement of students at all levels of decision making within schools and a parallel movement encouraging the utilization of students as peer helpers. These movements have widespread implications for personnel workers but particular applicability for consultants. Students can provide information about pupil needs, ideas about appropriate resolutions of needs, evaluate the services and serve as resources for change.

A revolutionary study was conducted by Gray, Graubard, and Rosenberg (1974) in which students were trained as behavioral engineers to modify their environment. The results indicated that students could successfully and responsibly engineer change in the behavior of teachers, parents, and peers. Although it would be difficult for counselors to undertake a project of that magnitude, the notion of training students as change agents is an intriguing one indeed.

Parents

Interaction with parents has been shown to influence the self-concept, attitudes, vocational choice and many other aspects of human behavior. Parents are therefore in a unique position for making a positive impact on the development of their child.

Parents may promote development of their child by being open to new ideas, participating in parent education programs, and developing skills which will permit them to facilitate development of their child in a positive manner. Parents may encourage their children to participate as fully as is possible in the totality of the educational process and supply pertinent information to school personnel which will enable them to meet student needs. Parents may provide the opportunity for children to gain valuable experiences appropriate for continual development. Equipped with the proper skills, parents can serve as consultants to their children and to other parents.

Community

Resources in the community could be utilized to their fullest through making present services available to students and their families through the referral and placement services of the school. Often families are not aware of the available resources and schools can dispense the information when it is needed.

Counselors, retired workers, community agency personnel, clergy, and other organizations' members can contribute to development of students by becoming involved with the educational enterprise. They could provide input into program planning, supply feedback on community needs, as well as make experience available to students through their agencies. Community members may seek out school personnel to participate in planning and development of programs for they have access to information about needs of students to which agencies can respond. Community personnel should also seek, when needed, the cooperation of the school in meeting student and family needs.

Other Pupil Personnel Specialists

Counselors do not operate within schools in isolation but exist along with other pupil personnel specialists from programs also designed to facilitate the total development of the individual. Counselors and other pupil personnel specialists work collaboratively to coordinate their respective services for the benefit of students. Most pupil personnel specialists may be grouped into three categories: counselors, school psychologists, and school social workers.

School psychologists and school social workers, like the counselors, perform an important consultative function. They provide consultation services to the school as a whole, particularly to teachers and other staff concerning child growth, development, and problems of adjustment. They assist in gathering information about students, providing in-service training to the faculty on the application of mental health principles in the classroom, and by conducting parent consultation and parent discussion groups.

The three groups of pupil personnel workers all have varying degrees of expertise in working with community agencies. Working together, they may be successful in matching the broad needs of children and families with available community services, thereby creating a mutually beneficial relationship between the community and the school. Through consultation and coordination the pupil personnel team can avoid duplication of effort, professional rivalry, and can capitalize on the strengths of each team member.

Differential Aspects of the Service for Various Levels of the Educational System

Differentiating between the consulting service for the various levels of the educational system will be difficult. The consulting process and its goals are basically the same for any level and to attempt a distinction by level would be superficial at best. Therefore, attempts to clarify the process will be based primarily on focus or direction of the intervention.

The degree to which counselors serve as consultants to students or adults is influenced by the level of involvement of the two groups in the decision-making process. As reflected by the developmental level of elementary school children, their participation in decision making is minimal. As individuals grow and mature, they become increasingly more able to contribute to planning and choosing for themselves. Significant adults tend to be intimately involved in making decisions for or with young children. As shown in figure 8.2, adults' participation in decision making tends to decrease as students' ability to make decisions increase.

This inverse pattern is a very simplistic way of portraying the complex relationship between individual developmental patterns and their interaction with behavior of significant adults.

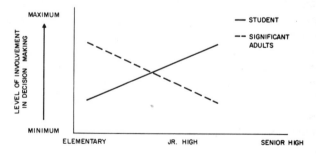

Figure 8.2. Levels of involvement in decision making.

However, it does seem to clarify some of the shifts in foci that occur in the consulting activity at various levels of the educational system.

Elementary School. The rationale for guidance consultation at any level stems from the basic belief that humanizing and personalizing the educational process and environment can facilitate the human potential of all children. This notion is dependent on two basic ideas about the elementary school: (1) that the teacher is the key to the educational process, and (2) that guidance should be developmentally oriented rather than remedial. It follows then that the belief upon which the counselor in the elementary school must operate is that guidance can be improved and extended to all children through increasing the effectiveness of teachers.

Consultation in the elementary schools focuses first on teachers because of their responsibility for the learning environment in schools. The second major concern is parents. Parents are much more attuned to schools and children at the elementary level than at any other time, which reinforces the notion of a high parental involvement rate at that level. This situation may be influenced by the fact that parents perceive young children as being more dependent on them and also by the legal responsibility that parents have for children at this stage. If counselors use their skills with parents and teachers at the elementary level, their work can have greater potential for prevention and development than one can expect in later years. Facilitating change in the family and school environment at the elementary level is viewed by the author as the optimal time for intervention.

Junior High School. Students in the junior high school are those of preadolescent and early adolescent years, a period roughly characterized by erratic physical, psychological, and social development. It is a time in which students are searching for social and emotional independence and attempting to develop skills needed to function on a more mature level.

The consultative process at this level would seek to provide home and school climates that allow students to test, question, explore and operate without being blocked at every turn. There are a number of factors in schools and society which unintentionally prevent or discourage students from assuming responsibility for themselves. According to Carlson and Mayer (1971), these factors prevent youth from gaining experience in making decisions, thereby predisposing them to ineffective living which could be characterized by high dropout and divorce rates and much vocational transfer. The consultant must take a close look at schools, homes, and the community for forces or practices that tend to dehumanize or penalize students. The focus of consulting is first on collaborative work with school personnel and the curriculum committee. Consulting with the administration concerns developing a flexible, open, nontraditional school atmosphere which allows for student involvement at different levels. Students may evaluate instructional programs and provide input to curriculum committees, may participate more fully in determining school regulations, and also might collaborate with teachers on planning unique opportunities for learning inside and outside the school.

A second group that is involved is students. The consultant enters a relationship with a student or a small group of students to help them develop the needed skills for self-exploration and decision making. Students are interested in evaluating their environment and may need help in looking at alternative ways of responding.

A third group through which the consultant may work is parents. As previously noted, parents tend to decrease their input and participation in decision making. However, it was not made clear that parents do maintain the ability to influence children. It is important that counselors help parents to recognize their influence and look for ways in which it can be used to encourage independence on the part of their children.

Consultants at the junior high level direct their effort toward creating the kind of environments in which students can be secure, open to others, free to explore themselves and free to manipulate the milieu. The goal is to provide opportunities through which students can develop skill in decision making.

High School. The consultant will find work at the high school level similar to the junior high school level. However, consulting with students may take some priority in that students are more aware of their problems and the aspects of the milieu that are facilitative as well as those that block development. Students also have more skills for participating in the process of sensitizing the learning environment to meet their needs.

Counselors may consult either with students or adults at the high school level to indirectly influence the academic and social progress of the student. In contrast to elementary students, the high school students are more skilled at making decisions and changing their behavior. Even so, at certain times individuals can only modify their behavior when significant others in their lives change their behavior toward them. The goal of consulting would be to intervene whenever necessary in order to help students develop to their fullest potential.

Ethical Consideration

Consultation is the role through which school personnel can provide help to each other and also to parents, students, and administrators. For the counselor, a clear distinction must be made between counseling and consulting with peers, for traditionally it has not been ethically advisable for counselors to enter into a professional counseling relationship with a colleague (*APGA Code of Ethics*). Faust (1968) suggested that success or maintenance of the consulting relationship depended largely on the degree to which the focus remained on some external unit rather than on the significant adult's internal need structure.

There appears to be a general conclusion that significant adults threatened with self-disclosure will be less willing to enter into a collaborative relationship for the benefit of the client. It has also been suggested that counseling with colleagues can create potential relationship problems for the counselor and the individual. It must be considered that significant others enter consulting because they are experiencing some difficulty and are willing to actively participate in procedures to help the client, thereby reducing or eradicating the problem. As Dinkmeyer and Carlson (1973) state, "the client problems are originally discussed with an awareness of the implications for the consultee. In some instances, the client problem really is associated with a crisis which exists in the consultee. In other instances the problem exists in the social system and necessitates dealing with the total organization" (p. 162). Lundquist and Chamley (1971) suggested that the counselor should serve as a consultant and counselor to teachers. They suggest, as an example, that the counselor "help the teacher or teachers to develop an awareness of how their intrapersonal feelings affect and influence their roles in the educative process with children" (p. 364). Counseling with teachers is being supported more in professional realms (Dinkmeyer, 1968; Tyler, 1969; Brown and Srebalus, 1972). Munson (1970:

121-129) described the consulting relationship as a tri-level process which builds on the first contact. The first level concentrates on external matters while levels two and three are more intense and focus on the personness of the teacher in a supportive way. However, he suggested that the advanced stage of the relationship should not be used to commence a psychotherapeutic relationship with the teacher. The implication may be that the counselor would have to conceptualize the client's problem and intervene where necessary—with the consultee, the client, or the milieu. One way for the counselor to resolve the ethical dilemma is to realize the student is the client and that intervention with colleagues is one way of facilitating students' development.

A second ethical concern that counselors will have to react to involves the conception of the consultation process as a manipulative strategy. A major concern arises when the counselor collaborates with others to change or control a client's behavior without the client's permission. Consultation is a process that is designed to bring about client's behavior change but the focus is more on change in environmental contingencies which elicits in turn a changed response from the client. From this frame of reference, consultation can be ethically viewed as creating facilitative climates in which clients can realize their potential.

Counseling may often be expected to be identified as a natural extension of an effective consulting relationship. When students are involved as consultees—the transfer to a counselor-client relationship is a simple process. However, when significant adults are involved, the process is more complex. Are counselors to ignore the needs of staff for additional assistance? Must they refer when they realize that the consultee is likely not to follow-through on the referral? Although counseling with teachers and other significant adults may create relationship problems, it is recognized that the future needs of the school may bring about a change in this practice. The role conflicts that emerge in providing service to the total system may require clarification of the consultant role, particularly as it relates to providing supportive services to significant adults within the client's milieu.

Training the Counselor-Consultant

Counseling and consultation differ in several ways but the roles are not mutually exclusive. Consultation has been viewed as a distinctly different profession from counseling. However, the type of consultation being described in this chapter is viewed as an extension of the role of the counselor. Whether the consultant is a distinct professional or a counselor, the consultant's primary responsibility is to facilitate human development. The consultant does not focus on assisting the individual to adjust to the environment but seeks to create the kind of environment which enhances individual development. The consultant must be a behavioral scientist with knowledge of the individual, the institution, the society, the interrelationships among them, and have skill in bringing about change at all three levels. The consultant is a change agent who might be conceived of as a leveler, a disturber, a personal threat, or as an advocate. Recognizing the dimensions of the task, Blocker (1966) questioned whether the counselor was qualified by training and experience to be such a change agent. What kind of training does one need to function effectively as a consultant?

Patouillet (1957) proposed the training of child development consultants as a way of providing mental health services in the schools. He suggested that child development consultants be trained in a two-year program of graduate study including courses in guidance, developmental psychology, school psychology, social work, administration, and curriculum. Dinkmeyer and Carlson (1973) also suggested a two-year course of studies for the preparation of the consultant. They state:

> the professional preparation of the consultant will place an emphasis upon creating an awareness of the significance of the school climate, the total milieu, and the way in which consultants may work through group procedures to influence the milieu. The consultant would be trained in counseling and learning theory and group process because they are basic to many of the skills of consultation. He would have special expertise in group dynamics and group procedures. The program for the consultant would provide intensive training in counseling so that he might utilize the process in working with pupils, parents, and teachers. (p. 21)

They also suggest that courses in community psychology, research, sociology, anthropology, and appraisal procedures would be necessary for developing a solid knowledge base. They further suggest that the consultant must be much more than the product of a set of courses but must have certain personal qualities and capacities if one is to function as a facilitator of human potential. The training program must emphasize both the development of cognitive skills and an awareness of one's self and the impact one might have upon others.

Both approaches indicate that preparation should be multidisciplinary in nature and concentrate on the development of cognitive and personal skills. One other unique aspect that should be included in the training program is to help counselors realize their position within the school's organization. The counselor must be able to realistically evaluate the skills and attitudes necessary to bring about change and to operate effectively in areas where he has little protection in the form of vested authority. In a staff position, the counselor can only suggest, recommend, or advise changes. However, in order to be effective, the counselor must be able to stimulate and generate change in a nonthreatening, supportive way. This task is almost impossible since change is viewed as a threat by many people. Several models have been developed that indicate that individuals without an authority base can emerge and generate enough power to initiate change within an organization (Cook, 1971).

It is apparent that specific skills and expertise are required to be a consultant, most of which the school counselor possesses. If counselors are to be effective consultants and agents of change, they must develop additional skills in research, organizational change, strategies for working with adults, in-service programming, and community development. These skills may be acquired through in-service training by counselors in the field or included in the counselor preparation programs. Counselor training institutions will have to expand the course offerings and the field experience base to fully equip the trainee to function as a counselor and a consultant.

Evaluation of Consultation

Consultation, as an intervention strategy, has become considerably popular among counselors and other human services professionals. Counselors across the country are increasingly beginning to integrate consulting activities in their work. In addition, some counselor education programs are now offering courses in consulting and intervention practices and strategies. However, there are questions about consultation such as, does it work?

Consultation, like all other services, must lend itself to evaluation in order for its usefulness to be determined. The available research on the evaluation of consultation as a guidance service is limited because the activity is relatively new. What research there is mostly resulted from experiences of mental health workers providing consulting service to the school as objective outsiders. Some of the research will be considered here but the emphasis will be on the effect of consultation rather than on the person (internal or external consultant) providing the service.

A number of mental health consultation studies were conducted with school personnel. One study by Tyler (1971) evaluated the effectiveness of consultation on the consultee by the amount of time spent with consultees. Tyler divided the teachers into three groups, giving one group intensive consultation the second group limited consultation and a control group no consultation. Pre- and post-analysis reports on understanding of the child indicated that those teachers who received intensive consultation changed significantly more than teachers in either of the other groups. Two studies evaluating the effect of consulting on the client indicate some success. Ginter (1963) conducted a study in which he used two groups of elementary science students and their teachers as subjects. In the first group the science consultant worked only with the teachers in planning the unit, and in the second group the consultant worked with the students directly once a week. Teachers in the second group followed up the consultant's work during the rest of the week. Using students' achievement test scores as criteria of change, he found that there was greater learning by the group of students who worked only with the teacher. Taylor and Hoedt (1974), in the study mentioned previously, evaluated change in client behavior as a result of consultation. Their results indicated that change in client behavior can be influenced without any direct intervention with the client.

Of the studies mentioned in this section, there was diversity in what was called consultation but they all indicated positive results and indicated that consulting does work. The intention here is not to imply that all consultation is successful. Needless to say, there are numerous studies in the literature that did not exhibit positive results. A number of the studies mentioned here and in the literature pointed up a need for additional research in the area, particularly the kind of research that follows good research methodology and from which meaningful conclusions could be reached.

Consultation with teachers, parents, administrators, and students is the kind of process that lends itself to the establishment of goals and/or objectives. As a result, the establishment of objectives provides the basis on which consultation can be evaluated and researched. Care must be given in determination of objectives so that they are specific—not general, explicit—not implicit, and immediate—not long-term. Objectives should be constructed in such a way that the outcome or terminal behavior is identifiable. Through determination of the objectives, the consultant can evaluate the effectiveness of consultation to the consultee, the client, and to the client system. Also, utilizing carefully designed research methodology, one could evaluate process as well as outcome variables and use this information for improvement of the consultative procedure. Evaluation can only be effective where accurate and immediate feedback is available. The counselor must design the kind of procedure necessary for collecting and using feedback.

References

ACES-ASCA Joint Committee on the Elementary School Counselor. Report of the ACES-ASCA Joint Committee on the Elementary School Counselor. Washington, D.C.: *American Personnel and Guidance Association,* 1966. Mimeographed

American School Counselors Association. Policy for Secondary School Counselors. Washington, D.C.: *American Personnel and Guidance Association,* 1964.

Atlas, J. W. Consulting: Affecting change for minority students. *Journal of Non-White Concerns* 3 (4) (1975):154-60.

Banning, J. and Kaiser, L. An ecological perspective and model for campus design. *Personnel and Guidance Journal* 52 (6) (1974):370-75.

Bedford, J. H. History of vocational guidance in the United States. In O. J. Kaplan ed., *Encyclopedia of Vocational Guidance.* New York: The Philosophical Library, Inc., 1948.

Berenson, B. and Carkhuff, R. *Sources of gain in counseling and psychotherapy: Readings and commentary.* New York: Holt, Rinehart, and Winston, 1967.

Blocher, D. H. *Developmental counseling.* New York: The Ronald Press Company, 1966.

———. Can the counselor function as an effective agent of change? *The School Counselor* 13 (4) (1966):202-05.

———. *Developmental counseling* (2d ed.). New York: The Ronald Press, 1974.

Blocher, D. H. and Shaffer, W. F. Guidance and human development. In D. R. Cook ed., *Guidance for education in revolution.* Boston: Allyn and Bacon, 1971.

Brown, D. and Srebalus, D. J. *Contemporary guidance concepts and practices: An introduction.* Dubuque, Iowa: Wm. C. Brown Company, Publishers, 1972.

Brubaker, D. L. and Nelson R. H. *Creative survival in educational bureaucracies.* Berkeley, California: McCutchan Publishing Corporation, 1974.

Carlson, J. and Mayer, G. R. Fading: A behavioral procedure to increase independent behavior. *The School Counselor* 17 (1971) 193-97.

Combs, A. W. et al. *Florida studies in the helping professions.* Univeristy of Florida Monographs, Social Sciences no. 37. Gainsville, Florida: University of Florida Press, 1969.

Cook, D. R. ed. *Guidance for education in revolution.* Boston: Allyn and Bacon, 1971.

Dinkmeyer, D. C. The counselor as consultant: Rationale and procedures. *Elementary School Guidance and Counseling* 3 (1968):187-94.

———. The 'C' group: Focus on self as instrument. *Phi Delta Kappan* 52 (10) (1971):617-19.

Dinkmeyer, D. and Caldwell, C. *Developmental counseling and guidance: A comprehensive school approach.* New York: McGraw-Hill, 1970.

Dinkmeyer, D. C. and Carlson, J. *Consulting: Facilitating human potential and change processes.* Columbus, Ohio: Charles E. Merrill Publishing Company, 1973.

Dreikurs, R. and Soltz, V. *Children: The challenge.* New York: Hawthorn Books, Inc., 1964.

Ellena, W.; Stevenson, M.; and Webb, H. *Who's a good teacher?* Washington, D.C.: American Association of School Administrators, 1961.

Faust, V. *The counselor-consultant in the elementary school.* Boston: Houghton Mifflin, 1968.

Fullmer, D. W. Family group consultation. *Elementary School Guidance and Counseling* 7 (1972):130-36.

Gilmore, J. V. Parent counseling: Theory and application. *Journal of Education* 154 (1) (1971):40-49.

Ginter, J. R. Achievement in sixth grade science associated with two instructional roles of science consultants. *Journal of Educational Research* 57 (1963):28-33.

Ginzberg, E. *Career Guidance.* New York: McGraw-Hill, 1971.

Gordon, T. *Parent effectiveness training.* New York: Peter H. Wyden, Inc., 1970.

———. *Teacher effectiveness training.* New York: Peter H. Wyden, Inc., 1974.

Gray, F.; Graubard, P.; and Rosenberg, H. Little brother is changing you. *Psychology Today* 7 (10) (1974):42-46.

Halpin, A W. and Croft, D. *The organizational climate of schools.* U.S. Office of Education Research Report. Salt Lake City: Utah University, July, 1962.

Harris, T. *I'm ok-you're ok.* New York: Harper and Row, 1969.

Helpern, J. M. G. The role of the guidance consultant at the elementary school. *Journal of Education* 146 (1964):16-34.

Kaczkowski, H. The elementary school counselor as consultant. In D. C. Dinkmeyer ed., *Guidance and counseling in the elementary school.* New York: Holt, Rinehart & Winston, 1968.

Leacock, E. The concept of culture and its significance for school counselors. *Personnel and Guidance Journal* 46 (1968):844-51.

Lippitt, R. Dimensions of the consultant's job. *Journal of Social Issues* 15 (2) (1959):5-12.

Love, L. R. et al. Differential effectiveness of three clinical interventions for different socio-economic groupings. *Journal of Consulting and Clinical Psychology* 39 (3) (1972):347-60.

Lundquist, G. W. and Chamley, J C. Counselor-consultant: A move toward effectiveness. *The School Counselor* 18 (1971):362-66.

Mannino, F. V. and Shore, M. F. The effects of consultation: A review of empirical studies. *American Journal of Community Psychology* 3 (1) (1975):1-21.

Mayer, G R. Behavior consulting: Using behavior modification procedures in the consulting relationship. *Elementary School Guidance and Counseling* 7 (1972):114-19.

McGehearty, L. Consultation and counseling. *Elementary School Guidance and Counseling* 3 (1969):155-63.

Mosher, R. and Sprinthall, N. Psychological education: A means to promote personal development during adolescence. *Counseling Psychologist* 2 (1971):3-84.

Munson, H. L. *Elementary school guidance: Concepts, dimensions, and practice.* Boston: Allyn & Bacon, 1970.

Patouillet, R. Organizing for guidance in the elementary school. In D. C. Dinkmeyer ed., *Guidance and counseling in the elementary school.* New York: Holt Rinehart & Winston, Inc., 1968.

Satir, V. *Conjoint family therapy.* Palo Alto, California: Science and Behavior Books, Inc., 1967.

Smith, C. M. History of high school guidance. In O. J. Kaplan ed., *Encyclopedia of vocational guidance.* New York: The Philosophical Library, Inc., 1948.

Smith, H. and Eckerson, L. *Guidance services in elementary schools: A national survey.* Washington, D.C.: Superintendent of Documents, U.S. Government Printing Office, 1966.

Stern, G. *People in context: Measuring person-environment congruence in education and industry.* New York: Wiley, 1970.

Taylor, W. F. and Hoedt, K. C. Classroom-related behavior problems: counsel parents, teachers, or children? *Journal of Counseling Psychology* 24 (1) (1974):3-8.

Tyler, L. E. *The work of the counselor* (3rd ed.). New York: Appleton-Century-Crofts, 1969.

Tyler, M. M. *A study of some selected parameters of school psychologists—teacher consultation.* Unpublished doctoral dissertation, University of Kansas, 1971.

Wrenn, C. G. *Counselor in a changing world.* Washington, D.C.: American Personnel and Guidance Association, 1962.

———. The counselor in a changing world revisited. *Teachers College Journal.* Terre Haute, Indiana: Indiana State College, 1965.

Chapter 9

AN INTRODUCTION TO CAREER EDUCATION

United States Office of Education Position Paper

Career education represents a response to a call for educational reform. This call has arisen from a variety of sources, each of which has voiced dissatisfaction with American education as it currently exists. Such sources include students, parents, the business-industry-labor community, out-of-school youth and adults, minorities, the disadvantaged, and the general public. While their specific concerns vary, all seem to agree that American education is in need of major reform at all levels. Career education is properly viewed as *one* of several possible responses that could be given to this call.

Conditions Calling for Educational Reform

The prime criticisms of American education that career education seeks to correct include the following:

1. Too many persons leaving our educational system are deficient in the basic academic skills required for adaptability in today's rapidly changing society.
2. Too many students fail to see meaningful relationships between what they are being asked to learn in school and what they will do when they leave the educational system. This is true of both those who remain to graduate and those who drop out of the educational system.
3. American education, as currently structured, best meets the educational needs of that minority of persons who will someday become college graduates. It fails to place equal emphasis on meeting the educational needs of that vast majority of students who will never be college graduates.
4. American education has not kept pace with the rapidity of change in the postindustrial occupational society. As a result, when worker qualifications are compared with job requirements, we find overeducated and undereducated workers are present in large numbers. Both the boredom of the overeducated worker and the frustration of the undereducated worker have contributed to growing worker alienation in the total occupational society.
5. Too many persons leave our educational system at both the secondary and collegiate levels unequipped with the vocational skills, the self-understanding and career

decision-making skills, or the work attitudes that are essential for making a successful transition from school to work.

6. The growing need for and presence of women in the work force has not been reflected adequately in either the educational or the career options typically pictured for girls enrolled in our educational system.
7. The growing needs for continuing and recurrent education of adults are not being met adequately by our current systems of public education.
8. Insufficient attention has been given to learning opportunities which exist outside the structure of formal education and are increasingly needed by both youth and adults in our society.
9. The general public, including parents and the business-industry-labor community, has not been given an adequate role in formulation of educational policy.
10. American education, as currently structured, does not adequately meet the needs of minority or economically disadvantaged persons in our society.
11. Post-high-school education has given insufficient emphasis to educational programs at the subbaccalaureate degree level.

It is both important and proper that these criticisms be answered, in part, through pointing to the significant accomplishments of American education. Growth in both the quality and the quantity of American education must be used as a perspective for answering the critics. Such a perspective, of course, is not in itself an answer. The answers given to such criticisms must take the form of either refutation of the criticisms or constructive educational changes designed to alleviate those conditions being criticized. The prospects of refuting these criticisms, to the satisfaction of the general public, seem slight. Thus, an action program of educational reform appears to be needed. Career education represents one such program.

Answering the Call for Educational Reform: The Rationale for Career Education

Each of the eleven criticisms cited centers on relationships between education and life-styles of individuals. Any comprehensive program of educational reform designed to answer such criticisms must be based on some common element inherent in each of them. Such a common element must be one that can logically be related to the societal goals for education as well as to the individual personal growth goals of learners.

One such element that seems appropriate to consider for use is the concept of work. For purposes of this rationale, "work" has this specific definition:

> "Work" is conscious effort, other than that involved in activities whose primary purpose is either coping or relaxation, aimed at producing benefits for oneself and/or for oneself and others.

This definition, which includes both paid and unpaid work, speaks to the survival need of society for productivity. It also speaks to the personal need of all individuals to find meaning in their lives through their accomplishments. It provides one possible societal basis for supporting education. Simultaneously, it provides one clearly recognizable reason for both educators and students to engage in education. It emphasizes the goal of education, *as preparation for work,* in ways that neither demean nor detract from other worthy goals of education. It is a concept which, while obviously encompassing economic man, reaches beyond to the broader aspects of productivity in one's total life-style—including leisure time.

As such, it serves as a universally common answer to all who ask, "Why should I learn?" The fact it may represent, for any given individual, neither the only answer nor necessarily the most important answer to this question is irrelevant to this claim for commonality.

Proposals for educational change made in response to any criticism or combination of criticisms cited above can all be accomplished through use of the concept of work. It accommodates the productivity goals of society in ways that emphasize the humanizing goals of American education. It is this quality that lends credence to career education as a vehicle for educational reform.

A Generic Definition of Career Education

In a generic sense, the definition of "career education" must obviously be derived from definitions of the words "career" and "education." In seeking a generic definition for career education, these words are defined as follows:

"Career" is the totality of work one does in his or her lifetime. "Education" is the totality of experiences through which one learns.

Based on these two definitions, "career education" is defined as follows:

"Career education" is the totality of experiences through which one learns about and prepares to engage in work as part of her or his way of living.

"Career," as defined here, is a developmental concept beginning in the very early years and continuing well into the retirement years. "Education," as defined here, obviously includes more than the formal educational system. Thus, this generic definition of career education is purposely intended to be of a very broad and encompassing nature. At the same time, it is intended to be considerably less than all of life or one's reasons for living.

Basic Concept Assumptions of Career Education

Based on the generic definition of career education and its rationale as cited above, the career education movement has embraced a number of basic concept assumptions. These assumptions include:

1. Since both one's career and one's education extend from the preschool through the retirement years, career education must also span almost the entire life cycle.
2. The concept of productivity is central to the definition of work and so to the entire concept of career education.
3. Since "work" includes unpaid activities as well as paid employment, career education's concerns, in addition to its prime emphasis on paid employment, extend to the work of

the student as a learner, to the growing numbers of volunteer workers in our society, to the work of the full-time homemaker, and to work activities in which one engages as part of leisure and/or recreational time.

4. The cosmopolitan nature of today's society demands that career education embrace a multiplicity of work values, rather than a single work ethic, as a means of helping each individual answer the question, "Why should I work?"

5. Both one's career and one's education are best viewed in a developmental rather than in a fragmented sense.

6. Career education is for all persons—including the young and the old, the mentally handicapped and the intellectually gifted, the poor and the wealthy, males and females, students in elementary schools and in graduate colleges.

7. The societal objectives of career education are to help all individuals to: (a) want to work, (b) acquire the skills necessary for work in these times, and (c) engage in work that is satisfying to the individual and beneficial to society.

8. The individualistic goals of career education are to make work (a) possible, (b) meaningful, and (c) satisfying for each individual throughout his or her lifetime.

9. Protection of the individual's freedom to choose—and assistance in making and implementing career decisions—are of central concern to career education.

10. The expertise required for implementing career education exists in many parts of society and is not limited to those employed in formal education.

Taken as a whole, these ten concept assumptions represent a philosophical base for current education efforts. Career education makes no pretense of picturing these assumptions as anything more than the simple beliefs they represent. certainly, each is debatable and none has sufficient acceptance as yet to be regarded as an educational truism.

Programmatic Assumptions of Career Education

Operationally, career education programs have been initiated based on a combination of research evidence and pragmatic observations. While subject to change and/or modification based on further research efforts, the following programmatic assumptions are intended to serve as examples of the truth as we presently know it. Each is stated, insofar as possible, in the form of a testable hypothesis. By doing so, it is hoped that further research will be stimulated.

1. If students can see relationships between what they are being asked to learn in school and the world of work, they will be motivated to learn more in school.

2. No single learning strategy exists that is best for all students. For example, some students will learn best by reading books, and others will learn best by combining reading with other kinds of learning activities. A comprehensive educational program should provide a series of alternative learning strategies and learning environments for students.

3. Basic academic skills, a personally meaningful set of work values, and good work habits represent adaptability tools needed by all persons who choose to work in today's rapidly changing occupational society.

4. Increasingly, entry into today's occupational society demands that those who seek employment possess a specific set of vocational skills. Unskilled labor is less and less in demand.

5. Career development, as part of human development, begins in the preschool years and continues into the retirement years. Its maturational patterns differ from individual to individual.

6. Work values, a part of one's personal value system, are developed to a significant degree during the elementary school years and are modifiable during those years.

7. Specific occupational choices represent only one of a number of kinds of choices involved in career development. They can be expected to increase in realism as one moves from childhood into adulthood and, to some degree, to be modifiable during most of one's adult years.

8. Occupational decision making is accomplished through the dynamic interaction of limiting and enhancing factors both within the individual and in his present and proposed environment. It is not, in any sense, a simple matching of individuals with jobs.

9. Occupational stereotyping hinders full freedom of occupational choice both for females and for minority persons. These restrictions can be reduced, to some extent, through programmatic intervention strategies begun in the early childhood years.

10. Parent socioeconomic status acts as a limitation on occupational choices considered by children. This limitation can be reduced, to a degree, by program intervention strategies begun in the early years.

11. A positive relationship exists between education and occupational competence, but the optimum amount and kind of education required as preparation for work varies greatly from occupation to occupation.

12. The same general strategies utilized in reducing worker alienation in industry can be used to reduce worker alienation among pupils and teachers in the classroom.

13. While some persons will find themselves able to meet their human needs for accomplishment through work in their places of paid employment, others will find it necessary to meet this need through work in which they engage during their leisure time.

14. Career decision-making skills, job-hunting skills, and job-getting skills can be taught to and learned by almost everyone. Individuals can effectively use such skills, once learned, to enhance their career development.

15. Excessive deprivation in any aspect of human growth and development can retard career development. For persons suffering such deprivation, special variations in career development programs will be required.

16. An effective means of helping individuals discover both who they are (in a self-concept sense) and why they are (in a personal awareness sense) is through helping them discover what they can accomplish in the work they do.

17. The attitudes of parents toward work and toward education act as powerful influences on the career development of their children. Such parental attitudes are modifiable through programmatic intervention strategies.

18. The processes of occupational decision making and occupational preparation will probably be repeated more than once for most adults in today's society.
19. One's style of living is significantly influenced by the occupations he or she engages in at various times in life.
20. Relationships between education and work can be made more meaningful through infusion into subject matter than if taught as a separate body of knowledge.
21. It can increasingly be expected that education and work will be interwoven at various times in the lives of most individuals rather than occur in a single sequential pattern.
22. Decisions individuals make about the work they do are considerably broader and more encompassing in nature than are decisions made regarding the occupations in wich they are employed.
23. Good work habits and positive attitudes toward work can be taught effectively to most individuals. Assimilation of such knowledge is most effective if begun in the early childhood years.
24. The basis on which work can become a personally meaningful part of one's life will vary greatly from individual to individual. No single approach can be expected to meet with universal success.
25. While economic return can almost always be expected to be a significant factor in decisions individuals make about occupations, it may not be a significant factor in many decisions individuals make about their total pattern of work.

This list is intended to be illustrative, rather than comprehensive, in nature. The prime point is that, in formulating action plans for career education, we can not, even at this stage, be forced to operate out of complete ignorance. While much more research is obviously needed, we know enough right now to justify and to undertake the organization, installation, and implementation of comprehensive career education programs. The call for educational reform, to which career education seeks to repond, need not and should not wait for further research before we begin to answer it.

Career Education Tasks: Initial Implementation

To the greatest extent possible, initiation of comprehensive career education programs should be undertaken utilizing existing personnel and existing physical facilities. The assumption of new roles by some staff members can be accomplished in most educational systems with no serious loss in total institutional productivity. While the emphasis and methodology will vary considerably from one educational level to another (e.g., the emphasis on vocational education will be minimal at the elementary school level and the emphasis on the home and family component will be minimal at the adult education level), the following kinds of tasks are essential for initial implementation of a comprehensive career education effort.

A.   All classroom teachers will:

1. Devise and/or locate methods and materials designed to help pupils understand and appreciate the career implications of the subject matter being taught.

2. Utilize career-oriented methods and materials in the instructional program, where appropriate, as one means of educational motivation.
3. Help pupils acquire and utilize good work habits.
4. Help pupils develop, clarify, and assimilate personally meaningful sets of work values.
5. Integrate, to the fullest extent possible, the programmatic assumptions of career education into their instructional activities and teacher-pupil relationships.

B. Some teachers, in addition, will be charged with:

1. Providing students with specific vocational competencies at a level that will enable them to gain entry into the occupational society.
2. Helping students acquire job-seeking and job-getting skills.
3. Participating in the job-placement process.
4. Helping students acquire decision-making skills.

C. The business-labor-industry community will:

1. Provide observational, work experience, and work-study opportunities for students *and* for those who educate students (teachers, counselors, and school administrators).
2. Serve as career development resource personnel for teachers, counselors, and students.
3. Participate in part-time and full-time job placement programs.
4. Participate actively and positively in programs designed to reduce worker alienation.
5. Participate in career education policy formulation.

D. Counseling and guidance personnel will:

1. Help classroom teachers implement career education in the classroom.
2. Serve, usually with other educational personnel, in implementing career education concepts within the home and family structure.
3. Help students in the total career development process, including the making and implementation of career decisions.
4. Participate in part-time and full-time job placement programs and in follow-up studies of former students.

E. Home and family members with whom pupils reside will:

1. Help pupils acquire and practice good work habits.
2. Emphasize development of positive work values and attitudes toward work.
3. Maximize, to the fullest extent possible, career development options and opportunities for themselves and for their children.

F. Educational administrators and school boards will:

1. Emphasize career education as a priority goal.
2. Provide leadership and direction to the career education program.
3. Involve the widest possible community participation in career education policy decision making.
4. Provide the time, materials, and finances required for implementing the career education program.
5. Initiate curriculum revision designed to integrate academic, general, and vocational education into an expended set of education opportunities available to all students.

Until and unless performance of these tasks is underway, we cannot say that implementation of a comprehensive career education program has taken place. While bits and pieces of career education are obvious in many educational systems at present, very few have fully implemented these intitial tasks. American education cannot be credited with responding to the demands for educational reform by simply endorsing the career education concept. Only when action programs have been initiated can we truly say a response has been made.

Learner Outcomes for Career Education

Like the career education tasks outlined above, specific learner outcomes for career education will vary in emphasis from one educational level to another. For purposes of forming a broad basis for evaluating the effectiveness of career education efforts, a listing of developmental outcome goals is essential. In this sense, career education seeks to produce individuals who, when they leave school (at any age or at any level), are:

1. Competent in the basic academic skills required for adaptability in our rapidly changing society.
2. Equipped with good work habits.
3. Capable of choosing and who have chosen a personally meaningful set of work values that foster in them a desire to work.
4. Equipped with career decision-making skills, job hunting skills, and job-getting skills.
5. Equipped with vocational personal skills at a level that will allow them to gain entry into and attain a degree of success in the occupational society.
6. Equipped with career decisions based on the widest possible set of data concerning themselves and their educational-vocational opportunities.
7. Aware of means available to them for continuing and recurrent education once they have left the formal system of schooling.
8. Successful in being placed in a paid occupation, in further education, or in a vocation consistent with their current career education.
9. Successful in incorporating work values into their total personal value structure in such a way that they are able to choose what, for them, is a desirable life-style.

It is important to note that these learner outcome goals are intended to apply to persons leaving the formal educational *system* for the world of work. They are not intended to be applicable whenever the person leaves a particular school. For some persons, then, these goals become applicable when they leave the secondary school. For others, it will be when they have left post-high-school occupational education programs. For still others, these goals need not be applied, in total, until they have left a college or university setting. Thus, the applicability of these learner outcome goals will vary from individual to individual as well as from one level of education to another. This is consistent with the developmental nature, and the basic assumption of individual differences, inherent in the concept of career education.

Basic Educational Changes Championed by Career Education

The actions of students, educational personnel, parents, and members of the business-industry-labor community, no matter how well intentioned, cannot bring about educational reform so long as the basic policies of American education remain unchanged. None of the basic educational policy changes advocated by career education is either new or untested. Yet, none has become common practice in a majority of educational systems. No one of these changes can or should come quickly. Each will require considerable study, debate, and public acceptance before it is initiated. In spite of the obvious difficulties and dangers involved, each of the flowing basic educational policy changes is championed by the career education movement:

1. Substantial increases in the quantity, quality, and variety of vocational education offerings at the secondary school level and of occupational education offerings at the postsecondary school level.
2. Increases in the number and variety of educational course options available to students with a de-emphasis on the presence of clearly differentiated college preparatory, general education, and vocational education curriculums at the secondary school level.
3. The installation of performance evaluation, as an alternative to the strict time requirements imposed by the traditional Carnegie unit, as a means of assessing and certifying educational accomplishment.
4. The installation of systems for granting educational credit for learning that takes place outside the walls of the school.
5. Increasing use of noncertificated personnel from the business-industry-labor community as educational resource persons in the educational systems total instructional program.
6. The creation of an open entry-open exit educational system that allows students to combine schooling with work in ways that fit their needs and educational motivations.
7. Substantial increases in programs of adult and recurrent education as a responsiblity of the public school educational system.
8. Creation of the year-round public school system that provides multiple points during any twelve-month period in which a student will leave the educational system.
9. Major overhaul of teacher education programs and graduate programs in education aimed at incorporating the career education concepts, skills, and methodologies.
10. Substantial increases in the career guidance, counseling, placement, and follow-up functions as parts of American education.
11. Substantial increases in program and schedule flexibility that allow classroom teachers, at all levels, greater autonomy and freedom to choose educational strategies and devise methods and materials they determine to be effective in increasing pupil achievement.
12. Increased utilization of educational technology for gathering, processing, and disseminating knowledge required in the teaching-learning process.
13. Increased participation by students, teachers, parents, and members of the business-industry-labor community in educational policy making.

14. Increased participation by formal educational institutions in comprehensive community educational and human services efforts.

There are three basic implications inherent in the kinds of educational changes cited here which must be made very explicit.

First, we are saying that while initial implementation of career education programs will be relatively inexpensive, total educational reform is going to be expensive. No matter how much current educational budgets are realigned, there is no way that this total reform can be carried out with sums now being expanded for the public school and public higher education systems.

Second, we are saying that a substantial portion of the additional funds required could be found in remedial and alternative educational systems that, supported with tax dollars, now exist outside the structure of our public school system and our system of public postsecondary education. Career education represents a movement dedicated to avoiding the creation of a dual system of public education in the United States. A single comprehensive educational system will be both less expensive, in the long run and more beneficial in meeting educational needs of all persons—youth and adults—in this society.

Third, we are saying that the days of educational isolationism are past. It is time that our formal educational system join forces with all other segments of the total society, including both community service agencies and the business-industry-labor community, in a comprehensive effort to meet the varied and continuing educational needs of both youth and adults. Rather than complain about or compete with other kinds of educational opportunities, all must collaborate in providing appropriate educational opportunities for all citizens.

Unless these kinds of long-range educational reforms are made a basic part of the career education strategy, it is unlikely that the kinds of criticisms that led to establishment of career education will be effectively answered.

Conclusion

As a response to a call for educational reform, career education has operated as a paper priority of American education for the last three years. During this period, it has demonstrated its acceptability as a direction for change to both educators and to the general public. Its widespread application to all of American education has not yet taken place. If successful efforts in this direction can now be made, the result should be complete integration of career education concepts into the total fabric of all American education. When this has been accomplished, the result should be abandonment of the term "career education" and adoption of some other major direction for educational change. The call for educational reform, to which career education seeks to respond, is still strong and persistent across the land. That call can no longer be ignored. It is time that this vehicle be used.

Chapter 10

ROLES OF TEACHERS, COUNSELORS, ADMINISTRATORS, AND THE COMMUNITY IN CAREER EDUCATION

Robert L. Crawford

Career education implementation does not require drastic changes in the present role definitions of educators. Rather, it provides all educators with a means to reduce the disparity between the way in which roles are defined and the way in which roles sometimes are acted out.

Classroom teachers state that their role includes strengthening student feelings of self-esteem, but some classroom teachers exhibit an inadvertent, but nonetheless onerous, form of work prejudice which is harmful to some students' feelings of self-esteem. Classroom teachers state that their role includes motivating students to strive for academic excellence, but some classroom teachers fail to provide a suitable answer to the question: "Why should I learn that?" Classroom teachers state that their role includes attempting to involve students' parents in school activities, but some classroom teachers make no attempt to involve parents in other than "parents' night" events. School counselors state that their role includes working with classroom teachers and groups of students, but some school counselors spend their time working with students on a one-to-one basis. School counselors state that their role includes helping students make their own decisions about which school courses to take, but some school counselors—faced with students who do not have the information and skills necessary to choose wisely—make the decisions for the students. School administrators state that their role includes management of the process of education, but some school administrators spend their time on care of the building and administrative minutia. School administrators state that their role includes collaboration with community, business, and labor groups to get their input into educational decision making, but some school administrators make no efforts to initiate such collaboration.

Included in the career education activities listed below are specific actions educators can take to fulfill the roles they already have defined for themselves.

Dr. Robert L. Crawford is Assistant Professor of Counselor Education at Memphis State University, Memphis, Tennessee.

Role of the Classroom Teacher

It is by design the teachers' roles in career education are discussed before the roles of others, because the classroom teacher is the most important person in career education implementation. Career education, simply defined, is a teaching strategy by which all instructors teach their academic subject areas—reading, writing, arithmetic, etc.,—with a sensitivity to the career usefulness of the subject areas, and implicitly suggest to the students that they begin considering how they might use these learnings in their lives. Career education in a school takes place in direct proportion to the amount of teacher involvement. Career education implementation depends on integration into the existing curriculum, and classroom teachers control the curriculum. Curriculum is what happens in the classroom when the door is closed, not what is written down in a curriculum guide.

General Responsibilities

The Position Paper on Career Development adopted by the American Vocational Association/National Vocational Guidance Association Commission on Career Guidance and Vocational Education (1973) states that the career guidance responsibilities of all academic teachers are to:

1. Provide for easy transition of students from home to school, from one school environment to another, and from school to further education or employment.
2. Provide students with curriculum and related learning experiences to insure the development of basic concepts of work and the importance of those who perform work.
3. Provide group guidance experiences, with appropriate aid from guidance specialists and vocational educators, to regularly demonstrate the relationship between learning and job requirements.
4. Help parents understand and encourage the career development process as it relates to their children.
5. Provide opportunities within the curriculum for students to have decision-making experiences related to educational and vocational planning.
6. Assist students in synthesizing accumulated career development experiences to prepare them for educational transitions.
7. Provide career exploratory experiences to help students gain an understanding of worker characteristics and work requirements.
8. Provide experiences to help students increase their understanding of their own capabilities, interests and possible limitations.
9. Provide for career preparation experiences that will enable the individual to acquire skills necessary to enter and remain in the world of work at a level appropriate to his capabilities and expectations.
10. Provide, as an extension of the in-service learning experience, opportunities for the individual to experience work firsthand in a nonthreatening environment. (pp. 15, 16)

Additional general responsibilities of classroom teachers include assisting in identifying school and community resources, serving as resource persons for vocations and avocations in which the teacher has expertise, and assisting in planning and coordinating of the school's career education efforts.

Use of Teaching Aids

Classroom teachers are responsible for making use of appropriate teaching aids as part of their efforts to implement career education. School librarians and school information services are valuable assets for career education implementation. However, teachers should exercise care to assure that the teaching aids contribute to the teaching of their basic academic subjects rather than substitute for it. If films about occupational activities, television programs about job-related value questions, etc., are not related by the classroom teacher to academic subject learnings, then the use of these teaching aids has not contributed to career education implementation.

Classroom teachers should acquaint themselves with various technological means of delivery of educational services and with various programs and materials developed by commercial companies, exemplary career education projects, and others. Prospective users are faced with an almost overwhelmingly large array of materials from which to choose. Teachers should devise an instructional design for career education involving the systematic development of instruction using all resources available, and this design should form a basis for making decisions as to what materials and equipment the librarian should procure for classroom use.

Use of Community Resources

Classroom teachers must make use of community resources in order to provide their students with opportunities to learn about specific occupations, work site environments, workers' attitudes toward their jobs, job stability, occupational career ladders, routes of occupational entry, and the use of basic academic skills in occupations. Community resources, properly used, should increase teachers' knowledge and understanding as well as that of students. Teachers should plan and coordinate their use of community resources through the school career education team. Coordination is necessary to avoid making unreasonable demands on the time of some resource people, to avoid duplicative experiences and overexposure of students to certain occupational clusters, and to provide students with exposure to a wide range of occupational clusters.

Parents and families of students. Each classroom teacher should identify possible resources from among the families of students. A simple checklist can be used to gather information about vocations, avocations, and specific employment positions of students' parents or guardians. In many cases, parents will be given time off their jobs to visit schools, but in many cases students will be able to explain parents' or guardians' occupations to their peers. This activity, whether completed by student reports or by family member visits to school, should result in strengthened feelings of self-worth as well as in increased knowledge about occupations. This activity should create a bond between schools and homes, and it should reinforce the tendency of students and parents to discuss school and work activities.

These good things can happen if classroom teachers implement career education practices, and career education practices include having teachers exhibit equally positive feelings about all the occupations reported. They should carefully refrain from imposing their own middle-class-oriented occupational values. Teachers should take great care to avoid inadvertent expressions of value judgment. Some studies (Suchman et al., 1969; Yee, 1968) have found that teachers express negative attitudes toward low-income groups, and that they tend to dominate and exhibit negative attitudes toward students from low socio-economic backgrounds. As a group, teachers are less dominant and exhibit positive attitudes toward more advantaged children. Students are likely to be as impressed with the vocational competence of parents who are telephone linepeople and hair stylists as with the vocational competence of parents who are tax lawyers and dentists. Classroom teachers have the responsibility to assure that the school curriculum does not demean certain work and exalt certain other work.

Field trips. Classroom teachers should plan field trips to meet specific objectives in their instructional design. Field trips should be planned and coordinated with the help of the school career education team. The difficulty and expense of field trips demand that they avoid duplication and meet as many needs as possible. Teachers should plan field trips which will provide students an opportunity to observe how workers carry out responsibilities, how workers use academic skills currently being taught in the classroom, and how work environments vary among occupations.

Several people, including administrators, counselors, parents, and community volunteers often are involved with teachers in solving scheduling, transportation, liability, and chaperoning problems which are associated with field trips. However, teachers alone are responsible for preparing for the trip and following up on the trip. Preparation should include readings, discussions, and student activities related to the trip's learning objectives, practice in student conduct as guests at work sites, and practice in observing on work sites. Follow-up should include readings, discussions, and student activities related to the trip's learning objectives.

All students should get out into the work world and experience the sights, sounds, smells, etc., associated with work environments. Most exemplary career education projects have accomplished such visits. However, there is not a workable plan for accomplishing such visits by all schools rather than just a few classes in a few schools. Classroom teachers can provide students with at least a vicarious field trip experience by backpacking a TV camera along on a visit by one class of students, and televising the visits for viewing by other students. For many students, such experiences might be the only alternative to no experiences.

Classroom guest speakers. As with field trips, the use of visiting speakers should be planned and coordinated with the help of the school career education team. Such sharing will help classroom teachers identify potential resource people. Teachers may wish to "swap" resource people from among their students' families. In some instances, classes may be combined for sessions with visiting speakers. If the school has the appropriate television facilities, several classes can view a speaker's presentation, or the presentation can be taped for later viewing by other classes.

Although the school career education team should participate in the planning and coordinating of speaking visits, individual teachers should assume part of the responsibility for contacting prospective resource speakers, gaining their cooperation, preparing them for the visit, and sending letters of appreciation to speakers after their visit.

In every case, classroom teachers have the responsibility for planning to use speakers to meet specific instructional objectives, for preparing the students for the visit, and for following up the guest speaker with discussions and activities in the classroom. Specific objectives should relate to the career development stage of students as well as to their academic level. For example, these instructional objectives might include learning about occupational clusters, specific jobs, specific avocations, and overlap of certain vocations and avocations. Since the primary role of classroom teachers is to teach academic subjects, all career-related activities, including classroom guest presentations, should have the objective of increasing student academic subject learnings, and motivation to learn academic subjects by relating activities to the career usefulness of specific academic subjects.

Classroom teachers should prepare students by developing class interest in the speaker's subject, explaining who the speakers are and why they are visiting the class, pointing out how the speakers' visits fit into the work of the class, having students role play to practice asking questions of the speakers, and helping them prepare to respond to questions which the speakers might ask them.

Teachers should conduct follow-up of visits by leading class discussions on the speaker's subject, asking students to evaluate the experience, assigning study activities which will help students understand how academic subjects are used in the speakers' occupations, and assigning practice in the use of academic subjects as used in the occupations. Teachers should evaluate the activity, keep a record, and consider the evaluation when planning future use of resource persons. If several classes have participated in the speaker's presentation, not all teachers need feel obligated to write to the speaker. However, at least one teacher, or representative of all the teachers involved, should write to the speaker to express appreciation for the visit, inform the speaker of positive evaluations by students, and invite the speaker to evaluate the activity, or make other suggestions concerning the purpose of the visit. Teachers of upper elementary, junior high, and senior high school pupils also should have at least one student write a thank-you letter on behalf of the students.

Use of Curriculum Materials

Classroom teachers control the career education curriculum not only because they decide what portion of recommended curricular materials they actually will use, but also because they have the expertise to write the needed materials. Administrators, counselors, vocational educators, exemplary career education project staff members and teachers, commercial companies, and community resource people all have certain unique contributions to make in creating career education materials. Some members of these groups already have created some valuable materials, but these are often too limited in number and scope to be considered as other than starting points for use by the teachers who must create materials which are of sufficient number and depth to integrate career education in the entire curriculum. It is the responsibility of many classroom teachers to create career education curriculum materials, and it is the responsibility of every teacher to adapt materials for appropriate use in individual classrooms.

As a first step toward creation or adaptation of career education curricular materials, teachers must assume the professional responsibility for facilitating students' career growth as well as intellectual growth. Classroom teachers traditionally have ignored responsibility for facilitating students' career growth. They have argued that their role should be to enrich students' lives by exposing them to "belles lettres," and that inclusion of practical utility of school subjects would destroy their aesthetic value. To the contrary, career education proponents believe that utility and aesthetics are not mutually exclusive. The teacher's role in career education is to create, adapt, and use curriculum guides and lesson plans which will assure that education is both career related and intellectually provocative. This curriculum will assure that education leads to increased understanding and appreciation of human values as well as occupational opportunities, and will be of sufficient academic rigor to assure that students gain the academic skills necessary both for vocational competence and aesthetic appreciation.

For classroom teachers to be able to exhibit such teaching skills, they first must have understanding of student career development growth patterns and knowledge of occupational usefulness of academic subjects. It is the responsibility of teachers to strive to acquire such knowledge and understanding, and to cooperate with other educators to accomplish the professional staff development necessary for career education implementation.

All classroom teachers should begin at least a modest effort to implement career education by modifying present curricular materials to include their present knowledge of their subject's career utility. As a first step, teachers should compile a list of occupations which relate to their subject. As an example, a foreign language teacher could list travel guide, travel agent, flight stewardess, stenographer, receptionist, missionary, social worker, customs inspector, FBI agent, physician, diplomat, business executive, and salesman among the many occupations which make direct or indirect use of foreign language skills. However, a classroom teacher whose knowledge stops at job lists is likely to present a sterile, boring picture of career uses of academic skills. For example, any teacher can list some occupations, such as umpire and professional athlete, which require good physical health, and many teachers can teach methods of reaching and maintaining good health standards. A career education classroom teacher, however, knows that many occupations require that certain health standards be met, and uses this knowledge in motivating students to learn and practice good health habits.

Classroom teachers are responsible for seeking out and adapting the material already developed for career education implementation. However, teachers should not wait to acquire special materials to implement career education. They should begin where they are with what material they have. They should modify existing materials, and work on creating at least a modest number of new lesson plans. Teachers should identify lesson plans according to career cluster, subject, area, grade level, broad developmental objectives, specific behavioral objectives, and career-related learning activities. The teacher should choose career-related activities which are appropriate for either sex, offer a reasonable chance for success for every pupil, are inexpensive, safe, interesting, appropriate to the age of the pupils, and which provide opportunity for pupils to practice the academic skill taught in the course.

Summary

Career education does not change the primary role of classroom teachers, but career education implementation requires that they all become master teachers. To accomplish this professional growth, teachers should acknowledge career education as an improved way to teach. They should then extend their knowledge of occupations, synthesize this occupational knowledge with their knowledge of academic subject areas, and teach with a sensitivity to the career usefulness of academic subjects. Teachers also should extend their knowledge of career development stages as one aspect of human development. They should extend their knowledge of teaching aids, so that as career education continues to grow, a variety of media will be used in schools as a partial substitute for regular visits of large numbers of students to the real work setting.

If classroom teachers do their part of the job, career education implementation will be accomplished with relative ease. If classroom teachers do not do their part, it is unlikely that career education implementation will be accomplished.

Role of the Counselor

School counselors' professional identity will not be swallowed up in career education. Counselors in career education programs will continue to provide unique guidance experiences which students do not receive through classroom experiences. In addition to the unique duties which counselors alone will perform, they should play a major role in collaborating with other people, both in and out of school, who have roles in career education. Hoyt (1974) emphasized this point by stating that "the most appropriate and productive role counselors could play is to enthusiastically endorse and enter into the collaborative efforts of the career education movement." However, Hoyt (1974, 1975) further emphasizes that implementation of career education calls for a change in counselor practice.

Need for Change in Counselor Practice

Counselors have had a central leadership role in career education from the first theoretical statement to the latest practical development. A majority of the financial and administrative support for career education efforts thus far has come from vocational education sources, but a majority of the theoretical and leadership support has come from guidance. Hoyt (1974) stated that, of people nominated by local school districts to attend a series of national leadership "miniconferences," more were from guidance backgrounds than from any other educational specialty. This finding was supported by data compiled for the Council of Chief State School Officers (Crawford and Jesser, 1975) which indicated that, although a majority of state department career education leadership positions were supported by vocational education funds, a majority of the positions were held by people with guidance backgrounds.

There is clear evidence that counselors have given more leadership than any other professional group to the development of career education, but there also are distressing indications that counselors have done more than any other professional group to interfere with career educaton implementation. Hoyt (1974) reports that, although people with counseling backgrounds were in the majority among local school district representatives to the national "miniconferences" on career education, when conference participants were asked to name factors currently acting to impede career education in the senior high school, counselors were among the most frequently mentioned "roadblocks" named. The writer has heard this same report from state and local career education leaders in several states, although a majority of these leaders themselves were trained guidance counselors. It is apparent that those who are counselors must put their own house in order before they can be effective change agents for career education implementation.

Counselors first should analyze their feelings about career education. It is probable that a thoughtful self-analysis will reveal to some counselors that they are apprehensive about career education because their own background has not prepared them to understand and work with the career development of students, and that they spend their time with educational counseling because that is what they understand better than other aspects of counseling. It is probable that a thoughtful self-analysis will reveal to some counselors that their one year of counselor training did not change the attitudes and practices they learned during their four years of teacher training, and that they still think and act as traditional teachers rather than as innovative counselors. It is probable that a thoughtful self-analysis will reveal to some counselors that they are permissive and yielding both by nature and by training, and that this permissiveness results in their being passive reactors rather than active initiators. It is probable that a thoughtful self-analysis will reveal to some counselors that their training and experience have not prepared them to do the teacher and student group work which career education requires, and they spend their time in one-to-one counseling sessions because they already are comfortable with this technique. In every case, counselors should examine themselves, and strive for whatever growth might be necessary for them to think and act as change agents.

Other reasons for counselors' career education inactivity are externally imposed. They include lack of clerical help, inflexible school schedules, high counselor-student ratios, inefficient course scheduling systems, the tendencies of some school administrators to use counselors as assistant-assistant principals, criticism instead of cooperation from teachers, and excessive demands on counselors' time by some college-bound students and their parents. It is apparent to the writer that these externally-imposed limitations on counselors' activities are strong reasons why they should become active as change agents for career education. If counselors continue to accept a system that does not permit them to function effectively, they will contribute to the obsolescence and eventual elimination of public school counseling.

The Counselor as Change Agent

After counselors have engaged in introspection to sort out their feelings about career education, they should familiarize themselves with all aspects of the concept. Then, they should prepare to work with students' career development, and with teachers to help them understand career development. Counselors should familiarize themselves with studies such as the one conducted by the American College Testing Program (Prediger, Roth, and Noeth, 1974) which show a general need for career education. In addition, they should conduct a needs assessment for their own schools. Much of the information for school needs assessments likely exists in the form of statistics such as dropout rates, percentage of graduates who go on to college, percentage of those college entrants who graduate from college, and the percentage of graduates and school leavers who had a job entry skill when they left the school. In addition to this statistical information, counselors should compile data about the career development levels of currently enrolled students. Counselors should involve representative students, teachers, administrators, parents, local labor leaders, and local business leaders in delineating desirable career development needs for various grade levels.

This local involvement is extremely important in mobilizing forces to implement career education. Some career education proponents (Bailey and Stadt, 1973) have recommended that students develop a tentative career choice by the beginning of high school, and that they "crystallize" this choice during high school. There is evidence (Super, 1969) that vocational maturity in the ninth grade and twelfth grade has predictive validity for vocational success in young adulthood. Although such theories and findings are interesting and helpful, they are much less effective than local opinion in motivating local support for career education. It is psychologically axiomatic that people tend to support a given change in direct proportion to the degree that they perceive a need for the change. If people have input in describing desirable goals, they are more likely to be concerned when the subsequent needs study finds that there is marked disparity between these goals and students' actual growth.

Counselors can find many suggested needs assessment techniques and aids, including standardized instruments in a guide (Development Associates, Inc., 1974) developed for local school districts. There are examples of needs assessment instruments in the reports of some exemplary career education projects, or counselors can devise their own instruments.

In cases where it is not possible to conduct a needs assessment, counselors should make observations about career development levels of their counselees. Such clinical judgments should be written down and used as evidence of need when discussing career education with people in and out of the school system.

In every case, counselors should seek out people, including other counselors, administrators, vocational educators, academic subject teachers, parents, business and labor leaders, and others, who share interest in and concern about student career development. Together with these people, counselors should assert themselves by working both formally and informally for career education implementation.

Counselor Activities in Career Education Programs

The American Personnel and Guidance Association (1974) adopted a career education position paper which listed the following counselor role statements as appropriate for career education:

1. Provide professional leadership in identification and programmatic implementation of student career development tasks appropriate for the educational level at which the counselor is functioning.
2. Provide professional leadership in the identification, classification, and dissemination of educational and career information to students and to other educational personnel involved in the career education program.
3. Provide professional leadership in the assimilation and application of career decision-making methods and materials in the total career education program.
4. Provide professional leadership in eliminating the influence of both racism and sexism as cultural restrictors of educational and career opportunities pictured as available to minority persons and to females.
5. Provide professional leadership in expanding the variety and appropriateness of assessment devices and procedures required for sound educational and career decision making.
6. Provide professional leadership in emphasizing the importance and carrying out the functions of professional educational and career counseling. (pp. 1-2)

Career education requires that counselors spend much of their time conducting group sessions for students, teachers, and parents. However, career education does not require that these group sessions deal entirely with career-related topics. To the contrary, they provide counselors the opportunity to work with the entire gamut of human development needs. Counselors should use regular group meetings to help students clarify their values and develop decision-making skills, as well as consider personal and social concerns. Counselors should use regular group meetings to help parents understand and work with career development needs of students, but these series of meetings also can include helping them relate to and communicate with their children. Except in cases where there is a favorable counselor-student ratio, there should be very little one-to-one counseling in a career education program. Counselors should spend most of their time in group, placement, information, consultation with teachers, and appraisal activities of the type which are described elsewhere in this book.

The school counselor has a responsibility to serve on the school career education team and to support and extend its work. However, counselors should keep in mind that establishing and directing the career education team is within the purview of school administrators rather than the purview of counselors. In cases where counselors are asked to serve as coordinators of the team, they should make an effort to involve as many other groups as possible in the planning and coordinating of career education activities. Regardless of who is designated as the coordinator of career education, the school counselor should strive to help other staff members understand that career education is the responsibility of the total staff, and assist them to meet this responsibility.

Summary

Counselors have a dual role in career education. They should act as change agents to implement career education. During and after implementation, they should perform duties unique to counseling services and serve on school teams for planning and coordinating career education activities.

Role of the Administrator

Career education is everybody's business, but too often everybody's business in theory becomes nobody's business in practice. The role of the administrator is to provide leadership which assures that all do their part in taking care of career education business. Career education implementation requires that educational administrators identify career education as a priority, that they gain official support for it by recommending adoption of a policy statement by school boards, that they arrange for the necessary staff development, that they devise and implement a system of planning and coordinating activities within and between schools, and that they monitor, evaluate, and, if necessary, modify the program.

There are historical as well as current practical reasons for administrators to assume the leadership responsibility for career education. Career education gained national attention because it was a top priority of a national educational administrator (Marland, 1971). However, the American Association of School Administrators (AASA Commission on Imperatives in Education, 1966) previously had identified preparation for the world of work as one of nine imperatives in education and recommended that schools provide developmental guidance programs to include focusing the curriculum on career objectives and interweaving career information with individual self-understanding. Additionally, the other eight imperatives identified by AASA include subgoals which directly relate to career education. These two examples of national administrative endorsements of career education have resulted in some national career education implementation, but it is the responsibility of local school administrators to provide leadership for local implementation.

Responsibilities of System-Wide Administrators

The school superintendent first should state behavioral goals for desired student growth through education. Where they do not already exist, career development goals should be stated. Involvement of diverse groups in goal stating, as was discussed above in the section dealing with counselor roles, is extremely important in setting goals for the entire school system. It is important that goal statements deal with acquisition of basic academic skills, citizenship development, aesthetic enjoyment, career development, and any other specific growth goals which the system uses to justify expenditure of public funds. These goals should form the basis for current needs assessments and future evaluations for the entire local school system. Superintendents should assure that current levels of attainment of all local educational goals will be used in future evaluations of the effect of career education.

After stating goals and conducting a needs assessment, superintendents should identify alternative actions to meet needs. If career education is identified as an action to take, the superintendent should recommend that the school board adopt a policy statement calling for career education integration into the curriculum.

Responsibilities of the Career Education Task Force

After the school board adopts this policy, the superintendent should appoint a task force to devise strategies for implementation. This task force, while it might include representatives from diverse groups, should primarily be composed of people who have the influence to carry out at least the first portion of their plan. Generally, since career education involves all areas of instruction, the director of instruction is the most logical person to name as chairperson of the task force, and, generally, the vocational education director is the least logical person to name as chairperson. Too many people already confuse the terms "vocational" and "career" education. However, the vocational education director should be named to the task force. The superintendent should point out to the task force the previous activities which established the "what," "why," "whether," and "when" of career education and should emphasize that their charge is to identify the "who," "where," and "how."

In carrying out their charge, the task force should contrast existing resources, such as professional personnel, materials, equipment, community resources, and organizational structure, with resources needed. Next, they should outline a plan with specified first steps, short-range implementation goals, long-range implementation goals, specified monitoring procedures, and specified regular times to meet and consider any time-frame changes or other modifications which may be indicated by unexpected progress or problems.

It is likely that the greatest need will be in the area of staff development, and the first step in meeting this need should be to identify resource people to train the staff. Counselor educators, teacher educators, state department of education supervisors, etc., whose positions require that they offer staff development assistance should be involved in the training. Some of these people already are prepared to assist with career education staff development. In using staff development resource people, however, the local school should see to it that the resource people deal with the specified local needs.

Staff development is of primary importance in carrying out the task force's plan. The staff development program should be aimed first at having administrators identify career education development and implementation as their responsibility. If this step is successful, the "ripple" effect will result in the involvement of other staff members. Staff development is necessary in order to meet other needs. The task force should acquire only the materials and equipment necessary to assist in staff development; the professional educators then should assist in creating, adapting, or adopting other necessary materials. Elementary general supervisors should assist in the staff development of elementary teachers, and then should work with them in developing materials. Likewise, all other general supervisors or administrators should act to implement career education in their area of responsibility.

Long-range goals should include articulation between schools so that students transferring from one school to the same grade level in other schools, and students promoted from elementary schools to junior high schools, etc., will not face duplicative experiences or miss being exposed to important career-related activities. Both short-range and long-range goals should include coordination between schools to assure that some community resources aren't overused and/or other community resources ignored. The director of instruction and the general supervisory staff are responsible for providing such articulation and coordination between schools. Additionally, they are responsible for encouraging and assisting school principals to provide articulation and coordination within schools.

Responsibilities of Building Administrators

The principal's role is to encourage and coordinate career education implementation in a specific school building. Selection of in-service education activities and faculty meeting topics, assignment of space and personnel, purchase of equipment and materials, selection of a class and activities scheduling system, evaluation of programs and staff, choice of administrative style, and selection of administrative organizational structure all are aspects of the principal's work which should express career education leadership.

In-service education experiences and faculty meetings should be used to translate broad goals into specific goals for the school, to identify present and desired resources, to plan specific action to reach the desired goals, and to take the first steps to implement the plan. In order to reduce boredom, encourage active participation, and set an example for teachers to follow in their use of teaching methods, principals should strive to assure that methods of conducting workshops and meetings are varied to reflect the varying environments of diverse work sites.

Evaluation of staff should include consideration of career education competencies. For example, a classroom teacher's evaluation should include consideration of the teacher's attitude toward career education, knowledge of direct and indirect vocational and avocational uses of academic subject matter, provision of career-related activities for students, and creation of a career environment in the classroom.

Responsibilities of the School Career Education Team

Administrative structure should include establishment of a school career education team. Generally, existing heads of departments should be named to the team, but it always should include representatives from each grade level, curriculum area, library, and counseling services. The principal should advise and assist the team. Everyone should be kept aware of the fact that the team is reflecting, rather than replacing, the principal's leadership. The school team should assist in identifying school and community resources and should coordinate the use of resources so that all are used, plan and coordinate activities so that all occupational clusters are included equally, and provide articulation between grade levels and curriculum areas so that students will not experience duplicative activities as they progress through the school program. In cases where several teachers are participating in an activity utilizing community resources, the team should coordinate the arrangements so that teachers share evenly in contacting, preparing, and follow-up of community resource people, and that such arrangements are not left to chance. The team should assist in monitoring and evaluating the progress being made toward reaching career education implementation goals, and, if necessary, recommend revision of the plan.

Summary

Educational administrators and supervisors should include career education development and implementation in carrying out all aspects of their present jobs. Local superintendents should state goals, assess needs, recommend career education policy statements to school boards, and carry out the policy statements with the assistance of career education task forces. Principals should accept and carry out the responsibility for career education implementation in the school, and should establish a school career education team to assist in coordinating the school's career education efforts.

Role of the Community

Career education cannot be fully implemented without collaborative efforts of schools and community resource people. The halls of ivy and the cloistered atmosphere of schools in "the good old days" has been praised in prose and poetry. The fact that multitudes of children, especially those who were subject to the inhuman child-labor sweatshops of "the good old days," couldn't participate in those cloistered experiences hasn't seemed to diminish the social myths which have grown out of those experiences. Today's society, in which the blackboard jungle has replaced the halls of ivy, has schools which oppress students in an opposite, but still onerous fashion. Many of today's schools oppress students by cloistering them from the real world. The privileged few students, whose parents can arrange and pay for experiences which allow them to understand themselves and the world of work, and then to make decisions based on both understandings, still are the people who leave school with a long headstart in the race for the good life. Other less fortunate children whose career development experiences now occur mainly within the traditional school boundaries of two covers of a book and four walls of a classroom, already are career-retarded by the time they leave school. The bright but financially poor young person of past generations, who had to drop out of school to take some low-status job, has been replaced by the bright but financially poor young person who graduates from high school or college with no job-entry skill, and then takes some low-status job.

Such oppression of students can be replaced by opportunities only when schools and communities collaborate. Currently, community groups generally offer more assistance to schools than schools accept, but these efforts generally have been designed by the community groups to meet their own ideas of student needs.

The role of the community in career education is to continue and extend practices of cooperation with schools, and to modify these practices according to collaborative agreements based on the community agencies' ideas and the schools' goals. The following discussions deal with some of the community influences on student development.

Parents

The Position Paper on Career Development adopted by the American Vocational Association/National Vocational Guidance Association Commission on Career Guidance and Vocational Education (1973) contains the following eloquent and accurate statement about the role of parents:

> Parents—Without question parents can and should be the most influential role model figures and counselors to their children. Having some measure of direct control over the environment in which their children have been reared, they have the unique opportunity of exposing them to experiences appropriate for self-fulfillment. As their children enter public education, parents share but do not give up, the responsibility for their development. Parents who take full advantage of the information given them by school staff members concerning the interest, aptitudes, failures and achievements of their children can use this background of information to provide:
>
> 1. Assistance in analyzing their children's interests, capabilities and limitations.
> 2. Explanations of the traits required, the working conditions and life styles of work areas with which they are most familiar.
> 3. Discussions of work values developed as a result of past experiences and of the consequences they have experienced.
> 4. Discussions of the economic condition of the family as it applies to the children's education and training needs, and assistance in planning a course of action.
> 5. Help in using the knowledge, experience and service of relatives, friends, fellow workers and other resources in exploring the world of work and in planning and preparing for their role in the work society.
> 6. A model and counsel to their children during critical developmental periods of their lives in an attempt to have children establish and maintain positive attitudes towards themselves and others.
> 7. Exemplification of the attitude that all persons have dignity and worth no matter what their position in the world of work.
> 8. Situations that allow children to experience decision making and to accept responsibility for the consequences of their decision.

9. Maintenance of open communications between school and home so that the experiences of both settings can be used in meeting student needs.
10. Opportunities for children to work and accept responsibilities of the home and community. (pp. 17-18)

Labor Unions

Labor took an active part in the early development of career education, and generally continues to endorse the career education concept. Certain labor representatives, such as Sessions (1974), have expressed concern that career education might be misdirected by placing too much emphasis on the occupational, and too little emphasis on the humanistic aspects of career education. However, these expressions of concern indicate interest in, rather than opposition to, career education. Sessions served on the advisory comitttee which helped to develop the "Bread & Butterflies" (Agency for Instructional Television, 1974) television career education aids. The advice of this committee influenced the creation of the strongly humanistic flavor of "Bread & Butterflies." Career education efforts of individual state and local educational agencies have been influenced and supported by labor unions. For example, Charleston, West Virginia's Experience-Based Career Education program flourished after getting advice and support from the labor movement.

Labor councils can and should offer help to school career education efforts by providing advice and support of a general nature. Craft unions can and should support career education awareness and exploration efforts by describing and demonstrating their work. Additionally, the apprenticeship programs supported by the craft unions provide valuable career preparation training.

Labor unions should continue to influence and support career education so that the humanistic aspect of career education always will remain a top priority. Labor unions understand that certain work situations can be alienating and dehumanizing, and they should help schools structure their curriculum to avoid practices and situations which are damaging to student human dignity.

Business Organizations

Various Chamber of Commerce groups have endorsed career education. Both the Chamber of Commerce of the United States (1975) and the Michigan State Chamber of Commerce (Easterling, 1974) printed and distributed booklets designed to aid career education implementation. Many state and local Chamber of Commerce groups have aided the promotion of career education by offering a variety of services to schools. Printed lists of part-time job opportunities, community resources, and diverse educational offerings are examples of services provided by local Chamber of Commerce groups. The National Alliance of Businessmen has provided funding for career guidance training for counselors and funds for training educators to upgrade career guidance skills have been provided by several private corporations.

Business organizations provide resource speakers, opportunity for observation in various work settings, and experiences in performing work. Hundreds of businesses and business organizations have provided schools with free brochures about a wide variety of occupations.

The role of business organizations in career education is to continue and extend their efforts to help schools increase student career knowledges. These efforts should be modified, on the basis of school requests to meet specific local school needs.

Other Community Agencies

The above discussions of labor and business roles in career education made no attempt to include a complete listing of the scope of services provided by these resource people; such a list would require printing a separate volume. Likewise, this paragraph makes no attempt to include a complete listing of other community resources and the career education services they provide. Such a list would require several printed volumes. The National Urban Coalition, Women's American O.R.T., The Boy Scouts of America Exploring program, and the Junior League are examples of the many community groups which have expressed interest in, and support for career education. Some of these groups, such as the National Urban Coalition, have expressed concern that career education not be allowed to increase, rather than diminish, the distance between our society's "haves" and "have-nots." However, this expression of concern, like that of some labor union representatives, indicates interest in and involvement with career education. Such influence is extremely important in shaping and implementing these programs.

Summary

The community has a dual role in career education. The community should collaborate with schools to plan for and provide experiential career learning activities for students, and the community should monitor, evaluate, and, if necessary, help redirect career education toward the goals of total self-development of students.

Conclusion

Teachers, counselors, administrators, parents, community agencies, labor, and business all have unique roles in career education. However, there are areas of overlap from each role to all the other roles. Career education is the responsibility of all and the domain of none. Further, no group's unique responsibilities for career education can be met independently of the other groups. Collaboration of all concerned, based on mutual dedication to maximum total opportunities for student growth, is essential for career education implementation.

References

Agency for Instructional Television. *Bread & butterflies: community action plans.* Bloomington, Indiana: Author, 1974.

American Association of School Administrators. *Imperatives in education.* Washington, D.C.: American Association of School Administrators, 1966.

American Personnel and Guidance Association. *Career guidance: Role and functions of counseling and personnel practitioners in career education.* Washington, D.C.: Author, 1974.

American Vocational Association-National Vocational Guidance Association. *Position paper on career development.* Washington, D.C.: NVGA/AVA, 1973.

Bailey, L. J., and Stadt, R. W. *Career education: New approaches to human development.* Bloomington: McKnight, 1973.

Chamber of Commerce of the United States. *Career education: What it is and why we need it.* Washington, D.C.: Chamber of Commerce of the United States, 1975.

Crawford, R. L. and Jesser, D. L. *The status and progress of career education.* Washington: Council of Chief State School Officers, 1975.

Development Associates, Inc. *Handbook for the evaluation of career education programs.* Washington: Bureau of Occupational and Adult Education, U.S. Office of Education, 1974.

Easterling, L. C. *Career education: A prospectus for businessmen and the community.* Lansing: Michigan State Chamber of Commerce, 1974.

Hoyt, K. B. *Career education: Challenges for counselors.* Paper presented at the All Ohio School Counselors Association, Columbus, September, 1974.

———.*Career education and counselor education.* Paper presented at the Association for Counselor Education and Supervision meeting, 1975 APGA Convention, New York City, March, 1975.

Marland, S. P., Jr. *Career education now.* Address to the 1971 Convention of the National Association of Secondary School Principals, Houston, Texas, January 23, 1971.

Prediger, D. J.; Roth, J. D.; and Noeth, R. J. Career development of youth: A nationwide study. *The Personnel and Guidance Journal* 53 (1974):97-104.

Sessions, J. Misdirecting career education. *Update* 2 (1) (1974):9-11.

Suchman, E. A., et al. *The relationship between poverty and educational deprivation.* A Report to the Learning Research and Development Center, Pittsburgh University, Pennsylvania, August, 1968, U.S. Office of Education, Bureau of Research. Washington: U.S. Government Printing Office, 1969. (ERIC Document Reproduction Service No. ED 023 769)

Super, D. E. Vocational development theory: Persons, positions, and processes. *The Counseling Psychologist* 1 (1969):2-9.

Yee, A. H. Source and direction of causal influence in teacher-pupil relationships. *Journal of Educational Psychology* 59 (1968):275-82.

Chapter 11

VOCATIONAL EDUCATION AND GUIDANCE: A PARTNERSHIP

Richard L. Lynch

One group of persons within the educational environment that can and should have a great deal of impact upon the career development of youth and adults is vocational educators. They are the group that can be most instrumental—by virtue of their education, training, and work experience—to guide the occupational exploration and skill development of students. However, the cooperative spirit and harmonious working relationship of guidance specialists and vocational educators within the schools has apparently yet to be realized.

The criticism of school guidance personnel and programs is well known to anyone who reads professional or popular journals or attends meetings of vocational educators. The guidance counselor is often accused by the vocational educator of being a former academic teacher who could not cut the mustard in that capacity and was therefore transferred into guidance by the principal who didn't want any more damage done to students. The image is further developed that the guidance counselor spends an undue amount of time encouraging her (and, according to vocational educators, it usually is a she) "academic" students to go on to college. Those students possessing something less than the desired level of intelligence or those who are generally viewed by the counselor as "nonconformists" are shuttled off to the shops and home economics laboratories in the basement.

The guidance programs have been accused—and perhaps rightly so—of neglecting the career development and occupational interests of the noncollegebound students. Numerous studies, conference proceeding reports, Congressional hearings, and reports from vocational education advisory councils have emphasized the lack of appropriate guidance services for vocationally-oriented students and the lack of career development services for all students.

Conversely, counselors too have had their comments to make with respect to vocational education programs. The "basement image" of vocational education programs has not always allowed conscientious counselors to encourage students to enroll in such programs. Some research and position papers have attempted to prove or theorize that vocational programs are only concerned with entry-level job skills (often which can be developed in a very short period of time and more efficiently in the actual employment environment), and that such programs do not enhance the theoretical thinking ability of students. Furthermore, many persons in educational leadership positions feel that vocational programs close out occupational options

Dr. Richard L. Lynch is Associate Professor of Vocational Education at Virginia Polytechnic Institute and State University, Blacksburg, Virginia.

for students by forcing them into a specialized vocational program much too early in life. For all these reasons—either true or imagined—counselors sometimes have been reluctant to recommend vocational programs for students, other than those who are failing in academic or general education courses.

It is interesting to note that neither group—the guidance counselors nor the vocational educators—will disagree with the common goal of the educational process: that is providing a curriculum that will enable the student to progress toward a life personally rewarding and meaningful to society. However, the manner in which each operates seems to be the basic misunderstanding between each group.

Some progress has been made in recent years to increase the understanding on the part of vocational educators of the guidance process and to inform guidance personnel of the objectives and operational procedures of various vocational education programs. Several universities, State Departments of Education, and/or local school systems have been sponsoring joint activities with guidance personnel and vocational educators. The primary purposes of these activities have been to increase the understanding of each others role and mission in the educational system and to begin jointly planning for an effective career information and training system that can benefit all students.

Much of the impetus for joint undertakings and planning sessions has come about as a result of Federal funding through the Vocational Education Amendments of 1968 and the recent emphasis on career education. More and more, all educators are realizing the importance of preparing young persons and adults for productive and rewarding careers. Educational leaders are becoming aware of the necessity for career-oriented guidance personnel who are knowledgeable of the processes involved in choosing, preparing for, and maintaining employment. Leadership personnel in universities and other educational institutions are also becoming aware of the inadequate vocational preparation of guidance counselors and are thus providing avenues for them to become informed about vocational offerings, as well as the skills, attitudes, and knowledges needed by workers in various occupations at entry, career, and managerial levels.

Vocational educators too have greatly benefited from increased contact with guidance counselors. They have received assistance in understanding and coping with the uniqueness of individuals, the importance of the self-concept as manifested within an occupation, the theory and research indicating vocational choice and occupational decision-making as a lifelong process, and the importance of teaching fundamental skills (i.e., reading, mathematics, communications) and life adjustment competencies (i.e., human relations) within the framework of occupational training. No longer are vocational educators teaching skills without parallel instruction in decision making, value clarification, attitude formation, and human relations.

The purpose of this chapter is to further increase the dialogue between guidance personnel and vocational educators. The chapter is written to provide beginning students of the guidance process with an understanding of vocational education—its mission in public education and its programs designed to achieve this mission. The chapter is also concerned with the role of guidance in the vocational education programs and offers suggestions of ways in which guidance personnel can be of assistance to vocational students and teachers. Finally, the chapter concludes with a section devoted to suggestions for vocational educators in order that they might assist guidance personnel in their work with students. Interwoven throughout the chapter is the premise that guidance personnel and vocational educators need to work together cooperatively to assist students in identifying appropriate educational experiences to insure a life rewarding to the student and meaningful to society.

Vocational Education—Programs and Processes

A prevalent complaint among vocational educators regarding guidance and counseling personnel in the school systems is that the guidance people appear to have little understanding of the vocational programs. This is and should not be surprising in view of the fact that nearly all demographic studies published about guidance personnel indicate that few of them have had formal training in or direct contact with programs of vocational education. Few states require their counselors to obtain any type of work experience outside of the field of education or require any formal course work in vocational education.

Furthermore, as pointed out by Hohenshil (1974), most administrators of guidance services in educational institutions received their training in the days when counselor training programs greatly emphasized the importance of counselors encouraging students to go on to college upon high school graduation. When the National Defense Act of 1958 was passed, its provisions specifically charged school counselors with the responsibility of "identifying talented youth and guiding them into careers in engineering and the physical sciences" (p. 62). Therefore, according to Hohenshil, since guidance administrators as a group were trained in this era and have academically-oriented backgrounds, it seems logical that they may consciously or unconsciously place greater emphasis on college programming as opposed to vocational programming. Hohenshil also analyzed the vocational interests of guidance administrators in the Ohio public schools and found these interests closely aligned with white-collar professional-type jobs. Since guidance administrators do influence the tenor and priorities of the guidance and counseling department, it should not be too surprising to have more of an academic orientation within the counseling staffs.

Thus, despite the fact that federal vocational education legislation has provided funds for guidance and counseling services, it should not be assumed by vocational educators that guidance personnel are truly knowledgeable of the programs. Few have ever been enrolled in a vocational education program, few have had college credits in vocational education, and few have occupational experience or interests in blue-collar or other occupations normally associated with vocational programs. As summarized by Hoyt (1970), "The typical school counselor does not have sufficient background to do what the amendments (federal vocational education legislation) specify should be done." (p. 62)

For the beginning student of the guidance process, it is therefore important to become familiar with the vocational education programs operating within educational institutions. As the public clamors for more accountability in its schools, as increased emphasis is placed upon vocational programs in the schools, as state legislatures mandate that the schools either prepare a student for college or provide the student with job skills (as the legislature so mandated in the state of Virginia), and as students demand a curriculum more relevant and applicable to their needs, counselors will be called upon to describe, interpret, and analyze the vocational programs. Thus, this section of the chapter is devoted to an explanation of vocational education programs and the processes by which program objectives are achieved.

Vocational Education Programs

There are those that say all of education is for vocational purposes and ultimately designed to assist students in choosing, preparing for, and obtaining personal satisfaction within an occupation and to be able to perform work in a satisfactory manner. Thus, such persons would say that medical schools, law schools, and even colleges of education are in fact vocational schools.

In general, however, personnel in most educational agencies and institutions regard vocational programs as those which receive special funding from monies earmarked through federal, state or local appropriations for purposes of providing programs of vocational education. The federal government has provided special funding since 1917 for programs of vocational education within public educational institutions. Currently, federal funds are made available for vocational education programs through the 1968 Amendments to Vocational Education. In this act, vocational education is defined and uses for this specifically-earmarked money are identified as follows:

> The term vocational education means vocational or technical training or retraining which is given in schools or classes (including field or laboratory work and remedial or related academic and technical instruction incident thereto) under public supervision and control or under contract with a state board or local educational agency and is conducted as part of a program designed to prepare individuals for gainful employment as semiskilled or skilled workers or technicicans or subprofessionals in recognized occupations and in new and emerging occupations or to prepare individuals for enrollment in advanced technical education programs, but excluding any program to prepare individuals for employment in occupations which the Commissioner determines, and specified by regulation, to be generally considered professional or which requires a baccalaureate or higher degree; and such term includes vocational guidance and counseling (individually or through group instruction) in connection with such training or for the purpose of facilitating occupational choices; instruction related to the occupation or occupations for which the students are in training or instruction necessary for students to benefit from such training; job placement; the training of persons engaged as, or preparing to become, teachers in a vocational education program or preparing such teachers to meet special education needs of handicapped students; teachers, supervisors, or directors of such teachers while in such a training program; travel of students and vocational education personnel while engaged in a training program; and the acquisition, maintenance, and repair of instructional supplies, teaching aids, and equipment but such term does not include the construction, acquisition, or initial equipment of buildings or the acquisition or rental of land. (90th Congress, 1968, pp. 6-7)

All federal monies earmarked for vocational education are transmitted to a state agency (usually the State Board of Education) for dissemination to local school districts for programs of vocational education. In addition to the federal monies available, most states and localities apportion a percentage of their tax revenue for educational purposes to programs of vocational education.

Since the passage of the first vocational education act in 1917 (the Smith-Hughes Act), several specialized programs of vocational education have been developed and are available in the public schools, vocational-technical centers, and community colleges. The Smith-Hughes Act originally appropriated funds for three specialized programs in vocational education:

agricultural education, trade and industrial education, and home economics education. In subsequent federal vocational education acts, four additional vocational programs received funding: distributive education, business education, health education, and technical education. Although current legislation does not contain funds specifically earmarked for these seven occupational areas, most educational institutions do organize programs in each of these occupational areas. Thus, a brief description of each of these seven occupational programs is warranted.

Agricultural education. Nearly all secondary schools in rural areas and many schools in suburban and urban areas have vocational agriculture education programs. Community colleges and other post-secondary institutions have recently been adding specialized agricultural programs to their vocational curricula. These programs are organized to assist young persons and adults in acquiring the knowledge and skills needed for occupations in agricultural subjects. Typically, schools organize agricultural education programs in farming, agri-business, mechanics, food processing and marketing, horticulture, and conservation.

Business education. In nearly all high schools, vocational-technical centers, and community colleges in the country, a vocational program in business education is offered. Traditionally the enrollment in the curriculum has been dominated by females who enrolled in courses in shorthand, typing, office practice, and bookkeeping. In recent years, however, boys and men have enrolled in business education courses in larger numbers and curricular offerings have been increased to include data processing, computer programming, and office management.

Distributive education. A vocational program with great potential as the American economy continues to shift from goods producing to service orientation is distributive education. Young persons and adults enrolled in such programs are preparing for careers related to the marketing, merchandising, and management of products and services. The people-oriented phase of vocational education, distributive occupations are usually found in such areas of economic activity as retail and wholesale trade, finance, insurance, real estate, services and services trades, manufacturing, transportation, utilities, and communications. Activities include selling, buying, transporting, storing, promoting, financing, marketing research, management, and the provision of leisure and recreational services.

Health occupations. Another vocational program receiving increased attention by vocational educators is the health education program. Offered to a limited extent at the high school level and to a greater extent at the post-secondary level, health education programs are designed to train workers for the health care occupations. Some of the occupations for which educational institutions are providing training include nursing, nursing home workers, hospital assistants, and other health paraprofessional personnel.

Home economics. Nearly every high school, most junior high schools, and many post-secondary institutions offer a program in home economics. Until a few years ago, most of these programs were designed for young girls who were going to be homemakers. Generally, courses were offered in cooking, sewing, and family relationships. Later, courses were added in child development, consumer education, and home management. Today, many schools are also offering occupational preparation through the home economics vocational education programs. These programs are available for young men and women and include training in such occupational areas as the care and guidance of children (i.e., nursery school and day care workers);

clothing production and related services; food management, production and services; home furnishings; and institutional and home management services.

Trade and industrial education. Traditionally referred to as the "shop area," many high schools and community colleges offer vocational training in the trade areas. All vocational-technical centers house laboratories designed to train workers for various trades. Programs in the trade areas vary greatly from state to state and depend, to a large extent, on the industries located in the geographical area served by the school. Typical trade programs include brick laying, auto mechanics, drafting, printing, cosmetology, dry cleaning, electronics, and appliance repair.

Technical education. Most technical programs are offered only at the post-secondary level and are designed to prepare students for a cluster of job opportunities in a specialized field of technology. Technical education prepares for the occupational area between the skilled craftsman and the professional person such as the doctor, the engineer, and the scientist. The technician frequently is employed in direct support of the professional employee. Typically, two-year technical degrees are available in engineering, medicine, electronics, business management, and scientific fields. Other technical programs may be available in law enforcement, mining, and specialized fields needed by businesses and industries in the geographical territory served by the appropriate school.

Vocational Education Processes

Within the public schools, vocational-technical centers, and community colleges, there are a number of delivery systems utilized by vocational educators to develop the knowledges, skills, and attitudes needed by the students for the appropriate occupational program. Each of the systems is designed in consideration of the objectives of the program, the complexity of the job skills needed, and the geographical environment in which the school is located. Just as guidance personnel need an understanding of the vocational program descriptions, they also need to know the system utilized to develop the competencies needed by the students. In many schools, counselors are responsible for the scheduling of classes and students for the classes. Since nearly all vocational programs require a different format for scheduling as compared to academic or general education courses, counselors should understand the delivery system for the various programs.

In-school laboratories. The largest percentage of vocational students will be enrolled in a program which utilizes an in-school laboratory. The lab or "shop" is equipped with machinery, tools, merchandise, and equipment similar to that used in business or industry. The trade and industrial programs will have huge laboratories for auto mechanics, welding, printing, electronics, brick laying, cosmetology, etc. The health programs may have a laboratory designed to simulate a hospital room where training is provided in patient care. The business education laboratories will house secretarial desks, typewriters, transcription machines, duplicating machines, electronic data processing machines, etc. The distributive education laboratory will often consist of a graphics department, model store, stockroom, sign-making machine, cash register, and receiving and marking area.

The school laboratories are designed to simulate the business/industrial environment, and all competencies needed by workers in the occupations for which the program has been designed are usually taught within the laboratory. Oftentimes, the labs are open to the public. Parents and other residents in the geographical area can make use of the services and products associated with the various vocational programs. For example, students in auto mechanics classes often will agree to service and repair cars for the public; distributive education students often sell goods in their school store to the public; and persons in cosmetology classes often cut and style hair or give manicures to the public. The laboratories are also often used in the evening for training and retraining of adults in the various occupational areas.

In order to develop the competencies needed by workers in the various occupations, vocational students must spend a considerable portion of their school day in the appropriate laboratory. For most programs, three hours of the six to seven hour school day is usually required. For other programs, two hours a day in the laboratory may be sufficient time in which to develop the competencies. Generally, one hour each day is spent in occupationally-related instruction (i.e., attitude development, provision of occupational information, job application, citizenship development, etc.) and one to two hours in specific technical competency development.

Cooperative education. Since the passage of the 1968 Federal Amendments to Vocational Education, increased emphasis has been given to providing programs of vocational cooperative education. Prior to 1968, cooperative education was only widely used in vocational education by distributive educators and some industrial education programs had a cooperative element in the training of workers for selected trade areas. Today, cooperative education programs are popular in all vocational education programs.

The cooperative education program is a specially-designed method of delivering vocational education. It is unique in that the student is employed in a local business or industrial firm directly related to the student's in-school vocational program. Both the job and in-school classroom experiences are jointly planned and supervised by representatives from the employing firm and the school. The student is paid for the employment by the cooperating firm. Thus, the student not only receives classroom instruction and training in a vocational program of his/her choosing, but is also receiving instruction and training on a job directly related to the in-school vocational program. Both the job and school experiences are jointly planned, supervised, and evaluated by the representatives from the cooperating firm and the school. The school representative is usually the teacher who instructs the student in the vocational class. The student is usually given credit for both the in-school class and on-the-job position.

Under the cooperative program in the secondary schools, most students attend classes at the school in the morning. Their afternoon "classes" are then held in the cooperating firm which, in effect, serves as the vocational laboratory. Thus, instead of reporting to an auto mechanics laboratory in the school, a student enrolled in an auto mechanics cooperative education program would report to a job in the local community where the student would actually be involved in the servicing and repair of automobiles. The student would be paid, and both the in-school teacher and on-the-job supervisor would plan, supervise, and evaluate the student's work. The teacher, too, would actually leave the school environment to coordinate the educational experiences with cooperating business/industrial firms.

In the community colleges and some vocational-technical schools, a variation of the A.M. class, P.M. work schedule is offered. In these educational institutions, a student may spend a quarter or semester in study and then a quarter or semester in full-time employment. However, the same principles as previously described for the cooperative education program are applicable.

Other delivery systems. In addition to the in-school laboratories and the cooperative education program, there is also a proliferation of other types of systems that have been designed to deliver variations of vocational education. Most of these are a less-structured version of the cooperative education program and are designed to utilize the work environment for general education purposes. Thus, the *work study* program was designed to permit fifteen to twenty-one year olds from low-income families to commence or continue a vocational program in the secondary or post-secondary schools. The student enrolled in work study must be employed in a public institution (i.e., a school, hospital, library, university), is limited in the number of hours to be worked, and the money earned is primarily paid out of federal funds. The student does not need to be employed in a job related to his/her vocational program or career interest, and school credit is usually not given for the work.

Students enrolled in the *Work Experience and Career Exploration Program* (WECEP) have been diagnosed as potential dropouts, underachievers, or "nonconformists." This federally-funded experimental program was designed to determine if the work environment could be utilized as a motivator to retain fourteen and fifteen year olds until they qualified for the regular vocational programs. All enrollees are to be employed in the private sector of the economy and are to be closely supervised by a school-employed coordinator who also teaches social skills and human relations competencies to the students. The hope for this program is that the enrollees will come to appreciate the value education can play in subsequent employment and will thus earn at least a high school diploma. Students are usually given credit for enrolling in the WECEP program.

Work experience or *work release* programs are a third variation of the cooperative education program. In these programs, students are usually released from school for a portion of the day in order that they may work. The work may or may not be related to a vocational program and is usually not supervised by a representative from the school. Credit is usually not given for participation in this program.

A final program being given impetus in the public schools is that of *job placement*. Again, this program is not really related to vocational programs, although it should be carefully coordinated with the cooperative education program. Most job placement programs are apparently a part of the function of the school's guidance services. A person in the guidance office is given the responsibility to coordinate the job placement program, which usually means assisting currently-enrolled students in locating part-time employment or graduating seniors in locating full-time employment.

There are other types of creative and experimental programs that are currently being offered in public schools, private vocational schools, public vocational-technical schools, and community colleges. Each one seems to have its own unique purpose or operational procedure. As the programs are developed and implemented, they further add to the confusion of those who are responsible—directly or indirectly—for their implementation. These include guidance counselors, vocational educators, and members of the business/industrial community who are being asked to absorb the products of these programs in their firms. It is crucial that guidance counselors attempt to understand the objectives and operational procedures of all of these programs. Only then can they appropriately counsel and guide students who could best benefit from the varying programs.

Guidance in the Vocational Programs

Shortly after the passage of the National Defense Education Act with its emphasis on identifying and "channeling" academic students into scientific studies, a state director of vocational education was said to have remarked at a state vocational conference: "Don't depend upon your guidance counselors to help you with your vocational programs. You'd best learn to work around them!"

Fortunately, the public and personnel employed in public education have come a long way in their thinking regarding vocational education. Today, nearly 50 percent of all secondary school students enroll in one or more courses in vocational education. The 1974 Gallup Poll of Attitudes Toward Education indicated that the public felt "good" schools should provide "enough variety in the curriculum to interest students who are not college bound" (Gallup, 1975, p. 28). Furthermore, the 1973 Gallup poll indicated that nine out of ten persons surveyed felt schools should give far more emphasis to career education. According to the pollsters, "Few proposals receive such overwhelming approval today as the suggestion that schools give more emphasis to a study of trades, professions, and business" (Gallup Poll, 1973, p. 163).

School guidance personnel, too, are becoming more interested and involved in the vocational education program. There is apparently more emphasis placed upon career counseling in counselor education programs in graduate school as well as through in-service education. An increasing number of conference reports, journal articles, graduate research theses, etc., seem to indicate that leaders in the guidance and counseling field are devoting more attention to the theory, roles, responsibilities, competencies, and "how to's" of vocational guidance.

As the guidance profession becomes more involved in the vocational education program, improvement should occur in every phase of students' vocational development. As Ryan (1974) and Hoyt (1974) recently pointed out in separate publications, it is hoped—and anticipated—that school counselors will continue to examine their practices and work to change guidance from an auxiliary (or ancillary) service to a systematic and productive part of the vocational education system. Ryan suggested that the counselor must shift from providing remedial services and information on a "crisis oriented process" to a procedure which involves the teachers and administrators in the provision of a comprehensive career development program for all students. Hoyt further suggested that counselors no longer "hoard their material" or isolate themselves from those engaged in teaching; they must share their expertise with other vocational educators to create an improved system for all. Wallace (1975) further elaborated on Hoyt's statements by suggesting that the counselor "expertise" to be shared include "competencies in the entire range of services encompassed by the career development concept—self-awareness programs, interpersonal relations training programs, career information centers, testing programs, behavioral techniques, and decision-making programs" (p. 38).

The purpose of this section of the chapter is to suggest possible ways in which guidance personnel can be of assistance to vocational education teachers and students. The suggestions are not meant to be exhaustive, nor limiting in scope. They are a compilation of practices experimented with in various educational institutions and published in the literature, suggestions resulting from conferences of vocational education and/or guidance personnel, and the results of rap sessions conducted with vocational educators at various conferences or seminars.

(1) Perhaps the primary request that emerges from vocational educators is that guidance personnel provide students with accurate and unbiased information about vocational education programs. Many vocational educators have the perception—either correctly or incorrectly—that guidance counselors encourage the academically-talented students to enroll only in college preparatory-type courses. They feel that the counselors do not inform the students of vocational offerings, even though the vocational programs might be completely congruent with the student's interests. Vocational educators often reflect the perception that if a student mentions to a counselor that he or she is thinking of going on to college, the counselor immediately plans a preparatory program to include advanced mathematics and science courses, foreign languages, social studies, and English. Vocational educators seem to feel that counselors fail to mention to the student the value of acquiring a vocational skill with which to earn expenses while in college. They also feel that counselors ought to inform students of vocational offerings which can and should serve as a foundation for certain college academic programs. For example, distributive education teacher-coordinators feel that students planning to major in business administration in college ought to have at least one year of distributive education in the high school. According to the teachers, counselors rarely inform such collegebound students of the value of the distributive education offerings with respect to the student's subsequent college major.

A number of solutions have been proposed to inform students of the vocational offerings in schools. Assembly programs, bulletin board displays of the various vocational programs, feature articles in the school newspaper, career days/weeks in the schools, monographs or brochures disseminated to all students explaining the various vocational programs, group guidance sessions jointly conducted by counselors and vocational teachers, and students visiting vocational education classes and teachers for a day have proven to be effective. Hoyt (1970) further suggested that guidance personnel teach courses or sections of classes to prospective vocational students. He felt that such classes should emphasize three aspects of vocational decision making: the world of work; the world of vocational education, to include discussions of secondary, post-secondary, and manpower training programs as well as military and on-the-job training; and self-analysis, to include a study of aptitudes, interests, and aspirations with respect to the world of work.

(2) Guidance counselors can be of tremendous assistance to vocational educators by providing them with the information that has been assembled into the students' cumulative file. Vocational teachers spend a great deal of time with these students, often three to four hours a day. They are generally much closer to the student than other teachers as they work together in the vocational laboratory or analyze together various aspects of the on-the-job training program. Vocational teachers need to be aware of the results of standardized test data, attendance records, disciplinary problems, tardy records, health records, and other significant data which may affect the vocational and personal development of the student.

This data is especially important for coordinators of cooperative education and other work experience programs. In addition to the vocational teacher and guidance counselor, the employer now becomes a third party in the education and training of the student. Such factors as attendance, tardiness, health problems, etc., must be thoroughly discussed with the student before job placement. If the student has developed poor habits with respect to these factors, remedial measures must be undertaken. Very few employers are willing to continue paying wages to irresponsible students who are consistently tardy, absent, sick, or insubordinate. Unfortunately, employers may then become critical of the entire school—including its vocational programs and guidance department—on the basis of experience with a few students who were simply not ready to assume the responsibilities inherent in the worker role.

Oftentimes, if the vocational teacher or cooperative education coordinator is informed of the data in the cumulative folder, any necessary remedial action can be brought to the attention of concerned persons upon student entrance into the program. Vocational teachers with the help of guidance personnel often can effectively counsel with the student to modify ineffective behavior patterns, solicit the cooperation of parents and guardians, use the work environment or laboratory as an illustrative device and motivator to encourage the student to change behavior.

(3) Vocational educators need the assistance of the guidance counselor in standardized test selection, administration, and interpretation. Most school systems utilize some sort of a testing procedure to determine an aptitude, interest, and achievement profile for their students. Much of this data can be of tremendous use in identifying students who have the potential to benefit from vocational education. Profiles of students who have relatively high scores on test subscales related to occupational clusters ought to be shared with appropriate vocational education personnel. Furthermore, the interpretation of the test scores ought to be discussed by the counselor with the vocational teacher and the student. The student then ought to decide, based upon information provided by both the counselor and the vocational teacher, whether or not to enroll in the appropriate vocational program.

Few vocational education teachers are trained in test interpretation and do need the assistance of guidance personnel in accurate analysis of the data. In the absence of a standardized testing program, guidance personnel might work with vocational teachers in utilizing self-inventory methods such as Holland's (1972) "The Self-Directed Search," providing career information to students, or utilizing commercially-published career games. These types of devices are especially appropriate for exploratory or prevocational courses. Guidance counselors can be of great service by bringing these materials to the attention of prevocational and vocational teachers.

(4) Many vocational educators need the expertise of the guidance counselor who is competent by virtue of training in the broad curricula of human relations. Gysbers and Moore (1968), suggested that counselors work closely with vocational teachers in developing learning experiences and teaching content emphasizing the psychological and sociological aspects of occupations. They especially felt cooperative education students need this type of instruction with emphasis on human relations skills, feelings toward jobs, attitudes toward work, etc.

With their training in counseling and discussion techniques, counselors can be of immense assistance to vocational teachers in developing instructional units in human relations. All research on job failure indicates that the vast majority of persons are dismissed from or quit jobs because of their inability to relate to people within the work environment. In general, persons do not quit or are dismissed because of inadequate skills or poor training. It is therefore crucial that this whole area be effectvely taught in vocational education classes.

Furthermore, guidance personnel can be of help in assisting the vocational teacher in one-to-one counseling relationships that may be necessary because of ineffective human relationships. Counselors can help the vocational teacher in the identification and solution of academic and/or social problems. In nearly all cases, the vocational teacher sincerely wants to help the student modify ineffective behavior which may be causing dissatisfaction in the work, laboratory, or school environment. However, the teacher lacks the counseling techniques to encourage student self-disclosure and the tools to assist the student in modifying the behavior. The well-trained and sensitive counselor can be of tremendous assistance to the vocational educator in such endeavors.

(5) Guidance personnel can be of assistance to the vocational education program (as well as the total school program) by simply being visible within the geographical territory served by the schools. Unfortunately, some counselors are reluctant to leave the sacred halls of the school environment. Counselors cannot truly be effective in serving the needs of the students if they are unaware or ill-informed of the numerous vocational and educational opportunities available in the community.

It is suggested that guidance personnel be active in local civic and professional organizations, such as the Chamber of Commerce, the local chapter of the American Management Association, the local chapter of the National Association of Manufacturers, Business and Professional Woman's Club, etc. They should also establish a close working relationship with the State Employment Service, Youth Opportunity Center, personnel connected with the United States Department of Labor Comprehensive Employment and Training Act (CETA), and other groups actively involved in the support and training of youth. Counselors should be in contact with the armed services regarding career opportunities in the military.

Guidance personnel should also be aware of company training programs and employment opportunities for students graduating and/or completing vocational programs from their schools. They should be familiar with the personnel directors at each of the major companies in the geographical area in which the school is located. Frequent, on-site visits to these companies (accompanied by the vocational education teachers) should be a part of the counselor's job tasks. To truly do an effective job of educating and guiding students, counselors and vocational educators need a thorough grasp of the competencies needed and opportunities available for all employees in the local community—entry-level through management.

Furthermore, it is suggested that guidance personnel frequently accompany the school's cooperative education and other work experience coordinators as they supervise the on-the-job training programs of the students. This provides an excellent opportunity to study the local community training and employment needs and opportunities, as well as to obtain a perception of the effectiveness of the total school program as perceived by employers cooperating with the school's work programs.

Throughout this entire community-involvement process, it can be of immense help to vocational educators if the guidance personnel share their information. As they learn of full- or part-time job opportunities, the information should be shared with appropriate vocational education teachers. As they learn of job requirements, union policies, apprenticeship training opportunities, entrance skills needed, etc., the information should also be shared with the vocational education personnel.

(6) Guidance personnel should be of assistance to vocational educators in a consulting

capacity in many aspects of the vocational education program. If possible, guidance specialists should serve as ex-officio members of the vocational education program advisory committee(s). They can provide leadership to vocational personnel in the design of occupational survey instruments. They can assist in the design and conduct of follow-up instruments of formerly-enrolled vocational students. They can advise vocational and prevocational teachers in the design of curriculum activities and experiences related to the career development process, especially in the areas of occupational choice making, career exploration, value clarification, and decision making. They can assist the vocational teacher with job placement and post-secondary educational placement. Finally, they can assist in follow-up studies of formerly-enrolled vocational education students.

Vocational Education in the Guidance Program

As emphasized in the previous section, guidance personnel can be of tremendous assistance to the effectiveness of the vocational education program. Conversely, vocational educators have the expertise and should contribute significantly to the total school guidance program. As Cote (1968) pointed out, vocational educators need to realize that the guidance counselor cannot be an expert in psychology, sociology, college placement, remedial techniques, plus provide occupational information in over 40,000 occupations. Counselors do need assistance, and the vocational educator is in a prime position to assist in various phases of the guidance program, especially those aspects related to the career development of students.

Cote recommended that vocational teachers do three things to fully utilize their potential as counselors: (1) learn more about the counseling process, (2) involve themselves in the guidance program, and (3) overcome any negative bias towards guidance. He has suggested that vocational teachers enroll in guidance survey courses in universities to study the guidance process and then utilize such training by assisting with various aspects of the guidance program. Cote's main contention is that vocational educators are ill-informed regarding the role and tasks of guidance counselors. They often have aspirations regarding the accomplishments of guidance personnel which are totally unrealistic. In their quest for sufficient student enrollments and a "quality" program, vocational educators often tend to blame the counselors for what they consider to be inappropriate or "inferior" students. Furthermore, vocational educators often fail to understand the purpose of vocational guidance, which as described by Super (1951) is "the process of helping a person to develop and accept an integrated and adequate picture of himself and of his role in the world of work, to test this concept against reality, and to convert it into a reality, with satisfaction to himself and benefit to society" (p. 92). Cote further stated: "It is (my) strong conviction. . .that no vocational teacher who studies guidance to any significant degree and who conscientiously devotes a part of his energies to assisting the counselor can long maintain a negative bias toward that program, the success of which means so much to every student" (p. 55).

The purpose of this section of the chapter is to encourage vocational educators to become involved in the guidance process within their local schools and to suggest specific strategies which may be appropriate for involvement. Many of the suggestions have a basis in the "Position Paper on Career Development" jointly prepared by an AVA-NVGA Commission on

Career Guidance and Vocational Education, W. Wesley Tennyson, Chairman. Other suggestions have been gleaned from the literature or as a result of personal experience in various educational environments.

(1) Vocational educators can and should provide realistic and current occupational information to school staffs and students based on their knowledge and day-to-day contacts with personnel in the work settings appropriate to their program specialty. Vocational educators—especially cooperative education coordinators and other work experience coordinators—are usually very familiar with actual and anticipated full- and part-time job openings. They know the competencies and entry-level requirements that are needed for such employment. They usually have first-hand knowledge of the potential career progression available in local firms and the requirements for progressing to new job responsibilities and/or salary scales within the firm. They are often familiar with employment policies, union concerns, salary and fringe benefit figures, and the procedure for job applications. This information should be shared with appropriate guidance personnel, faculty, and students.

(2) Based upon their knowledge of occupational needs and worker competencies, vocational educators should assist appropriate educational curriculum specialists and guidance personnel in the design of career-related curricula. There is certainly no group of school personnel that is as knowledgeable of occupational information as the vocational educators. They can and should be of tremendous help in consulting on the development of instructional materials and learning experiences at the awareness, orientation, and exploration stages of the school's career development program.

They can also easily assist academic or general education personnel in identifying appropriate activities, field experiences, projects, in-class examples, etc., to illustrate the fundamental concept that all of education has meaning in a vocational sense. As examples, they can supply mathematics teachers with problems of relevance to retail store buyers, machinists, and engineers; they can supply English teachers with job application forms, names of personnel managers to whom letters of application should be addressed, and business correspondence letters that need editing; and they can provide science teachers with equipment typically found in health-care facilities to be used in biology and other science classes.

(3) Vocational teachers can recommend and recruit resource persons from the business/industrial community to assist in various aspects of the school program. Vocational teachers are usually familiar with personnel officers, managers, and foremen in the various firms and businesses. They can often identify speakers for classes, career days, and other functions. They can often identify persons who would be helpful and facilitative for various school programs, i.e., fund-raising projects, advisory committees, adult education programs, in-service education programs, etc. Furthermore, vocational education teachers often have the type of rapport with persons in the employment sector that might permit the arrangement of field observations, field interviews, and part-time employment for students and school staff in order that they might learn more about occupations and work settings.

(4) Vocational educators, themselves, should also serve as resource persons throughout the school system. Other teachers and guidance personnel ought to be able to utilize the vocational teachers as role models in other classes and for career development activities. The vocational educators ought to exemplify persons typically found in their occupational areas. The persons should be available to discuss occupational information with respect to their vocational

program with students in other classes. Vocational teachers should also provide exploratory experiences in vocational classrooms or laboratories for students not enrolled in occupational classes. Finally, these persons should be able to suggest exploratory field observations, interviews, and other experiences that could be undertaken by nonvocational students in the local business/industrial community.

(5) Within their own programs, vocational educators can and should incorporate the current theory and supportive research which indicates that students should be prepared with sufficient competencies to enter a number of jobs within an occupational cluster. Furthermore, students should be prepared to adjust, progress within, and change jobs within an occupational field. In some vocational fields, this has not always been the prevalent manner of operation. Many have trained students in the skills needed for just one type of job; only to find out that there were no employment positions for persons with those skills. For young persons enrolled in vocational programs, career development theory indicates that they should be informed of and reasonably prepared in a wide range of occupations for which their vocational instruction is applicable.

Finally, career development theorists would also encourage vocational educators to develop within the students the ability to analyze and interpret vocational experiences in terms of self-concept and personal satisfaction with the performance of the job tasks within the simulated or actual job environment.

(6) Much of the responsibility for identifying students who can benefit from the vocational education program should rest with the appropriate vocational teachers. For many years guidance personnel have taken abuse from vocational educators about the inappropriateness of certain students in the vocational programs. It is the vocational educator who is and should be responsible for his/her program. The provision of occupational information with respect to the teacher's vocational specialty, the provision of information to the student body about the vocational specialty, the promotion of careers within the vocational specialty, and the necessary provision of prevocational information and prerequisite competencies needed to enter the vocational specialty should be the responsibility primarily of personnel within that particular vocational program. This, of course, does not mean to imply that guidance personnel should not actively be involved in this process. They should—and usually will—cooperate and assist in every phase of the process. However, it is the contention of this writer that vocational educators can no longer assume responsibility for only the skill phase training of vocational education students. They must also be actively involved in the recruitment, identification, information provision, exploration, and other phases of the career development process. When vocational educators realize this and do become involved in the guidance process, they will then truly be training students who do need and can benefit from vocational instruction.

Conclusion

The central theme throughout this chapter is one of simplicity and common sense: guidance personnel and vocational educators need to cooperate more fully and form a partnership to develop and implement a career delivery system that will enable students to progress toward a life which is personally rewarding and meaningful to society. Each has expertise to bring to such a partnership. The guidance personnel have training and competencies in student appraisal, analysis of and modification techniques with respect to human behavior, career development, test analysis and interpretation, and counseling techniques. The vocational educators have training and competencies in occupational skill development methodologies, occupations needed for satisfaction and satisfactoriness in the industrial/business sector, methodologies for delivering career information, and current information with respect to the labor market. Both groups are student oriented. Both groups are knowledgeable of curriculum and pedagogical processes and the importance of the total development of students. By combining their commitment to youth and adults of all ages and capitalizing upon the expertise each can bring to a partnership, guidance personnel and vocational educators *together* can develop and implement a viable educational and training program that truly serves the personal, social, educational, and vocational needs of students.

References

Cote, T. J. The counselor's most logical helper. *American Vocational Journal* 43 (9) (1968):11-12, 55.

Elam, S. ed. *Gallup polls of attitudes toward education 1969-1973.* Bloomington, Indiana: Phi Delta Kappa, Inc., 1973.

Gallup, G. H. Sixth annual Gallup poll of public attitudes toward education. *Phi Delta Kappan* 56(1) (1975):20-32.

Gysbers, N. C., and Moore, E. J. Cooperative work experience as a guidance setting. *American Vocational Journal* 43(9) (1968):16,61.

Hohenshil, T. H. The guidance administrator and vocational education: how interested? *American Vocational Journal* 49(5) (1974): 62-3.

Holland, J. L. The self directed search—a guide to educational and vocational planning. Palo Alto, California: Consulting Psychologists Press, 1972.

Hoyt, K. B. Career ed altering counselors' roles. *Guidepost* 17 (1974):3.

———. Vocational guidance for all—new kinds of personnel needed. *American Vocational Journal* 45(5) (1970):62, 64,65.

90th Congress. Public law 90—576, H. R. Bill 18366. Washington, D.C.: United States Superintendent of Documents, October 16, 1968.

Ryan, C. Career development for youth and adults. *American Vocational Journal* 49(9) (1974):21.

Super, D. E. Vocational adjustment: implementing a self concept. *Occupations. . .The Vocational Guidance Journal* 30(2) (1951): 88-92.

Wallace, W. G. Counselor collaboration in staff improvement. *American Vocational Association* 50(4) (1975):38-39.

Chapter 12

LEGAL ISSUES IN GUIDANCE

David Alexander

Introduction

This chapter was designed to present the beginning student with some of the basic legal aspects of public education which might arise in the area of guidance and counseling. It is not intended to be exhaustive and more in-depth study should be pursued by the student in selected areas of interest.

The first section of the chapter examines some of the basic constitutional rights of public school students. Its main purpose is to focus on the aspect that public school students do have certain rights under the constitution and it behooves all educators to be aware of these rights. The second area examines some of the legal-ethical questions that might arise in the pursuit of a professional counseling career. These areas are ethical standards versus legal rights in the context of confidential and privileged communications, licensing and certification, and defamation. The third area examines the relationship of public records to the rights of privacy of the individual.

Due Process

The concept of due process has been around in this country since the Bill of Rights was written and even before in the writings of the Magna Charta.[1] In 1215 the King of England signed the historic Magna Charta which provided that individuals could not be imprisoned, outlawed, banished, prosecuted, or hurt in any way unless they were judged by their peers according to the law.[2] In other words, a person has certain rights which can be negated only by the judgment of one's peers as related to appropriate law. Later, this concept was written in the Constitution of the United States and encompasses the fundamental idea that before a basic right can be taken away an individual must be afforded due process.[3]

The due process clause was first enunciated in the Fifth Amendment, which stated:

> . . .nor shall any person. . .deprived of life, liberty, or property without due process of law;. . .[4]

Dr. David Alexander is Associate Professor of Educational Administration at Virginia Polytechnic Institute and State University, Blacksburg, Virginia.

This basic concept was later written in the Fourteenth Amendment. The Fourteenth Amendment provides that no *state* shall deprive a person of life, liberty, or property without due process of law.[5] Positively stated, this means that a state may deprive a citizen of life, liberty, or property but first must afford that individual due process.[6] The Fifth Amendment applies to the federal government while the Fourteenth Amendment applies to the state.[7] Since education is not mentioned in the federal constitution it is, therefore, left to the states through the reserved powers of the Tenth Amendment.[8] The Tenth Amendment states:

> The Powers not delegated to the United States by the Constitution, nor prohibited by it to the States, are reserved to the States respectively or to the people.[9]

Student rights cases are usually brought under the provision of the Fourteenth Amendment.[10] This comes about because education is reserved to the states through the Tenth Amendment and the Fourteenth Amendment provides that no *state* shall deprive a person of life, liberty or property without due process of law.

In recent years the courts have expanded the interpretations and applications of student rights. The concept of due process, which embodies one of the basic precepts of a democratic society, has been applied to the rights of public school students only in the past decade.

The reasons for the expansion of the rights of students is that education was considered a privilege rather than a right. At one time students were removed at the pleasure of school officials.[11] But as society has moved from an agrarian economy to a highly technological multiphased economy, greater emphasis has been placed on education. Therefore, the federal courts no longer adhere to the privilege doctrine and view education as an important right.[12]

The famous *Brown* v. *Board of Education of Topeka* case expressed the importance of education when the court said

> Today education is perhaps the most important function of state and local government. . . . Today it is a principal instrument in awakening the child to cultural values, in preparing him for later professional training, and in helping him adjust normally to his environment.[13]

In the celebrated *Tinker* decision the United States Supreme Court recognized the constitutional rights of a student. The court said

> School officials do not possess absolute authority over their students. Students in school as well as out of school are "persons" under our Constitution. They are possessed of *fundamental rights* which the State must respect. . . In our system, students may not be regarded as closed-circuit recipients of only that which the State chooses to communicate. They may not be confined to the expression of those sentiments that are officially approved. In the absence of a specific showing of constitutionally valid reasons to regulate their speech, students are entitled to freedom of expression of their views. . .,[14] [Emphasis added]

The "fundamental rights" that were referred to in the *Tinker* decision are those liberty and property rights that a public school student possesses.

The problem that faces most educators is determining what are liberty and property rights of the student. In *Board of Regents* v. *Roth* the court spoke about liberty and property rights. The court said

> Liberty and property are broad and majestic terms. They are among the great constitutional concepts. . .purposely left to gather meaning from experience. . . . They relate to the whole

domain of social and economic fact, and the statesman who founded this nation knew too well that only a stagnant society remains unchanged.[15]

School officials whether they be teachers, administrators, or counselors should be cognizant that students do have liberty and property rights under the Constitution. Therefore, before students can be deprived of these rights they must be given due process.

There are two types of due process.[16] The first to be interpreted and defined by the courts was procedural due process, which had its origin in the Fourteenth Amendment. Procedural due process means that a prescribed procedure must be followed before a person may be deprived of rights, particularly life, liberty and property.[17] The second type is "substantive due process" which was first applied to the substantive content or meaning of the law in 1923.[18] The following definition by an Arizona Court distinguishes "substantive due process" from "procedural due process."

> The phrase "due process of law," when applied to substantive rights, as distinguished from procedural rights, means that the state is without power to deprive a person of life, liberty or property by an act having no reasonable relation to any proper governmental purpose, or which is so far beyond the necessity of the case as to be arbitrary exercise of governmental power.[19]

Today both substantive and procedural due process apply to the relationship between government and students. Schools have the right to make rules and regulations but these must be reasonable and cannot be arbitrary or capricious or they are unconstitutional under substantive due process. The United States Supreme Court said ". . . the authority possessed by the state to prescribe and enforce standards of conduct in its schools, although very broad, must be exercised consistently with constitutional safeguards."[20]

The substantive areas of due process are very important because only after a substantive issue of liberty of property has been affected would the school be required to give the student procedural due process.

The court in speaking to this point said

> The requirements of procedural due process apply only to the deprivation of interests encompassed by the Fourteenth Amendment's protection of liberty and property. When protected interests are implicated, the right of some kind of prior hearing is paramount. But the range of interests protected by procedural due process is not infinite.[21]

Therefore the substantive aspects of due process are the foundation from which due process is built. Because of the enormity of the litigation, it is beyond the scope of this chapter to attempt to explore all substantive rights of students. Therefore only some of the basic aspects of substantive due process will be examined.

Substantive Due Process

The basic constitutional rights of students have a substantive base found in the First, Fourth, Fifth, and Fourteenth Amendments of the Constitution.[22] Some of these rights are freedom of religion, freedom of speech, freedom of association, freedom of assembly, and others that are found in the Constitution that may be applied to students.[23] One basic question pertaining to the students' substantive rights is "what are the liberty and property rights of public school students, and under what circumstances may these rights be limited by school authorities?''[24] This is an extremely important question because the federal courts will only intervene if a constitutional right has been violated.[25]

A federal circuit court said:

> For better or for worse, our jurisdiction attaches only when the Constitution has been violated—not every time a principal acts arbitrarily or unfairly.[26]

Two examples relating to substantive due process will be discussed in this chapter; the first will be the First Amendment right of freedom of expression and the second the Fourth Amendment freedom from unreasonable searches.

Tinker v. *Des Moines* was the landmark decision in the area of constitutional rights of students under the First Amendment. The court, in referring to the student, said:

> . . . he may express his opinions, even on controversial subjects. . . if he does so without 'materially and substantially interfering with the requirements of appropriate discipline in the operation of the school.'

The court further stated:

> . . . the record does not demonstrate any facts which might have led school authorities to forecast substantial disruption or material interference with school activities. . . .[27]

There are two key elements to the language of the Supreme Court in *Tinker* relating to the substantive rights of students.[28] First, the student does have substantive rights of freedom of expression as guaranteed by the constitution and, second, these substantive rights do have limits. The students' substantive rights may be limited if they "materially or substantially disrupt" the educational process or disruption can be reasonably predicted by school officials.

The courts have refused to protect a student's substantive constitutional rights when the student's action disrupted the educational process. The courts have found for the school districts when students blocked hallways and threatened teachers,[29] staged sit-ins,[30] wore racially inciting patches or buttons,[31,32] and many other cases of a similar nature.

It is now well established in law that students have a substantive right to freedom of expression, but it is equally well established that these rights are limited if school officials can show disruption of the educational process or reasonably predict such disruption is eminent.[33] Johnson stated that "a school official who attempts to limit the student's nondisruptive freedom of expression may well violate substantive due process."[34]

Another significant area of substantive due process for school officials is the Fourth Amendment to the Constitution which states:

> The right of the people to be secure in their persons, houses, papers, and effects, against *unreasonable* searches and seizures, shall not be violated, and no warrants shall issue, but upon probable cause, supported by Oath or affirmation, and particularly describing the place to be searched and the persons or things to be seized. [emphasis added][35]

The courts have ruled that it is not *unreasonable* for school officials to search students when the officials have "reasonable grounds" that state laws or school regulations have been violated.[36] If school officials have "reasonable grounds" then the students' substantive rights are not violated by the prohibition of the Fourth Amendment against unreasonable search.

The courts have applied this reasoning and upheld school officials when they searched lockers,[37] required students to empty the contents of their pockets[38] and also searched a student's jacket, even when the student objected.[39]

The student's substantive rights under the Fourth Amendment have been interpreted differently than those under the First Amendment. Although the substantive rights of the student under the Fourth Amendment have been recognized, the school has been given broader powers to limit the rights of students than under the First Amendment. One of the reasons for the difference in the interpretation of the two amendments is that search and seizure usually involve dangerous weapons, illegal drugs, bomb threats or other situations that may be hazardous to the health and safety of all school pupils.

Procedural Due Process

The courts originally interpreted procedural due process as applying to judicial proceedings, "i.e., a person's right to a trial by jury."[40] The courts have since given a broader interpretation to procedural due process. Now procedural due process must also be afforded to individuals by administrative agencies,[41] which includes public schools.

If there is the potential loss of a liberty or property right, such as the right to attend school, then the student must be afforded procedural due process.[42]

In the landmark case of *Dixon* v. *Alabama State Board of Education,*[43] the courts for the first time said that a student who was faced with the disciplinary actions of suspension or expulsion has a right to notice and a hearing. There was no attempt to establish strict procedural guidelines for due process, but schools were expected to afford the student minimal procedural due process which would constitute "fundamental fairness." It was specified that "the notice should contain a statement of the specific charges and ground which, if proven, would justify expulsion. . .the nature of the hearing should vary depending upon the circumstances of the particular case."[44]

A number of cases after *Dixon* provided some clarification of the procedural due process requirements. In *Due* v. *Florida A & M*[45] the court outlined three minimal requirements for cases of *severe* disciplinary action. These minimal requirements were: (1) adequate notice of the charges and the nature of evidence which supported those charges; (2) a hearing at which the student had an opportunity to explain his position; and (3) that any action taken must be supported by the evidence presented at the hearing.

Therefore, procedural due process for severe disciplinary proceedings, i.e., expulsion, was established by the courts. The courts have agreed that procedural due process is a flexible concept and the formality of the procedure depends upon the circumstances of that case. "The touchstones in this area are fairness and reasonableness."[46]

After the *Dixon* case there was agreement among the courts on the fact that if students are to be given a long-term suspension or expelled from school, they must be afforded some minimal procedural due process which constitutes a basic fairness. But there was much disagreement among the courts concerning whether students should be given due process for short-term suspensions.[47] (See note 47 for different interpretations by federal courts concerning due process prior to the *Goss* decision.) In January of 1975, the Supreme Court in *Goss* v.

Lopez[48] settled the dispute regarding due process for short-term suspensions. Short-term was defined as ten days or less. It was determined that due process must be afforded students if they are temporarily denied access to an education. The court said

> Students facing temporary suspensions have interests qualifying for protection of the Due Process Clause, and due process requires, in connection with a suspension of ten days or less, that the student be given oral or written notice of the charges against him, and if he denies them, an explanation of the evidence the authorities have and an opportunity to present his side of the story. The clause requires at least these rudimentary precautions against unfair or mistaken findings of misconduct and arbitrary exclusion from school.[49]

The court also said that for short-term suspension, students *did not* have a right to legal counsel. . . "to confront and cross-examine witnesses supporting the charge or to call their own witnesses to verify their version of the incident." To formalize the suspension process would be too costly and would destroy the suspension's effectiveness as an educational process.

The court also ruled that when disruption or disorder takes place or an emergency situation arises in the school that it might be necessary to remove the individual immediately for the health and safety of all concerned. If this takes place, due process should be afforded the pupil who has been removed from school as soon as the disruption or disorder has subsided.

Therefore, it is clear that a student who is suspended for a short term (fewer than ten days) must be afforded due process. But this due process need not be as formal as for long-term suspension or expulsions. This informal procedure still must encompass notice, either written or oral, to the student concerning what specifically is the violation and a decision based on what took place at the informal hearing. This informal hearing allows students to tell their side of the story.[50] The disciplinarian may conduct the hearing immediately after the violation. School officials should act in a fair manner before removing a student from school even for a very short period of time.

Guidelines

Expulsion or suspension for more than ten days will require more formal procedures.

If your state has specific statutory laws concerning either short-term suspensions or long-term suspensions or expulsions they must be adhered to exactly.[51] In the absence of statutory law the minimum element of due process should be established. The following check points should be observed for long-term suspensions or explusions:

1. The student should be aware that he may be expelled or suspended if he disrupts the educational process or endangers the health and safety of other individuals.
2. Until a due process hearing is conducted the status of the student, his right to attend classes, should not be altered unless his conduct endangers the health, safety, and well being of others.
3. The student should be aware of the specific rules of conduct so as to be reasonably informed as to what is prescribed.
4. The student should be given notice in writing as to the specific charges against him. The notice should specify the rule or regulation that has been violated and the evidence you have to establish the specific violation.

5. The student should be notified of the procedural rights available at the hearing along with the date, time, and place of the hearing.
6. The student should be allowed reasonable time to prepare a defense.
7. The hearing should be fair and conducted by an impartial person or the appropriate tribunal. The hearing does not have to follow the technical rules of a court of law. The hearing should be a fair forum for the student to present his side of the incident. The hearing committee can be composed of administration, faculty and students and should be empowered to make a decision regarding the case.
8. The burden of proof is with the officials bringing the charges.

There are a number of procedural questions regarding long-term suspensions or expulsions which the courts still have not resolved. Some of these are the student's right to legal counsel, the right to confront and cross-examine witnesses, and the right to have a transcript of the hearings. The courts have had a tendency to keep the hearing out of the realm of quasi-criminal procedures because of time, effort, and expense involved. Therefore, they have maintained that these hearings are only administrative hearings to insure the fairness of disciplinary actions.[53]

In summary, a student must be afforded due process when suspended whether for a short period or for an extended length of time. But the due process procedures must positively correlate with the severity of the punishment. The more severe the penalty the more formal the procedure and vice versa.

Legal Aspects of Counseling

The role of the counselor in public education is different from what it was a decade ago. Because of societal changes, the role of the counselor has changed from the early purposes of dispersing educational information and vocational guidance to a much more comprehensive range of tasks. The counselor today is engaged in a broad range of professional activities including personal counseling, either individually or in groups, plus a diversity of other activites. These activites are designed to meet the needs of the pupil population served by public education. Because of the need to adapt to changing times, the counselor is now faced with more complex legal problems and a higher professional demand has been placed on the counselor as evidenced by new legislation and the standards of professional associations.[54]

In 1974 the American Personnel and Guidance Association published *Ethical Standards* for counselors, guidance and student personnel workers, and for others working in the profession. The counselor should be aware of all areas of this document but certain areas are more significant than others because of the possibility of ethical and legal conflicts. Two areas of particular concern, Section A, General and Section B, Counselor-Counselee Relationship, are listed below:

Section A: General

2. The member has a responsibility both to the individual who is served and to the institution within which the service is performed. The acceptance of employment in an institution implies the member is in substantial agreement with the general policies and principles of the institution. Therefore, the professional activities of the member are also in accord with the objectives of the institution. If, despite concerted efforts, the member cannot reach agreement with the

employer as to acceptable standards of conduct that allow for changes in institutional policy conducive to the positive growth and development of counselees, then terminating the affiliation should be seriously considered.

Section B: Counselor-Counselee Relationship

To the extent that the counselee's choice of action is not imminently self- or other- destructive, the counselee must retain freedom of choice. When the counselee does not have full autonomy for reasons of age, mental incompetency, criminal incarceration, or similar legal restrictions, the member may have to work with others who exercise significant control and direction over the counselee. Under these circumstances the member must apprise counselees of restrictions that may limit their freedom of choice.

1. The member's *primary* obligation is to respect the integrity and promote the welfare of the counselee(s), whether the counselee(s) is (are) assisted individually or in a group relationship. In a group setting, the member-leader is also responsible for protecting individuals from physical and/or psychological trauma resulting from interaction within the group.

4. When the counselee's condition indicates that there is clear and imminent danger to the counselee or others, the member is expected to take direct personal action or to inform responsible authorities. Consultation with other professionals should be utilized where possible. Direct interventions, especially the assumption of responsibility for the counselee, should be taken only after careful deliberation. The counselee should be involved with the resumption of responsibility for his actions as quickly as possible.

5. Records of the counseling relationship including interview notes, test data, correspondence, tape recordings, and other documents are to be considered professional information for use in counseling, and they are not part of the public or official records of the institution or agency in which the counselor is employed. Revelation to others of counseling material should occur only upon the express consent of the counselee.[55]

These are the ethical standards which have been established by the profession and should be recognized and respected by all members of the profession. But situations can arise where the legal standards take precedence over the ethical standards.

The counselor in private practice can perform his or her professional responsibilities more on a counselor-counselee relationship with little intervention of third parties, except in special situations. However, the public school counselor is in a unique position not only legally but ethically. The *Ethical Standard,* Section A:2 states "The member has a responsibility both to the individual who is served and to the institution within which the service is performed." Not only do counselors have a special relationship to the students that they are working with, but they also have a special relationship to the other students in the school and to the school institution as a whole. This second relationship which intervenes into the counselor-counselee relationship has its legal origin in the police power of the state. The police power of the state is the authority for requiring children to attend school under compulsory attendance statutes.[56] The courts have ruled that compulsory attendance statutes are a valid exercise of police power.[57] The police power of the state has been defined:

No jurist has dared to attempt to state the limit in law of that quality in government which is exercised through what is termed the "police power." All agree that it would be inadvisable to attempt it. Yet very broadly and indefinitely speaking, it is the power and obligation of government to secure and promote the general welfare, comfort, and convenience of the citizens, as well as the public peace, the public health, the public morals, and the public safety. . . . The good sense and the honest judgment of each generation must after all furnish the real limit to the police power of government. For each age must judge—and will judge—of what is hurtful to its welfare, or what endangers the existence of society.[58]

Another court explained police power as it related to public education:

We are of the opinion that the legislature, under the constitutional provision, may as well establish a uniform system of schools and a uniform administration of them. . .the object of the public school system is. . ., providing and receiving a higher state of intelligence and morals, conserve the peace, good order, and well-being of society.[59]

The courts have interpreted education as a vital instrument to the welfare of citizens of the state.[60] Therefore, since children are required to attend schools the professional personnel owe all children a high standard of care to protect them, within reasonable limits, from harm. The guidance counselor has not only a special relationship to protect the counselee but also a duty to protect all other children.

Because the counselor has a responsibility to all children, in some instances the counselor may become an arm of the administration in special situations which would override the counselor-counselee relationship. Although *Ethical Standard* B-1 says that *the* ". . .primary obligation is to respect the integrity and promote the welfare of the counselee(s). . ." there may be instances where the welfare of the counselee may become secondary to welfare of the student body. Even the principles of Medical Ethics of the American Medical Association (1957), section 9, says "A physician may not reveal the confidences entrusted to him in the course of medical attendance. . .unless he is required to do so by law or unless it becomes necessary *in order to protect the welfare of the individual or of the community.*" [emphasis added] In *Tarasoff* v. *Regents of University of California*[61] the court said, "the protective privilege ends where the public peril begins" and the confidential standard for the counselor would not be as high as that of the physician.

Therefore, the ethical issue is that the counselor must inform the student of the limitations of the relationship. The counselor-counselee relationship has been predicted upon the free exchange of information and complete trust and any limitation would impede this relationship, but it is the duty of the counselor to make the counselee aware that there are limits to the relationship. This is a precarious ethical-legal position that must be balanced to insure the counselees of their rights and to insure the rights of others.

The standards also state that the counselor should agree to the policies and principles of the institution. If agreement cannot be reached between the counselor and the institution concerning policies and principles, then, as a professional, the counselor should seriously consider terminating employment.[62]

Aubrey states that the counselor is trapped because of the institutional limits upon the counselor-counselee relationship and that this destroys the counselor's flexibility. These limitations are antithetical to the objectives of the counselors. Besides institutional limitations of the philosophical nature, it has been shown that the secondary school counselors spend as much as 50 percent of their time performing clerical or administrative responsibilities which are required by the institution.[63]

The counselor is not autonomous but is a member of the institutional team. No one member of the team can be autonomous and function effectively. The counselor, in conjuction with teachers, administrators, parents, and students has to establish common goals. Counselors can operate more efficiently if they work within the framework of an integrated team rather than becoming suspect by the institutional staff.[64] It should be recognized that the ultimate authority for not only the guidance program but all school programs rests with the school administration.[65]

Communications: Confidential and Privileged

The terms confidential communications and privileged communications are often used synonymously but they are not the same.[66] The basic difference is a legal distinction.[67] Confidentiality has been defined as: ". . .an ethical term referring to the decision made by a professional that he will not reveal to others what he has learned in private interaction with a client."[68] Another author explains it as: "Confidentiality in the ethical sense, refers to a professional's decision that he should not and will not divulge what has been revealed to him in his contact with a client."[69] It is standard to the literature relating to counselors that confidentiality is an ethical term. The counselor would, therefore, have an ethical duty to maintain the confidential relationship with the client and not release information that results from this relationship.[70]

Privilege has been defined as: ". . . the legal privilege certain professionals have not to disclose certain information in a court of law."[71] Another similar definition is: "Privileged communication refers to the right of the counselor to refuse to divulge any confidential information while testifying in a court of law."[72]

Privileged Communication

Privilege is granted either by common law or by legislative action. Common law privilege has been established for communication between husband and wife, attorney and client, priest and penitent, government and informer, and between jurors. Professional groups have been granted privilege communication through statutory law in some forty-five states.[73] Legislative action has established this privilege for professional groups such as physicians, psychologists, journalists, and accountants.[74]

The established standards that have been used to determine whether confidential communications should receive privilege status are:[75]

1. The communications must originate in a confidence that they will not be disclosed.
2. This element of *confidentiality must be essential* to the full and satisfactory maintenance of the relationship between parties.
3. The *relation* must be one which in the opinion of the community ought to be sedulously *fostered.*
4. The injury that would inure to the relation by the disclosure of the communications must be greater than the benefits thereby gained for the correct disposal of litigation.[76]

Litwack and associates state that the counselor-counselee relationship meet the four criteria for establishing privileged communication for counsels. Apparently, legislators have in recent years agreed that the privilege standard is a necessary component for the functioning guidance counselor. Litwack reported that only two states, Michigan and Indiana, provided privileged protection.[77] Swanson reported that fourteen states have enacted statutes that provided for privileged communication between the counselor and students,[78] and with the passage of legislation in Kentucky there are now fifteen. (See note 79 for states given by Swanson plus the Kentucky statute.) The Kentucky legislation states:

> Any certified counselor who meets the requirements issued pursuant to the authority of KRS 161.030, and who is duly appointed and regularly employed for the purpose of counseling in a public or private school of this state, shall be immune from disclosing in any civil or criminal court proceeding, without the consent of the student counselee, any communication made by the student counselee to the counselor in his professional character, or the advice thereon. If the student counselee is less than eighteen years of age, neither the communication nor advice thereon shall be disclosed in the court proceeding without the consent of the student counselee and his parent or legal guardian.

Legislators have weighed the need for testimony from the counselors in a court of law against the need to protect the communications between the counselor-counselee. Because of the amount of recent legislation in this area it would appear that legislators are deciding that protection of the communication takes precedence over the need for testimony in a court of law.[80]

Counselors should realize that the extension of privileged communication is for the protection of the counselee. Some counselors believe that the privilege is to protect them but this is not the case. The purpose of the privilege is to protect the rights of privacy of the counselee. The counselee would have a right to waive this protection and let the counselor divulge the communications, but the counselor would not be forced to divulge the communications[81] unless the public is in peril.[82]

If no statutory privilege exists, then the counselor can be subpoenaed and required to testify in court. The counselor could be required to testify concerning the confidential communications between the counselor and counselee. If the counselor[83] refuses to answer then the counselor can be held in contempt of court. Two solutions expounded by Swanson to alleviate the above situation are:

1. The honoring by a judge of a counselor's request not to be required to testify, especially when it is felt that the probative worth of the testimony would be minimal.
2. Rigid adherence by the counselors to their ethical standards. This, of course, could lead to being held in contempt of court. The counselor should at least request that the judge not require him to testify as this would violate the confidential relationship and his professional ethics.[84]

Confidential Communication

A counselor has an ethical responsibility to maintain in confidence any communications that take place in the counseling session. As previously noted, this confidential relationship should be maintained short of contempt of court. When can the counselor make an exception to this rule of confidentiality? The *Ethical Standards* provide that where there is a clear and imminent danger to the counselee or to others, the counselor may divulge to the proper authorities what has transpired in conference with the counselee. The clear and imminent danger rule would apply whether there was a privilege statute or not. The counselor would be obligated to take action even if it breached the confidentiality of the relationship if there was danger to the counselee or to the public.[86]

The confidential relationship may not be legal but may be moral, social, domestic, or merely personal.[87] The legal definition of a confidential relationship is quite broad. One definition is: ". . .whenever one person occupies toward another such a position of advisor or counselor as responsibly to inspire confidence that he will act in good faith for the other's interest. . ."[88]

Counselors would have an ethical responsibility to not convey confidential information except in certain cases, but would have a legal responsibility also to the client not to convey this confidential information. If the counselor arbitrarily conveys the confidential information to a third party where the third party had no "need to know" then this could amount to invasion of privacy.

Even in those states that do not have privilege laws the counselor should not reveal the confidential information except when a clear and imminent danger to the counselee or the public exists. The counselor should use every conceivable means within the "system to maintain confidentiality before releasing the information.

License, Certification

Counselors in public schools are now certified to practice in the public schools by some state agency, usually the State Department of Education, the same as teachers.[89] There has been quite a clamor in recent years that counselors should be licensed rather than certified. It has been proclaimed that licensing would provide greater legal status and reduce some of the legal-ethical conflict. If counselors were licensed then this would give them status equal to other professionals such as private psychologists. Some of the advantages for licen ing are proffered by Vacca. These are:

1. Increased legal status and acceptance as professionals;
2. Clients in schools (students and their parents) will be protected as statutory privilege of communication will be eventually extended to counselors in schools—now limited to licensed psychologists in schools; and
3. Standards for entry into school counseling will be upgraded, thus the profession would be assured stricter control over practice with a result of more ethical conduct in practice. Thus there will be less chance of irresponsible statements made in evaluating students.[90]

It is extremely difficult to define the commonality among the various states as it pertains to licensing and certification. In some instances the term certification and licensing are synonymous.[91] The Code of Virginia differentiates between licensing and certification for counselors in the private sector. The code defines these as:

Certification means the process whereby the Commission, Department or any regulatory board on behalf of the Commonwealth issues a certificate to any person certifying that he has minimum skills properly to engage in his profession or occupation and that it knows of no character defect that would make him a bad practitioner of the same.

Licensing means a method of regulation whereby the practice of the profession or occupation licensed is unlawful without the issuance of a license.[92]

It must be remembered that both of these definitions apply to the counselor outside the realm of public education. The above definitions apply generally to counselors in private practice where the authority for certification or licensing rests with some state agency other than education. This separation between counselors and public school counselors is defined in the statutes. The law provides

> . . . nor shall the provisions of Chapter 5.2 apply to persons regularly employed and within scope of their employment as guidance or personnel counselors by *public educational institutions* or a *private educational institution* approved or accredited by the State Board of Education. . .[emphasis added] [93]

The statutes further provide that whenever adequate regulations cannot be achieved through other means, such as certification, then the state agency would have the authority to set up licensing standards. The rationale for establishing any licensing regulations is to protect the public health and welfare.[94] The factor that licensing is for the protection of the clients that avail themselves and not to enhance the status of the occupational group is sometimes forgotten.

If the necessary statutory law is passed by the legislature to allow public school counselors to be licensed, it should be noted that these individuals would still be state employees and have to be concerned with the goals of the institution and the welfare of all pupils. Even if public school counselors were licensed, they would not have the autonomy that counselors in the private sector would enjoy.

Records

Pupil records date back to the 1820s in New England when schools started keeping registers of enrollment and attendance.[95] Two major movements spurred the growth of pupil records. These were (1) the scientific movement[96] and the (2) whole child concept.[97] These are not mutually exclusive as each is dependent on the other to a great extent.

The scientific movement revolved around the concept of more sophisticated measuring devices such as surveys, tests and other measuring devices. Because of these devices the school could better evaluate the development of the child. This movement made it necessary to have more data within the pupil records and made records of attendance impertinent.[98]

The "whole child" concept was a major change in educational philosophy; no longer was the primary purpose of the school to teach reading. The philosophies of education had evolved to encompass the social, emotional, mental, and physical variables which relate to the child's education. Therefore, more comprehensive documents had to be kept which would meet the needs of the child.[99]

In 1925, a NEA committee recommended that not only the previous aspects of student records be kept, but also recommended that guidance and psychological records be maintained. In 1941 the American Council on Education made available the first cumulative record folder[100] which stressed that attention be given to the description and evaluation of behavior.[101]

From these early beginnings the record keeping process has progressed to where it is today. No longer is the pupil record limited to matters of grades, test scores, and daily attendance. These school records have evolved into student *dossiers*[102] which often contain information relating to all aspects of pupils' life.[103]

With the increase in technology, the information gathering process has become very extensive, not only in public education but in all forms of governmental and business operations. The advent of computerized multi-level information systems[104] and other technological advances in electronic equipment have stimulated public concern with all agencies that collect information. This has also coincided with greater awareness of individual rights as evidenced by numerous court decisions affecting the individual.[105] Because of societal changes the rights of the individual have become more fully recognized by all elements of society.

The need for pupil records is well recognized. The National Committee for Citizens in Education has observed: "Schools must keep basic records about children. Names, addresses, birthdates, courses taken and grades received must be recorded for review by teachers, counselors, college admission officers, employers and others. Problems begin to form around what different people in different places define as a record, what entries should be made into it, who should use it, and who should not see it." The present record system is often unclear.[106]

Because of the growth in use of pupil records and the new emphasis on the rights of the individual, a major question has arisen. Where is the line drawn between the student's right of privacy and the public right to know?

Authority to Maintain Pupil Records

Legislatures are required by constitutional provisions of each particular state to provide a school system for the purpose of educating children.[107] The legislature may exercise this power in any manner not expressly prohibited by the state constitution.[108] The legislature with the power and authority to establish an educational system usually delegates certain powers to local education agencies. These local educational agencies operate the school[109] systems with powers expressly conferred or implied which are necessary to carry out the assigned objectives.[110]

Since the powers of local education agencies must be either expressly conferred or implied as necessary, the authority for maintaining pupil records varies from state to state depending on statutory law. Carey reports that most state statutes are not clear and the scope of the files are at the discretion of either the state or local authorities.[111]

Some states make reference to records and pupil records at various places throughout the state code. Virginia is an example. Section 22-275.15 of the Virginia School Code states:

> *Teachers to keep daily attendance records.*—Every teacher in every school in the Commonwealth shall keep an accurate daily record of attendance of all children. Such record shall, at all times, be open to any officer authorized to enforce the provisions of this article who may inspect or copy the same, and shall be admissible in evidence in any prosecution for a violation of this article, as prima facie evidence of the facts stated therein.[112]

In another section of the Code of Virginia, it states:

> The State Board of Education is further authorized to promulgate rules and regulations governing the retenion of pupil personnel records in public schools.[113]

In Kentucky, pupil records are referred to in several places. Section 159.160 of the Kentucky Revised Statutes says:

> The principal or teacher in charge of any public, private or parochial school shall report to the superintendent of schools of the district in which the school is situated the names, ages, and places of residence of all pupils in attendance at his school together with any other facts that the superintendent may require to facilitate carrying out the laws relating to compulsory attendance and employment of children. The reports shall be made within the first two weeks of the beginning of school in each school year.[114]

Kentucky Revised Statute 159.140 subsection 8 under Duties of Directors of Pupil Personnel says:

> Keep the records and make the reports that are required by law, by regulation of the State Board of Education and by the Superintendent and Board of Education.[115]

A State of Missouri statute provides that each agency head must "make and maintain records. . .designed to furnish information to protect the legal and financial rights of the state and of persons directly affected by agency's activity."[116]

Therefore, school districts have the power to maintain pupil records either through powers expressly conferred, such as the statutes above, or through powers implied as necessary to carrying out the objectives of the state.

Purposes of Maintaining Pupil Records

The purposes of maintaining records are varied and complex. One reason pupil records are kept is because they are required either by statute or regulation. The statute of Mississippi required the keeping of a cumulative folder containing the following information: pupil's date of birth, record of attendance, grades, mental and scholastic abilities, personality traits and characteristics, occupational interest and aptitudes, and health information.[117] The state of Montana requires by regulation that each school shall keep pupil files that include name, addresses of the parent or guardian, birthdate, academic work completed, level of achievement, and the attendance of the pupil. The Montana regulation also states that other information may be kept if in conformance with the district policy.[118] Therefore, one purpose of keeping records is to be in compliance with the law.

Two other purposes of keeping records that have been proffered are (1) to help pupils better understand themselves and then, in turn, chart their future with greater assurance, and (2) to provide information for the teachers, guidance specialists, administrators, and parents to furnish guidance for the pupil.[119] Because of this complexity of legal requirements and educational philosophies, a problem arises concerning not the basic purpose of keeping records but the type and extent of information that will be retained. Because of this, some very germane, ethical and legal questions are being asked about the purposes of student records.

Pupil Records

Pupil records must be viewed in association with public records. As the rights of privacy become better enumerated,[120] more questions are raised concerning the conflict between the public's right to know, and have access to documents and the personal rights of individuals.

In 1972 Butler and others reported forty-seven states had public record statutes. Although the statutes have similarity in that they all define public records, there is considerable variation among the states on the scope and language.[121] The New Jersey statute defines public records as

> . . .(A)ll records which are required by law to be made, maintained or kept on file by any board, body, agency, department, commission or official of the State or of any political sub-division thereof. . .shall, for the purpose of this act, be deemed to be public records.[122]

The New Jersey statutes further define public records in Section 47: 3-16 entitled, Destruction of Public Records, as:

> . . . (A)ny paper, written or printed book, document or drawing, map or plan, photograph, microfilm, sound-recording or similar device, or any copy thereof. . .that has been received by any such officer, commission, agency or authority of the state or of any political subdivision thereof, including subordinate boards thereof, in connection with the transaction of public business and has been retained by such recipient or its successor as evidence of its activities or because of the information contained therein.[123]

The New Jersey statute is definite but the Indiana statute is rather brief in its definition of public records:·

> The term "public records" shall mean any writing in any form necessary, under or required, or directed to be made by any statute or by any rule or regulation of any administrative body or agency of the state or any of its political subdivisions.[124]

In *MacEwan* v. *Holm* the court said that whether or not a record is to be considered as a public record in a certain situation depends upon the "purposes of the law which will be served by so classifying it. A record may be a public record for one purpose and not for another."[125] There appears to be no single definition of a "public record" which applies in all situations.[126] Generally, the elements essential to constitute a public record are that it be (1) a written memorial, (2) made by a public officer, (3) authorized by law, and (4) accurate and durable.[127]

Cases: What Are Public Records

In *Papadopoulos* v. *Oregon State Board of Higher Education,* the plaintiff, a faculty member, claimed that a report submitted to the University Administration on the functioning of the School of Science Department was a public record. The report which was made by out-of-state consultants was claimed by the administration to be confidential, and, therefore, not a public record. The court ruled the breach of the promise of confidentiality was not of sufficient harm to the public interest to prevent full disclosure of the report and, therefore, it was a public record.[128]

In New Jersey a citizen's group requested that the school board release the mean and median scores for standardized achievement tests on a grade-by-grade and school-by-school basis. The citizen's group stated that such information was a public record under the state statute. The board contended that since no law required them to administer comprehensive achievement tests, the results were not public records. The court reasoned that although no law mandated the test be given, an administrative rule did so require. Therefore, the citizen's group had a right to such documents. It is important to note in the above case that individual scores were not requested—only the mean and median score for each grade of each school.[129]

In an interesting case where the student refused to wear a cap and gown at graduation exercises because the garments were not sanitary, the board refused to release the grades and other documents claiming that they were the private property of the school officials. The decision was against the board because the grades and records were". . .in a sense, public records. . ." Therefore, the records were of a public nature and the student had a right to copies of such records as maintained by the school officials.[130]

Cases: What Are Not Public Records

A number of cases have been decided which have classified certain types of documents as not being public records. A consultant was hired by a school board to seek out prospects for the position of superintendent. It was contended that the files used by the consultant to make a report to the school board were public records. The court decided that all reports when turned over to the board were public records, but the private files of the consultant were personal property.[131]

In *Conover* v. *Board of Education* the court said that there is no formula for determining what is or what is not a public writing. In each situation the terms had to be defined, facts observed and previous decisions relied upon. In this particular case, it was determined that the untranscribed notes of the board clerk were not public writings. To find these notes to be public records would "deify doodling."

Public writings are to be interpreted from one end of the continuum to the other with the determination of their character being made where "reason shows brightest."[132]

Other cases have found that work sheets[133] and daily logs by various government officials are not public records. To adopt the interpretation that every document made by a public official is subject to scrutiny and examination is refuted by ". . .legislative history of the statutory definition. . ."[134]

Inspection of Public Records—Right-to-Know

When examining public records and corresponding state statutes, one has to consider the right of inspection. After determining whether a record is public, the question arises—which records are open for inspection and which are not?

In *Sanchez* v. *Board of Regents of Eastern New Mexico University,* the court said:

> In few if any states has the legislature attempted to define public documents for purposes of their inspection statutes or to spell out the circumstances under which inspection may be required. Rather, such matters have been left to the courts. Study of many cases, texts and law reviews convinces us that the leading case on the subject is *MacEwan* v. *Holm*. . .[135]

In *MacEwan,* the right to inspect public records was viewed in a broad respect. The nature of public records is broad; therefore, the nature of inspection is correspondingly broad. Only when the writing lacked sufficient guarantee of authenticity could there be justification for a narrow interpretation of the inspection right.[136]

At common law the public has certain limited rights to inspect public records or government documents.[137] The modern day philosophy of democratic institutions does not allow the extent of the holding of old English common law of restriction on government documents. Still a few states follow this common law doctrine while others have passed legislation which is[138] usually known as the right-to-know doctrine.[139] Although there are a number of states that have statutory right-to-know laws, this doctrine largely emanates from judicial interpretation and writings.

Cases: Right-to-Know

The right to inspect public records has been questioned in numerous cases. In a community college case, it has been ruled that minutes of the board of trustees are open to the teacher's association and taxpayers of the county. These records are not confidential. The rights of citizens and taxpayers to inspect these documents are fundamental and the purpose of inspection is immaterial.[140] Taxpayers have a right "to inspect and copy purchase records of student's desks, chairs and replacement parts. . ." Because these are public records, the reasoning of the board that it was inconvenient is not sufficient to deny the right of inspection of public documents.[141]

A superintendent cannot deny a school board member the names and addresses of pupils enrolled in certain schools of the district. Although the majority of the board had passed a rule not to divulge the names and addresses of pupils to anyone, the court said that since the state law allowed inspection of public records the board could not contravene this law and the board member had a right to the names and addresses of pupils.[142] In a similar case a school board member wanted to have the names and addresses of all pupils enrolled in a special program. The purpose for obtaining the names and addresses was to write letters to the pupils enrolled in a special program stating that the school board member opposed the program. The majority of the board felt that such criticism would be detrimental to the program and refused access. The court said that the right to inspect official records could not be negated by a resolution of a majority of the board.[143]

In two recent New Hampshire cases relating to negotiations, the court ruled in the first that the education association had a right to inspect public records to determine the names and addresses of all employees during a teacher strike. The purpose of this request was to determine the credentials of the substitutes. Since no hardship existed, these were public records and the association had a right to know.[144] The second case was where a reporter wanted to be admitted to the negotiation session between the board and teachers. The plaintiff contended the right under the law to attend such sessions. The court decided that the legislature did not intend the right-to-know law to apply to negotiation sessions. Also emphasized was the fact that any official action that came out of these sessions would be approved in an open meeting in accordance with the right-to-know statute.[145]

A few cases have involved pupil records as they relate to court proceedings outside of the realm of official school action. Where a father had received visitation rights to his child under court order, the school was required to provide the forwarding address of his child. A key element in the case was that there was no evidence that the child was in any physical danger from the father.[146] In another similar case, the plaintiff wanted access to the names and addresses of a particular high school class of which the plaintiff was a member for the purpose of preparing a defense for a criminal action. The school had a policy that did not allow private detectives, solicitors, collectors, or others of like nature to receive information about students or former students from school records. The court said that this was a very laudable policy but there had to be a balancing of the individual rights against the confidentiality of records. Since the individual was charged with a criminal offense, the person had a greater right; therefore, the information had to be provided. The court quoted *Matter of Wenfel* v. *Fitzgerald* 260 N.Y.S. 2d 791 (New York, 1965) which said:

> Where the defense of a person accused of a crime requires access to public records or even to records sealed from general examination, the right of inspection has a greater sanction and must be enforced.[147]

In *People* v. *Sharp*[148] the defendant in a rape case wanted to subpoena the school records of the victim before the victim had been called to testify. The court denied the request based on a number of cases[149] which held that school records are privileged and only the parent or student could disclose the contents. But the court went on to say that the request for a subpoena would be reviewed in line with *Davis* v. *Alaska* 451 U.S. 308, 94 S.Ct. 1105 which says that the policy of protecting the confidentiality of juveniles would be waived in favor of the defendants' constitutional right of confronting witnesses. Therefore, the record would be used for "cross-examination to show bias."[150]

A mandamus was requested to compel the board to produce the records of a student involved in a negligence and malpractice suit. The purpose of securing the record was to prove the previous mental ability of the child. The board, although not involved in the negligence suit, refused to release the records saying that the plaintiff could subpoena the records at the time of the trial. The court required the board to produce the records because as a matter of law parents are entitled to the information in student records.[151]

Public records are generally open to inspection by any person and as a general rule most state statutes allow the records to be inspected during normal office hours at reasonable times.[152]

Although the right-to-know doctrine prevails, there are exceptions to this rule for certain types of records. In *Mans* v. *Lebanon* a group of citizens claimed that under the "right-to-know" law, they should have had access to the name and salary of each school teacher.[153] The court said that this issue was governed by the right-to-know law, permitting freedom of access to public records. The law provided that: "Every citizen during the regular or business hours of such bodies or agencies, and on regular business premises of such bodies or agencies, has the right to inspect all public records. . ." The court said that citizens, therefore, had the right to the salary and name of each teacher, but explicitly pointed out that personal school records of pupils were *exempt* from the provisions of the law. Also exempt from the law are ". . .internal personnel practices, confidential, commercial, or financial information, personnel, medical, welfare, and other files whose disclosure would constitute invasion of privacy."[154] The teacher's salary is not so intimate as to constitute an invasion of privacy under *Griswold* v. *Connecticut,* 381 U.S. 479. This case illustrates that certain types of documents are open to the public and certain tyes are not open.

In *Getman* v. *National Labor Relations Board* in reviewing the exemption clause of the Freedom of Information Act, which dealt with exempting personnel and medical files and similar files, the court said the issue was to be determined by a balancing of the interests. To balance the interest test requires that the right of privacy of the affected individual be measured against the right of the public to be informed.[155]

Pupil Records v. *Public Records*

Because of the rights of the individual to privacy or confidentiality, school records are neither clearly "public records" or "private records." In *Allen* v. *McCleary* it was stated, "It serves no useful purpose to enter into the classification of school records of pupils as being 'public records' or 'private records.' " The court said they are public in the sense that they are required to be maintained and supported by taxes[156] but remain private because of the confidentiality of their nature. This conflict between the "right" to inspect and the "right" to remain private has been recognized and resolved by a few states either through statutes, regulations, attorney general opinions, or court decisions or a combination of all.[157] Because of the previously mentioned conflicts, and exemptions from right-to-know laws, pupil records have been classified as quasi-public records by a number of sources.[158,159,160]

Do Parents Have a Right to Inspect Pupil Records?

May parents obtain access to the records of their children? In *Van Allen*[161] school officials said that a pupil needed psychological treatment and therapy. The parent after obtaining the services of a private physician wanted the school's psychological findings conveyed to the physician. The school refused. The court said,

> Petitioners rights, if any, stem not from his status as taxpayer seeking to review the records of a public corporation, but from his relationship with school authorities as a parent under compulsory education has delegated to them the educational authority over his child. Thus, the common law rule. . .to the effect that when not detrimental to the public interest, the right to inspect records of a public nature exists as to persons who have sufficient interest in the subject matter, is a guide. . .as a matter of law the parent is entitled to inspect the records.[162]

In the *Matter of Thibadeau* the Commissioner of Education of the state of New York ruled ". . .progress reports, subject grades, intelligence quotients, tests, achievement scores, medical records, psychological and psychiatric reports, selective guidance notes and the evaluations of students by educators. . ." to be privileged which prevent disclosure from third parties other than the parents. The parents have, as a matter of law, the right to all information collected by the school.[163]

From reviewing the cases, statutes, attorney general opinions, and state board guidelines, it would appear that pupil records in a strict sense are not public records. Pupil records are quasi-public records which must be considered in respect to the balance of interest test. The pupil's rights of confidentiality and privacy must be balanced against the rights of the public to know. Persons who want to inspect student records must have a sufficient interest which is greater than the student's interest such as obtaining evidence for criminal proceedings. Parents have as a matter of law a right to inspect the records of their children although there are some exceptions. In *Marquesano* v. *Board of Education of City of New York*,[164] the court ruled against the parent as no educational interests were involved. The parents wanted the records to enforce visitation rights. The court said that an issue not involving the education of the child but relating to divorce proceedings was not of sufficient interest to release names and addresses of children.

Public Law 93-380—Protection of the Rights and Privacy of Parents and Students

In 1974, a new federal law relating to pupil records went into effect. This law was passed by the United States Congress as Section 438 of Public Law 93-380 (Education Amendments of 1974).[165] Section 438 which is entitled, "Protection of Rights and Privacy of Parents and Students," says that any educational institution receiving federal funds will lose those funds unless it complies with this section of the federal law.

Parents who have children attending an educational institution must be given the right to examine and challenge their children's official school records. The official school record specifically includes, but is not limited to "academic work completed, level of achievement (grades, standardized achievement test scores), attendance data, scores on standardized intelligence, aptitude and psychological tests, interest inventory results, health data, family background information, teacher or *counselor* ratings and observations, and verified reports of serious or recurrent behavior patterns." Parents have the right to challenge the records "to insure the records are not inaccurate, misleading, or otherwise in violation of the privacy rights of students and to provide an opportunity for correction or deletion of any such inaccurate, misleading, or otherwise inappropriate data. .."

This act also provides that the *parents* must give *their* consent before the records are released or shown to outside or third parties except those excluded by the act. Students eighteen (18) or over or attending an institution of post-secondary education must be given the same rights.

Student records, that are personally identifiable, may not be released without the written consent of the student's parents or students eighteen or older. The parents or older students must be notified if records are released under judicial order or lawfully issued subpoena.

In addition, all institutions or school agencies must notify parents or students eighteen years of age or older of the rights accorded them by this section of the federal statute.

Although federal guidelines are still being constituted it is clear from the law that any institution, under the penalty of loss of federal funds, must make student records available to parents or students who have reached the age of majority (eighteen years of age or older).

Summary

The first section of this chapter deals with the basic constitutional rights of students. Public school educators should recognize that students have constitutional rights but these rights do have limits. Reasonable rules and regulations may be promulgated.

Courts have noted that discipline and order are essential if the education function is to be performed. Educators not only have a responsibility but a duty to operate an orderly environment where education may be promoted, and that the rights of students do not extend so far as to allow disruption of the process.

Section two focused on the legal and ethical, or professional standards that face the modern day counselor. The counselor not only has a responsibility to the counselee but to all students attending school. Therefore, there are limits to this relationship the same as there are limits to the constitutional rights of students. The legal as well as the moral and ethical limitation in both situations are correlated with the rights and well being of other students or citizens.

The cases, statutes, attorneys general opinions, guidelines, and regulations reviewed in the third section would suggest that pupil records are not "public records" nor are they "private records." Pupil records are quasi-public records because they are generally required by law to be kept at public expense and serve an important public function. Yet pupil records are "private" in the respect that they contain personal data about individuals. Therefore, educators should be aware of the delicate balance between the right of the pupil and the right of the state.

Very clear and concise policies should be adopted by school districts in order to avoid any misuse or misunderstanding surrounding pupil records. Below are some summary elements which might be helpful in formulating guidelines:

1. Parents have a right to examine their child's records. There are possible exceptions to this statement when the purpose has no relationship to the educational process of the child.
2. School officials should be aware of the federal law (Public Law 93-380) and any state statutes, regulations, guidelines, or opinions.
3. School officials should be aware that parents and pupils have a protected right to privacy.
4. The parents and pupils right to privacy can only be overridden when the public has a greater interest.
5. Parents should be informed of all policies pertaining to pupil records.
6. The courts may subpoena a pupil's records for legal proceedings.
7. Pupil records should not be released to third parties without the consent of the parents in the absence of authority from statutes or regulations.
8. The professional staff of a school would have access to pupil records if they have a valid educational interest.
9. Material that is *not* relevant to the educational progress of the child should be expunged from the records.
10. The federal statute (Public Law 93-380) requires records be made available to eighteen-year-old pupils without consent of parents.

References

1. Alexander, Kern and Solomon, Erwin S. *College and University Law,* The Michie Company, Charlottesville, Virginia, 1972, p. 430. Also, see T. Page Johnson, "Due Process in Pupil Control," unpublished speech, Conference on Legal Issues in Education at Virginia Polytechnic Institute and State University, October 13, 1975.
2. Howard, A. E., *Magna Charta,* Thirty-ninth chapter of Magna Charta, The University of Virginia Press, Charlottesville, Virginia, 1964, p. 43.
3. Johnson, see note 1, p. 1.
4. United States Constitution, Amendment V.

5. United States Constitution, Amendment XIV.
6. Alexander, Kern; Corns,Ray; and McCann, Walter; *Public School Law: Cases and Materials,* West Publishing Company, St. Paul, Minnesota, 1969, p. 539.
7. Frankel, Osmond K. *The Rights You Have,* Warner Paperback Library Edition, New York, New York, 1972, p. 35.
8. Alexander; Corns; McCann; op. cit. p. 35.
9. United States Constitution, Amendment X.
10. Alexander; Corns; McCann; loc. cit.
11. Phay, Robert. "Student Rights and Responsibilities," M. D. Alexander et al. eds., *Legal Rights of Teachers and Students,* Gainesville, Florida: Maxwell-King Publishers, 1974, p. 78.
12. Johnson, op. cit. p. 10.
13. Brown v. Board of Education of Topeka 347 United States 483, 74 S.Ct. 686.
14. Tinker v. Des Moines 393 United States 803, 89 S.Ct. 733.
15. Board of Regents of State College v. Roth 408 United States 564 (1972).
16. Alexander; Corns; McCann, op. cit. p. 539.
17. Alexander; Corns; McCann; loc. cit.
18. Adkins v. Children's Hospital 261 United States 525 (1923).
19. Valley National Bank of Phoenix v. Glover 152 p. 2d 292.
20. Goss v. Lopez 419 United States 565 (1975).
21. Board of Regents v. Roth supra.
22. Alexander, Solomon, op. cit. 414.
23. Johnson, op. cit. p. 8.
24. Johnson, op. cit. p. 3.
25. Johnson, op. cit. p. 5.
26. Murray v. West Baton Rouge Parish School board 472 F. 2d 438.
27. Tinker v. Des Moines supra.
28. Johnson, op. cit. p. 10.
29. Hernandez v. School District #1, 315 F. Supp. 289.
30. Gebert v. Hoffman 336 F. Supp. 694.
31. Melton v. Young 465 F. Supp. 1332.
32. Guzick v. Drebus 431 F. 2d 594.
33. See E. Edmund Reutter, *The Courts and Student Conduct,* National Organization on Legal Problems of Education, Topeka, Kansas, 1975 for comprehensive analysis of court cases relating to student conduct.
34. Johnson, op. cit. p. 14.
35. United States Constitution, Amendment IV.
36. Johnson, op. cit. p. 14.
37. Kansas v. Stein 456 P. 2d 1 (1969); People v. Overton 249 N.E. 2d 366 (1969).
38. People v. Stewart 313 N.Y.S. 2d 253 (1970)
    Mercer v. State 450 S.W. 2d 715 (1970).
39. State v. Boccino 282 A. 2d 869 (1971).
40. Alexander; Corns; McCann; op. cit. p. 177.
41. Alexander; Corns; McCann, op. cit. pp. 177-78.
42. Alexander, Kern; Corns, Ray; and McCann, Walter, *Public School Law: Cases and Materials,* 1975 Supplement. St. Paul, Minn.: West Publishing Company, 1975, p. 177.
43. Dixon v. Alabama State Board of Education 297 F. 2d 150.
44. Dixon supra.
45. Due v. Florida A & M, 233 F. Supp. 396.
46. Phay, op. cit. p. 9.
47. Since the landmark decision of the Court of Appeals for the Fifth Circuit in Dixon v. Alabama State Board of Education,294 F. 2d 150 (1961), the lower federal courts have uniformly held the Due Pro-

cess Clause applicable to decisions made by tax supported educational institutions to remove a student from the institution long enough for the removal to be classified as an expulsion. The lower courts have been less uniform, however, on the question whether removal from school for some shorter period may ever be so trivial a deprivation as to require no process and, if so, how short the removal must be to qualify. Circuit courts have held or assumed the Due Process Clause applicable to long suspension, to indefinite suspensions, the addition of a thirty-day suspension to a ten-day suspension, to mild suspensions, and to a three-day suspension, to a suspension for "not more than a few days," and to all suspensions no matter how short. The Federal district courts have held the Due Process Clause applicable to an interim suspension pending expulsion proceedings, to a ten-day suspension, to suspensions of under five days, and to all suspensions, and inapplicable to suspensions to twenty-five days, to suspensions of ten days, and to suspensions of eight days. (Taken from note in Goss v. Lopez United States 565).

48. Goss v. Lopez, 419 United States 565.
49. Goss supra.
50 Johnson, op. cit. p. 32.
51. Phay, op. cit. p. 8.
52. Alexander, Supplement, op. cit. pp. 182-85.
53. Johnson, op. cit. pp. 27-28.
54 Ohlsen, Merle M., *Guidance Services in the Modern School,* New York: Harcourt, Brace, Jovanovich, Inc., 1974 pp. 7-18.
55. American Personnel and Guidance Association, *Ethical Standards,* 1974.
56. Alexander; Corns; McCann; op. cit. pp. 19-26.
57. Reutter, op. cit. p. 501.
58. Berea College v. Commonwealth, 94 S.W. 623.
59. Leeper v. State, 53 S.W. 962.
60. Reutter, loc. cit.
61. Tarasoff v.Regents of University of California, 529 P. 2d 553.
62. American Personnel and Guidance Association, *Ethical Standards,* A:2.
63. Aubrey, Roger, F. "Organizational Victimization of School Counselors," *The School Counselor,* vol. 20, no. 5, May 1973, pp. 346-347.
64. Hays, Donald G. "Responsible Freedom for the School Counselor," *The School Counselor,* vol. 20. No. 1, September 1972, pp. 93-94.
65. Aubrey, loc. cit.
66. Litwack, Lawrence et al. "Testimonial Privileged Communication and the School Counselor," *The School Counselor,* vol. 17, No. 2 November 1969, p. 109.
    Also see John J. Pietrofesa and John Vriend,*The School Counselor as a Professional,* F. E. Peacock Publishers, Itasca, Illinois 1971, p. 105.
67. Swanson, Carl D. "Duties and Liabilities of Counselors," Richard Vacca ed., *The Law of Guidance and Counseling,* Cincinnati, Ohio: W. H. Anderson Co. Publication Date 1976.
68. Pietrofesa, see Note 56, p. 105.
69. Litwack, op. cit. p. 108.
70. Swanson, op. cit. p. 5.
71. Pietrofesa, loc. cit.
72. Litwack, loc. cit.
73. Pietrofesa, op. cit. p. 109.
74. Litwack, op. cit. p. 110.
75. Pietrofesa, op. cit. p. 105. Also, see Litwack, op. cit. p. 111.
76. Wigmore,J. H. , *Evidence in Trials at Common Law,* vol. 8, McNaughton revision; Brown / Little Brown, 1961.
77. Litwack, op. cit. p. 109.
78. Swanson, op. cit. p. 19.

79. List of states as cited by Swanson plus Kentucky:
   1. Connecticut (Conn. Gen. Stat. Ann. Sec 10-154a, Supp. 1973).
   2. Delaware (Del. Stats. Tit. 14 Ch. 41 Sec 4114, 1970).
   3. Idaho (Ida. Code Sec 9-203, Supp. 1973).
   4. Indiana (Ind. Ann. Stat. Sec 28-4537, 1970).
   5. Maine (Me., Rev. Stat. Ann. Tit. 20, Sec 801, Supp. 1973-4).
   6. Michigan (Mich., Stat. Ann. Sec 27A, 2165, Supp. 1973).
   7. Montana (Mont. Rev. codes Ann. Sec 93-701-4, Supp. 1973).
   8. Nevada (Nev. Laws Chap. 49, 1973).
   9. North Carolina (N.C. Gen. Stat. Sec 8-53.4, Supp. 1973).
   10. North Dakota (N.D. Cent. Code Sec 31-01-06, 1, Supp. 1973).
   11. Oklahoma (School Law, Sec 49).
   12. Oregon (Ore. Rev. Stat. Sec 44.040, 1971).
   13. Pennsylvania (Pa. Stat. Ann. Tit. 24, Sec 13-1319, Supp. 1973-4).
   14. South Dakota (S.D. Compiled Laws Ann. Sec 19-2-5.1, Supp. 1973).
   15. Kentucky (KRS 421.216).
80. Swanson, loc. cit.
81. Pietrofesa, op. cit., p. 107.
82. Tarasoff, supra.
83. Swanson, op. cit. p. 16.
84. Swanson, op. cit. p. 18.
85. American Personnel and Guidance Association, *Ethical Standards,* 1974, B-4.
86. Tarasoff, supra.
87. 15A Corpus Juris Secundum at 355.
88. 15A Corpus Juris Secundum at 353.
89. Swanson, op. cit. p. 8.
90. Vacca, Richard. "Student Personnel Records in Public Schools: An Examination of Legal and Professional Problems," *Legal Issues in Education,* M. D. Alexander et al. eds., Virginia Polytechnic Institute and State University, Blacksburg, Virginia 1975, p. 7.
91. 14 Corpus Juris Secundum at 112.
92. Virginia Annotated Code,   4-1.4.
93. Virginia Annotated Code,   4-102.3.
94. Virginia Annotated Code,   4-1.8.
95. Divoky, Diana "Cumulative Records: Assault on Privacy." *Children, Parents and School Records,* National Committee for Citizens in Education, Columbia, Maryland, 1974, p. 9.
96. Butler,Henry E. Jr.;Morgan, K. D. and Vanderpool, Floyd A. Jr.; *Legal Aspects of Student Records,* National Organization on Legal Problems of Education, Topeka, Kansas, p. 9.
97. Divoky, loc. cit.
98. Butler, et al., op. cit. p. 1.
99. Divoky, loc. cit.
100. Butler, et al. op. cit. p. 2.
101. Divoky, op. cit. p. 10.
102. Vacca, op. cit. p. 4.
103. Divoky, op. cit. p. 9.

The mushrooming effects of record keeping in public education is vividly illustrated by those records required or recommended for each child in the New York Public School System:

a buff-colored, cumulative, four-page record card that notes personal and social behavior, along with scholastic achievement, and is kept on file for fifty years;

a blue or green test-data card on which all standardized test results and grade equivalents are kept, also for fifty years;

a white, four-page, chronological reading record;

a pupil's office card;

an emergency home-contact card;

a salmon-colored health record—one side for teachers, the other for the school nurse and doctor;

a dental-check card;

an audiometer screening-test report;

an articulation card, including teacher's recommendations for tracking in junior high school;

a teacher's anecdotal file on student behavior;

an office guidance record, comprised of counselor's evaluation of aptitude, behavior, and personality characteristics;

a Bureau of Child Guidance file that is regarded, though not always treated, as confidential, and includes reports to and from psychologists, psychiatrists, social workers, various public and private agencies, the courts and the police;

and all disciplinary referral cards.

104. Hogan, John C., *The Schools, The Courts and the Public Interest.* Lexington, Mass.: Lexington Books, 1974, p. 144.
105. Some cases involving the rights of individuals: Tinker v. Des Moines, 93 United States 503 (1969), Wisconsin v. Yoder, 406 United States 250 (1972), Loving v. Virginia, 388 United States (1967), Roe v. Wade, 410 United States 43 (1973), Griswold v. Connecticut, 381 United States 479 (1965), Eisenstadt v. Baird, 405 United States 438 (1972).
106. *Children, Parents and School Records,* National Committee for Citizens in Education, Columbia, Maryland, 1974, p. 3.
107. Harmony Grove School District v. Camden School District No. 35, 302 S.W. 2d 281 (Arkansas, 1957).
108. Harris v. Burr, 52 p. 17 (Oregon, 1898).
109. Riccio v. Hoboken, 55 A. 1109, (New Jersey, 1903); Malone v. Williams, 103 S.W. 798, (Tennessee, 1907).
110. Bopp v. Clark, 147 N.W. 172, (Iowa, 1914); Malone v. Williams, 103 S.W. 798, (Tennessee, 1907).
111. Carey, Sara "Students, Parents, and the School Record Prison: A Legal Strategy for Preventing Abuse," National Committee for Citizens in Education, Columbia, Maryland, 1974, p. 26.
112. *Virginia Code Annotated,* 22-275.15.
113. *Virginia Code Annotated,* 22-53.1.
114. *Kentucky Revised Statutes,* 159.160.
115. *Kentucky Revised Statutes,* 159.140.
116. *Missouri Annotated Statutes,* 109.240 (3), 1965.
117. Chapter 24, House B. 11 No. 15, General Acts, Extraordinary Legislative Session, 1953, As Amended by Chapter 26, House Bill No. 250, General Acts of the Regular Legislative Session, 1954.
118. Standards of Accreditation of Montana Schools, Adopted by Board of Education, December 10, 1971.
119. Mortensen, Donald G. and Schmulle, Allen M. *Guidance in Today's Schools,* New York: John Wiley and Sons, Inc., 1966, p. 203.
120. See footnote 95.
121. Butler et al., op. cit. p. 16.
122. *New Jersey Statute Annotated,* 47: 1A-2.
123. *New Jersey Statute Annotated,* 47: 3-16.
124. Burns Indiana Statute Annotated, Chapter 6, 57-602 (1)
    Other examples of the scope of definition of public records:

    Kansas: All official public records of the state, counties, municipalities, townships, school districts, commissions, agencies, and legislative bodies, which records by law are required to be kept and maintained. . . Ch. 45-201.

Oregon: "Public Record" means a document, book, paper, photograph, file, sound recording or other material, such as court files, mortgage and deed records, regardless of physical form or characteristics, made, received, filed or recorded in pursuance of law or in connection with the transaction of public business, whether or not confidential or restricted in use. . .ORS 192.005 (5).

125. MacEwan v. Holm, 359 P. 2d 413 (Oregon, 1961).
126. Linder v. Eckard, 152 N.W. 3d 833 (Iowa, 1967).
127. 76 Corpus Juris Secundum 112.
128. Papadopoulas v. Oregon State Board of Higher Education, 494 P. 2d 260, ct. 263, (Oregon, 1972).
129. Citizens for Better Education, et al. v. Board of Education of City of Camden, 308 A. 2d 35 (New Jersey, 1973).
130. Valentine v. Independent School District, 174 N.W. 334, (Iowa, 1919).
131. State v. Sharp, 300 So. 2d 750 (Florida, 1974).
132. Conover et al. v. Board of Education of Nebo School District. 267 P. 2d 768 at 770 (Utah, 1954).
133. Kottschade v. Lundberg, 160 N.W. 2d 135 (Minnesota, 1968).
134. Town Crier, Inc. et al. v. Chief of Police of Western, 282 N.W. 2d 379, (Massachusetts, 1972).
135. Sanchez v. Board of Regents of Eastern New Mexico University, 486 P. 2d 608 at 613 (New Mexico, 1971).
136. MacEwan supra.
137. 76 Corpus Juris Secundum 113.
138. Papadopoulos supra.
139. Butler, loc. cit. Examples of Right-To-Know Statutes:
   (1) Virginia Freedom of Information Act, Chapter 21   2.1-342 (a),
      Except as otherwise specifically provided by law, all official records shall be open to inspection and copying by any official of this State having a personal or legal interest in specified records during the regular office hours of the custodian of such reocrds. Access to such records shall not be denied to any such citizen of this State nor to representatives of radio and television stations broadcasting in or into this State.
   (2) Kentucky Revised Statute 171.650—This statute applied to state agencies but has not been applied to schools.
      Unless otherwise provided by law, all papers, books, and other records of any matters required by law or administrative rule to be kept by any agency, and all records arising from the exercise of functions authorized thereby, are public records and shall be open to inspection by any interested person subject to reasonable rules as to time and place of inspection established under KRS 12.080. A certified copy of any public records, subject to any public record, subject to any such rules in effect, shall be furnished by the custodian thereof, to any person requesting it, upon the payment of such reasonable fee therefore as may be prescribed by law or by administrative rule.
   (3) Burns Annotated Statute, Chapter 6, 457-602 (1)
      Pursuant to the fundamental philosophy of the American Constitutional form of representative government which holds to the principle that government is the servant of the people, and not the master of them, it is hereby declared to be the public policy of the State of Indiana that all of the citizens of this state are, unless otherwise expressly provided by law at all times entitled to full and complete information regarding the affairs of government and the officials of those whom the people select to represent them as public officials and employees. To that end, the provisions of this act shall be liberally construed with the view of carrying out the above declaration of policy.
140. Cline v. Board of Trustees of Schenectady County, 351 N.Y.S. 2d 81 (New York, 1973).

141. Application of Welt, 328 N.Y.S. 2d 930 (New York, 1972).
142. Wagner v. Redmond, 127 So. 2d 275 (Louisiana, 1961).
143. King v. Ambellan 173 N.Y.S. 2d 98 (New York, 1958).
144. Timberlane Regional Educational Association et al. v. Crampton 319 A. 2d 633, (New Hampshire, 1974).
145. Talbot et al. v. Concord Union School District, 323 A 2d 912 (New Hampshire, 1974).
146. Dachs v. Board of Education of New York, 277 N.Y.S. 2d 449 (New York, 1967).
147. Marmo v. New York City Board of Education, 56 Misc. 2d 517, 289 N.Y.S. 2d 51 (New York, 1968).
148. People v. Levon Sharp 355 N.Y.S. 2d 295 (New York, 1974).
149. See Matter of Thibadeau 1 Education Department Rep. 607: Matter of Wilson II Education Department Rep. 208; Matter of Van Allen v. McCleary 211 N.Y.S. 2d 501; Matter of Johnson v. Board of Education of City of New York 220 N.Y.S. 2d 362.
150. Sharp, supra.
151. Johnson v. Board of Education of City of New York 220 N.Y.S. 2d 363 (New York, 1961).
152. Butler, op. cit. p. 16.
153. Mans v. Lebanon School Board 290 A. 2d 866 (New Hampshire, 1974).
154. Mans, supra at 867.
155. Getman et al. v. National Labor Relations Board 450 F. 2d 670 (D.C., 1971). See also *Papadopoulos* supro, and *MacEwan* supro.
156. Van Allen, supra.
157. Van Allen supra.

    (1) Letter from William J. Guste, Jr., Attorney General of Louisiana by Louis Carruth, Ass't. Attorney General, January 31, 1974.

    "We reaffirm the conclusions reached in our 1958 opinion and we also add the opinion that a student, in entering a public school, retains his constitutional rights, including the right of privacy, and that school may not reveal a student's confidential records except by his or her parent's consent, or for the purpose of the State's conduct or other activities, e.g., to other educational institutions, law enforcement officials, or the order of the court."

    (2) *Recommended Guidelines for Pupil Records,* Indiana State Department of Public Instruction.

    Any record of an individual pupil maintained by an officer or employee of the school district for the use of professional members of the school staff is a pupil record. When placed in the student's cumulative folder and used by the school district in the educative process, such material, no matter how informed or incidental, is part of the pupil record. Pupil records are considered "quasi-public" records and are open to "real parties of interests."

    (3) Delaware Code Annotated Title 14, Chapter 41, Sec. 4114 (1970).

    All personal records of pupils in all public schools in Delaware and in all private schools in Delaware, including but not limited to, test scores, marks given according to a school grading system, psychological or medical reports, reports related to discipline, personal and anecdotal reports, reports by guidance counselors are deemed to be confidential and not to be disclosed or the contents thereof released to nonschool personnel except in the following circumstances. ..

158. Butler, op. cit. p. 22.
159. *A Legal Memorandum,* National Association of Secondary School Principals, Reston, Virginia, p. 1 September, 1971.
160. See footnote 21, Section (2).
161. Van Allen, supra at 503.
162. Van Allen, supra at 505.
163. Matter of Thibadeu, supra.
164. Marquesano v. Board of Education of City of New York 191 N.Y.S. 2d 713 (New York, 1959).
165. Public Law 93-380. (Education Amendments, 1974).

Chapter 13

ISSUES, TRENDS, AND THE FUTURE OF CAREER GUIDANCE

Dean L. Hummel

Issues, or concerns with which there are divergent views, require conceptualization before action can be taken for their resolution. Delineating all the issues inherent in the guidance process would prove a monumental task. Indeed, such an endeavor may not serve in promoting understanding, much less conceptualization, or resolution. Nor would it seem productive to identify issues with criticisms, since criticisms of guidance arise from a diverse and confusing host of expectations and from a complex array of functions. The purpose of this chapter, therefore, is to enumerate conceptualizations of issues in guidance with a narrative attempt to stimulate reader discussion and clarity in understanding as a reference point from which resolutions may be achieved and trends can be viewed. Conceptualizations are synthesized under four major rubrics, in the form of questions, followed by an enumeration of trends. The issues dealt with in this chapter probably suggest author biases, and the trends and future predictions contain an element of crystal ball gazing.

The careful reader of the first twelve chapters of this book will already have identified numerous issues concerning the expectations of guidance and its functions in the educational enterprise. A synthesis of the related content will provide the student with a foundation for conceptualization and a basis on which responsiveness toward solutions can be developed.

Guidance, whether viewed as a point of view, a process, a set of organized services, or method for facilitating human learning activities, has become accepted as a vital aspect of educational programs in schools and colleges, in agencies, in business, and in industry. The underlying basis for almost universal acceptance is that guidance has come to be thought of as a process of helping individuals examine their life experiences with the goal that they will understand and know themselves and their environment to the degree that purposeful, creative, and effective actions will result (Hansen and Tennyson, 1975).

The issues presented in this chapter will be presented along with influential trends in guidance. From a synthesis of the diverse issues related to guidance, four major conceptualizations are presented. Without a more accurate understanding of trends related to and resulting from these issues, and a thorough analysis related to local situations, applied guidance practices will be less responsive to the issues and to the purposes for which guidance is intended.

Dr. Dean L. Hummel is Professor of Counselor Education at Virginia Polytechnic Institute and State University, Blacksburg, Virginia.

Various issues and trends in guidance have developed as a result of the origin of their intended services, disciplines from which the services are drawn, particular national, state or local
crises, and images practitioners of guidance may create. Even today, a particular issue may be
shaded by influences and unemployment, economic conditions, needs of special populations, or
a particular national, state, or local thrust. It seems as though guidance is in a continual state of
flux, with issues related to both practitioners and to the functions they are expected to perform.
The "other" counselor, teacher, or personnel worker continually seems to be the object of
search. The "passing parade" of guidance workers and their "contacts with reality" provide
the stuff from which issues are surfaced.

Four major conceptualizations of issues based on trends appear to formulate the basis
upon which guidance in the educational enterprise will enhance the probability of resolving the
issues.

Should Guidance Be Problem Centered?

Although most objectives of various personnel areas include a statement identifying services for *all,* or for *each individual,* many guidance programs are problem-centered in their
orientation. In addition to the administrative direction of services and to the particular point of
view of guidance practitioners in schools and agencies, three conditions tend to influence a
problem-centered approach. The first of these conditions generally relates to limited staffing of
professionally prepared guidance practitioners. Personnel available in such a situation are
usually forced to work with problem cases and conditions in an effort to save the group from
the problem person or condition. In the schools, for example, it often seems to teachers,
parents, and to pupils themselves, that the counselor is for problem children rather than for
every child who experiences normal concerns of development (Hummel and Bonham, 1968).

A second influence pertaining to the problem centered issue is related to the lack of
guidance program direction through organization and administration. Without a board level
administrative office with power to develop and enforce policies, acquire needed staff and
budget, establish system wide guidance practices, and coordinate programs, a building oriented
guidance program frequently lacks support and direction. Building principals, in this case, tend
to be directly responsible for the guidance functions of staff. Such a condition generally leads
guidance to priorities related to problem cases and situations. When a school's guidance effort
is directed toward special problems identified with the gifted, the misbehaver, the
underachiever, or the disturbed, or when guidance personnel are assigned administrative paper
work, disciplinary and other sundry duties, the majority of students are deprived of necessary
guidance services.

A third influence creating the problem-centered program is related to the major societal
and educational problems identified at any given time. As we know from past experiences,
special attention has been given to the slow learner, the job seeker, the gifted pupil, the college-
bound, the drop-out, the juvenile delinquent, and now, the disadvantaged. When local or national problems of this nature are identified (often for reasons external to the individuals and
their situations), the major program effort in guidance services is diverted in the direction of the
problem.

During the past several decades, local, state and national spotlights with a rainbow of colors have been focused on guidance and the school counselor's work. At the national level, through congressional action, and through the United States Office of Education, assistance has been provided for the improvement and expansion of state programs of guidance services. Recognition of the need for improved and expanded programs of guidance services is reflected at the state levels by legislative support, State Department of Education action, and state level research. And locally, schools have responded to the guidance recommendations for the modern school.

An example of this interest was evident in the *1960 White House Conference on Children and Youth.* Recommendation 190 of the report states that "guidance and counseling programs be strengthened, expanded, and coordinated at all levels, and that the role of the guidance and counseling program be clearly defined" (Golden Anniversary White House Conference on Children and Youth, 1960. p. 19). This interest was reinforced in the Rockefeller Report, sometimes referred to as *The Pursuit of Excellence* (1958) which emphasized the role of guidance in the success of our present day school system. Guidance services were prominently mentioned in the Conant Report which was published under the title *The American High School Today* (Conant, 1959). This report also placed improved guidance services as the number one recommendation for the workable, comprehensive American high school. The high priority given to guidance culminated in *The National Defense Education Act of 1958* (1958, p. 35). This piece of national legislation provided assistance to the state to be administered to the local schools for the improvement and expansion of the guidance programs in the secondary schools. Concern for school guidance preparation was also indicated by Congress with the passage of Part B, Title V of the National Defense Education Act. Proof of professional educator's concern for guidance is evident in the adoption of policies for guidance by the regional college and school accreditation associations. And since 1960, nineteen federal education and manpower laws have been enacted, all of which called for counseling and guidance services. However, most of these efforts have been crisis oriented, each directed at a particular problem or group.

The problem-centered issue has resulted in raising the voices of numerous critics, with a resounding "call for change." Rather than problem centeredness, the call emphasizes guidance for all—a program "to improve the quality and quantity of guidance and counseling services to all individuals—youth and adults" (National Advisory Council on Vocational Education, 1972).

Are There Contributing Guidance Roles Which Can Be Supported in the Educational Enterprise?

Originally, the term guidance was proposed as a description of a set of activities within the educational enterprise (Shertzer and Stone, 1971). Most guidance practitioners focused on information giving and advisement. As guidance became identified with an organized set of "services" (see chapters 3 through 8), school counselors and other pupil personnel specialists concerned with guidance, tended to be viewed as performing roles ancillary to the major function of the educational enterprise. While the issue of contributing roles fluctuates between the view that "everybody is a guidance worker" to "guidance is the counselor's job," the resolution of the issue will depend upon delineating guidance roles and differential staffing.

Mayer (1973) in *Education for a New Society,* sees the role of guidance as drawing upon contributions of all staff and on community resources. He suggests that learning and individual development is stimulated and reinforced in school and community environments. Unfortunately, some teachers view the classroom as the sacred domain of the teacher and any attention given pupils by outsiders is a challenge to this domain. Those who hold this view and concede that individualized approaches to assist pupils in self-understanding and self-direction are important, nevertheless often resist the specialized services of a guidance program. Some teachers feel that any attention of a personal nature is disrupting to the main task of the classroom—teaching subject matter. In the observation of the author, this view is held more often by teachers and others in the junior and senior high schools than in elementary schools.

A common thread running throughout modern views of guidance services in schools is the provision of helping services to individuals. Perhaps Kehas (1970), in calling for a "redefinition of education," provides the clearest rationale for guidance role contributions in the educational enterprise. He proposes that both cognitive and personal learning are necessary. What then are some of the contributing guidance roles of school curricula and teachers?

It seems plausible that well-designed curricular learning experiences, more than any other single aspect of the educational enterprise, set the tone for guidance.

A coordinated curriculum provides student orientation for course choices. It assists in student selection and educational planning. It individualizes instruction in the light of student potential and within the range of minimum and optimum standards required by the curriculum.

Contributing guidance roles of teachers are performed through study of cumulative records and consultation with counselors and other teachers concerning students' problems. They review with individual students, progress and relation to goals they might have set and demands of course work. They hold conferences with parents and employers concerning students' plans. They challenge students to achieve at the level of their optimum potential. They listen patiently when students want to talk out problems. They refer students to the school counselor and other resource personnel when the need seems to demand it. They help provide educational and occupational information whenever possible. They assist in placement which results in appropriate planning for the next steps in school or out of school. Through career education, teachers utilize nonschool resources consistent with career guidance goals.

Resolution of the issue of contributing roles will require the educational enterprise to develop and adopt guidance role definitions for teachers, administrators, and other school personnel. Likewise, identification of contributions through learning activities, nonschool resources, and students' participation will provide the clarity of roles for resolving this issue.

Is Guidance More Than a Selection and Placement Process?

Several aspects of this issue provide a foundation for a response consistent with goals of the education enterprise. Two major aspects of the guidance process in the educational enterprise in a democratic society mandate that it is more comprehensive than selection and placement. These aspects are related to values and freedom of choice and the responsibility of guidance practitioners.

To achieve educational goals of our society and to assist indiviuals in self-development, guidance practitioners must have values in which a majority of our members believe. We should be deeply disturbed with the frequency of suggestions for guidance workers that imply neutrality, objectivity, and duplicity. The support for guidance in learning institutions and the effectiveness of guidance work with youth depend upon a quality performance consistent with values of the democratic ideal. We must be for values that are definable in terms of social and educational goals, that are consistent with our beliefs about man and his development, and that are demonstrable through social interaction.

Goals, according to the democratic ideal, are to guard the rights of the individuals, to ensure development and to enlarge opportunity. Major emphasis and responsibility supporting the concept of democratic government rest on a system of universal education. Our educational philosophy must encompass an appreciation of the worth and dignity of the individual, realization of individual differences among persons, and a recognition of a person's inherent rights of self-direction and choice. Over the years, we have maintained our beliefs in these concepts in the face of many challenges, and we have made great progress in providing basic educational experiences resulting in scientific and social accomplishments unequalled among nations of the world. We have been considerably less successful in direct assistance to individuals (through counseling and teaching) when conflict of values are in question.

Generally recognized in accord with goals of education is the realization that effective teaching through social interaction is the core of any school program. It is also recognized that this task is largely dependent upon accurate knowledge of the learner's personal characteristics which include his potential, his interests and his ambitions. Recognition of these individual factors, along with the adaptation of instruction and the provision of a healthy environment for learning provide for the motivational factors for individual development and learning. Furthermore, it is recognized that realistic self-direction on the part of the learner relies on a continuous understanding of self in relation to potential, opportunities, obligations, and responsibilities in our society. The school, the subsociety in which the junior generation spends so many years, must interact in all its endeavors to provide a situation conducive to maximum self-development. The valuing guidance worker whose work is consistent with values of the democratic ideal in our schools, serves as the interacting agent for goal attainment.

The Conflict Between Goals and Performance

With regard to the educational setting, an obvious and prominent type of predicament is the conflict between the expectations of the specific social institution and the values of the general society; for example, it is generally expected by the school that the student will work diligently in order to achieve to the fullest extent of his intellectual potentiality and creativity. Accordingly, the student must be motivated to sacrifice immediate ease for ultimate attainment. However, recent commentaries suggest that our social values tend to prize ease and sociability more than intellectual independence and achievement. In this sense, the criteria of worth in the classroom and in society at large are incongruent, and to the extent of such incongruence, counselors, teachers and students are immersed in conflict. Several of the conflicts between values and performance are obvious from what we say we value and how we act.

1. We value the individual's potential and right to make his/her own decisions. But, we often show an unexpressed bias and a discomfort that prompts us to feel that a decision will be more valid if it matches the one we have selected for the individual.
2. We value the notion that there is no single niche into which an individual fits. We believe that for each individual there are alternative choices. But, we tend to overemphasize so-called objective data in selecting the best pigeonhole for the individual.
3. We value the dignity of all work. But, we also believe that each should fulfill his/her highest potential, so we urge the bright to enter status professions and overlook others, especially in the realm of social and governmental services.
4. We value the teaching-learning process as focusing on the total development of the individual, but we allow this process to be influenced by whatever pressures our time and culture press on us.
5. We value communication as a basic aspect of social interaction through counseling. But, we assume that the spoken word has usually the same meaning for counselor and client.
6. We value the premise that every individual is a unique personality. But, we have a stereotype of the ideal, and we typify some by their background and by our own.
7. We value the proposition that the student brings to the counselor's office the sum total of all his experiences. But, we often act as if counseling were an isolated process unrelated to the world of which the student is a part.
8. We value the idea that all children and youth deserve the acceptance, understanding, and assistance of a professional counselor. But, we often relegate such efforts to problem situations with no time for the rest.
9. We value the importance of a significant model for growing individuals. But, as the senior generation, we often tend to isolate ourselves from true helping relationships through social interaction in which such a model can be perceived by students.
10. We value the significance of the relationship that can be developed behind the closed doors of the counselor's office. Yet, this may not be where the action is with the younger generation. The real action may be political, economic or social in the form of protest, dissent, withdrawal or even going to pot—usually in the name of individual freedom or social justice.

Conflict Regarding Freedom and Responsibility

On the one hand, students have always striven for freedom and self-control in their development toward maturity. At the same time social institutions have always been concerned with control of behavior. It would seem that youth and the generation they represent, and social institutions and the generation they represent, are basically in conflict with regard to the responsibility involved in freedom and control objectives.

Some disquieting questions are included in any discussion of the freedom-control conflict. Control suggests control by someone or something. *Who* should control individual behavior?

Persons themselves? Perhaps the controlling forces would be some aspect of the individual's mind. Such a view would not be supported by the behavioral sciences. The assumption of a fragmented view of the self would only add confusion. Neither would it be acceptable to view society as the single controlling force of individual behavior, for society is simply composed of individuals whose behavior it would be proposed to control.

The proposal sometimes made in educational and psychological conferences that computers can determine our goals, that technicians decide our policies would probably be construed as the most serious of errors. For one thing, computers cannot tell us what our goals ought to be. However, in an era of confusion and anxiety, it is not surprising that the machine is in fashion, sometimes justified by expressions of efficiency, objectivity, and feasibility. The danger is to tend to ask only the questions the machine can answer, to teach only the things the machine can teach, and to limit our research to the quantitative work the machine can do. Followed through to the bitter end, it takes no stretch of the imagination to predict a 1984 in which the image of man would be overhauled into the image of the very machine by which we study and control him (Toffler, 1970).

Viewed as a lifelong process, guidance in any educational enterprise includes selection and placement as two of the several aspects of a comprehensive program. Program objectives will provide for individual skill development, self-understanding, and decision-making strategies for freedom of choice with responsibility.

Job placement and follow-up services must be considered as important aspects of career guidance programs. Placement and follow-up services should be critical ingredients of a comprehensive set of practical career guidance and counseling services that should be available to all students in each school. This idea needs at least two clarifications. First, follow-up services should entail more than data collection on students who have received placement assistance. Follow-up help should be provided to youths so they maintain the career development progress in effect before they were placed. Second, both types of follow-up—data collection and further career guidance—are expensive. All schools need to provide the long-term assistance; therefore, staff and budget priorities will have to be reconsidered.

Placement and follow-up services must include career planning assistance and follow-up for all areas of careers. Suitable job placement and follow-up must be an integral part of the education for students planning to enter work upon leaving school. Issues growing out of a concern for successful placement tend to relate to several contemporary conditions related to practice.

First, job placement and follow-up services are not now being routinely provided as an important part of counseling and guidance programs.

Second, too frequently, placement is separated from follow-up services, while both are separated from career guidance and counseling. These piecemeal efforts do not support a continuous, developmental approach to youth careers.

Third, most investigators and program personnel who use placement success as a criterion not only limit it to job finding but also concentrate on the number of actual placement contacts made.

Finally, students don't see a relationship between educational activities and tentative career considerations.

Without follow-up and job placement procedures, counseling is incomplete. The high unemployment rate for youth as compared to other age groups indicate their difficulties in making transition from school to work.

Hipp (1973) in an article entitled "Job Placement: Organize and Advertise," described the many benefits to be gained by establishing a vital, functioning, part-time job placement service in a high school. In addition to giving students an opportunity to earn money while in school and meeting the needs of employers in the community, such a placement service provides the following occupational orientation for students: (a) experience in filling out a comprehensive job application form; (b) experience in being involved in job interviews; and (c) experience in working in a variety of occupations, which can often give a student an idea about what kinds of occupations he does or does not want in the future.

Who Should Be Accountable for Career Guidance?

Although the term "accountability" has only recently found its way into the educational vocabulary, few would doubt its general meaning or its importance to educational practices. Accountability has rapidly become the watchword of those served by and supporting education. It provides serviceable techniques for responsible management and for allocation of resources. Several of the antecedents of the concept of accountability are: (1) federally and state intensified emphases on evaluation of school systems and their programs (i.e., The Commonwealth of Virginia Standards of Quality and Program of Action); (2) the trend to view educational enterprises in terms of cost effectiveness; (3) increasing emphasis on education for the disadvantaged and handicapped as a priority responsibility for schools; and (4) the demand for making educational programs more responsive to their supporters and clientele (Barro, 1970). Since accountability relies on educational outcomes, the process for its determination requires the establishment of well-defined performance objectives, the development and implementation of learning activities to achieve stated objectives, and the assessment of outcomes.

Because career guidance is a total school program, the accountability issue is many faceted. When individual values and freedom of choice are viewed as dimensions of the guidance process, a bundle of variables, not always definable, tend to contaminate the accountability picture. Nevertheless, counselors are frequently held responsible (accountable) for objectives of career guidance. When professionally trained counselors are unable to conceptualize, understand, and take leadership roles in resolving the issues, they deserve to be singled out as the scapegoats by critics. If counselors lack the competencies to carry out the objectives of guidance, they deserve to be replaced by practitioners who possess required competencies. The same rules should apply to other professionals—teachers, administrators, supervisors, pupil personnel staff and paraprofessionals, "Those who work as practitioners in the field are—and should be—held accountable for both the success and failures of students in specific programs" (Cochran, 1974).

An example of a public demand for accountability for career guidance is contained in the *Sixth Report-Counseling and Guidance: A Call for Change* (National Advisory Council on Vocational Education (1972). The report is a critical statement on career guidance, on who is responsible, and recommends solutions for change. Counselors, generally viewed as leadership persons in career guidance, must accept their share of responsibility for the present state of affairs. They may also take heart in *The Gallup Polls of Attitudes Toward Education* (Phi Delta Kappa, 1973) in which the sample polled, responded to the following: "How do you feel about having guidance counselors in the public schools? Do you think they are worth the added cost?" *No children in school,* yes worth it—69 percent, No opinion—14 percent; *Public School Parents,* Yes, Worth it—79 percent, No opinion—14 percent; *Parochial School Parents,* Yes, Worth it—79 percent, No opinion—9 percent, and High School Juniors and Seniors, Yes, Worth it—83 percent, No opinion—1 percent (Phi Delta Kappa, 1973, p. 72).

Concommitant Issues

In the view of the author, there are a series of concommitant issues that can be derived from, or which have some influence on, the questions posed above. The five categories of concommitant issues listed below are grouped into general categories, followed by brief comments and selected references for further study.

Guidance Organization, Administration, and Support

What organizational structure will provide for the most effective guidance services?

This issue suggests numerous questions left unanswered by practice or research. On the one hand, guidance programs are building or unit oriented so that guidance practitioners are viewed as staff of a particular school. On the other hand, program policy should be developed on a system-wide basis.

Perhaps the administrative structure poses a more crucial issue. Without an administrative structure reaching to the highest levels of curriculum, business and personnel administration, guidance priorities tend to take a back seat. Allocation of staff and budget for materials and resources are frequently placed on low-priority levels. Worse still, in times of economic stress, cuts in guidance are among the first to be made as evidenced during the recent economic recession.

Guidance Workers' Preparation and Certification

Should all guidance practitioners be required to complete preparation related to competencies required for their assigned roles? All state departments presently require a specified level, normally a master's degree or beyond in the area of counseling and guidance for school counselors. School administrators and supervisors generally are required to have minimal preparation in guidance. However, few teacher certification regulations require even a single course in the field of guidance. It seems ironical that paraprofessionals are required to have more training in guidance than certified teachers whose guidance roles are crucial to the program. Furthermore, with an ever increasing emphasis on career guidance and career education, it seems paradoxical that teachers are not required to have some preparation in the field. Should it be suggested that preparation be offered through in-service training? Who among the school staff possesses the skills to conduct a program?

The Why People Work Question

Since the time Parsons advanced his theory, strategies on helping people make vocational choices have been based on some common understanding of work. However, the term has different meanings and interpretations as indicated by the thirty-seven different listings in *The American Heritage Dictionary of the English Language* (1970). Today, an understanding of why people work may be vital to a teacher's and counselor's understanding of the student's motivation to choose a particular curriculum to follow. A review of some of the authors concerned with work and career development indicate a variety of answers to the questions, Why do people work?

Super (1957), in his book *The Psychology of Careers* lists three major needs for which a person seeks satisfaction in work: (1) the need for human relations—to be recognized as a person, to be independent, autonomous, and for status or prestige; (2) the need for activity—a means of self-expression, to use skill and knowledge, to express interest, and to express personal adequacy; (3) the need for a livelihood—to provide a standard of living, security, and satisfaction.

Levenstein (1962), in *Why People Work* postulates that work links people to society, to other individuals, and provides a means of self-development, growth, and fulfillment.

Significant reasons for working as given by Taylor (1968) in *Occupational Sociology* are for money, security, status, working conditions, intrinisic values, and as an activity.

In *Work and Its Discontents,* Bell (1956) states that people no longer work because they are hungry, but because ". . .now a standard of living has become a built-in automatic drive." Work is a means of ". . .confronting the absurdity of existence and beyond" (p. 89).

Kaplan (1960), in *Leisure in America: A Social Inquiry,* describes the reasons for working: "In work, man has gone much further than mere sustenance; in it he has found the core of his life" (p. 52).

Silberman (1966), in *The Myths of Automation,* describes why people work in terms of loss of work through unemployment or retirement. "It is even harder if a person is unemployed, for unemployment can make the most secure person feel useless and unwanted" (p. 18). Some people do not know what to do with themselves when they retire or are out of work.

In his study, "Vocation: A Religious Search of Meaning," McDaniels (1965) adds another dimension as to why people work in identifying the religious significance of work as a calling, a total life purpose, a vocation.

Green (1968), in *Work, Leisure, and the American Schools,* states, "We have learned to view work as the way in which a man defines for himself who he is and what he shall do with his life" (p. 113). The motive and incentive for "doing one's work well" has been the work ethic in which dignity, worth, and properness were attributed to work.

Clearly, the answers to the question, "Why do people work?" are complex and they are significant as human values which are not singular but pluralistic; so that the reason for working is inevitably related to the meaning of work to the individual. In schools and colleges the meanings will be as varied as the diversity of the student body; however, for the individual, the meaning of work may be any one or a combination of those cited above. In any case, the developing student must, in the process of understanding self in relation to the world of work, come to grips with the reason or reasons why he plans to work.

Legal and Ethical Aspects of Guidance

The issues in this area relate to testing programs, confidentiality and use of information, privacy rights legislation and a myriad of related questions. Silliman, in chapter 5, deals with testing related issues and Alexander, in chapter 12, provides the bases for legal and ethical practices in guidance. The major issue in this category is concerned with the question, who establishes the policies, and how are policies enforced? The personal issue of the guidance practitioner is concerned with liability protection and ethical practice.

Guidance Roles and Practices

Although contributing roles were discussed earlier in this chapter, issues yet to be resolved are: What are the differential guidance roles of counselors, teachers, and other pupil personnel workers at the elementary level? Who should coordinate the elementary school guidance program? And, what should be the nature of the program?

A major contemporary issue to be resolved throughout the entire school system is related to roles and practices in career education. Chapter 9 presents a thorough discussion and offers generally accepted guidelines on this issue.

Obviously, there are numerous issues concerning career guidance that could be discussed. For the counselor, as another practitioner in the educational enterprise, a major issue relates to professional affiliation and to whom guidance should turn for professional leadership.

Trends and the Future

Career Guidance Practices

Without question, there has been a trend, since the late 1960s, in the development of innovative practices to facilitate career development. Guidance and career education in the schools provide a new basis for a total school effort to bring career guidance and the curriculum into a collaborative relationship. Although there are resistances to the new emphasis in career education, usually based on philosophical differences, most school systems have attempted some new career guidance practices. It frequently appears that resistance to change and lack of know-how are the major blocks to developing comprehensive and effective career guidance systems. Objectives for programs tend to be developed with ease, but issues arise regarding practices to be employed in career guidance. From a review of the literature, it appears that several practice issues presently receiving attention by practitioners portray influences on future trends.

Career Information Systems and Their Use

According to Campbell, Walz, Miller, and Kriger (1973), most studies in follow-up of recent high school graduates indicate that students felt schools did not provide enough help in understanding career opportunities which were available. The recent statewide study by the Virginia State Advisory Council on Vocational Education (1973) supported the above observation and the Sixth Report of National Advisory Council on Vocational Education (1972) was especially critical of the lack of, or inefficiency of, the use of career information systems.

While filing plans and classification systems, information kits, films and filmstrips, and computer assisted approaches are providing a response to the needs for career information, the delivery to and use of information by students will require a local planning effort consistent with the school and communities' needs.

Among the many systems approaches for providing meaningful career information, (Du Bato, 1968) reported an effective method of needs assessment through a demonstration system of occupational information for career guidance. Such locally based demonstration approaches appears to be a trend in the development of systems approaches.

Economic and Manpower Education as a Factor in Understanding the World of Work

An outstanding example suggesting a trend in economic and manpower education as a contributor to career guidance resulted from the experimental work of Darcy (1968). As director of the Center for Economic Education at Ohio University he conducted an experimental project to provide the schools with instructional materials, evaluation instruments and a realistic classroom educational program for bridging the gap between school and work. Some major objectives were to: (1) identify appropriate course content for economic and manpower education, (2) develop instructional materials, and (3) develop evaluation instruments and procedures. Eighth, ninth and tenth grade classes in three school systems within a seventy-five-mile radius of Athens, Ohio were selected for the pilot project. Pre- and post-tests designed to measure understandings and attitudes were administered to treatment and control groups matched on mental ability and socioeconomic characteristics. Some conclusions were: (1) Eighth graders enrolled in the experimental course increased their test scores by 33.4 percent more than the control group, (2) The experimental course did not induce changes in student attitude toward manpower and economic issues, and (3) Students enrolled in the experimental course reflected more interest in school and a lower dropout rate. The appendixes contain 316 pages of textual material, the 140-page teacher manual, and evaluation instruments.

As a result of Darcy's project, a course guide, *Manpower and Economic Education, Opportunities in American Economic Life* (Darcy and Powell, 1968) was published by the Joint Council on Economic Education and is in wide use throughout junior high schools.

Modeling and Learning Vocational Behaviors

Social modeling has long been a behavioral counseling technique (Crites, 1974) and appears to be an influential factor in shaping a future trend in experiential learning in career guidance.

According to Bank (1969), during the elementary school years, it would appear that boys and girls are in need of experiences which can provide maximal opportunity for vocational inquiry. A broader base for vocational choice can be developed during these formative years in the lives of elementary school students. The counselor can be instrumental in building an expanded careerland in which they are exposed to the world of work and workers at an early age. The individual's choice of alternatives in future years of development may be enhanced by the effectiveness of exposures during these formative years.

Numerous innovations in providing modeling approaches including use of videotapes, group counseling, sociodrama, and on-the-job training models are in vogue and appear to indicate a trend in career guidance.

Teaching Career Decision-Making Skills

Whereas in the past the major emphasis in vocational guidance was in providing information and learning experiences of a content nature, a definite trend is the focus on personal skills.

Probably the most emphasized of these skills in career development is decision making. Although Katz (1966) and others previously challenged that decision making as a teachable skill had yet to be established, Hewer (1968), Kagen (1964), and Hoppock (1967) are but a few of the proponents for teaching these skills, and have shown their effectiveness through a variety of techniques.

Among the approaches to teaching decision-making skills is a program developed by the College Entrance Examination Board. The CEEB program, *Deciding, A Decision Program for Students* (1972) is presented in the form of a course of study. It encourages the development of decision-making skills in junior and senior high school students. The program, through student and leader materials, provides a course of study that can be taught in group or classroom settings. The program includes exercises, group activities, simulations, and discussion guides aimed at helping students learn and apply the decision-making process to the personal, educational and vocational decisions they face in the early secondary school years. The adaption of and use of such programs tend to indicate that the future trend will be to operationalize materials and approaches to teach personal skill development in career decision making.

To the above predicted trends should be added presently developing practices (Campbell, Walz, Miller and Kirger, 1973) in the following:

1. Simulation as a method to facilitate career exploration;
2. Parental and community involvement in career guidance;
3. Integrating career guidance and career guidance, and;
4. Special training for guidance personnel to provide differential staffing in carrying out career guidance objectives.

The above practices are dealt with in previous chapters in this volume and provide support to predicted trends in the future.

The Future

Trends in career guidance are illustrated by the authors' point of view and are well documented throughout the fourteen chapters of this volume. Issues raised in this chapter lend additional support to the identified trends.

The future of career guidance holds an optimistic outlook. *First,* career guidance is concerned with major objectives which have persisted since the beginning of the vocational guidance movement at the turn of the century. *Second,* career development is a central factor in the life development of the individual's personal, social, and educational pursuits. It is the chief means by which persons achieve identity and self-fulfillment. A person cannot choose a physical stature, a color, a culture of a family with which to be born, but the great American ideal provides for most of its citizens the freedom to choose a career. *Third,* national policy demands effective individual career development if our democratic system is to achieve its ideals and to survive as a free people. *Fourth,* technology, and more effective systems are being developed for career guidance, which are both humanistic in nature and relative to the environment in which persons live.

As predicted by Wrenn (1962) in his classic volume, *The Counselor in a Changing World,* the future of guidance will be influenced by "1. The pressure of populations; 2. Jobs in the future; 3. The changing family; 4. Clustering together; 5. The growth in wealth; 6. The impact of the federal government; and, 7. The world next door.'' From Wrenn's seven, the dice can be rolled to a sure winner for career guidance; 8. Technology for ecology and energy needs; 9. Expanding equal opportunities for women and minority group persons; 10. Increasing career opportunities and preparation for the handicapped and aged; and, 11. The increasing awareness of the need for people to live together peacefully. Any of the above numbers means jobs, and careers, and they require career guidance.

References

American heritage dictionary of the English language, New York: American Heritage Publishing Company, 1970.

A study of counseling and guidance in the public schools of Virginia. Blacksburg, Virginia: Virginia State Advisory Council on Vocational Education, 1973.

Bailey, L. I. and Stadt, R. W. *Career education: new approaches to human development.* Bloomington, Illinois: McKnight Publishing Company, 1973.

Bank,I. M. Children explore careerland through vocational role models. *Vocational Guidance Quarterly* 17 (4) (1969):284-88.

Barro, S. M. An approach to developing accountability measures for the public schools. *Phi Delta Kappan* 41 (4) (1970):196-205.

Bell, D. *Work and its discontents.* Boston: Beacon Press, 1956.

Borow, H. ed., *Career guidance for a new age.* Boston: Houghton Mifflin Company, 1973.

Campbell, R. E.; Walz, G. R.; Miller; J. V., and Kriger, S. F. *Career guidance: a handbook of methods.* Columbus, Ohio: Charles E. Merrill Publishing Company, 1973.

Cochran, L. H. Counselors and the non college-bound students. *The Personnel and Guidance Journal* 52 (4) (1974):582-85.

College Entrance Examination Board. *Deciding, a decision-making program for students.* Princeton, New Jersey: CEEB, 1972.

Conant, J. B. *The American high school today.* New York: McGraw Hill Book Company, Inc., 1959.

Crites, J. O. Career counseling: a review of major approaches. *The Counseling Psychologist* 14 (3) (1974): 3-23.

Darcy, R. L. *An experimental junior high school course in occupational opportunities and labor market processes.* (Final Report). Athens, Ohio: Ohio University, Center for Economic Education, 1968.

Darcy,R. L. and Powell, P. E. *Manpower and economic education: opportunities in American life.* New York: Joint Council on Economic Education, 1968.

DuBato, G. A vocational guidance unit for the noncollegebound. *Vocational Guidance Quarterly* 8 (1) (1961).

Green, T. *Work, leisure, and the American schools.* New York: Random House, 1968.

Hansen, L. S. and Tennyson, W. W. A career management model for counselor involvement. *The Personnel and Guidance Journal* 53 (9) (1975):638-45.

Hewer, V. H. Group counseling. *Vocational Guidance Quarterly* 43 (4) (1968).

Hipp, E. W. Job placement: organize and advertise. *The Personnel and Guidance Journal* 51 (8) (1973):561-64.

Hoppock, R. *Occupational information.* New York: McGraw-Hill Book Company, 1967.

Hummel, D. L. and Bonham, S. J., Jr. *Pupil personnel services in schools: organization and coordination.* Chicago: Rand McNally and Company, 1968.

Kagen, N. Three dimensions of counselor encapsulation. *Journal of Counseling Psychology* 39 (6) (1964).

Kaplan, M. *Leisure in America: a social inquiry.* New York: John Wiley and Sons, Inc., 1960.

Katz, M. A model of guidance for career decision making. *Vocational Guidance Quarterly,* 15 (1) (1966):2-10.

Kehas, C. D. Toward a redefinition of education: a new framework for counseling in education. In B. Shertzer and S. C. Stone eds., *Introduction to guidance: an introduction.* Boston: Houghton Mifflin Company, 1970.

Levenstein, A. *Why people work.* New York: The Crowell Collier Press, 1962.

McDaniels, C. O. Vocation: a religious search for meaning. *Vocational Guidance Quarterly* 47 (3) (1965):p. 28.

Mayer, F. *Education for a new society.* Bloomington, Indiana Phi Delta Kappa Educational Foundation, 1973.

Phi Delta Kappa. *The Gallup polls of attitudes toward education 1969-1973.* S. Elam ed., Bloomington, Indiana: Phi Delta, Inc.

Shertzer, B. and Stone, S. C. *Fundamentals of guidance.* 2nd ed. Boston: Houghton Mifflin Company, 1971.

Silberman, C. *The myths of automation.* New York: Harper and Row, 1966.

Sixth report, counseling and guidance: a call for change. Washington, D.C.: National Advisory Council on Vocational Education, 1972.

Super, D. E. *The psychology of careers.* New York: Harper and Row, 1957.

Taylor, L. *Occupational sociology.* New York: Oxford University Press, 1968.

The pursuit of excellence, education and the future of America. Panel Report V of Special Studies Project. Garden City, New Jersey: Doubleday, 1958.

Toffler, A. *Future shock.* New York: Bantam Books, 1970.

Wrenn, C. G. *The counselor in a changing world.* Washington, D.C.: American Personnel and Guidance Association, 1962.

Chapter 14
CAREERS IN COUNSELING

Richard Warner and Richard Hawk

The purpose of this chapter is to examine the field of counseling as it is found in diverse settings. In doing so, the authors are hopeful that they can provide a foundation of information upon which a prospective counselor can base a meaningful career decision. As with any chapter of this type the reader does need to keep in mind that the field is in the process of change and some of the figures or facts presented here, while true when this is being written, are subject to change. Nonetheless, it is felt that the basic information about various career possibilities within the counseling profession that are discussed here will remain basically unchanged over the next few years.

The chapter will examine career possibilities within the counseling profession as found in schools, colleges, rehabilitation agencies, employment services, mental health agencies, governmental agencies, and other public and private agencies. Within each section, the authors will discuss the need upon which the service is based, the actual roles performed, the job setting, benefits, and job outlook.

Before beginning the discussion of specific career possibilities within the profession, it should be helpful to consider the reasons for the emergence of the general profession of counseling. Counseling has largely been a child of the twentieth century. The cultural and social pressures of this time period molded the profession into its present form and will continue to mold it as it moves into the future.

The advent of the industrial revolution gave birth to the increasing urbanization of this country; and this development coupled with the rapid increase in our population brought increased pressures on individuals to fit themselves into a rapidly changing society. As the industrial revolution progressed, it became more difficult for persons to live the life of the rugged individualist. Whether the individuals wanted to or not, they were forced to deal in more intimate and cooperative ways with other people. At the same time that it was becoming literally impossible for individuals to live their own lives without having an impact on others and it was becoming increasingly more difficult to choose one's life work. When the country was in an agrarian period, a person's occupational choices, even though they were very limited, were visible. Children who wanted to follow in their fathers' footsteps could literally do that very thing. They could observe the work with their fathers and in so doing, could develop an understanding of the work required. Even if children wanted to enter an occupation different from their fathers, they were able typically to observe the chosen field before entering that field. The age

Dr. Richard Warner is Associate Professor of Counselor Education at Auburn University, Auburn, Alabama, and Dr. Richard Hawk is Assistant Professor of Counselor Education at Tuskegee Institute, Tuskegee, Alabama.

of technology was to change much of this. Individuals began to find employment in places where it was not possible to be observed by one's children. Indeed, it became quite difficult for a father or mother to explain to a child just what he or she did for a living. Hence, what for many years had been a relatively smooth process of moving from childhood into adulthood and the world of work became a process so complex that many individuals needed help in moving through this stage.

A second outcome of the industrial revolution and the resulting urbanization of this country was a rapid change in social mores and customs. As growing numbers of immigrants poured into this country, it became an overwhelming task to amalgamate everyone into the system and indeed it became increasingly more difficult for an individual to cope with all the changes. Such a period of change pushes a society toward disintegration rather than integration. Individuals within the society feel pressured, for while they know they must change, the basis for making those changes becomes very difficult to understand. In effect, individuals are confronted with so much information and so few guidelines that they are often thrown into a state of anxiety and fear. Such was the case for many individuals during this period of rapid change. Individuals in the small arm community had few options open to them either in terms of a choice of vocation or in choice of goals by which to live. As these same individuals moved into the urban areas or as the urban areas moved to them, they were confronted with more and more options and less clear cut criteria to apply to their choices if they were to survive.

It was in response to these two social needs that the profession of counseling was to develop. The historical antecedents of the occupation were mentioned in an earlier chapter and will not be repeated here, but it is necessary that the reader remember that counseling began in response to social NEEDS. If the needs disappear, either because the needs are satisfied or if the occupation fails to respond to those needs, then it can be expected that the progress toward a profession of counseling will be impeded. As Shoben (1955) has indicated, "A new profession emerging because of its capacity for vigorous and useful service to people, is caught up in a battle for position in the public eye and for the legal status that it needs to carry out most effectively its socially desireable work" (p. 196). It is not enough that those in the occupation feel that they are performing their particuar function in order to satisfy the needs of individuals or the society; the society at large must feel likewise if its professional stature is to flourish and continue their work.

Against this background and in response to the social needs of individuals, the counseling profession has become a large and highly diversified group of practitioners working with people in a wide variety of settings. A large percentage of counselors are located in educational institutions from elementary schools through college. Another large percentage of counselors is employed by rehabilitation agencies, and yet another fairly large segment is employed by state employment bureaus. Finally, there is an increasing number of counselors being employed by public and private agencies. As might be expected in examining the characteristics of the jobs and the counselors in such diverse settings, noticeable differences can be found on almost any dimension from "position titles and job descriptions to methods of selection, educational requirements, working conditions, supervision, and salary scales" (Feingold, 1965, p. 132). In short, "counselor," means many things and the functions to be performed are highly dependent upon the particular agency, school, or other work setting in which the counselor operates. This point needs to be kept in mind while reading the following sections. What will be presented in each section is an overview of counseling, in differing types of work settings; however, each specific work setting will have its own unique characteristics. For example, the first section will discuss counseling in the schools, but it should be expected that public schools will each be somewhat unique.

School Counseling

Counseling in the schools began as a direct outgrowth of the vocational guidance movement popularized by Parsons in the early 1900s. While the Vocational Bureau continued the work of Parsons, men such as Weaver in Brooklyn, Davis in Detroit, and Boyden in Westport, Connecticut, were establishing vocational guidance within the school systems. From these early beginnings was to spring that branch of the profession known as school counseling. While it is impossible to separate these early beginnings from a strict vocational concern of the society, it is interesting to note that even in these early days there was some contradiction between what those in the profession felt they should be doing and what the society was expecting. For example, Davis (1914) in his book *Vocational and Moral Guidance,* devoted a great deal of attention to the moral and spiritual needs of individuals. Hence, from its very beginnings, those counselors that operated in the schools were apt to define their role more broadly than did the society at large. Nevertheless, it is clear that the branch of the profession known as school counseling received it impetus from the needs of the society to find a means by which it could more easily and efficiently move people into appropriate lines of work.

This impetus has resulted in a tremendous growth in the numbers of individuals employed in the elementary and secondary schools in this country. It is now estimated that there are some 35,000-40,000 school counselors in the United States. This growth is also reflected in the number of institutions whose focus is on preparing school counselors. While in the early days of the movement there were few requirements for professional training, there are now some four hundred institutions of higher learning in this country that are offering master's degrees in counseling. These figures, in and of themselves, provide rather strong evidence that school counseling has received some form of social recognition. Even such strong critics of the public schools as Conant (1959) point out that counseling may be one of the avenues for improving our educational system. Such statements also lend support to the notion that school counseling has become a recognized position within the school structure. It is also clear, however, that while counseling may be an accepted position within the schools, there is no clear acceptance or agreement on what kinds of responsibilities entailed within the position. One has only to examine the status of certification of school counselors to understand the confusion over what is a school counselor.

Entry Requirements

As with any staff position in schools, school counselors must meet the educational requirements established by state boards of education. Over the past fifty years state departments of education have developed and attempted to enforce certification requirements for school counselors. Most of this activity on the part of state departments has taken place since the passage of the NDEA Act in 1958. As reported by Houghton, in the period from 1963 to 1966 alone some tweny-two states changed their requirements for school counselors. By January 1, 1966 fifty-three states and territories had specified requirements for secondary school counselors, and three of those states also had separate requirements for elementary counseling (1967). In a study of certification for school counselors conducted by Dudley and Ruff (1970) it was found that every state except Michigan has specific requirements for certification, and that state was instituting requirements as of July 1, 1971. In a recent survey of certification conducted by Thorsen (1972) for the American Personnel and Guidance Association it was found that only five states had not changed their requirements since the 1966 study by Houghton (1967). For all this activity, however, there is little evidence of cooperation among the states (Thorsen, 1972). In order to develop an understanding of the complex nature of certification of school counseling using as a base line the end of 1971, it may be helpful to examine the information in tabular form. Table 14.1 presents the various requirements of the fifty states and the District of Columbia.

As one examines the table it becomes quite clear that there is no single accepted way of certificating school counselors. As one might expect most states still require some form of school experience, whether teaching or an acceptable internship in the schools. As indicated in a survey of state requirements conducted by Boller (1972), however, the trend is away from this requirement. Only twenty-one states now require some form of teaching experience. Five states no longer require a counselor to hold a valid teacher certificate. Eight other states use the certificate as one form of entry into the profession but also provide for alternatives to teaching experience as an entry requirement. Ten states require a teaching certificate but no actual teaching experience or some alternative (Thorsen, 1972). This development takes on added significance when one considers that in most states, as shown in the table, the certification of counselors is still in the hands of state boards of education. It is worth noting that five states surveyed by Thorsen (1972) reported work under way toward the development of performance based criteria for certification. This would appear to be a real step in the right direction.

Another example of the increasing acceptance of school counseling is indicated by the data in table 14.1. Of all the states including the District of Columbia, only four still permit individuals to receive permanent certification as a school counselor who have not completed at least a master's degree or its equivalent. One state, New York, has changed its requirements for permanent certification to sixty hours beyond the bachelor's degree, and most states are increasing their requirements.

The data in table 14.1, however, also indicates some areas in which there is still the lack of agreement as to how education prepares a school counselor. One such indication is the lack of specificity in type of certificate required for counseling practice. Van Hoose and Carlson (1972) report that only twenty-four states at this point in time recognize the difference between an elementary and secondary counselor, even though thirty-six states have some published guidelines for elementary counselors. Such a situation indicates that many do not recognize the basic differences in preparation required to work with children at these two different age levels; a recognition that is given when the question is one of teacher certification. Hence, one might believe that in many states counselors are not recognized as having competencies as specialized as those of the classroom teacher. Despite the differences in certification requirements, preparation programs and job situations there are some generally agreed upon tasks which are normally performed by school counselors. Because the nature of these tasks differs from

TABLE 14.1

Certification Requirements for School Counselors in the Fifty States
and the District of Columbia*

	Type of Certificate				Master's Degree Required		Teaching Experience Required	Agency That Certifies or Recommends Changes in Certification							Reciprocity with Other States
	Nondifferentiated	Secondary	Junior High	Elementary	Temporary	Permanent		State Board of Education	State Comm. on Certification	State Certification Dept.	State Guid. and/or P. P. Dept.	Professional Organization	State Legislation	Other	
Alabama	X				X	X	X	X	a						no
Alaska	X							X							no
Arizona	X					X	X		a	X		a			b
Arkansas		X		X		X	X	X			a	a			b
California	X					X		X							no
Colorado		X		X		X	X	X			a	a	a		b
Connecticut	X				X	X			a			a	a	X	New England
Delaware		X		X		X		X							no
District of Columbia		X	X			X									
Florida	X					X		X							b
Georgia	X					X	X	X		a					no
Hawaii	X					X		X		a	a				b
Idaho	X					X	X	X	a		a				b
Illinois	X					X			a		a		X		no
Indiana	X				X	X	X	X		X					b
Iowa		X		X	X	X	X	X	a			a			c
Kansas		X		X	X	X	X	X							no
Kentucky	X				X	X	X	X							d
Louisiana	X					X	X	X	a			a	a		no
Maine		X		X	X	X	X	X	a						New England
Maryland	X					X		X	a			a			d
Massachusets	X							X	a						b
Michigan		X		X		X	X	X							no
Minnesota	X				X	X	X	X	a						b
Mississippi	X				X	X	X	X	a						no

*Adapted from data provided in Dudley and Ruff (1970) and Thorsen (1972).

a = Groups that may recommend changes in certification; no authority to carry our recommendation.
b = Some informal arrangements are usually made. Such arrangements usually involve a time requirement and the requirement that the new state's requirements be met.
c = Recommended by training institution.
d = Master's degree is acceptable.

TABLE 14.1 (continued)

	Type of Certificate				Master's Degree Required		Teaching Experience Required	Agency That Certifies or Recommends Changes in Certification							Reciprocity with Other States
	Nondifferentiated	Secondary	Junior High	Elementary	Temporary	Permanent		State Board of Education	State Comm. on Certification	State Certification Dept.	State Guid. and/or P. P. Dept.	Professional Organization	State Legislation	Other	
Missouri		X		X		X	X				X	a			no
Montana	X					X	X	X							d
Nebraska		X		X		X	X	X	a						no
Nevada		X		X		X	X	X		a		a			b
New Hampshire	X					X		X							yes
New Jersey	X					X	X		a						b
New Mexico	X					X	X								no
New York		X		X	X	X			a						PA. and New England
North Carolina	X				X	X		X	a						no
North Dakota	X					X	X		X			a			b
Ohio	X				X	X	X		X						d
Oklahoma	X				X	X	X	X	a						no
Oregon	X					X	X	X	a						no
Pennsylvania		X		X	X	X		X		a					no
Rhode Island	X					X	X	X	a			a			no
South Carolina		X		X	X	X	X	X	a		a				yes*
South Dakota	X					X	X	X	a						no
Tennessee		X		X		X	X	X	a						no
Texas	X					X		X	a						b
Utah	X					X		X		a	a	a			no
Vermont	X					X		X	a						yes
Virginia	X					X	X				a				no
Washington	X					X					a	a	a	X	no
West Virginia	X					X		X	a	a	a	a			no
Wisconsin	X					X					a	a		X	b
Wyoming	X				X	X	X	X	a	a		a			d

*South Carolina now has a certificate called "Associative Guidance Counselor." This certificate can be obtained through an undergraduate program.

a = Groups that may recommend changes in certification; no authority to carry our recommendation.

b = Some informal arrangements are usually made. Such arrangements usually involve a time requirement and the requirement that the new state's requirements be met.

c = Recommended by training institution.

d = Master's degree is acceptable.

elementary to secondary schools, the tasks of the elementary and secondary school counselor will be examined separately.

Role of Secondary School Counselor

A model through which the general role and the specific tasks of the counselor might be examined is shown in figure 14.1. The model, adapted from one developed by Swisher (1971),

Services	Modes of Delivery		
	Individual	Group	Indirect
Administrative			
Counseling–remedial			
Counseling–developmental			
Consulting			
Student appraisal			
Referral			

Figure 14.1. Diagramatic view of the role of the secondary school counselor.[1]

takes into account the interaction between several types of services typically the responsibility of the counselor and the modes through which those services might operate. For example, the service called educational or vocational counseling might be offered through the mode of individual counseling, or group counseling or perhaps through an indirect mode. In point of fact a good developmental counseling program might include the use of all three modes. A counselor might, for example, utilize a group procedure to provide occupational information to students. The counselor might follow this up with individual sessions, and finally the counselor might set up vocational exploration experiences in the world of work for students; an indirect mode. Not all services would utilize all three modes. One might expect that most remedial counseling would utilize only the individual and group modes, while the administrative and consulting service are most often indirect services to students. The point of all this is that the services expected to be offered by a counselor may be rather inflexible, but each individual counselor does have some options as to how services are offered. This option allows counselors to utilize the strengths they possess. The actual nature of the services generally offered by a secondary counselor are as follows:

(1) *Administrative.* Regardless of how much counselors and counselor educators may protest this role, there is no evidence that school counselors can escape some administrative functions. The particular tasks that most often fall under this service are the actual scheduling of students into classes, issuance of work permits, direction of orientation activities, and other miscellaneous duties which the building principal may delegate. Discipline, once seen as a guidance function, is now typically handled by an assistant principal.

(2) *Counseling—Remedial.* This service is generally considered the most exciting by prospective counselors. The authors believe that is unfortunate. There is no question that counselors need to be prepared to offer a helping service to troubled students. Such a service

1. Adapted from model developed by Swisher (1971).

should help them better understand themselves and others, and to help them develop coping behaviors which will enable students to more adequately deal with environmental pressures and internal conflicts. Counselors should keep in mind however that it is generally easier to prevent problems than it is to solve them once they have developed.

(3) *Counseling—Developmental.* This service is designed to help students move through the myriad of developmental tasks which occur during the secondary school years. It is through this service that the counselor seeks to offer programs which will facilitate the personal, social, educational, and vocational development of young people. Programs designed to help students clarify values, develop decision-making skills, and make educational and career plans are examples of the kinds of activities that should be offered under this service.

(4) *Consulting.* This is an increasingly recognized important indirect service to students. The counselor's function here is to work with the significant others in the student's life (i.e., parents, teachers, administrators) so that these individuals can enhance the development of the student. Specific tasks might be to help teachers understand particular students, to help teachers identify students with problems, help parents communicate with their children, or to provide information to administrators which would help them make decisions which affect the entire student body.

(5) *Student Appraisal.* Counselors are most often the individuals responsible for the gathering and maintaining of test and nontest data on students. Frequently this service simply entails the gathering of achievement, ability, personality, interest, and demographic data. The most important task of this service, which is often overlooked, is the interpretation of the data to students, parents, teachers, and administrators.

(6) *Referral Service.* The counselor is most often the individual who refers students to either other specialists within the school (i.e., special therapist, psychologist), or specialists associated with other agencies (i.e., vocational rehabilitation, employment service, psychiatric clinic).

Role of Elementary School Counselor

Generally the elementary counselor is expected to offer similar services to those offered at the secondary level. There is, however, a difference in the priorities given to the services. The elementary counselor is seen much more as a developmental specialist. Hence, the remedial counseling role is down played and the consulting and developmental counseling services receive top priority. Thus, at the elementary level the counselor will spend much more time working directly with classroom teachers. Often instead of removing students from the classroom in order to work with them, the elementary counselor and the teacher will work with students in the classroom.

Increasingly elementary counselors are being looked to for leadership in helping teachers provide affective experiences and career education experiences for children. These activities also take place in the classroom rather than in the counseling office.

The elementary counselors will also generally spend more time working with parents than does their counterpart at the secondary level. The goal of such work is to enhance the development of young children. Many of these programs are a form of parent education.

Working Conditions

Most school counselors are now provided adequate physical facilities in terms of private office space for individual counseling. Many counselors, however, will find very limited physical facilities in terms of space to conduct group work. As new school plants are built this problem is being somewhat alleviated. Major problems still exist in the areas of secretarial help and in the numbers of students for which any individual counselor is responsible. Most counselors operate with student loads far above the recommended 250-1 ratio at the secondary level or 500-600-1 at the elementary level.

Salaries

Public school counselor's salaries are generally tied directly to a school district's teacher salary schedule. In some areas counselors receive slightly more than a classroom teacher based on a responsibility index. Counselors also often work a longer school year, particularly those at the secondary school level, than the classroom teachers and are paid accordingly. The average starting salary from the latest government statistics is around $7,000 to $10,000.

Prospects of Employment

School counseling at the secondary level moved through a boom period during the 1960s. The 1970s have seen a leveling off effect, and in some areas there have been cutbacks in the number of counselors employed. Present economic conditions plus the reduction in birth rate make it difficult to predict the future. Certainly there is still a need for counselors, but whether there will be financial support for such positions remains a question mark.

Elementary counseling positions have opened up at a rapid rate during the last decade. Even with present economic conditions it can be expected that there will continue to be a demand for elementary counselors. The rate of growth may be somewhat slower than in the last decade, but the openings at this level will still outstrip the demand at the secondary level.

Counseling in Higher Education

A body of counselors are employed in various institutions of higher education. The terms student personnel worker or student development specialist have been used to describe people in all types of positions at the college and university level. The positions typically include financial aids, student counseling, placement, foreign student advisement, housing, recreational services, and admissions. The common denominator to these positions appears to be that they are all concerned with services to students that are not directly concerned with the academic nature of the institution. While the academic instructors are responsible for providing the necessary atmosphere and substance for learning and the administrators are responsible for the general operation and management of these institutions, it is the student personnel worker who has the responsibility for responding to those psychological and physical needs of students which affect their ability to learn effectively. Quite obviously, the preceding is built on the assumption that once the individual enters an institution of higher learning it is the responsibility of that institution to guide the development of the total individual. As Wrenn (1951) has indicated in his classic work on student personnel services, *Student Personnel Work in College;* "Institutions of higher education are responsible for developing in their students essential 'interpersonal skills and understandings' as well as civic, vocational, and personal knowledges and skills" (Wrenn, 1951, p. 25).

While the preceding may be the most important reason for the existence of present day student personnel services, it is not clear that they were begun in response to that need. Crowley (1937) indicated that the development of student personnel services was largely because the institutions of higher education then in existence were primarily interested in the development of the religious character of their students. He points out that this period of interest in the total individual on the basis of religious beliefs lasted until about 1870 when a period of almost absolute interest in intellectualism became the dominant force in education. During this period, there was a decline in interest in the well being of the entire individual, but beginning in 1920 with an ever increasing student population, college administrators turned once again to a consideration of how to meet the needs of all of their students. Important to this development was the work of such individuals as Cattell and Hall, whose work emphasizing the nature of individual differences in the field of psychology was beginning to show results (Wrenn, 1951). It was becoming increasingly clear to educators that individuals could no longer all be treated the same and that one could not simply educate the mind, but must work with the total individual.

Two other developments in the social milieu of colleges were to have a profound impact on the development of student personnel services. The first was the initial admission of women into college which began at Oberlin College in 1837, but was not to really gain momentum until the latter part of the century. The second development was the increased numbers of indivduals who were attending college from other than the very upper socioeconomic strata of society. Increasingly college populations were becoming more heterogeneously mixed and institutions of higher education were being forced to recognize that they were dealing with student populations that had a wide variety of needs. Certainly, a dean of men could not respond to all the needs of women, so as institutions admitted women, it became necessary to create the position dean of women, if for no other reason than to be guardians of the young women's morals. At first, the dean of men and women were seen only as regulators of behaviors, but gradually they began to work with students in counseling relationships. Hence, student personnel services came into being out of a need to respond to the ever changing needs of the student populations at institutions of higher learning. Perhaps even more important than this most obvious reason for the establishment of these services is that college administrators as well as other leaders within the society began to view the college and university as a vehicle for social change. Education began to be viewed as the great leveler of people. It was the vehicle that made equal opportunity for all a potential reality. As such, there was a need to provide a wide variety of services to individuals who came to these institutions in order to meet the needs of a wide variety of individuals; persons who came from all socioeconomic levels and differing family and societal backgrounds. Certainly this trend continues today, as more and more special programs are established at institutions of higher learning which are geared to special groups of individuals within the larger society and with the advent of junior, two-year, and community colleges.

Role of College Counselor

The diversity of American higher education makes it very difficult to discuss the general role of a counselor in this setting. More than in any other setting in which counselors are employed the actual tasks performed by individuals trained as counselors are dependent upon the particular institution in which they work. Generally accepted as services to be performed by counselors in collegiate settings in addition to the kinds of services offered by a secondary school counselor are admissions, student activities, financial aid, housing, and discipline. Generally the smaller the institution the more of these services will be performed by one or two individuals. In larger institutions all of these services may be under one administrative head but each service will have its own specialists. It may be helpful at this point to briefly examine each of the services that may be offered under the general rubric of student development.

(1) *Counseling.* As indicated earlier most of the services discussed under the role of the secondary school counselor apply to a college counselor. All of these services the authors include under the general title of counselor. That is, they will typically be offered by someone called a counselor. Typically the other services offered at the college level are offered by someone who has the preparation of a counselor, but works under a different title.

This service is critical in all types of institutions but may be most critical at two-year, junior and community colleges where many of the students have a greater need for assistance with educational, vocational, and personal planning.

(2) *Admissions.* This service not only involves the actual admitting process, but also usually involves high school visitations for talks with prospective students and their parents. Individuals in this role are often the most visible representative of the institution. Orientation of new students often falls within the domain of this service. Financial aid is also often connected directly with this service.

(3) *Financial Aid.* In large institutions financial aid is not part of the admissions service but is a separate office. In an era of increased governmental support of students this has become an exceedingly complex job. It involves knowing where aid can be obtained, and deciding whom shall receive aid and often the amount of that financial aid.

(4) *Student Activities.* This service is designed to provide direction to all activities and organizations on campus which concern students. One might say that this service is designed to provide an optimal program of extracurricular activities designed to further the development of the student.

(5) *Housing.* Individuals involved in campus housing (i.e., housing director, resident advisor) are responsible for the control of the actual building and the activities that take place there. Currently the popularity of living in dorms is again on the upswing as housing officials permit more individual expression (i.e., painting of own rooms) and more individual freedom. A position in housing is often an entry level job for student personnel workers. Of late, however, it is developing into its own area of specialization.

(6) *Discipline.* As an outgrowth of dean of men and women's offices, student personnel has retained much of the responsibility of administering the student discipline program. It is a legislative, administrative, and judicial function in that individuals working in this area,

working in conjunction with student representatives, are often responsible for establishing the rules and regulations of campus life, with enforcing those rules and regulations, and for operating the judicial system when a purported violation has occurred.

Entry Requirements

Most entry level positions in college student personnel require at least a master's degree in counseling or student administration. Some resident hall positions either require no specific degree or a bachelor's degree. Increasingly actual counseling positions in college counseling centers require the doctorate degree.

Working Conditions

The settings for the college student personnel worker are as diverse as colleges and universities.

Future

Student personnel work has grown to the point that it was estimated in 1965 by Hitchcock that there was some 4,000 student personnel workers across the country in four-year institutions with another 1,500 to 2,000 being employed in two-year institutions. It should be pointed out that these are very rough figures, because the very diversity of the field makes it difficult to identify all those that should be classified as student personnel workers and the field, particularly at the two-year institutions, has expanded rapidly since 1965. Nonetheless, it can be said that there is a substantial number of such specialists engaged in counseling as well as other helping services who find their major employment and allegiance in college and university work. This will undoubtedly be true in the near future even with a drop in college enrollments. Over the long term positions in higher education may become slightly more difficult to find particularly at the entry levels. Starting salaries range from $9,000 at entry to $17,000+ with experience and a terminal degree.

Employment Service Counselor

Another result of the social need to efficiently move people into appropriate occupations was the establishment of that branch of the occupation known as employment counseling. As early as 1915, Bloomfield wrote in his book, *Youth, School and Vocation,* about the need for the establishment of bureaus designed to facilitate the vocational placement of individuals. Unlike other writers, he did not feel that the school would be the only agency responsible for the vocational placement of individuals. He encouraged the further development of employment services which at that time only a few states had. The depression years of the 1930s were to heighten the awareness of the need for more vocational services than could be provided to individuals within the school setting. Certainly, during that time period, discussion of counseling as part of the employment service among those in the agency took a second seat to the importance given to the problems of finding the most qualified individuals for available jobs; nonetheless, people came to accept the employment service as an agency that provided counseling services. For example, in 1946, the United States Employment Service reported that they had handled some one million counseling cases during that year (Stocking, 1947). In addition, as part of the counseling service, research was begun which led to the development of one of the finest test batteries in existence today; the General Aptitude Test Battery. Yet another development under the auspices of the Bureau of Labor that was to have a tremendous impact on the profession of counseling was the development and publication of the *Dictionary of Occupational Titles.*

These early developments have led to a federal-state network of employment services that encompasses some 2,000 local employment offices (Feingold, 1965). These local offices are under the overall supervision of the Federal Bureau of Employment Security, a bureau within the Department of Labor; however, the local offices are staffed and administered by the fifty states under their own state standards. It is estimated that about half of the individuals employed in these agencies spend up to fifty percent of their time providing counseling services to individuals, with the rest of the time being spent in placement activities. It is clear, however, that the trend is for the amount of time spent in counseling services to continue increasing. At least part of this trend is attributable to the growing demand for counseling services for individuals who in their thirties, forties, and fifties, with many years of work ahead of them, find their job skills are suddenly obsolete. It is also because legislation such as Manpower Development Training Act (MDTA), the Area Redevelopment Act, and the various pieces of antipoverty legislation have included counseling services in these agencies as an active part of manpower policy. The pace of change which causes so many individuals difficulty within our society is occurring even more rapidly, hence, the promise is that increasingly there will be a need to provide counseling services of some sort over the entire life span of individuals. Such a demand will require even more from the employment services than they are currently able to provide.

Role of Employment Service Counselor

The employment service counselor works in State Employment Offices within the State's Civil Service System. Broadly conceived, their primary function is to assist applicants experiencing difficulty with job choice, change, or adjustment (Employment Service (ES) Manual).

Job choice is usually associated with an applicant who has never held a full-time job and could include recent graduates, veterans leaving the service, and women entering the labor market after a period of time away from work outside the home.

Job change essentially is the same as a choice situation with the added considerations of loss of seniority, possible reduction in income or change in locale, and lifestyle to the established worker.

Job adjustment refers to the counselor assisting the applicant to cope with some disturbing influences in the present employment situation, i.e., communication with co-workers, superiors or subordinates, or some affect about the work itself.

As indicated earlier, recent years have seen some change in emphasis in the employment service counselors' work. Their job description now includes job training and work motivation for the disadvantaged. These programs include screening for the Job Corps, referring to or developing Manpower and Development Training Act courses, and the most recent addition, responsibility for the Work Incentive Program. The counselors' responsibilities for Job Corps referral include assisting the sixteen through twenty-two-year-old applicant who meets the "disadvantaged" criteria to determine whether the Job Corps experience will be useful for applicants. Job Corpsmen are paid a small allowance while in training. MDTA trainees are usually older than the Job Corpsmen and receive a more substantial support with increments for dependents while in training. MDTA trains men and women in vocational skills at a training site organized for MDTA training or through an established vocational school. The employment service counselors' responsibilities include assisting with appropriate occupation and school selection. Occasionally, there is a need for assisting with budget management, procuring emergency funds for travel to the training site or maintenance and subsistence until the training money checks arrive. Adjustment to the training situation may require professional counseling assistance.

In the WIN program the counselor works with a group of welfare recipients. In its initial conception the WIN program provided, as necessary, a combination of basic adult education and work training. The counselors and a "Coach" coordinate the education, training, job motivation, and survival skills through a combination of individual and group counseling, behavior modification, and direct intervention. The coach is one of the trainees who is selected to serve as a model for the other trainees, and a peer who can take more direct measures than the counselor such as going into a home to get a trainee out of bed, dressed, and on the way to class. Recent trends are to eliminate the training and concentrate on immediate employment.

Entrance Requirements

Employment service counselors are required to possess a bachelor's degree with some training in psychology, testing, and introductory counseling courses. Several states have had assistance programs for ES counselors who wished to obtain a master's degree.

Working Conditions

Employment offices are usually modern, well-lighted business offices. Unfortunately, counselors in the employment service have not always had private offices even though the Federal Government has recognized the need for privacy in counseling situations and this need is reflected in the state's manual. Counselors work on a twelve month basis, receive three weeks vacation, fifteen days sick leave a year (cumulative to 90 days) and have the usual medical and insurance programs offered to civil service employees.

Outlook

Although employment service counselors are state civil service employees, the number of positions is controlled by federal funding and this can appear whimsically uncontrolled. For example, in the late sixties, employment service counselors in Pennsylvania were receiving financial support to earn master's degrees. Then, in the early seventies over one hundred counselors in the state were laid off due to a cutback in federal spending. Some other states are still receiving funds to upgrade the employment service counselor's educational background, but simultaneously, reductions in the number of counselors occurred in the Ohio and Tennessee regions. According to the United States Bureau of Labor the long-range outlook for counseling positions in the employment service is very good especially for those with master's degrees in counseling.

Rehabilitation Counseling

Yet another branch of counseling found its origins in the world of work. The rehabilitation counseling movement, however, was generated not in response to a need to place people into work, but rather in response to a felt need to take care of those injured while working. As Obermann (1965) suggests in his excellent text on the history of the rehabilitation counseling movement, the initial impetus for the rehabilitation movement was the concept of workman's compensation. As he points out, the concept of the employers having legal responsibility for their workers can be found in writings as old as the Old Testament, where in the twenty-first chapter of Exodus, it is pointed out that employers must take care of their injured servants. This basic concept carried across the centuries and was incorporated in English Common Law. It should be noted that even though it was part of common law, it was beyond most employees' resources to bring anyone to court. The first evidence of real support for the working man injured on the job was a cooperative insurance law passed by Maryland in 1902. This law provided for fixed benefits to be paid to workers for certain injuries. From that time forward, the number of states who adopted workman's compensation laws rapidly expanded. By 1921, forty-five states had laws on the books. While the purpose here is not to trace in any detail the history of the workman's compensation laws it is important to remember that it was from this context that the rehabilitation movement began.

As the world moved more and more into an industrial society where work-related injuries became more common, it became increasingly clear that to simply pay an individual for an injury received was not a complete answer to the problem. This feeling was given added credence with the return of veterans from World War I who had suffered disabling injuries in the service of their country. As Obermann(1965) reports, the evidence of the impact of this feeling was first seen in Wisconsin where Regina Dolan was commissioned by the state to study the employability of disabled workmen. Following the completion of this study, she was employed to place these disabled workers in jobs, thus becoming the first rehabilitation worker. At roughly the same time, the Minnesota Department of Labor and Industry made a study of injured workers that had been awarded damages from industrial injuries. The report was sent to the governor and he in turn established a commission to draw up appropriate legislation. On April 23, 1919, a rehabilitation act was passed and operations under the act began on July 1, 1919. A similar, but more restrictive act had passed in Massachusetts in May of 1918. The Minnesota Act called for the rehabilitation of persons injured in industry or in other ways (Obermann, 1965). The rehabilitation movement was under way but progress over the next few years was slow. By 1930, there were some forty-four states participating in the Federal State Vocational Rehabilitation network, but in these states only 143 rehabilitation workers were on the payrolls (Lamborn, 1970). This number has now grown to close to 4,000 full-time rehabilitation counselors employed in the state and local agencies alone.

Role of Rehabilitation Counseling

The vocational rehabilitation counselor is often called upon to serve two roles: one a provider of services, the other a personal counselor. As a provider of services the "rehab" counselor must be knowledgeable about and be able to procure for clients as needed, the whole range of services including diagnostic, medical and psychological examinations, treatment, remedial and advanced education and training, financial support, and successful job placement. During any and perhaps all of these potential phases in the rehabilitation process, the counseling skills, sensitivity, awareness, empathy, knowledge of human behavior, pathology, and all the other counseling skills are used to assist the client to successful termination. While there are those who recognize a dichotomy in these roles of provider of services and counselor (Stone and Shertzer, 1972), Lamb and Makota (1975) argue that the two are essentially inseparable. In the final analysis the counselor's personality and the particular demands of the local agency will determine where the emphasis is placed.

Rehabilitation counselors are employed in a variety of settings: hospitals, private agencies, Veteran's Administrations, and each state Bureau of Vocational Rehabilitation. Recent legislation has added the socially disadvantaged to those who are eligible for Vocational Rehabilitation services. This enables the "rehab" counselor to provide services to the criminal offender as well as the mentally and physically impaired.

Rehabilitation counselors should have a desire to work with people, and the ability to work with the handicapped without being overly sentimental or sensitive to severe mental retardation, missing limbs, or disfiguring scars. Tolerance for a large number of forms and for the pressure to obtain a specified number of "closures" or completed cases, is helpful. A pleasant personality coupled with interviewing skills help to obtain the necessary information in the early stages of counseling. Decision-making and vocational counseling abilities are necessary to develop a rehabilitation plan. Periodic interviewing or counseling sessions are held to assist the client through the plan, maintain the relationship, and provide any additional support or services that are necessary. Because rehabilitation clients are sometimes provided services which take them away from home, the counselor needs to be aware of the client's family situation as well as the individual's condition.

Entry Requirements

Preparation requirements range from a bachelor's degree with specified specialized courses to master's or doctoral degrees. Even though the requirements for employment are not standardized, the degree requirements are fairly uniform and require eighteen to twenty-four months of education for the master's degree and up to six years for the doctorate.

Work Setting

The vocational rehabilitation counselor will usually have a pleasant well-lighted office. The counselors who work for the State Bureau of Vocational Rehabilitation will usually work for a "district office" which requires periodic travel to that office for clerical services, consultation with superiors, and reporting. Some counselors in rural communities use their homes as offices, meet clients at the Employment Service Office, some other social service agency, or the schools. Generally, "rehab" counselors working for state vocational rehabilitation agencies work with either a general caseload or specialize in a particular disability such as blindness, heart disease, or mental problems.

Starting salaries for bachelor or master degreed counselors range from $7,000-$10,000, depending on the agency and location, to $15,000 for directors of agencies. State civil service positions usually require a written examination although this is not a uniform practice. The outlook for rehabilitation counselors seems to be holding steady. New fields such as prison and probation work may provide new positions for the rehabilitation counselor graduate. Another reason for continued openings will be job turnover through retirement, promotion, and resignations. Data from several sources show dissatisfaction with the position to have caused substantial turnover in the rehabilitation field.

Outlook

The latest estimates indicate that there is a need for close to 1,000 new rehabilitation counselors each year if demands are to be fully met. Graduate school training for these professionals, which was begun in 1954, has spread to more than forty institutions. Commensurate with this growth is the continuing expansion in federal funding of rehabilitation. In 1930, the funding level was under 2 million, in 1950 it was slightly under 30 million, and by the 1960s it had reached 80 million (Lamborn, 1970). In the early 1970s there has been some reduction in federal support, but the long-range outlook for employment possibilities in rehabilitation counseling is excellent.

Special Government Programs

There are many diverse governmental programs in which counselors are employed. For example many rehabilitation counselors often work in governmental programs particularly in the Veteran's Administration. The V.A. also employs individuals with doctoral degrees in counseling psychology. Also, the military services are providing active duty servicemen and their dependents counseling and social work services. These programs normally are confined to military installations. Because these programs are ever changing it is difficult if not impossible to describe them or predict their future with any certainty. We will however describe one such program in which counselors are employed which is a representative of many similar governmental programs.

Job Corps

Origins: The Job Corps was initiated as part of the war on poverty. The intent was to provide educational, vocational and social skills to disadvantaged youths thus enabling them to rejoin society with the skills necessary to be successful. Job Corps centers were set up in two types of locations; small, rural or forestry centers designed to teach basic education and working habits; and large urban centers which continued the educational development and taught vocational programs in curriculums ranging from cooking to electronic data processing. In both settings, counselors were provided to assist with the developing and changing of attitudes and habits, providing educational and vocational guidance, administering tests, and assisting with referrals.

Counselor Role

Counseling in any program of this type is essentially a remedial function. Most of the participants in these governmental programs come to the program with low self-esteem, poor work habits and a variety of self-defeating behaviors. In the truest sense of the word the counselor in this setting must be able to facilitate the development of individuals. Counseling, individual and group, is an integral part of the process, but much more is required. Counselors operating in this setting must be able to function as an outreach worker in the community. They must be able to work with families, employers, and others who affect the lives of their clients. In many ways counselors in this setting need to take on the role of big brothers or sisters to their clients working with them both within and outside of the counseling office.

Entry Requirements

For the remaining positions potential employees will need a completed master's degree in counseling, rehabilitation or psychology. Experience or education in working with the disadvantaged would be extremely helpful. Starting salaries for persons with a master's degree are usually at the GS-9 level.

Outlook

During the first Nixon term, funds for Job Corps were severely cut resulting in many centers closing and a sharp reduction in the number of available counselor positions. The outlook for counseling services with the Job Corps are dependent on federal money. The recent trend to reduce money for assistance to the disadvantaged means that few, if any, new positions will be created and in some cases positions created by transfers, terminations, and retirement may go unfilled.

Corrections

A growing number of individuals trained as counselors are finding employment in the fields of corrections and parole. This trend is due to the increased emphasis in both fields on providing remedial services to individuals who have experienced difficulty with the law.

Corrections Oriented Counseling

The corrections field was originally intended to be solely custodial; but the "prison" system is becoming the "correctional" system with an emphasis on returning a rehabilitated offender to productive use in society (Oswald, 1973). The change is occurring as new facilities are built and old ones remodeled, new community or cluster living arrangements are made, new personnel requirements emphasizing behavioral science training rather than physical size are implemented (Hendricks, 1973; Kline, 1973; Beckmeyer, 1974), and most important, because of a change in philosophy from punishment to rehabilitation (Malcolm, 1975; Bradley, 1975; Dillon, 1975). As in any system or philosophy which undergoes a change of direction, the corrections field has many diverse situations from old, castlelike prisons with formidable walls, armed guards and chains, to community-based facilities defined as any type of correctional activity that takes place in the community (National Advisory Commission on Criminal Justice Standards and Goals, 1973). In some community programs, the "inmates" are confined at night while in others they are "diverted" from incarceration and remain free, although under the court's jurisdiction. In both programs the daytime activities are structured to assist the client's vocational, educational, social, or personal development. Many of the newer programs call for staff personnel with the ability to "counsel" with both juvenile and adult offenders.

Most changes are reportedly occurring in the federal system which operates both penitentiaries and correction institutes. The former are usually maximum or medium security facilities designed for "repeat" offenders or those with long-term sentences. The federal correctional institutes tend to be newer, more modern, and house first offenders or those with short sentences.

At the state level the changes seem to be in juvenile correction. Some states have upgraded their correctional programs, but at this time the federal government leads the way. These duties, listed in an Alabama announcement for a youth service counselor, seem related to counselor training, such as compiling background data, arranging for specialized

> medical, psychological and psychiatric examinations if necessary, as part of the rehabilitation process for juvenile delinquents. Consults and coordinates. . . Provides counseling services to encourage. . .efforts to obtain meaningful educational and vocational careers. . .making use of available community resources. (State of Alabama Job Description 4384, March, 1975)

Kentucky has undertaken the task of improving the correctional environment by building new facilities, increasing staff training, publishing rules so inmates may have access to them, providing more "furloughs" from the institutions, and hiring more counselors and teachers (Bradley, 1975). Other states have initiated programs new to the criminal rehabilitation process. Oklahoma established professional standards for prison inmates and personnel in Transactional Analysis (Wright, 1975). These developments may be taken as indicative of the changes in state correctional systems, although little uniformity in program changes can be expected from one state to another.

Correctional efforts at the city and county levels in large cities are employing similar methods. Many local facilities are used for pretrial detention which imposes some additional legal implications since the inmates have not been tried and in the American system of justice a person is presumed innocent until proven guilty. Thus, local facilities confine some "innocent" people. In New York City the city detention facilities house many pretrail persons as well as convicted inmates. Nevertheless the programs new to penology have been introduced (Malcolm, 1975). Middlesex County, Massachusetts has increased their work release program and holiday furlough program (Dillon, 1975), further evidence of the "prison" reform at the local level. Small communities, however, tend not to provide these services for lack of adequate facilities and monetary support.

Counselors at correctional institutions, however, reportedly serve primarily as case managers with the power to recommend or not recommend parole. As such they are often viewed more as staff members who are to be "conned" or "snowed" into giving good recommendations rather than professional persons who help people change or grow. This situation may result from the parole recommendations or the status as former guards of some of the counselors.

Outlook

Current trends seem to favor an increase in the number of professionally trained people who will serve the inmate population as federal funding and the change in philosophy are combined to alter practice. Salary ranges vary from state to state, but starting salaries around $9,000-$10,000 with ranges up to $11,500 can be expected. Promotional opportunities are usually into supervisory and administrative positions. In Federal Civil Service, counselors with a master's degree usually can expect to start at Government Service Grade 9 (GS-9) at just under $13,000.

Probation Counseling

Some counselors are finding employment in probation work. This field expanded rapidly in late 1971 when federal money flowed through Law Enforcement Program Assistance (LEPA). Initially, these grants were almost entirely federal funds (90 percent federal—10 percent local or state). Since the intent was to foster ongoing programs, the federal funds decreased by 10 percent each year for five years at which time the federal government would no longer contribute to the support of the program. In some locations, the programs have been phased out or reduced as federal funding diminished.

Role of the Probation Counselor

The duties of the probation officer vary from locale to locale, and whether the probation case load is comprised of adults or juveniles. Common elements include building a case file on the probationer, including family background, work history, and court decisions. The probation officer also acts as case manager coordinating the activities of the various agencies (school, vocational rehabilitation, mental health, employment service) which may be providing services to the parolee.

Working Conditions

Probation officers are required to appear in court whenever requested or when one of their clients is on the docket. Probation officers are apt to do a great deal of their work out of the office. Juvenile offenders are seen at home, at school and a lot of family counseling can be expected.

The adult probation officer (counselor) works primarily in an office. While there is less likelihood of coordination with school officials, more work is done with the employment service and with family counseling agencies.

Entry Requirements

Education requirements are usually a bachelor's degree in psychology, sociology, social work, or counseling. Pay is commensurate with educational requirements, with starting salaries in the $7,000-$8,000 a year range.

These positions may or may not be covered by civil service. In Knoxville, Tennessee, for example, adult probation counselors are not covered under civil service. In other areas the probation officers are city managed, sometimes under a Model Cities Program.

Outlook

Employment prospects for new positions seem dependent on grantsmanship and therefore very difficult to predict. The usual replacement/retirement projections are also difficult to predict since state and local governments appear more willing to fund these programs when there are matching federal funds than when the programs are entirely supported by local money.

Counseling: Noneducational Settings

While there is no question that there are great numbers of counselors who work in community mental health centers, governmental programs, and other settings, it is impossible to deal with all of them in any comprehensive way in this chapter. The chief reason for this is that it is extremely difficult to define all the different kinds of counselors that are operating within these settings. It is even hard to estimate the numbers of individuals so employed though some estimates place the figure close to 3,000-4,000 counselors. This group encompasses individuals from all levels of formal preparation, including doctoral and master's level counselors as well as some with only bachelor degrees. It also encompasses all kinds of agencies including community mental health, private agencies, marriage counseling, vocational counseling, family counseling, governmental programs, etc. While it would be impossible in the space of this text to deal with the diverse reasons for the development of these varied services, it is at the very least safe to say that they developed in response to the felt needs of individuals. Most of these agencies have come into being out of a recognition that many individuals in all walks of life and at all ages need some help in dealing with the complexities of life. While it is not possible to describe all the types of private agencies it is possible to give a general albeit brief description of community mental health centers.

Community Mental Health

Community mental health centers are public agencies which receive the majority of their funds for operation from federal, state and local governments. Clients are generally charged for services on a sliding scale according to their ability to pay. Most of these centers are comprehensive in nature in that they provide a broad spectrum of services: psychiatric, psychological evaluation, individual and group counseling, alcoholic and drug counseling, day-care, and half-way house operations. The specific number and types of services often depends on the the size of the particular center.

Counselors operating in this setting are part of a comprehensive team which includes individuals from almost all if not all, of the helping services. Most mental health centers have the services of a consulting psychiatrist, staff psychologists, social workers, counselors, and paraprofessional aides. Because of this team approach, it is in many ways an ideal counseling setting if the various professional groups do work as a team. If not, it can be a very difficult situation in which counselors may find their professional skills questioned.

Counseling Roles

In most centers counselors provide remedial counseling, either group or individual, to individuals who are (a) experiencing emotional conflict in some area of their lives, (b) making the adjustment from a hospital setting to the outside world, (c) experiencing problems related to alcohol and/or drugs, and (d) experiencing problems related to mental or physical deficiencies. Most often these services account for the majority of the counselor's work load.

Most centers also attempt to provide preventive and educational services to the community and most particularly the schools. These services are limited by other demands on staff time and on financial backing. Most federal funds are designed for treatment programs, not education or prevention.

Counselor Preparation

As indicated earlier, individuals from a variety of fields with degrees ranging from bachelors to doctorates are hired as counselors in most mental health centers. As with other fields within the profession, the standards for entry level are being raised and few individuals with less than a master's degree are hired except in day-care programs. Generally the preparation program for counselors entering this field is somewhat broader based and longer (credit hours) than other counselor preparation programs.

Work Setting

As with any relatively new venture, mental health centers suffer growing pains. Consequently actual physical settings range from brand new buildings designed specifically for the center, to converted business sites, to converted mobile homes. Generally centers are understaffed, meaning that counselors have heavy workloads and most must work flexible hours including evenings.

Future

The demand for counselors in this setting is high and prospects are that the demand will continue as existing centers expand and more communities develop their own settings. Salaries range from $9,000-$16,000 depending on preparation and experience.

Religiously Affiliated Counseling Services

Many religious groups provide counseling services to individuals and many of these programs do not require the clients to be members of their own particular faith. Two such services are described here as examples of the kinds of positions a prospective counselor might find in such programs.

B'nai Brith Career Counseling Centers[2]

The B'nai Brith Counseling Service operates seven full-time offices and thirteen part-time offices in twenty cities located in thirteen states, mostly in the Northeast; however, California and Missouri each have one office. Six of the offices are sponsored jointly by the B'nai Brith Career Counseling Service (BBCCS) and the Jewish Vocational Service or other related Jewish agencies. Only the California agency offers full-time services. The thrust of the BBCCS has been to provide career counseling services to youth who wish to develop realistic career plans. Services are also offered to college students and adults. A full program of testing for interests, abilities, skills, and personality is offered as well as individual and group counseling. Most BBCCS offices maintain libraries of occupational and educational information and specialized information pertaining to minority group needs. These libraries are open to the general public without charge. A humanistic approach emphasizing individual responsibility for personal decisions is the philosophy underlying BBCCS.

The B'nai Brith Career Center Service counselors are sometimes called to participate in Project Outreach—a service offered to communities which do not have a BBCCS office. All materials are taken to the community to be served. Appointments are scheduled in advance. (Most clients are obtained by referral.)

2. The authors wish to express their appreciation to Dr. S. Norman Feingold for his cooperation in providing information about the BBCCS. Any inaccuracies are the responsibilities of the authors.

The BBCCS also develops and publishes career information at its Washington (central) office. These publications include the Counselor's Information Service, aides to counselors and parents, three occupational brief series, and pamphlets pertaining to the handicapped and rehabilitation.

A master's degree in counseling, psychology, or education is the minimum educational attainment required by the BBCCS. Many BBCCS counselors hold the doctorate degree.

Presbyterian Guidance Centers

The thirteen Presbyterian Guidance Centers (PGC) are operated by the Synod of the Southeast, a regional governing body of the Presbyterian Church in the United States. The centers' services are designed for individuals at the high school sophomore level or older. Individuals of any denomination are welcome to use the PGC's service.

The major thrust of the PGC seems to be the high school counseling program wherein a precounseling preparation begins at the home church under the direction of lay persons. The counseling sessions at the center consist of a two-day session devoted to individual and group testing, individual and group test interpretation, access to vocational information, and counseling sessions regarding decisions. Services are offered to college students who feel a need to reevaluate life, academic, or career goals, or who are experiencing academic difficulties. The thrust of the adult services is similar to those offered students—reassessment of life and career goals. Assistance is also offered adults with difficulties in interpersonal relationships. Marriage and family counseling are also available.

The thirteen centers are located in the states of Virginia, West Virginia, Tennessee, the Carolinas, Georgia, Florida, Mississippi, Missouri, and Texas.

References

Beckmeyer,G. H., II. Rational counseling with youthful offenders. *American Journal of Corrections* 36 (6) (1974):34.
Boller, J. D. Counselor certification: Who still needs teaching experience? *Personnel & Guidance Journal* 50 (1972):388-91.
Bradley, M. Kentucky's Commissioner Holmes changes correctional environment. *American Journal of Corrections* 37 (1) (1975):16-17.
Conant, J. B. *The American high school today.* New York: McGraw Hill, 1959.
Crowley, W. H. A preface to the principles of student counseling. *The Educational Record* 18 (1937):217-34.
Davis, J. B. *Vocational and moral guidance.* Boston: Ginn, 1914.
Dillon, J. T. Examining the role of maximum security in the rehabilitation process. *American Journal of Corrections* 37 (1) (1975):27.
Dudley, G. and Ruff, E. F. School counselor certification: A study of current requirements. *The School Counselor* 17 (1970):304-11.
Employment service manual. Montgomery, Alabama: State of Alabama, 1974.
Feingold, S. N. Issues related to a study of the influence of salary, methods of selection, working conditions, supervision, and mobility upon selection, training, and retention of counseling person-

nel. In *Counselor development in American society* Washington, D.C.: United States Department of Health, Education, and Welfare, 1965, 133-92.

Hendricks, W. J. Attitudes and the correctional worker. *American Journal of Corrections* 35 (3) (1973):31-32.

Hitchcock, A. A. Counselors, supply, demand, need. *Counselor Development in American Society.* Washington, D.C.: United States Department of Health, Education, and Welfare, 1965.

Houghton, H. F. *Certification requirements for school pupil personnel workers.* Washington, D.C.: United States Department of Health, Education, and Welfare, 1967.

Kline, R. H. School for criminals. *American Journal of Corrections* 35 (2) (1973):8.

Lamb, H. R. and Makato, C. Vocational rehabilitation counseling: A "second class" profession? *Journal of Rehabilitation* 41 (3) (1975):21-49.

Lamborn, E. The state-federal partnership. *Journal of Rehabilitation* 36 (1) (1970):10-15.

Malcolm, B. J. Incarceration. . .rehabilitation or vindictiveness? *American Journal of Corrections* 37 (1) (1975):21.

National Advisory Commission on Criminal Justice. *Standards and goals.* Washington, D.C.: United States Government Printing Office, 1973.

Obermann, C. E. *A history of vocational rehabilitation in America.* Minneapolis: T. S. Denison and Company, 1965.

Oswald, R G. A correctional administrator talks to the judges. *American Journal of Corrections* 35 (3) (1973):6-11.

Shoben, E. J. Some thoughts on interpersonnel relationships. *Journal of Counseling Psychology,* 2 (1955):196-201.

State of Alabama Job Description 4364. Montgomery, Alabama: State of Alabama, 1975.

Stocking, C. Contributions of the U.S.E.S. to guidance and personnel problems. *Occupations* 25 (1947):500-03.

Stone, S. C. and Shertzer, B. *Careers in guidance and counseling.* Boston: Houghton-Mifflin Company, 1972.

Swisher, J. D. A model for counseling services. Unpublished paper. Pennsylvania State University, 1971.

Thorsen, J. *Counselor certification 1971.* Washington, D.C.: American Personnel and Guidance Association, 1972 (mimeographed).

Wrenn, C. G. *Student personnel work in college.* New York: The Ronald Press, 1951.

Wright, R. J. Penologically speaking: Recent happenings in corrections. *American Journal of Corrections* 37 (1) (1975):33.

Appendix 1

Career Guidance: Role and Functions of Counseling and Personnel Practitioners in Career Education

Position Paper of the American Personnel and Guidance Association*

The Association recognizes that the methodologies employed in career education vary in focus, scope and magnitude. The Association endorses comprehensive career education activities centered upon career development that integrate the participation of educators with that of business, industry, labor and community personnel. This approach views the work and human development resources available in the broader community as important components of career education.

The American Personnel and Guidance Association recognizes and supports the concept that role statements can be formulated most appropriately for individual practitioners employed in specific settings. Thus, it is not possible or appropriate to formulate universal statements about their career guidance role in career education that are highly specific and/or restrictive.

The practitioner's assumption of an active career guidance role in career education programs is vital. The following set of counselor role statements is endorsed by the American Personnel and Guidance Association as appropriate and necessary for the conduct of career education in any setting.

1. *Provide leadership in the identification and programmatic implementation of individual career development tasks.* The Association supports career education that is organized around identified career development tasks (e.g., choice and preparation for work and leisure) facing individuals over the life span.
2. *Provide leadership in the identification, classification and use of self, educational and occupational information.* The crucial importance for comprehensive collection, careful organization and appropriate use of such information is affirmed here. Additionally, the Association supports practitioner efforts to share such information with other personnel who are participating in career education programs.
3. *Provide leadership in the assimilation and application of career decision-making methods and materials.* The Association supports practitioner efforts to involve other personnel in the use of career decision-making strategies.
4. *Provide leadership in eliminating the influence of both racism and sexism as cultural restrictors of opportunities available to minority persons, females, and others who may*

Adopted by APGA Board of Directors—July 14, 1974. Adopted by APGA Senate—March 26, 1975.

be affected. The Association views career education as a vehicle for use in the human rights movement and believes the career guidance practitioner represents the most appropriate person to provide leadership and direction in this effort.

5. *Provide leadership in expanding the variety and appropriateness of assessment devices and procedures required for sound personal, educational and occupational decision making.* The Association recognizes the need to use a wide variety of simulation and experiential activities as career assessment procedures to supplement the more traditional individual appraisal procedures. The career guidance practitioner is the professional qualified to guide the development and utilization of such procedures in the total career education process.

6. *Provide leadership in emphasizing the importance and carrying out the functions of career counseling.* Protection of freedom of choice for the individual rests upon self-understanding as the basis for educational and occupational decision making. Thus the crucial importance of counseling, individually and/or in groups, is viewed by the Association as a fundamental element in the formulation and operation of career education. The necessity for professionally prepared career guidance practitioners being assigned primary responsibility for counseling is asserted here.

In addition to these six inseparable leadership roles, career guidance practitioners should be active participants in several other key career education activities. Whether viewed in a leadership or a participatory sense, it is essential that these specialists be actively involved in the following functions:

1. *Serving as liaison between the educational and community resource groups.*
2. *Conducting career guidance needs assessment surveys.*
3. *Organizing and operating part-time and full-time educational, occupational and job placement programs.*
4. *Conducting follow-up, follow-through and job adjustment activities.*
5. *Participating in curriculum revision.*
6. *Participating in efforts to involve the home and family in career education.*
7. *Participating in efforts to monitor and assess operations and communicating the results of those activities to other practitioners and clientele, as appropriate.*

Implications for Members and the Association

The functions outlined above have implications for career guidance practitioners and for the Association. The changes in behaviors and practices of practitioners called for are far reaching and profound. In order to achieve such changes, massive in-service education must take place. Additionally, changes must be made in the educational programs that prepare the practitioner. Both of these efforts will require substantial investment of dollars, time, and energy. The American Personnel and Guidance Association commits itself to legislative efforts aimed at obtaining these resources. In general, it is the Association's intent to:

1. Support career education and actively champion it at federal, state, and local levels.
2. View the career guidance practitioner as a key, pivotal professional in career education.

3. Encourage the increasing use of paraprofessional or support personnel supervised by career guidance practitioners in career education.

4. Join in efforts aimed at providing in-service education for career guidance practitioners in the area of career education. It is the position of the Association that, with institutes and workshops, practitioners employed currently can increase their career guidance competencies and understandings required for effective participation in career education. The Association does not support the creation of a new specialty called the "Career Education Counselor." It is the position of APGA that it is preferable to include an expanded career development and guidance emphasis as a part of existing counselor education programs.

5. Support efforts aimed at changing counselor education programs in ways that advance sound career education practices.

6. Endorse and pledge support to the teamwork philosophy inherent in career education and the concomitant belief that career guidance practitioners should assume roles as team members in career education.

7. Represent career guidance practitioners as one of several kinds of professional personnel who should be seriously considered to coordinate and direct systemwide career education efforts.

8. Encourage the installation of career guidance activities in support of career education in settings that influence career development.

The American Personnel and Guidance Association recognizes the existence of the widely differing views held by its members with respect to career education. It encourages each APGA member to reflect carefully on the philosophical basis and substance of career education and to develop an individual point of view which will guide the member's professional actions in career education.

Appendix 2

Position Paper on Career Development

**AVA-NVGA Commission on Career
Guidance and Vocational Education, 1973**

The Process of Career Development

In order to be whole persons, men and women naturally must engage in activities they consider to be significant. The need to make judgments about using time and assuming roles recurs throughout life. A person formulates a career by continuously evaluating both what he wants to do with his life and the actions that will enable him to achieve his personal goals. Career development occurs as educational and vocational pursuits interact with other life pursuits. It continues throughout life.

Career Development as Part of Human Development

As with other normal aspects of human development, career development is not totally dependent upon external forces or programs. Rather, it reflects a personal growth pattern that, in some respects, differs for each individual. However, certain common patterns of growth, coupled with individual variations, allow generalization about usual developmental patterns and career sequences.

Certain basic principles regarding human development apply whether one speaks about physical, emotional, intellectual, social or career development. At least seven developmental dimensions are important in the design and implementation of programs for career development:

1. Development occurs during the lifetime of an individual. It can be described in maturational terms denoting progression through life stages and the mastery of developmental tasks at each stage. Although research evidence is lacking, it seems unlikely that intervention can substantially shorten this maturational process.
2. Individual development is influenced by both heredity and environment. Psychological, sociological, educational, political, economic and physical factors affect development. Appropriate intervention strategies which focus upon these factors can influence the quality of individual development.
3. Development is a continuous process. Individual development can best be facilitated by intervention strategies that begin in the early years and continue throughout the life of the person. Programs which focus only at certain points or at certain stages in the individual's life will have limited effectiveness.
4. Although development is continuous, certain aspects are dominant at various periods in the life span. Programs designed to facilitate career development should account for the dominant aspects at given stages.
5. Individual development involves a progressive differentiation and integration of the

291

person's self and his perceived world. Intervention strategies need to be designed to assist individuals during normal maturational stages of career development rather than to provide remedial assistance to individuals whose development has been damaged or retarded.

6. While common developmental stages can be observed and described during childhood and adult life, individual differences in progressing through these stages can be expected. Intervention programs should provide for these differences, making no assumption that something is "wrong" with those who progress at atypical rates.

7. Excessive deprivation with respect to any single aspect of human development can retard optimal development in other areas. Optimal human development programs are comprehensive in nature, not limited to any single facet; it is recognized that those who suffer from deprivation may require special and intensive assistance. Where deprivation is long-term, short-term intervention is not likely to be sufficient.

Building upon these principles only offers assurance that a program of career guidance will have a constructive and educative influence in shaping human potential and providing the means for its expression.

Work Values as Part of Human Values

Just as career development is a part of human development, the values a person formulates with regard to work and to himself as a worker are a part of his larger value system. Human values, including work values, begin to develop early in life. These values are influenced by society and by the attitudes and values held by family, associates and peers. The educational institution, as an instrument of society, plays a decidedly important part in value formation and clarification—particularly in the clarification of previously formed values that may not be fully understood. Through the clarification and formulation of values, an individual finds meaning, direction and purpose in life and participates as a responsible citizen. The values a person formulates about workers and their work form a topic which needs the attention of those who set goals and priorities for education.

The United States was founded when the classical work ethic was universally held. That ethic embraced a number of work values:

1. All honest work possesses worth and dignity.
2. A man is known best through his achievements and what he contributes to society.
3. A task well done is its own reward.
4. A worker should do his very best at all times and not quit a job until it is finished.
5. Hard work is the best and surest route to occupational success.
6. The pride an individual can find in himself is derived in large part from the pride he finds through achievement in his work.
7. A man deserves nothing that he has not earned through his work.

These values and beliefs have played a fundamental part in national progress. In recent years, the emergence of some new values and a change in the relative importance of others is markedly altering the nature of jobs and organizations and, for many persons, their career development. These changes have led to recognition that the United States is experiencing the evolution of a new epoch: the postindustrial era. In this present period of transition, it is difficult to speak with assurance about values and value positions. Several observations, however, seem to have validity.

First, for many workers, the classical work ethic no longer constitutes a viable set of work values. Although this ethic was eminently appropriate in the agrarian period when work was viewed as an essential prerequisite to individual survival, its base has been somewhat eroded. Today, technology increasingly provides for material needs and banishes somewhat the fear of scarcity.

Second, technological advances in industrial productivity, stimulated by both automation and cybernation, have created working conditions that have further eroded the bases for the traditional-work ethic. This is particularly true for individuals engaged in assembly line jobs where job tasks and responsibilities are narrowly defined and the worker is viewed and treated as an operating unit. While most employers would be pleased if the classical version of the work ethic were still regarded as meaningful by all employees, it is a fact that management decisions and assembly line techniques have affected worker motivation.

Third, the continuing substitution of mechanical and electrical energy for human energy in performing work will lead eventually to a somewhat greater emphasis on new careers calling for adaptability, self-expression, and interdependence. With machines increasingly absorbing tasks and activities that are programmable, future industrial workers will function in situations where programming is not feasible and where a high degree of variability exists. For those who will pursue production-oriented career, this change in job functions may lead to a revitalization of the traditional work ethic, though in modified form.

Fourth, as the nation moves into this postindustrial period, the provision of services will become increasingly important. An expansion of occupational opportunities in services is a natural consequence of automation and cybernation. The formulation of work values deeply rooted in a desire to help fellow humans may well motivate the career development of many individuals. Work viewed as service may assume a set of values that diverges considerably from those which underlie work conceived as a means to society's maintenance. Such services may still be offered for profit.

Many of the values which characterize the classical version of the work ethic remain alive and viable in the postindustrial period. Achievement, self-control, independence and delay of gratification are values that continue to hold great importance for many individuals, directing their vocational behavior and molding their career development. For others, however, and particularly for some young people, values of self-expression, interdependence, service and search for meaning in work are playing a more prominent role in the way they structure their work lives. In facilitating career development, educators should not attempt to impose any particular set of work values on all. Yet education must provide each student with the opportunity to develop a comprehensive set of personal values upon which he can rely when making career plans and decisions. Today more than ever before, there is every reason to allow students to explore their own basic natures and to formulate career plans in keeping with their own values.

Perhaps the single most important characteristic of the postindustrial era will be the tolerance it accords the individual's human values.

The Meaning of Career

One may view "career" from several perspectives. In general, the term is defined differently depending on whether the viewer seeks to relate it to institutions, organizations and occupations, or whether he intends to relate it to persons. At one extreme is the equation of career and occupation, including the advances a person makes in his occupation. At the other extreme is the view that career denotes a general life pattern which includes virtually all activites. Some writers would delimit the matter of interpretation by suggesting the major life domains which engage the individual in multiple roles—e.g., worker, family member, community participant and leisure time participant.

Between these two extremes, some sociologists and psycholoists have used the term "career" to refer to the sequence of occupations, jobs and positions held during the course of life. This definition may be applied in considering developmental movement through societal structures, but it conveys no sense of an active person interacting with his environment.

The position taken in this paper is that the term "career" means a time-extended working out of a purposeful life pattern through work undertaken by the individual. Career can easily be differentiated from the term "career development," which refers to the total constellation of psychological, sociological, educational, physical, economic and chance factors that combine to shape the career of any given individual.

The meaning of the word "career," then, is directly dependent upon the meaning attached to the word "work." Work, as conceived for this paper, may be defined as an expenditure of effort of civilization. It is not simply an arbitrary or gratuitous action, but something which, from some viewpoint within society, ought to be done. The concept carries the intention that human effort will lead to an improvement of the individual's own condition or that of some element of society.

Viewed in this way, work is not directly attached to paid employment; it may also include efforts of an educational or a vocational nature. Thus education for work, as well as certain elements of leisure undertaken to benefit society or which contribute to a sense of individual purpose and achievement, are included in this definition.

While these definitions provide a framework for the educator who will facilitate career development, it must be emphasized that a person's career does not unfold independently of other areas of his development. Ultimately the educator, whatever his title, must concern himself with the total development of a person, and this implies a consideration of how work and career mesh with other life pursuits in a reasoned style of living.

Freedom to Choose

A basic value, rooted deeply in the moral heritage, political philosophy, and traditions of western society, is the concept of individual freedom and responsibility. The strength of this nation in the past has rested in part upon the natural differences in individual talents and the freedom of each individual to develop and express his talents in a unique way. The theory underlying career development is consonant with this fundamental democratic value. Preservation of the individual's integrity disavows any type of prescriptive guidance which commits the individual to particular directions. Individuals, however, must be made aware of the values society places on different talents and the relative demands for different kinds of talents.

Career Guidance and an Intervention Process

The Need for Career Guidance

Today there are many social factors which converge to stimulate an interest in the career development needs of persons of all ages:

1. Growing complexity in the occupational and organizational structure of society which makes it difficult for a person to assimilate and organize the data necessary to formulate a career.
2. Evermore rapid technological change demanding human adaptability and responsiveness.
3. Increasing national concern with the need to develop all human talent, including the talents of women and minorities.
4. An ardent search for values which will give meaning to life.
5. The need for specialized training to obtain entry jobs.
6. The apparent disenchantment expressed by students who have difficulty relating their education to their lives.

Each one of these factors impinges on the individual in ways that make achieving self-fulfillment more difficult.

In the past, some managerial personnel in business and industry have held a "non-careerism" attitude which viewed the typical job as an isolated event in a person's life. Whether this attitude is tenable in the postindustrial period is seriously questioned today. The evolving view is that a job should be considered as a stage in an integrated, lifelong career—a step on a career lattice which involves both horizontal and vertical dimensions. On the horizontal level it involves patterns of choice at one point in time, such as: "Should I combine employment with study? Or should I engage in volunteer work along with my employment?" Vertically, it involves choices along a time line, such as: "How do my options or behavior at this point relate to options or behavior in the near, intermediate or distant future?" As new questions are raised about the opportunities work provides for learning and self-development, the need for expanded programs of career guidance becomes apparent.

The Nature of Career Guidance

The nature of guidance for career development cannot be viewed as a static, tradition based set of related services that assist individuals in making single occupational choices. The content of any career guidance program must be developed from initial assessment of the present and future career development needs of the individual; it must also account for impinging environmental factors that could affect the development and fulfillment of career expectations. Career guidance content can be organized in many ways to facilitate the individual's development. Whatever its form, the program should encourage the individual to assume responsibility for his own career development.

A career guidance program assists the individual to assimilate and integrate knowledge, experience and appreciations related to:

1. Self-understanding, which includes a person's relationship to his own characteristics and perceptions, and his relationship to others and the environment.
2. Understanding of the work society and those factors that affect its constant change, including worker attitudes and discipline.
3. Awareness of the part leisure time may play in a person's life.
4. Understanding of the necessity for and the multitude of factors to be considered in career planning.
5. Understanding of the information and skills necessary to achieve self-fulfillment in work and leisure.

An illumination of these content areas may include career guidance experiences to insure that each individual:

- Gathers the kinds of data necessary to make rational career decision.
- Understands the necessary considerations for making choices and accepts responsibility for the decisions made.
- Explores the possible rewards and satisfactions associated with each career choice considered.
- Develops through work the attitude that he is a contributor to life and the community.
- Determines success and failure probabilities in any occupational area considered.
- Explores the possible work conditions associated with occupational options.
- Shows an understanding of the varied attitudes toward work and workers held by himself and by others.
- Recognizes how workers can bring dignity to their work.
- Considers the possible and even predictable value changes in society which could affect a person's life.
- Understands the important role of interpersonal and basic employment skills in occupational success.
- Clarifies the different values and attitudes individuals may hold and the possible effects these may have on decisions and choices.
- Understands that career development is lifelong, based upon a sequential series of educational and occupational choices.
- Determines the possible personal risk, cost and other related consequences of each career decision and is willing to assume responsibility for each consequence.
- Systematically analyzes school and nonschool experiences as he plans and makes career-related decisions.
- Explores the worker characteristics and work skills necessary to achieve success in occupational areas under consideration.
- Identifies and uses a wide variety of resources in the school and community to maximize career development potential.
- Knows and understands the entrance, transition, and decision points in education and the problems of adjustment that might occur in relation to these points.

•Obtains necessary employability skills and uses available placement services to gain satisfactory entry into employment in line with occupational aspirations and beginning competencies.

Responsibilities for Facilitating Career Guidance

Effective implementation of career guidance in an educational setting necessitates that guidance leadership identify not only what has to be accomplished, but who has the capabilities for coordinating and delivering specific program elements. This is of particular importance if the education establishment is to reduce the past confusion and misinterpretation of who holds responsibilities for career guidance and when it should be accomplished. To some, career guidance means merely a body of content in which volunteers participate at will; others see its functions as solely those of the professionally prepared school counselor. Obviously, neither of these viewpoints is correct. A clear identification of those persons who have primary, secondary, and shared roles and responsibilities in meeting student career development needs is urgently required.

To assure program quality, consistency and sequence, some one person must be assigned responsibility for overall coordination of the career guidance program. The competencies needed by that person include:

1. A thorough understanding of career development theory and research;
2. Group process, human relations and consultative skills;
3. A knowledge of curriculum and how curriculum is developed;
4. An understanding of the relationship between values, goals, choices and information in decision making;
5. A knowledge of the history of work and its changing meanings;
6. An understanding of the changing nature of manpower, womanpower and economic outlooks; and,
7. Familiarity with various strategies and resources for facilitating career development, including the utilization of the school, the community and the home.

It is the position of this paper that the guidance specialist possesses many of these qualifications and is in a position to coordinate the career guidance program. Other educational personnel having these qualifications also are in a position to coordinate the program.

The advent of career education has focused the interest of school people upon the career development needs of young people and has provided an opportunity for all educational personnel to extend their involvement. To meet the career development needs of today's population, career guidance must be planned only after accounting for the needs of those to be served and the impinging environmental conditions that exist. This means, then, that the combined skills of the guidance team, vocational educators, academic teachers, administrators, parents, peers and others in the individual's environment need to be identified and appropriate learning experiences provided to make full use of the contributions they can provide. For descriptive purposes these role definitions will be discussed under the headings guidance specialists, vocational educators, academic teachers, principals, parents, peers, and employers and other community members.

Guidance Specialists

The guidance team has appropriate understandings and competencies to serve as facilitator and change agent in (1) assisting in school curriculum development and instructional methods; (2) assisting the individual in his career development; and, (3) communicating with parents and others. The guidance team is composed of a number of specialists including (but not limited to) education personnel with the following titles: Elementary Career Development Specialist, Elementary Counselor, Junior Career Exploratory Teacher, Orientation and Group Guidance Specialist, Occupational and Educational Information Specialist, Postsecondary Student Personnel Worker, Guidance Counselor, Cooperative Work Experience Coordinator, Vocational Appraisal Specialist.

The responsibilities of the guidance team are:

Program Leadership and Coordination

1. Coordinate the career guidance program.
2. Provide staff with the understanding necessary to assist each student to obtain a full, competency-based learning experience.
3. Coordinate the acquisition and use of appropriate occupational, educational and labor market information.
4. Help staff understand the process of human growth and development and assess needs of specific individuals.
5. Help staff plan for sequential student learning experiences in career development.
6. Coordinate the development and use of a comprehensive, cumulative pupil data system that can be readily used by all students.
7. Identify and coordinate the use of school and community resources needed to facilitate career guidance.
8. Coordinate the evaluation of students' learning experiences and use the resulting data in counseling with students, in consulting with the instructional staff and parents, and in modifying the curriculum.
9. Coordinate a job placement program for the school and provide for job adjustment counseling.
10. Provide individual and group counseling and guidance so that students will be stimulated to continually and systematically interrelate and expand their experiences, knowledge, understanding, skills and appreciations as they grow and develop throughout life.

Student Direction

1. Help each student to realize that each person has a unique set of characteristics and that to plan realistically, each must appraise himself fairly.
2. Enable each student to make use of available assessment tools and techniques in examining his personal characteristics.
3. Assist students in identifying realistic role models.
4. Assist students in developing the employability skills necessary for entry into employment where opportunities exist.

Vocational Educators

Vocational educators carry many of the same responsibilities as guidance specialists in facilitating the career development of students who are enrolled in vocational education courses. Their unique contributions to a comprehensive career education program may include:

1. Providing realistic educational and occupational information to students and staff based on knowledge of occupational fields and continuous contact with workers and work settings.
2. Identifying and recruiting resource persons in the employment community to assist in the school program.
3. Providing exploratory experiences in vocational classrooms, labs and shops for students not enrolled in occupational preparation programs and assisting those teachers who wish to incorporate "hands on" types of activities in their courses.
4. Identifying basic and academic skills and knowledge needed to succeed in the occupations of their field and communicating this information to academic teachers and guidance specialists.
5. Assisting academic teachers and guidance specialists in designing appropriate occupational exploration experiences.
6. Providing students with information about the kinds of careers for which students are prepared.
7. Assisting students enrolled in vocational programs to analyze and interpret their learning experiences for better understanding of self in relation to occupations and the world of work.
8. Planning and providing vocational instruction which prepares students to enter, adjust, progress and change jobs in an occupational field.
9. Assisting students in identifying a wide range of occupations for which their vocational instruction is applicable.
10. Encouraging employers to assist in expanding student awareness of career opportunities.
11. Arranging observation activities or part-time employment for students and school staff to help them learn more about occupations and work settings.
12. Participating in the planning and implementation of a comprehensive career education program.

Academic Teachers

The academic teacher also has a vital set of responsibilities in career guidance which require the ability to:

1. Provide for easy transition of students from home to school, from one school environment to another, and from school to further education or employment.
2. Provide students with curriculum and related learning experiences to insure the development of basic concepts of work and the importance of those who perform work.

3. Provide group guidance experiences, with appropriate aid from guidance specialists and vocational educators, to regularly demonstrate the relationship between learning and job requirements.
4. Help parents understand and encourage the career development process as it relates to their children.
5. Provide opportunities within the curriculum for students to have decision-making experiences related to educational and vocational planning.
6. Assist students in synthesizing accumulated career development experiences to prepare them for educational transitions.
7. Provide career exploratory experiences to help students gain an understanding of worker characteristics and work requirements.
8. Provide experiences to help students increase their understanding of their own capabilities, interests and possible limitations.
9. Provide for career preparation experiences that will enable the individual to acquire skills necessary to enter and remain in the world of work at a level appropriate to his capabilities and expectations.
10. Provide, as an extension of the in-school learning experience, opportunities for the individual to experience work firsthand in a nonthreatening environment.

Principals

The principal carrries ultimate responsibility in his building for the guidance program. More specifically his responsibilities are:

1. Providing active encouragement and support of the program.
2. Espousing the idea of career guidance as a responsibility of each staff member.
3. Committing himself to experimentation and flexibility in program and curriculum.
4. Arranging for in-service education of staff in career guidance and human relations.
5. Organizing and encouraging the development of a career guidance committee composed of staff members, students, parents and community leaders.
6. Providing necessary personnel, space, facilities and materials.
7. Encouraging constant evaluation and improvement of the program.

Although school staff members are extremely important in assisting youth in their career development, there are other persons who also provide valuable assistance. They include parents, peers, employers and other community members.

Parents—Without question parents can and should be the most influential role model figures and counselors to their children. Having some measure of direct control over the environment in which their children have been reared, they have the unique opportunity of exposing them to experiences appropriate for self-fulfillment. As their children enter public education, parents share but do not give up, the responsibility for their development. Parents who take full advantage of the information given them by school staff members concerning the interest, aptitudes, failures and achievements of their children can use this background of information to provide:

1. Assistance in analyzing their children's interests, capabilities and limitations.

2. Explanations of the traits required, the working conditions and life-styles of work areas with which they are most familiar.
3. Discussions of work values developed as a result of past experiences and of the consequences they have experienced.
4. Discussions of the economic condition of the family as it applies to the children's education and training needs, and assistance in planning a course of action.
5. Help in using the knowledge, experience and service of relatives, friends, fellow workers and other resources in exploring the world of work and in planning and preparing for their role in the work society.
6. A model and counsel to their children during critical developmental periods of their lives in an attempt to have children establish and maintain positive attitudes towards themselves and others.
7. Exemplification of the attitude that all persons have dignity and worth no matter what their position in the world of work.
8. Situations that allow children to experience decision making and to accept responsibility for the consequences of their decisions.
9. Maintenance of open communications between school and home so that the experiences of both settings can be used in meeting student needs.
10. Opportunities for children to work and accept responsibilities of the home and community.

Peers—As youth establish and experience interpersonal relationships with their peers, they need to understand how to analyze and use these experiences in their career development. A person's friends and associates have an intense effect upon his values, attitude formation and career expectations. Opportunities should be provided to allow young persons to share their ideas with each other.

The guidance team is in a particularly strategic position to capitalize upon the influence that young persons may have upon each other. Research is beginning to demonstrate that peer influence can be harnessed and directed to contribute to the favorable development of youth. The strategy involves teaching selected youngsters certain skills of counseling and human relations and then using these young persons in a paraprofessional capacity. The use of this or similar strategies will enable youth and young adults to perceive accurately the challenges and responsibilities of being an active member of the school's guidance team.

Employers and Other Community Members—As contemporary schools open their doors to allow for expanded community involvement, it is appropriate to discuss the possible roles members of the community may play. Employers, employees, clergy, retired workers, community agency personnel and others should be viewed as potential guidance team members. Educators and parents must be ready and willing to team up with other community members, especially when they find a child needs specialized information or assistance related to career development. Employers should provide work stations and observation experiences and be available as career speakers for school programs. Industry and business should demand a significant role in the education of youth, rather than the token role they've had in the past. Since employers can provide actual work settings, staff who understand the traits of workers and skill competenices needed for entry jobs and job retention, it would be tragic if education failed to utilize this resource. Career guidance specialists working in cooperation with vocational educators, can do much to encourage full use of all community resources available for the career development of young people.

Subject Index

Chapters

5
6
7
9
10
11